ACTION STATIONS

1 Wartime military airfields of East Anglia 1939-1945

ACTION STATIONS

1 Wartime military airfields of East Anglia 1939-1945

Michael J.F. Bowyer

 Patrick Stephens, Cambridge

First published in 1979

British Library Cataloguing in Publication Data

Bowyer, Michael John Frederick
    Wartime military airfields of East Anglia, 1939-1945.
    — (Action stations; 1).
    1. World War, 1939-1945 — Aerial operations, British
    2. Air-bases — England — East Anglia — History
    I. Title II. Series
    940.54'43'426   D786

    ISBN 0 85059 335 2

Photoset in 9pt and 10 on 11pt English Times
by Red Lion Setters, Holborn, London.
Printed in Great Britain on 100 gsm coated cartridge
and bound by The Garden City Press, Letchworth, Herts,
for the publishers, Patrick Stephens Limited,
Bar Hill, Cambridge, CB3 8EL, England.

Contents

Introduction   6

Glossary   8

Origins   11

Building the armoury   14

Five counties at war   17

Airfield architecture   24

The airfields   46

Index of units referred to in the text   228

Introduction

No area of the British Isles has seen as much air activity as East Anglia. Almost since the birth of flying there has been something in the air over the eastern counties. With so much flat land strategically placed it is little wonder that the region has contained more airfields than any other of comparable size. Indeed, at one time airfield circuits were so close that some overlapped. Within the five counties there were well over 100 airfields at the peak of activity in the 1939-1945 war. From them was woven a story unparalleled in the history of military aviation.

This book sets out to record concisely the activity that took place from these airfields and outline the squadrons and units which flew from them, the whole punctuated by some personal memories.

It does not set out to be a catalogue of runway lengths or hangar sizes; more is it concerned with what took place and from where, especially during the busy wartime days. Then, as many as 5,000 flights were being made daily over East Anglia.

It has been considered best to concentrate upon the 1939-1945 period, whilst remembering that some airfields had early beginnings, and some are still very active today. Wyton, where the mighty Nimrods now roar aloft, has known the frail biplanes of the past. Marham, resounding to the colossal power of the weighty Victor tankers, could recall some of the early entrants to the field of military flying. East Anglia is indeed a region steeped in history and sprinkled with memorials to the past. Past the site of Bassingbourn, for instance, its name deriving from a Saxon invader, must have tramped Roman Legions. Delving into the origin of the names of the airfields would provide a book on its own. To read through any list of names of those associated with the airfields is to take a detailed look into the complete history of the RAF. Turn the pages of the memorial books in Ely Cathedral and one cannot but feel deep sadness at the folly of man.

For three years the USAAF waged its tremendous war effort from places the names of which remain known to few. Inevitably, the rather primitive American wartime bases have nearly all been returned to agricultural use. Thus they have shorter, probably less interesting, histories than those of the long-sited RAF aerodromes. Yet action from these stations was as intense as any.

Civilian airfields have been few in number, although enhanced now by small privately owned landing strips which lie beyond the scope of this volume. Of one civilian airfield there has to be full mention for Marshall of Cambridge has made a most important contribution to the world of aviation, indeed is a name respected throughout the world with a history sufficient to fill a book.

The intention of this volume is that it be used as a guide, perhaps kept in the car, to be read at the places where the action took place, the events recounted came about. Visits to historic houses and famous sites are commonplace. Yet, why are airfields not looked upon as historic places? Perhaps it is that some are not aesthetic spots to linger in, but many are steeped in historic events or are the homes of famed warriors, and all are rich in nostalgia. The sad thing is that few carry any memorial to mark the past. Others, where there may be little to see, are highly evocative places.

Two points of advice, though. Some of the airfields remain in RAF or USAF hands and they are not for public viewing, except on their 'open' days. Many are in private hands and put to good agricultural purpose. Respect this, and please do not take it for granted that the beckoning old building is public property when it is almost surely privately owned.

This does not mean that viewing is impossible. There are often good vantage points. In some cases public roads cross the old airfield sites, and it may even be possible to travel along the line of a runway. If you must delve into today's activities then there is always the public viewing area at Mildenhall, an astonishing place for certainty.

The source of much of the material within these pages comes from my many years' association with military aviation in the area. Added to this has been the invaluable assistance of Peter M. Corbell whose fund of airfield knowledge is unsurpassed. I have added material from official releases and from official records and thereby acknowledge Crown Copyright on some of it. The United States Air Force has helpfully provided material and photographs and to them goes my thanks, as indeed it goes to many people who, over a very long period of time, have entertained me at so many of the stations and bases mentioned in this book. What memories it has brought back to me as I have worked upon its pages!

If you tour the region looking at these now almost ancient sites then it is to be hoped that David Dean's maps and diagrams will aid you. It might be a good idea to invest in the latest Ordnance Survey maps too, as the airfield references relate to the 1:50,000 series. You may be amazed to discover that in the case of the 25-inch series current airfield layouts are depicted in great detail whereas the disused ones do not merit much recording.

Keith Braybrooke, author of *Wingspan*, a history of Debden, has contributed the items on that station and also on Little Walden and Martlesham Heath, and to him I extend my thanks for his general help and advice with this book.

To Tommy Cushing I am greatly indebted. It was he who flew me over many disused airfields to obtain photographs from his Piper Cub, a delightful means of travel for sure. My thanks also to those who have lent photographs.

Much help has been given by the Staff of the Construction Industry Training Centre, Bircham Newton, and to them I am much indebted.

My thanks also to Michael Farrar and Cambridgeshire County Archives, and the Cambridge City Library for their patient assistance.

If you are not an East Anglian you probably think of this as a flat, unattractive part of England divorced from the modern world. This is quite untrue. Visit it on a lovely day when the clouds billow, the cowslips colour the verges as they do at one wartime airfield and the landscape is at its spring best. Then you will find it a region with its own brand of soft beauty — and you will discover a region with as great a history as any.

Cambridge,
May 1978.

Michael J.F. Bowyer

Glossary

AA Anti-aircraft.

AACU Anti-Aircraft Co-operation Unit.

A&AEE Aeroplane & Armament Experimental Establishment.

A&IEU Armament & Instrument Experimental Unit.

AATT Flight Anti-Aircraft and Target Towing Flight.

ACHU Aircrew Holding Unit.

ADGB Air Defence of Great Britain (previously Fighter Command).

AEF Air Experience Flight.

AFDS Air Fighting Development Squadron.

AFDU Air Fighting Development Unit.

AFS Advanced Flying School.

AI Airborne Interception (radar).

ANS Air Navigation School.

Anti-diver patrol to shoot down V1 bombs.

AOC Air Officer Commanding.

AOP Air Observation Post.

APC Armament Practice Camp.

APS Armament Practice Station.

ASH Narrow beam radar used for low-level operations.

ASR Air-Sea Rescue.

AWDS All-Weather Development Squadron.

AWFCS All-Weather Fighter Combat Squadron.

Baedecker raid German reprisal attack delivered upon historic city.

BAT Flight Blind Approach Training Flight.

BDTF Bomber Defence Training Flight.

BDU Bomber Development Unit.

BG Bomb Group (USAAF).

B&G Flight Bombing & Gunnery Flight.

BLEU Blind Landing Experimental Unit.

BSDU Bomber Support Development Unit.

CAACU Civilian Anti-Aircraft Co-operation Unit.

Calvert Bar landing light system A system of bars and intervening lights leading to the runway threshold.

'Carpet' operation Supply dropping sortie to Resistance forces.

CCRC Combat Crew Replacement Center.

'Circus' operation Fighter-escorted operation to entice enemy response.

CONUS USAF supply organisation (ie, Continental United States).

CSE Central Signals Establishment.

Darkie system Method of homing at night on radio bearings.

'Day Ranger' Operation to engage air and ground targets within a wide but specified area, by day.

DFCS Day Fighter Combat School.

'Distil' operation Fighter operation to shoot down enemy aircraft minesweeping, usually off Denmark.

Drem lighting System of outer markers and approach lights installed at many airfields in the early years of the war.

EBTS (*Coastal Command*) Elementary and Basic Training School.

ECM Electronic Counter Measures.

EFTS Elementary Flying Training School.

E&RFTS Elementary & Reserve Flying Training School.

ETO European Theatre of Operations.

Exercise 'Spartan' Exercise to establish methods of making entire airfield formation mobile.

FG Fighter Group.

FIDO Fog Investigation and Dispersal Operation.

'Fighter Night' patrol Fighter patrol over area where anti-aircraft gunners were ordered not to fire, sometimes restricted to certain altitudes.

'Firebash' sorties Sorties by Mosquitoes of 100 Group with the aircraft delivering incendiary or napalm loads on German airfields.

FTS Flying Training School.

'Gee' Medium-range radio aid to navigation equipment employing ground transmitters and airborne receiver.

GP (*bomb*) General Purpose high explosive bomb.

GRU General Reconnaissance Unit.
GSU Group Support Unit.
HE (bomb) High explosive bomb.
H2S Airborne radar navigational and target location aid.
IRBM Intermediate Range Ballistic Missile.
LAC Leading Aircraftman.
'Lagoon' Shipping reconnaissance operation off the Dutch coast.
LCN Method of identifying the load-weight characteristics of a runway.
LFS Lancaster Finishing School.
Lindholme gear Equipment dropped from air-sea rescue aircraft to crews ditched in the sea, developed at RAF Lindholme.
LNSF Light Night Striking Force of Mosquitoes of 8 Group.
Lorenz system Blind beam approach system.
MAEE Marine Aircraft Experimental Establishment.
'Mahmoud' sortie Night fighter sortie to specific point over enemy territory to engage his night fighters in that area.
'Mandrel' Airborne radar jamming device used by 100 Group.
MAP Ministry of Aircraft Production.
MCU Mosquito Conversion Unit.
MR squadron Medium Reconnaissance squadron.
MU Maintenance Unit.
'Night Ranger' Operation to engage air and ground targets within a wide but specified area, by night.
'Oboe' Ground-controlled radar system of blind bombing in which one station indicated track to be followed and another the bomb release point.
OCU Operational Conversion Unit.
Operation 'Aphrodite' Use of aged aircraft as radio-controlled bombers.
Operation 'Channel Stop' Attempt to close the English Channel to the passage of enemy shipping.
Operation Exodus Ferrying troops and displaced persons to and from Europe.
Operation 'Haddock' Code name for a force of Wellingtons sent to the South of France in 1940 to bomb Italy.
Operation 'Manna' Delivery of food and supplies to Holland by air in 1945.
Operation 'Musketeer' Code name for the Suez operation of 1956.
Operation 'Starkey' Large scale 'spoof' invasion of the Pas de Calais in September 1943, mounted to assess German reaction and bring his fighters to battle.
Operation 'Torch' Invasion of French North Africa in November 1942.
Operation 'Varsity' Airborne operation to facilitate the crossing of the River Rhine in March 1945.
ORTU Operational Refresher Training Unit.
OTU Operational Training Unit.
(P) AFU Pilots Advanced Flying Unit.
'PAMPA' Long-range weather reporting sortie.
PFF Pathfinder Force.
PFFNTU Pathfinder Force Navigational Training Unit.
POL depot Petrol, Oil and Lubricants depot.
POW Prisoner of war.
'Prata' Weather reconnaissance flight.
PRU Photographic Reconnaissance Unit.
PSP runway Pierced Steel Planking runway.
Pundit lights/letters Letters or lights displayed giving the airfield identity letters.
Q-site A site flashing lights to represent a mock airfield to attract enemy attention at night.
'Ramrod' Bomber raid escorted by fighters aimed at destruction of a specific target in daylight.
'Ranger' Usually a deep penetration flight to a specified area, to engage targets of opportunity.
RCAF Royal Canadian Air Force.
RCM Squadron Flight Radio Counter Measures Squadron Flight.
RDF Radio Direction Finding.
RFS Reserve Flying School.
'Rhombus' Weather reporting flight.
'Rhubarb' Low-level strike operation mounted in cloudy condition against enemy targets in Occupied Countries.
RLG Relief Landing Ground.
'Roadstead' Fighter operation mounted against shipping.
'Rodeo' Fighter sweep.
'Rover' Coastal Command armed patrol to search for enemy shipping.
RTC Recruit Training Centre.
SAC Strategic Air Command.
Sashlite bulb Photo-flash bulb used for training and experimental purposes.
SBC Small Bomb Container.
'Serrate' sortie Operation to locate and destroy enemy night fighters and combined with night bomber raids. Made use of airborne radar.
SHQ Station Head Quarters.
SLG Satellite Landing Ground.
SOE operations Operations under the control of the Special Operations Executive.
SRW Strategic Reconnaissance Wing.

'Sunray'   Overseas training flight for bomber crews.

SWO   Station Warrant Officer.

TAF   Tactical Air Force.

TAMU   Transport Aircraft Maintenance Unit.

TAW   Tactical Airlift Wing (USAF).

TDY   Temporary Duty Overseas (USAF).

TFW   Tactical Fighter Wing.

'Thum'   Weather reporting flight.

TRS   Tactical Reconnaissance Squadron.

UAS   University Air Squadron.

UP   A projector for firing Z rockets.

USAAC   United States Army Air Corps.

USAAF   United States Army Air Force (designated thus from June 20 1941, although the term Army Air Corps remained in common use long after that date).

USAF   Post-war formation from the USAAF, the United States Air Force.

USAFE   USAF Europe.

'Window'   Metallised paper strips dropped by bombers to disrupt enemy radar system.

Origins

East Anglia? No one appears to be really sure just where it is. Certainly it remains, fortunately, a rather undeveloped piece of land between London and Lincolnshire. But its precise boundaries in the south and west have always been disputed. If you were born in Norfolk or Suffolk you are a true East Anglian, and many who hail from Essex would claim that right. Cantabrians claim to be East Anglians, but it is doubtful whether the same can be true of those of the former Huntingdonshire. That county has been swallowed by Cambridgeshire whose masters now have the temerity to consider their whole county part of East Anglia. For sure, Bedfordshire is part of the East Midlands although some of its airfields had East Anglian leanings.

When it comes to writing about airfields and associated activity over East Anglia it makes more sense to overlook the niceties of territorial boundary and encompass a region which roughly stretches from King's Lynn almost to Bedford, by way of circumnavigating Peterborough, thence passing to Chelmsford and the Blackwater Estuary.

To the west of this region in the war lay largely training units. To the immediate south lies the zone where air activity and airfields have always been directly associated with the capital. East Anglia was the scene of the action stations.

It is not a flat, dull, uninteresting place as many would claim. In the south are the low East Anglian Heights which cut it off from the flat lands and salt marshes of Essex. To the west the sandy hills of Bedfordshire afford a changing landscape. Between that area and the sandy regions of north Norfolk runs a band of chalk downland fashioned by phases of the Quarternary Ice Age penning in the Fens. They have proven too wet to permit building of airfields except on islands which protrude from them. The coastal strip is, by contrast, slightly undulating, often sandy yet having firm foundations. Cambridgeshire is a mixture of these features, undulating land in the south rising to a windswept, uneven plateau bounded by the Cam Valley which leads to the Fens at Waterbeach leaving flat, wet land to the north which also forms part of the Fens. Travel west from Cambridge and the land immediately rises and again offers firm airfield territory stretching away to Bedfordshire. Thus, the scene.

The history of East Anglia as regards flying is long. Indeed, balloon ascents were being made here during the late 1700s, from Norwich, Cambridge and Bury St Edmunds. These towns, apart from Ipswich and the border bastions of Colchester and Chelmsford, have long been the only sizeable centres of population other than coastal towns and market hamlets, and they have had a bearing upon the siting of airfields.

There was plentiful experimentation with aeroplanes in this area during the dawn of powered flight. Flat grasslands attracted the Army around garrison towns. The great encampment of troops on Midsummer Common in Cambridge during the summer of 1912 brought along the airships 'Beta' and 'Gamma', to settle close to where Colonel Cody and Moorhouse had landed, the latter to 'buy a pair of shoes in town', an event which brought the crowds out to see his unusual mount.

The coming of the 'Great War' saw a veritable explosion of air activity. Great Yarmouth's famous Naval Air Station opened in the summer of 1914, able to accommodate land and sea planes. Orfordness Experimental Station for ordnance testing, and still in secretive use, was a going concern from 1912 and soon had an airstrip. Thetford, a major troop centre, had an airfield to the south of the town. The seaplane station at Felixstowe opened in August 1913 to specialise in experimental work and inland at nearby Martlesham Heath, a sandy waste near Ipswich, a landplane experimental station was opened in 1916.

When Boulton & Paul at Norwich began building aeroplanes they needed a testing ground, readily available on Mousehold Heath from 1915 and used until the outbreak of the Second World War. From Mousehold the company concentrated testing of the all-metal aeroplanes in which they specialised. Savages Ltd of King's Lynn, more associated with fairgrounds than aeroplanes, started building aircraft in the First World War, whilst at nearby Bircham Newton an airfield was built in 1916 and later accommodated four-engined Handley Page 0/1500s, part of the Independent Bombing Force which ultimately evolved as the germ of Bomber Command.

Training stations to supply crews for the forces in France were built at Wyton, Narborough, Fowlmere, Feltwell and Hardwick near Cambridge. With the coming of the Zeppelin raids fighter defence was brought into being.

The importance of airships was still very high on the list of suitable flying machines. In February 1916 the airship station at Pulham opened, a base for experiments, home of the R-33 used after the war for trials with fighters hooked on to the airship for defence. Home, too, for the R-34, the first airship to make a double Atlantic crossing. When Pulham closed, a giant hangar was transported to Cardington for the Royal Airship Works.

East Anglians took readily to flying themselves. The Suffolk Aero Club formed in 1925, the Norfolk and Norwich Aero Club in 1927. Ipswich airfield was opened in June 1930 by HRH The Prince of Wales, and in 1938 West Suffolk Aero Club opened at Westley, a small airfield near Bury St Edmunds where Taylorcraft monoplanes were to see peacetime and wartime usage.

Most important of them all, though, was the civilian organisation founded by Mr David Marshall of Cambridge. He had been attracted to motor cars before the 1914-1918 war and established a garage in Jesus Lane in 1909. After the war his interest proceeded to aviation and in 1929 he established Marshall's Flying School on a site near his old home, now covered by the Whitehill Estate. To this airfield came many of the great names in sporting flying during the 1930s, and Alan Cobham's Circus was a summer excitement.

Those were, indeed, memorable days. For a few shillings one could get aloft in an Avro 504 or that striking-looking Airspeed Ferry. On a wet Tuesday afternoon, hearing that Henri Mignet had come to display his 'Flying Flea', I craftily slipped out of school for a look. Amazingly, nobody ever seemed to notice my absence, proving that safe truancy is nothing very new! There Mignet stood, in the rain, a lonely figure in black beret looking every inch a pioneer. I was his only visitor. But alas, I had to leave before he flew. 'I'm sorry, little boy,' he said. 'The rain...' Fortunately I left just before a relative arrived to photograph the strange craft.

Little wonder that with so much air activity some East Anglians have felt that they must record their memories. My interest in all things that fly probably stems from another sight of youthful days. I was playing with a large tin model aeroplane that the wonder of Christmas had bestowed upon me when, suddenly, my mother swept me off my feet and into her arms. She rushed into the garden and there, in all its gigantic majesty, like a colossal silver cigar, appearing over the rooftops in the next street was the R-101. It was low enough to see the black letters on its side. Its passage seemed endless for the nose was over our rooftop before the tail had appeared. It was for me a magic moment for all time equalled only by my distant viewing of the airship shortly before it took off on its ill-fated voyage.

I screamed as the R-101 had passed over, half in fear half in ecstasy. Mum had told me all about the 'zepps' — I wasn't sure whether this was a left-over! Then we rushed along the passage by our house to see the massive airship slowly pass over the town towards Cardington. I was an aviation fanatic from that moment onwards.

'No, you can't got to see the Mildenhall Air Race, it's starting too early,' said my father, who presumably thought of a tiring day at work ahead. The MacRobertson Race was, without doubt, one of the aviation 'greats' of all time. There were 64 entries for this Mildenhall-Melbourne Air Race and the eager pilots set off at dawn on October 20 1934, some to join in Melbourne's Centenary. Jim Mollison and Amy Johnson were there, but the names we all came to associate with Mildenhall were of C.W.A. Scott and Campbell-Black who won in the amazing de Havilland Comet. How I have wished a hundred hundred times that I had been more persuasive and made Mildenhall, which had opened on October 16 as one of the first airfields of the Expansion Period. For ever my life-long friend Alan Wright would be able to remind me that he was actually there to see that DC-2 and all the other exciting entrants!

But at least I had one compensation. I did not miss the 1935 Jubilee Review at Mildenhall, a memorable event indeed with hundreds of silver biplanes drawn up in review order for viewing, and green Heyfords and 'Ginnys' as a backcloth.

In retrospect that event marked a watershed, for already the signs of war were emergent when Italy attacked Abyssinia and Hitler was yelling. It is with the active days beyond then that this book is mainly concerned.

Building the armoury

Major expansion of the RAF was announced in July 1934. Aircraft production needed to be matched by expanded support organisations and great increase in ground and aircrew training.

In 1934 there were only four active military airfields in East Anglia. The only feasible enemy had hitherto been France, an unlikely foe, and the Metropolitan Air Force existed primarily to feed the needs of Empire policing. True, the approaches to London were guarded by a ring of fighter stations stemming from the Steel-Bartholomew Plan of 1923, and updated in 1935 under the Fifty-Two Squadron Scheme and quickly by the Re-orientation Scheme. Army support squadrons were stationed in southern England and the few bomber bases sited where they would cause least public annoyance.

East Anglian stations of Great War vintage remaining in use were Bircham Newton and Felixstowe, with Duxford built just after the war as a training station and later used as a fighter base whose squadrons had to defend the whole of East Anglia and bar entrance to the East Midlands. The airship base at Pulham remained, but Cardington held the Royal Airship Works where now the balloon barrage scheme would be worked out. After the R-101 disaster nobody wanted to know about airships. Felixstowe housed the Marine Aircraft Experimental Establishment which carried out trials on a wide assortment of marine aircraft — useful for Empire and deep sea patrolling. Nearby Martlesham's Aeroplane & Armament Experimental Establishment tested landplanes, military and civilian, making the area in which these two stations were sited always one of extreme interest. A few civil fields were also available in East Anglia.

In 1923 the flourishing and large airfield at Fowlmere had closed, its hangars of Duxford style being demolished. Some less pretentious wooden wartime hangars remained at Bircham Newton, along with a small grass landing ground and areas of concrete around the hangars. To the rear of these were the stone-dashed buildings of the Technical Site, with the Domestic Site on the side of the road passing through the camp, as also at Duxford. Buildings generally had slate roofs, accommodation was spartan.

The RAF, starved of money, obviously considered a land of carrots, sugar beet and kippers barely worth defending. But as an unsinkable aircraft carrier East Anglia would later play a major part when war came.

In 1934 the first expansion airfields were begun and Mildenhall opened. Future bomber stations would have huge concrete and metal 'C' Type hangars with gabled roofing to allow the light to penetrate. Offices and small workshops were placed along their sides. There were four such hangars at bomber stations, one for each Flight of the two squadrons to be based there generally. Aircraft were always stored in hangars when flying ceased for the day, to protect them against bad weather.

'Double box' control towers — the RAF always referred to them as watch offices — were now provided, brick-built and replacing the wooden sheds which had been used previously as primitive communications centres. Concrete areas were laid down around the hangars and perimeter roads were later added for vehicles. There were no concrete dispersals pre-war, they did not come until 1940.

Domestic sites on the new stations were built to the rear of the Technical Site which was close to the hangars. Included was the Fire Section at first sited among the camp buildings and not by the watch office as was wartime practice. Elaborate workshops were also provided, but no longer an engine test rig. One of those may still be seen at Duxford.

The most striking landmark at expansion stations was the tall, rectangular water tower. Stations needed to be as self-supporting as possible, holding their own water supplies and generating their own power. In a flat region water supply had always brought problems and the tall towers ensured adequate pressure as well as home supplies.

General designs for the buildings were submitted to the Fine Arts Commission, and major buildings had a mock Georgian exterior. This was particularly true of Officers' Messes which remain a gracious feature of any pre-war station. Airmens' Quarters were usually planned on a two-storey H-pattern, each floor of each wing accommodating about 20 beds. The provision of indoor ablutions was a great advance, and floors were covered by linoleum. Vying for best grace was the Station Headquarters building which usually faced the camp Main Gate. It is surely worth noting that for decades the style of these buildings has given them a quite up-to-date appearance, added to which they have proven extremely substantial. As for the 10-gabled 'C' Type bomber hangars of 300-foot length and 150-foot width, they toned as well with a Hart as with a Canberra.

Acquisition of land for the new airfields in an agricultural region was very unpopular. Wyton and Marham were chosen to embrace sites used in the First World War. The constant fear was that new monoplane bombers would need very long take-off runs. One possibility was assisted or 'catapult' take-off. This was abandoned due to technical inflexibility and vulnerability to attack. Maximum runs of 600 yards were required at the airfields, quite inadequate for heavily laden bombers. Thus, some of the grass fields had to be extended giving runs of 1,000 yards or more.

As soon as the German threat was obvious the positioning of the new bombers was decided upon. Yorkshire, closest to Germany, came to house the longest-ranged bombers, for maximum penetration. Lincolnshire and East Anglia would accommodate medium and light bombers, the latter now intended to operate from France. That assumed available French aerodromes, which were never sufficient in number. At first Handley-Page Heyfords made up the main heavy bomber strength in East Anglia until Wellingtons began to join 3 Group in November 1938. Throughout the war, and indeed into the 1960s, 3 Group controlled the medium and heavy East Anglian bombers.

In the west, and in central East Anglia, were sited the light bombers of 2 Group on stations similar in size to those for the heavies at Marham, Stradishall, Mildenhall and Honington. Watton, Wattisham, Wyton and West Raynham were built with 2 Group in mind and housed Blenheims, the Battles being based at Upwood. All except Mildenhall were of standard expansion style, and Mildenhall still retains many features of the pre-expansion period.

Its proximity to the East Coast caused Bircham Newton to be switched to

Coastal Command in August 1936 and three 'C' Type hangars were built replacing the First World War sheds. The Domestic Site was updated, but First World War buildings may still be seen there in plenty. This is also true of Felixstowe where the Officers' Mess, still easily seen, is of First World War vintage, like the huge hangars for tall flying boats. By contrast are the more modern Married Quarters.

The only pre-war expansion period fighter station was Debden, opened in April 1937. Luckily the Spitfire and Hurricane were suitable for short grass fields and Duxford, whence the first Spitfires came, was able to accept them readily. Hangars at fighter stations were slightly shorter than those at the bomber bases, and the two hangars at Debden were intended for two fighter squadrons.

Ground defences were moved on to airfield perimeters during the Munich crisis, and searchlights were then deployed in fields around, manned mainly by Territorial Army personnel. Pre-war airfields were usually surrounded only by hedges without even barbed wire to keep out the unwelcomed.

Air traffic control was primitive in the extreme and not until 1940 was much development undertaken. Meteorological services, which hitherto had amounted to a phone call, were now provided in an office in the ground floor of the new watch offices where provision of teleprinters would revolutionise communications.

To the war many aircraft did not have R/T, and landings were made after a glance at the landing 'T' and the windsock. The provision of R/T in fighters came in 1935 and was a great advance.

Night flying, too, was a primitive business, with the landing lane on the grass marked by oil burning gooseneck flares which were still in use to the middle of the war on airfields without solid runways.

In 1939 a new type of airfield began to be built, its centre piece being two Type J hangars with oval roofing and more metal in their construction to speed building. A gradual switch to flat-roofed buildings was apparent, and control towers of revised form. Generally speaking such airfields were less sophisticated building-wise, and are typified by Waterbeach and Oakington. Gone, too, the tall water tower, replaced by two large tanks on scaffolding.

One feature, though, was apparent at all pre-war airfields — the parade ground. Usually it was sited close to the Airmens' Mess. Nowadays, with parades few, these large tarmac areas have become car parks and other wide concrete aprons serve for parades. Such is evolution.

Five counties at war

When war broke in September 1939 there were only 15 active military airfields and five satellite landing grounds in East Anglia. In May 1945 there were 107 within the region earlier defined. The increase in air activity had been phenomenal, and the area remains the busiest for military flying in Britain.

With mobilisation came the opening of the first SLGs (Satellite Landing Grounds), the most famous of which was at this stage surely Newmarket Heath which virtually had station status and where, when war broke out, armed Wellingtons of 99 Squadron stood clustered by the service road leading to the famous Grandstand.

The greatest need, however, was for fighter protection over the eastern counties. It was achieved by placing fighter detachments at Watton, and at Martlesham which accommodated aircraft from Debden.

Only one of the East Anglian airfields had fixed runways, the others merely marked grass tracks. Work was hastened on four new airfields commenced in 1939, of which the most important proved to be Coltishall. Its position caused its role to be switched from bomber to fighter at a late stage in its construction, and it became the Sector Station for a large area of East Anglia. Meanwhile, essential East Coast convoy protection flights and the 'Kipper Patrols' had to be flown over the fishing fleet by Coastal Command Ansons from Bircham Newton. Fighters operated from Martlesham where the hangars were assorted in size and shape and the buildings otherwise very aged.

One of the most interesting aspects of military flying in East Anglia throughout the war was the number of new types of aircraft which made their service entry at airfields in this area. The first to do so was the Boulton Paul Defiant at Martlesham in late 1939. East Anglia, though, would always be primarily a bomber area. Early in the war Stradishall, Bassingbourn and Upwood took on bomber training roles. There were only ever to be three Training Command airfields in the region.

Most operational Bomber Command stations had SLGs attached by the end of 1939, little more than grass fields with tented accommodation and soon a few wooden huts. Refuelling could be from bowsers sent from the main stations where arming and briefing took place. Small water trailers were placed at these sites, which were otherwise devoid of services at this period.

When the battle really broke in May 1940 the two fighter stations were too far from the scene of action to be of use, so their squadrons advanced to Hornchurch and to Horsham St Faith, which was incomplete, but from where Defiants flew their first memorable encounters. The first major airfield to open during the war was Coltishall, in June 1940.

That month brought the first night bombing attacks on the United Kingdom, some being delivered against East Anglian airfields. They were all too far north to play much part in the Battle of Britain, but the Wellington squadrons which had fought over Scandinavia were now pitted against German industry. By day the Blenheim stations mounted costly raids on Belgian and French targets and continued to fly such raids in the summer. Debden, Martlesham and Duxford were attacked, but the major participation in the Battle of Britain was made by the 12 Group 'Big Wing' which assembled daily at, and operated from, Duxford.

The most noticeable change in the appearance of operational airfields at the outbreak of war had been the dispersal of aircraft around their perimeters although no hard dispersals had been built. Aircraft were taken into hangars only for major servicing. Use was made of camouflage netting, but the time taken to place and remove it from large aircraft quickly brought an end to the scheme. At some stations aircraft were dispersed among nearby trees.

The war brought an immediate increase in accident rates and there were battle casualties to consider. At the start of September a small dump of crashed aircraft appeared opposite the railway station by Barnwell Bridge in Cambridge. Soon, a larger depot to accommodate the wreckage — first of a Vildebeest — was established opposite the then Cambridge Borough Cemetery. The organisation here, No 54 Maintenance Unit, gradually expanded into a large force which travelled far through the eastern counties salvaging parts from wrecked aircraft and, in November 1939, had the task of gathering the pieces from a mine-carrying Heinkel 115 floatplane which exploded on the foreshore at Sheringham. The site of the MU is now covered by a housing estate and its extensive sub-sites are clear of all remnants. One lies under the new Cambridge relief road by the Priory School, the other is now partly within the Cambridge Airport boundary.

The winter of 1940/41 brought a big problem. It turned out to be snowy and icy and when the thaw set in the airfields, not having properly settled, were turned into muddy surfaces. Some attempt at producing hardstandings came when coke and ashes from local gasworks were put down, but this could only be a temporary measure. Such sites were quickly made for the heavy Stirlings at Oakington, but that airfield was in such poor state that it was all but abandoned for the well-drained surface of Newmarket Heath. Drainage in an area noted for its high water table was to be a serious problem for many years.

Late 1940 saw the coming of the Nissen hut at dispersal points. These huts with their curved metal roofs, tortoise stoves and differing lengths were to become a feature of nearly every station, and were used as living quarters at many American bases. It was in 1941 that the 'Blister hangar' made its debut, with a curved roof and at its base a width of 45, 65 or 69 feet. One may still be seen on the one-time Snailwell airfield.

The biggest advance, though, came with the provision of concrete runways at bomber bases. Providing them at the heavy bomber stations took a long time to achieve, and policy was that new stations would have them from the start and older ones would acquire them in 1942-1943. In March 1941 Waterbeach opened with a 6,070-foot runway 150 feet wide serving as the main NE/SW runway and two 4,140-foot × 150-foot subsidiary runways running roughly SE/NW and N/S and connected by an encircling perimeter track from which exit points led to 33 circular concrete dispersal hardstandings. Provision of such runways took a long time: Bassingbourn and Wyton had them in 1942, but it was mid-1943 before they were laid at Marham.

The runways were to a similar pattern at all new airfields and many of the older ones. The main runway lay in the direction of the prevailing wind, roughly NE/SW, and was usually about 2,000 yards in length and 50 yards wide. Two subsidiary runways ran roughly N/S and NW/SE, each about 1,400 yards in length. Around 36 dispersals were normal, enough for two bomber squadrons. Runway siting partly depended upon obstructions and dwellings in the flight path. Airfield circuits were chosen with as much care as possible. Nevertheless, that at Waterbeach had to pass over Landbeach village, a feature never desirable but here impossible to avoid. One example of a possible obstruction which became well known in the war was the church at Orwell near Bassingbourn. The wall of its tower facing the aerodrome was painted white, a feature still visible. It was one of the first buildings to carry a red obstruction light, and at that time a red light had only one connotation! Siting of a 2,000 yard runway at Oakington in 1941-1942 brought an inevitable problem of those times, the closing of a local road linking two villages and forcing a lengthy diversion at a time when the most popular, and almost only, means of transport was the bicycle. Such closures of roads were avoided wherever possible, but the residents around Little Walden, Mildenhall and others suffered similar disturbances.

Every airfield was marked at night by a Chance Light placed on a vehicle mounting which was like a small lighthouse, and which could be revolved. By the watch offices in 1940 came two white identity letters, the pundit letters within the signal's square which afforded visual identity of each station. As in pre-war days a pundit light flashed these letters at night when the station was open, 'OA' for Oakington, 'MH' for Mildenhall, 'CI' for Cambridge, etc. Naval stations later used such letters for the tail identity of their aircraft. Within the signals square at every station was placed the signal mortar, a wide tube into which could be dropped a mortar bomb which would burst high to light the airfield and surrounding areas for an emergency landing.

The provision of runways brought one great advance for along their sides were built flush-lying high-intensity unidirectional flarepath electric lights. The general pattern of these was on the style of Drem Lighting. Threshold lighting is a post-war feature, funnel lights having normally been sited in wartime as a runway lead-in from the outer markers. Provision of power to outlying places brought great problems and needed a considerable effort if the station was attached to the grid system. Airfields had their own generating units which were used at remote stations. The East Anglian fens were without electricity until the 1960s.

Equally important was the linkage of water mains to airfields where as many as 2,000 personnel were stationed. This was done where practicable, and at a time when the country areas were devoid of such niceties. Again, not until many years after the war were many villages supplied with piped water. Little wonder that the RAF stations, which had to be self-supporting for emergencies, all acquired high water towers for storage of water which could be supplied under suitable pressure.

Vast quantities of cement were needed for the building of airfields, the individual costs of which often surpassed £1 million. Archaic as it now sounds some of the cement was carried to sites in the early war years by steam-powered British Portland Cement lorries. They had to negotiate winding roads far removed from any that remain today, so that airfield building required tremendous effort and care.

The biggest expansion period came in the late summer of 1942, by which time the Americans were arriving. To accommodate a new air force meant a vast building programme. Some RAF airfields had to be vacated, or intended RAF airfields relinquished. There was a limit to where squadrons could be redeployed, and some were drafted overseas. In July 1942 the first US Army Engineer Battalions arrived to aid British civilian contractors, and a host of new airfields were prepared under RAF surveillance for occupation in 1943. Many satellites were raised to full station status and had runways laid down. Labour did not exist for all airfields to have concrete runways and in 1942 PSP (Pierced Steel Planking) in the form of Sommerfeld Tracking began to be laid, for even fighters were getting too heavy to be able to operate in all weathers from grass surfaces. Duxford acquired such tracking in 1943, Bottisham had it in 1942. It was also widely used, particularly at American bases, for hard standings and taxi tracks.

Runway laying was not easy, for some of the older airfield surfaces were far from ideal without a lot of preparation. In the case of Lakenheath the sandy soil had a built-in springing motion, hardly suitable for the Stirlings based there.

It was in 1940 that attention began to be paid to the security of airfields. Gone was the mere hedge of pre-war days, coils of barbed wire now being placed to keep out intruders. Gun sites for airfield anti-aircraft defence were placed around the airfields in 1939 carrying light machine-guns or Bofors and manned by Army personnel until the RAF Regiment formed mid-war.

The increase in mid-war night flying brought considerable problems. In 1940-1941 crews homed on bearings transmitted from a considerable number of D/F stations, such as that which may still be seen fully intact at Warboys, within the Darkie system. By 1943 a novel idea in use consisted of a trio of searchlight beams which met over the 'open' airfield to assist bombers returning from night operations. There was no radar to assist in landing, and Ground Controlled Approach talk down did not come into use, initially with RAF Transport Command, until after the war. Crews found their own ways home, aided by Lorenz and Standard Beam Approach systems and even these were not universal. Any display of runway or flarepath lights was bound to attract intruders, and holding aircraft on the circuit when crews were most fatigued was equally dangerous. Many crews did become lost in the early war years and, as few airfields were open at night in non-operational areas of the country, crashes were all too frequent as fuel ran low.

From 1942 onwards hangar accommodation, now only used for major servicing, was answered by the erection of Tees-side Engineering's prefabricated transportable metal hangars, the 'T' Hangars whose size varied according to need. Generally they had a length of 240 feet and a width of 115 feet, the latter varying according to need. The 1942 *et seq* airfields usually had two T2 hangars 115 feet wide which allowed housing of the largest aircraft in use. Major servicing was often undertaken by parties from Maintenance Units, or working parties from civilian contractors like Marshall of Cambridge whose workers were to be found in many parts of Britain.

The vast increase in flying, with as many as 4,000, even 5,000 flights being made daily over East Anglia by 1944, put great demands upon flight planning which, even to the end of the war, was in its infancy. Every airfield had its control tower, and defence radar stations gradually provided more information on the positions of aircraft. The Observer Corps played a vital role in plotting all flights. The wonder is that there were so few mid-air collisions. Exit points for bomber operations were established and usually the bombers left our coast near Yarmouth, Orfordness or Cromer, so that any aircraft using another route could be seen likely to be hostile. The Luftwaffe was quick to appreciate the ease with which low-flying aircraft could escape detection, and intruders were able to creep in when clouds were low, doing so into 1942 after which the enemy relied upon speed and transit in the bomber stream to penetrate.

Late in 1943 FIDO (Fog Investigation and Dispersal Operation) was introduced to aid night landings when visibility was poor. One great advance came with the opening of the Emergency Landing Ground at Woodbridge which existed only to receive aircraft in distress. Hitherto they had to make safe landings wherever they could, most stations at some time receiving 'cuckoos'.

Backing the operational side at any airfield was Station Sick Quarters. A large RAF hospital was built at Ely at the start of the war to which seriously injured personnel had to be taken, the hospital having the appearance of a pre-war RAF station as regards its buildings.

By 1943 the USAAF was mounting fighter-escorted bomber operations with up to 1,000 aircraft airborne and later many more. These forces needed great airspace in which to take station early in the day, the place jockeying being something never to be forgotten. Brightly coloured leadships were involved and sometimes bomber forces gathered behind towed flares, it often taking well over two hours before the great cavalcade set forth in splendid array across a sky festooned with vapour trails.

Once gone it would be the turn of the RAF bombers flying training sorties or being air tested for the following night's operations. Such was the crowded nature of the British sky that Ansons and Wellingtons from OTUs and ANSs had to traverse East Anglia on training cross-country flights by day. A considerable amount of communications flying took place and by 1944 the sight of a UC-64 Norseman or a C-78 Bobcat was a common feature.

Gunnery practice and fighter affiliation training became more commonplace as the war progressed. There was beam approach training using Oxfords distinguished by their yellow triangles, and a surprising number of experimental aircraft traversed the area. At night Wellingtons of OTUs had to be routed this way, clear as it was of large cities, but it was the massed take-offs at dusk which posed the greatest traffic problems, the bombers generally circling their bases to gain height before progressing in the bomber stream. A malfunction, or worse a flying accident at take-off, could jeopardise a whole operation, so precise had timing become. Once the bombers were on their way training aircraft would cross the area, and the high intensity of training by the Stirling Conversion Units added to the control problems. All these aspects cannot be divorced from any consideration of airfield activities.

As an area of interest for any enthusiast East Anglia was unbeatable. Operational aircraft passed that way in thousands so that one acquired the feeling of 'oh no, not another 300 B-17s,' or 'it's only a Lancaster,' the singular sight of which today makes the pulse beat faster. Security at all airfields was, of course, strict; but it only whetted the appetite of the handful of enthusiasts of those days ever eager to locate a new airfield and identify its occupants. Often they could only be identified by some cunning detective work, and the appearance of new 'code letters' would bring a flurry of excitement. There was always the thrill of finding a newly opened airfield and seeing some new British or American unit in occupation. Usually there was careless talk and those of us with the interest and active minds would have what still seems an amazing picture of what was taking place.

Mix with this the sight of some exotic creature like a jet test bed Wellington which spent a few days at Newmarket in July 1944, enjoying watching the giant Hamilcar glider on trial, secret of course, and seeing the first Typhoon arrive for squadron service — not to mention the excitement of diving into a ditch when a low-flying Ju 88 appeared — these were daily thrills.

Some days would become indelible in the mind. September 12 1941 was one such. Local gossip revealed that late that day some German aircraft would arrive at Duxford. Three of us set off for a private view and at 1530 hours sure enough they came, the Heinkel He 111, AW177, and Ju 88A-6, EE205, escorted by Spitfires and Hurricanes, and they landed low over the side road now destroyed by the new motorway. We watched and waited and were well rewarded when Bf 109E, AE479, did some flying and at 1700 hours one of the early Typhoons took off. The second Whirlwind prototype, L6845, made some low passes before combating the Bf 109. Then a Fulmar trundled away and to round off the day we had some fine close views of the first Typhoons for 56 Squadron.

July 5 1942 was a typical fine day of that warm summer. My diary for that day begins with the noting of two low-flying Tomahawks, and during the morning I recorded Stirlings including MG:L and two from 1651 Conversion Unit, 'V' and 'G'; Tigers and Magisters from Cambridge; a Master 1,T8483; Blenheim IVs; Wellington lcs; a Hudson manouvering with a Folland 43/37 test bed; a Martlet IV; Typhoons in plenty; a Boston III; Lysander target tug on fighter affiliation with a Blenheim IV; Mustang 1 XV:S; one of the rare Wellington VIs based at Stradishall; a Whitley V and a Beaufort 1 which landed at Cambridge. In the afternoon a Boston III zoomed around, Typhoons and Wellingtons were active including some Mk IIIs like SR-O, SR-Q, SR-X and some of 75 Squadron; a Master III; Hudson with OS coding; Mustang 1s; Stirlings; Oxfords; Hurricane IIB; Wellington lc XW:I; Tomahawk IIB; Gladiator; two Mosquito IIs; Ansons; a Beaufighter 1; three Lancasters in formation; a Halifax II; a Beaufort in grey-green finish and in the evening a Lancaster crew took it into their heads to do some beat-ups. Just a normal day!

A year later July 5 1943 proved just as typically interesting. Again it was fine, but the evening was overcast. Stirlings were still active, also an assortment of Halifaxes and Lancasters. A Beaufighter with dihedral tailplane was an unusual sight, still. A few B-17Fs flew over and a Whitley V towed a Horsa across. In the afternoon eight Venturas made passage and an RAF Mitchell crew had fun with a P-47. Mosquitoes, Wellingtons, a Lysander, Whitley V, Albemarle and some B-26s were about and at 1325 came a moment of excitement when a Fortress 1 in a curious scheme of black upper surfaces and grey under surfaces took off for Driffield. Sixteen B-17Fs flew across with eight P-47s and an EZ-coded Whitley V. Next day brought even more excitement when a strange sound turned out to be the only Heston Phoenix, heading east out of Cambridge.

All the airfields from time to time had rare visitors. Rarities came fast as on July 24 1943 when the prototype Halifax III circled a few times then at 1740 hours a Stirling flew over in USAAF markings. Every day had something exciting to offer, for the large number of airfields attracted so many aircraft.

The demise of airfields and units after VE-Day was nothing short of amazing. They seemed to close in no time, it was unbelievable. The quietness of a forsaken airfield was quite eerie. Silent roads where once military vehicles abounded was equally strange. The large spectacle-like dispersals at so many American airfields looked odd without their occupants, but bomb craters were still a reminder of alarming moments. Some have never been filled and are marked by groups of shrubs thriving on the fertility of a land mine.

Removing the concrete for the return to farming has proven a weighty task — getting on for £1,000 million had been spent on the airfields. Never again is such a panoply of might likely to be assembled, and it is sad that so little remains now of airfields where happiness, pathos and courage were inextricably mixed. Perhaps one day people will visit such places as Deopham Green centuries hence to feel something of its history which, to them, will be as distant as the castles of the Middle Ages are to us. They will find little, and certainly not the memorial which one might expect. One thing is certain, they will never be able to appreciate the thrill of having been around when it all happened.

Airfield architecture

Before recounting the histories of the individual airfields some consideration of the architecture of the stations is worthwhile.

Buildings on East Anglian military airfields fall into these six categories:

   i) erected by 1918

   ii) completed immediately following World War 1

   iii) erected during the early 1920s to accommodate the peacetime Air Force and, additionally, further buildings dating from the late 1920s

   iv) erected on both old and new sites stemming from the 1934 Expansion Scheme which item also embraces airfields completed early in World War 2

   v) somewhat utility airfields laid down during the war and which were of three types: a) grass runway satellite airfields and Relief Landing Grounds, b) grass landing grounds to which runways were later added and c) airfields built to have runways, this latter type forming the largest number

   vi) airfields retained for post-war use and much modified. At the latter runways have been extended to about 10,000 feet in length, control towers have been much improved and many other modifications have taken place in respect of landing aids, etc.

History plays strange tricks, for who in 1939 would have envisaged that Alconbury — the first satellite used in the area — would become a major airfield, that Bentwaters which came late into use would also hold a major place and that strongly-built Stradishall would evolve into a prison?

1 Below left: *A view across the apron at Duxford, Chipmunk G-BBMV in the foreground and a Belfast Truss hangar behind.* 2 Above: *One of the 1917-style hangars at Martlesham in 1978.* 3 Below: *Bircham Newton's old workshop building. Note ducts to carry warm air to the adjacent hangar, now marked merely by its concrete floor.*

Without doubt the most architecturally interesting East Anglian airfield is Bircham Newton, probably the most historic in the region. It closed as an RAF station in 1962. Four years later it was revived to become the Construction Industry Training Centre. The landing ground has changed face as construction industry students learn their skills. The area of the bomb dump has suffered a similar fate, but for the most part Bircham Newton retains the appearance of an airfield comprised of buildings of the period 1917-1945.

There is no 'standard layout' for an airfield, yet all have similarities. Airfields may be grouped into those with runways and those without, there being few of the latter in East Anglia by 1945 (a notable exception being Docking). Another grouping comprises those with the Technical and Domestic Sites grouped as opposed to some where the two items are on opposite sides of the camp access road, as at Duxford and indeed Bircham Newton. Wartime airfields had much reduced technical facilities, and domestic sites were scattered within the airfield environs.

The dominating feature at all airfields is the hangar complex. At Duxford and Martlesham hangars of 1917 style may be seen. In the case of the former, Belfast Trusses in the roofs have given the name 'Belfast Type' to the sheds, whereas two of Martlesham's hangars are of even earlier vintage and remain in good condition (Photos 1, 2). Another hangar of similar vintage stands by the eastern edge of Marham. At Bircham Newton World War 1 hangars were demolished in the mid-1930s, although the bases of two hangars and door runners may still be seen. Adjacent to one of these hangars were the main workshops from which warm air ducts led into the hangar providing heating. The ducts are still in situ (Photo 3).

A fourth stage in hangar design is typified by C Type Aircraft Sheds. There are two versions of these. At Martlesham and Mildenhall may be seen C Type Gabled (plan reference 2029/34) (Photo 4). More common are C Type Hipped, the ends of the roof gables being slanted as at many sites including Bircham Newton (Photo 5). The first of the C Type were similar to Type A, but enlarged. Of B Type none has existed in East Anglia. They had doors opening along one side of the building. The C Type hangars were built in varying lengths. Fighter stations such as Debden had seven-bay hangars whereas the ten-bay type were built at bomber stations and at Bircham Newton (Photo 5). Details of hangar types may be seen in the diagrams on pages 28-30.

In 1939 hangar design was changed and stations laid down pre-war were completed with J and K Type hangars (drawing references 3084/39 and 5836/39 respectively) to the designs of Sir William Arrol & Co Ltd. These had curved ¼ in steel plate covering roofs. Offices along either side of the base of the hangars were added as with C Type. It was usual for those facing the landing ground to accommodate offices and crew rooms, leaving the others to be used for workshops. Such hangars may be seen at Oakington, Waterbeach (Photo 6) and one at Swanton Morley.

4: *The newest hangar still standing at Martlesham.*

During 1941 Blister hangars began to be quickly erected at many airfields. Most were of the Miskins Type of which three variants existed: a) Timber maximum open span of 45 ft 6 in, b) Over Type (Steel) with an opening of 65 ft 0¼ in, and c) Enlarged Over Type (Steel) with an opening of 69 ft. A much wider Dorman Long Blister was designed in 1943 with an opening of 90 ft 3½ in. Types 'a' and 'b' were the most common, sited on the perimeters of airfields as at Bircham Newton, and on satellite airfields where no hangars had previously been placed. Each Blister could accommodate one smallish aeroplane for major servicing. Very few Blister hangars remain in their wartime positions, but one may be seen in its original siting at Snailwell (Photo 7), and another is used by the private flying group at Cambridge and may be seen close to the A45.

Commonest hangars at airfields built during the war were the Bellman (8349/37) and Tees-Side Bridge & Engineering Company 'T' (transportable) Type of which the T2 with an open span of 113 ft was the most common. This variant

5 Above: *One of Bircham Newton's C Type (Hipped) hangars.* 6 Below: *The curved roof distinguishes this J Type hangar at Waterbeach.*

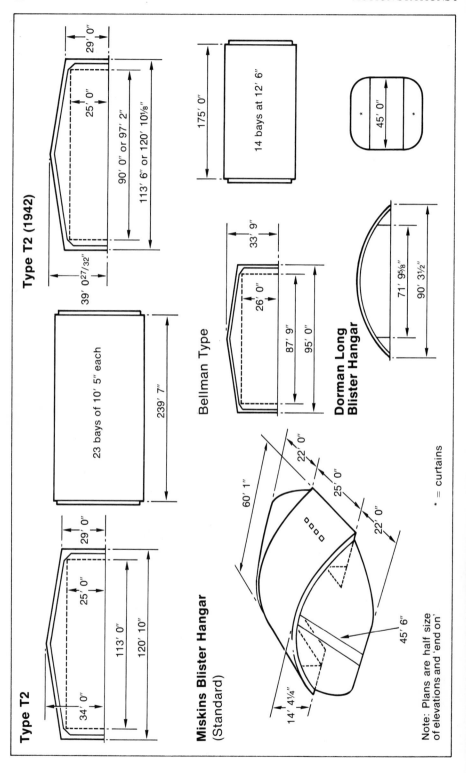

Type T2 (1942)

29' 0"

25' 0"

90' 0" or 97' 2"

113' 6" or 120' 10⅛"

39' 0²⁷/₃₂"

175' 0"

14 bays at 12' 6"

45' 0"

*

23 bays of 10' 5" each

239' 7"

Bellman Type

33' 9"

26' 0"

87' 9"

95' 0"

Dorman Long Blister Hangar

71' 9⅝"

90' 3½"

Type T2

29' 0"

25' 0"

113' 0"

120' 10"

34' 0"

Miskins Blister Hangar
(Standard)

22' 0"

25' 0"

22' 0"

60' 1"

45' 6"

14' 4¼"

* = curtains

Note: Plans are half size
of elevations and 'end on'

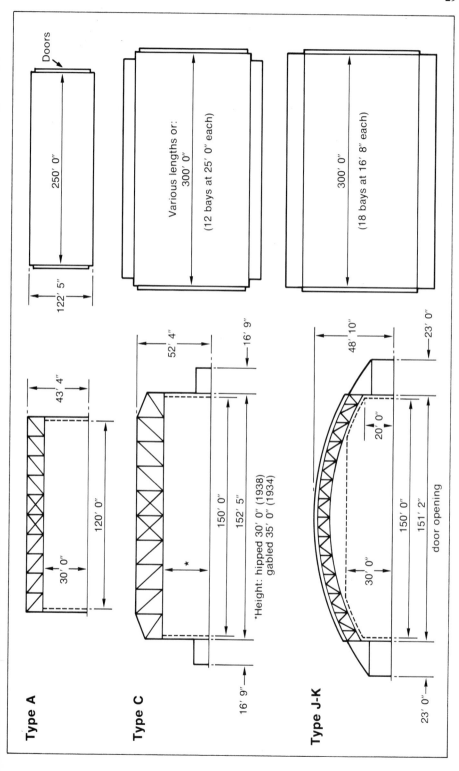

Type A

Doors

250' 0"

122' 5"

43' 4"

120' 0"

30' 0"

Type C

Various lengths or:
300' 0"

(12 bays at 25' 0" each)

52' 4"

16' 9"

150' 0"

152' 5"

*

16' 9"

*Height: hipped 30' 0" (1938)
gabled 35' 0" (1934)

Type J-K

300' 0"

(18 bays at 16' 8" each)

48' 10"

23' 0"

20' 0"

150' 0"

151' 2"

door opening

30' 0"

23' 0"

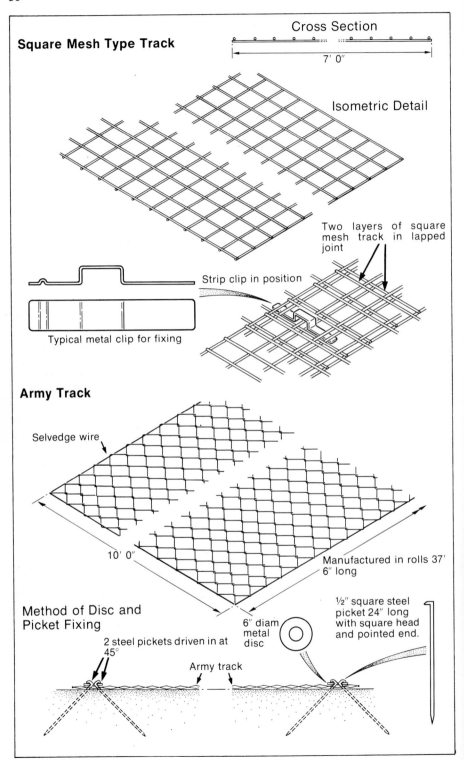

Square Mesh Type Track

Cross Section

7' 0"

Isometric Detail

Two layers of square mesh track in lapped joint

Strip clip in position

Typical metal clip for fixing

Army Track

Selvedge wire

10' 0"

Manufactured in rolls 37' 6" long

Method of Disc and Picket Fixing

2 steel pickets driven in at 45°

Army track

6" diam metal disc

½" square steel picket 24" long with square head and pointed end.

7: *In a sea of sugar beet stands Snailwell's last Blister hangar, one of the few left anywhere* in situ.

was known as Old Type T2 (8254/40) and was built of steel with cranked sheet covering. In 1942 the T series were re-designed and the T2 (Home) was evolved (6304/42) 270 ft 4 in long. The T2 (Home) Standard (3653A/42) had a length of 239 ft 7 in and this was the type normally erected. A shorter T2 (3669/42) had a length of 145 ft 10 in and a further variant was 135 ft 5 in long. In theory the number of bays could be extended, but common practice was to adhere to the lengths given.

Within the ranges two widths were available, with 90 ft and 97 ft 2 in clear openings. Thus the Old Type T2 was the only one large enough to accommodate four-engined bombers, the Bellman having a clear opening of 87 ft 9 in. Apart from the speed at which these transportable metal hangars could be erected, the T2 weighed only 172 tons compared with the 600 tons of the brick, steel and concrete C Type.

At first glance the Bellman and T hangars appear very similar, but the Bellman usually has end supports to the hangar door runners. The doors of the Bellmans run level with the top of the side panelling, whereas T hangars — without runner supports — have panelling above the doors before the roofing commences (see diagram on page 29). The T hangar is shown in Photo 8 and Photo 9 depicts a Bellman at Newmarket, one of two still standing.

Dominating the skyline at many military airfields is the water tower, necessary in East Anglia because the flatness of the region means that, to obtain sufficient water pressure for supply, water has to be pumped to a high tower prior to release. Bircham Newton has two such towers (Photo 10). To the right is the old circular tower and it stands alongside the standard wartime Braithwaite tank whose sections in 4 ft modules measure 8 ft x 8 ft and 8 ft x 4 ft and complete a tank 12 ft x 16 ft on high scaffolding. Some of these tanks remain in use for water storage such as the example of Framlingham used by the East Anglian Water Company.

At airfields laid down in the mid-1930s the water tank is enclosed in a tall brick encasement. Designs for such items were all submitted to the Royal Fine Arts Commission and the views of the Society for the Preservation of Rural

8 Above: *A common wartime sight, a Type T2 hangar, in this instance at Wratting Common.* 9 Below: *One of two Bellman hangars still visible at Newmarket.*

England were sought. Over 40 years old, the Expansion period buildings tone well with modern architecture and the countryside, as indeed do many of the buildings now frequently screened by trees. Similar tall structures were built around boiler house chimneys so that the unsightly tall chimney at Bircham Newton was replaced by more elegant structures, although the old pump house remains (Photo 11).

Always a prominent feature of any airfield is the watch office or control tower. In the 1920s and 1930s watch offices were small wooden huts placed somewhere about the apron or, as in the case of Duxford, situated on the corner of a hangar roof. In 1934 plans were drawn up for a twin box structure built of brick and placed by the apron. One of these remains at Bircham Newton (Photo 12) and another may be seen at Felixstowe (Photo 13) where it has been converted for office use. Although similar in appearance these watch offices were locally adapted to afford a view over the landing ground which meant some height adjustments to suit local terrain, Bircham Newton's tower being built in accordance with plan 1959/34. Placed near the tower was the Fire Tender Shelter and Fire Section office, and in front of the tower was laid out the signals square.

Buildings for technical purposes stemming from World War 1 are single-storey sloping roofed huts all similar in shape to the concrete and wood or stone-dash and wood hut-like buildings in the centre of Bircham Newton's technical

10 Right: *Bircham Newton's two water towers, the old circular one and the Braithwaite tower from World War 2.* 11 Below: *The old pump house at Bircham Newton.*

12 Above: *The Watch Office and tower built to pattern 1959/34 still standing, battered, at Bircham Newton.* 13 Below: *Felixstowe had a similarly shaped control tower, now used as an office block.*

14: *Hutments built about 1928 still stand in excellent condition at Bircham.*

site (Photo 14). Workshops, Stores, Armoury and MT Sections were all housed in buildings of this shape suitably adapted in size, and many remain at Duxford.

During the 1930s Expansion plain brick box-like structures were built for similar purposes, each having some characteristic of its own. The Photographic Section, largely a new feature, was often sited above the armoury (Photo 15), although not always so. Stores of similar shape were often to be found with barred windows and large doors for unloading. Operations blocks (Photo 16) were similar in shape. Such were often sited near Station Head Quarters (Photo 17) which again was a two-storey, box-like structure near the Main Gate. An older type may still be seen at Duxford dating to 1918.

Every airfield had its Guard House, a single storey building usually of two rooms with cell accommodation added. Few were as stylish as Bircham Newton's (Photo 18) built in 1923 and which now houses a branch of Barclay's Bank. Many were similar in design to that at Duxford (Photo 19).

Forming part of the Technical Site area were the Messes for Airmen and Sergeants. Again, a typical style of 1936 is that found at Bircham Newton where the Airmen's Mess is now used as a restaurant for students (Photo 20). Above the Mess Hall were placed games rooms and the library. The previous structure resembled large 1918-style huts, with metal frame and were of only one storey. NAAFI buildings were similar to the Airmen's Mess in appearance whereas the Sergeants' Mess was larger including accommodation for single men (Photo 21).

Airmen's accommodation in the 1920s was in huts similar in shape to those in Photo 14. Two-storey buildings, Barrack Block Type C to pattern 1100/28 were erected at Bircham Newton in 1929 and similar structures may be seen at Duxford and Martlesham Heath. They held accommodation for three NCOs and 64 men. Brick built, the barracks had sloping roofs (Photo 22).

Their replacement of the mid-1930s was the Barrack Block Type L (Photo 23) which was a two-storey, box-like structure having four or eight large rooms each with space for about 30 beds, with latrines and bathrooms to the rear. When two such blocks were linked the unit resembled, from the air, a letter 'H' in plan-form.

15 Top: *Building 75 at Bircham Newton, the Station Armoury with the Photographic Section sited on top. It was built to pattern 7616/37.* 16 Centre: *Building 22, the one-time Operations Block at Bircham Newton to pattern 7040/38. It now serves as the Training Centre Reception Block.* 17 Below: *Building No1, the Station Headquarters at Bircham Newton to pattern 1723/36, in use as an office block. On the wall of the one-time library hangs a board outlining the station's great history.*

18 Top: *Bircham Newton's stylish Guard House, to pattern 166 of 1923.* 19 Centre: *Duxford's Guard House built in the early 1920s. Doubtless, the faithful friend in the foreground would have been unwelcome in the war years!* 20 Below: *The 1936-style Airmen's Mess at Bircham Newton.*

21 Above: *Bircham Newton's Sergeants' Mess, to pattern 3484/36.* 22 Below: *Built in 1929, this Barrack Block Type C at Bircham Newton carries the evocative name 'Mons'.* 23 Right: *By contrast, a barrack block type 8/84 of 1938.*

The mid-1930s saw the building of somewhat gracious Georgian style Officers' Messes at many stations old and new where the standard of living was high. Many of these buildings remain little altered with living accommodation to the left of the vestibule and the ante-room to the right, to the rear of which is the dining hall.

Hutment accommodation during the war was of three basic types. Commonly seen still are the metal Nissen huts usually sited on a concrete base. They were built in three widths — 16, 24 or 30 feet and could be of any length and were built in sections of six feet. In 1941 Nissen huts began to be a feature of many airfields, particularly satellites and by dispersal points. Many American bases had them for accommodation and clerical use (see Photo 24).

Many men were accommodated early in the war in stout timber huts connected by brick latrine and toilet facilities, the unit being able to accommodate 150 men. Most of these huts were sold after hostilities. Later variants were Types X, Y and Z and were of a standard 18 feet in width but could be various lengths.

Romney and Iris huts were similar in appearance to Nissen huts, but were 35 feet wide and built in bays of eight feet, and were used mainly for storage purposes.

At many a wartime airfield one saw small concrete buildings (Photo 25). The Maycrete hut of 1941 was built around reinforced concrete posts with Maycrete slab walls and a felt and board roof. They measured 54 ft long x 16 ft wide, a larger edition being the Orlit hut of 1942 measuring 18½ ft x 60 ft. This had a pre-cast concrete roof.

In addition to these main buildings there were many others built for special purposes. Prior to, and even during, the war it was common practice to run aero engines on test rigs and the Engine Test Bay was a normal feature. At Duxford one remains as a metal structure upon which in the 1930s the Mercurys and

24 Above: *Nissen huts were seen in profusion on airfields in the last war. These stood on the domestic site at Thorpe Abbotts and still stand in 1979.* 25 Below: *Maycrete huts of varying sizes were also commonly seen, this relic still standing at Ridgewell.* 26 Right: *Bircham Newton's Engine Test House, Building 139, to pattern 8800/38.*

Jupiters were slung for running tests. Bircham Newton retains another type, brick built and open ended (Photo 26). Another specialised building housed the Parachute Section where the parachutes were examined and packed ready for use. Often it was set close to the Link Trainer building again of the standard box-like flat roof type. Flat roofing characterised many of the Expansion period buildings. A rare sight even in the war years was the astro building, a domed concrete structure upon the roof of which, by the aid of special projectors, star groups could be projected for navigational training purposes. One such building remains, at Langham (Photo 27).

Bomb dumps were usually buildings sunk and covered by grass mounds, and set well away from the airfield buildings. Siting of fuel tanks varied. Indeed, some of Bircham Newton's tanks were not far from the hangars and brought great alarm when they exploded during the war.

Radio Direction Finding stations were built in the 1930s close to many stations as part of a grid for radio navigation. The site was usually surrounded by a high metal strut fence within which were contained a single-storey brick building and a very distinctive radio mast and aerials. Few remain, but one may be seen fairly intact at Warboys.

No airfield was complete without its runways, which were grass strips in the pre-war days, often four in number and evident by their short grass. By 1940

27: *Never a common sight, an astro dome still in place at Langham.*

runway laying was underway although many pre-war stations continued well into the war without runways which were the norm for airfields built later. The latter usually had three runways laid to a triangular pattern, and they were usually built of concrete and sometimes protected by a layer of bitumen which proved a nuisance when jet aircraft were introduced for the covering was so easily burnt. Usually the longest runway was approximately 2,000 yards long and 50 yards wide, but precise lengths varied. The main runway was orientated roughly SW/NE to suit the prevailing wind. Until Woodbridge was built in 1943 Newmarket had the longest runway in the area, and one of longest in the country. Some of the grass fields, like Bottisham, had metal runways. Sommerfeld tracking was first used, but the American Universal Pierced Steel Planking was much superior and lengths may still be seen at old airfield sites. Details of these metal runways are shown in diagrams on pages 30, 43 and 44.

Prior to the war many airfields had a narrow perimeter road for vehicles, but when in 1938 it was decided to disperse aircraft around airfield perimeters a wider road was soon added so that aircraft could taxi. Later these tracks were linked to concrete hard standings, or dispersal pads. Originally these were circular in planform and later took on the 'spectacle' pattern to permit more aircraft to be dispersed.

Few inactive airfields now survive in such a good state as Bircham Newton. Little wonder that there are stories that it is haunted, and that ghosts have appeared on the 1917 squash courts. Many of the features still present at that station may be seen, if only in part, elsewhere.

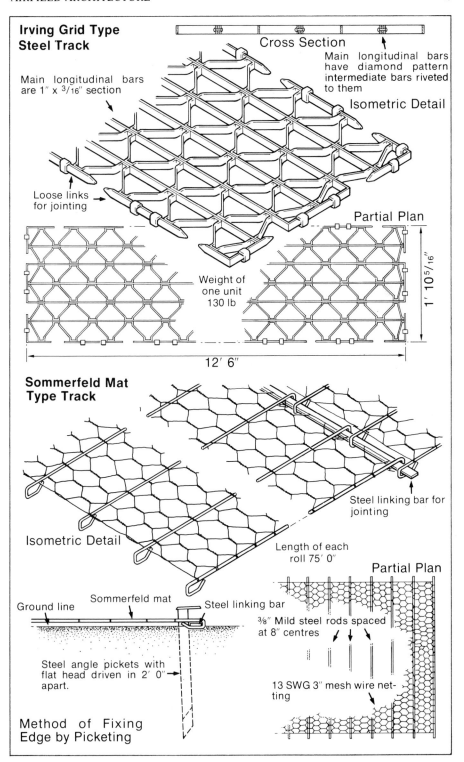

Irving Grid Type Steel Track

Cross Section

Main longitudinal bars have diamond pattern intermediate bars riveted to them

Isometric Detail

Main longitudinal bars are 1″ x ³/₁₆″ section

Loose links for jointing

Partial Plan

Weight of one unit 130 lb

1′ 10⁵/₁₆″

12′ 6″

Sommerfeld Mat Type Track

Steel linking bar for jointing

Isometric Detail

Length of each roll 75′ 0″

Partial Plan

Ground line

Sommerfeld mat

Steel linking bar

³/₈″ Mild steel rods spaced at 8″ centres

Steel angle pickets with flat head driven in 2′ 0″ apart.

13 SWG 3″ mesh wire netting

Method of Fixing Edge by Picketing

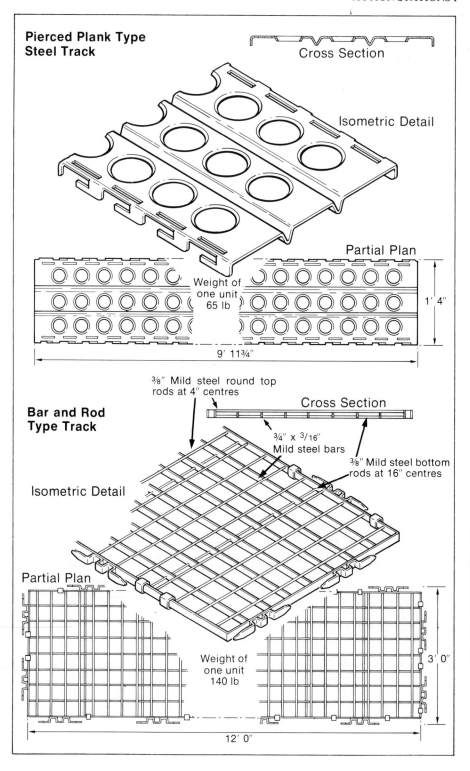

Pierced Plank Type Steel Track

Cross Section

Isometric Detail

Partial Plan

Weight of one unit 65 lb

1′ 4″

9′ 11¾″

Bar and Rod Type Track

⅜″ Mild steel round top rods at 4″ centres

Cross Section

¾″ x ³/₁₆″ Mild steel bars

⅜″ Mild steel bottom rods at 16″ centres

Isometric Detail

Partial Plan

Weight of one unit 140 lb

3′ 0″

12′ 0″

KEY
to symbols used on Airfield maps

LOCAL FEATURES

 Roads. Important roads in the area are numbered

 Railway lines, or the courses of disused lines

 Rivers, streams

 Wooded areas

Buildings

Groups of buildings – details not known

GENERAL FEATURES

80 ▲ Height of ground (Above Mean Sea Level)   394 ▲ Height of structures (Above Mean Sea Level)

AIRFIELD FEATURES

Except Bircham Newton & Felixstowe

Runways, concrete

Aircraft dispersal areas, and perimeter track

Buildings*   LA Light aircraft landing area

Groups of buildings – details not known

 Runway bearing. First two figures only of bearing area given due to compass deviation

Runway approach lights

Ç Control tower   § Signals Square   ► Windsock

Bircham Newton only

 Runways, grass

Airfield boundary

Air-raid shelters

 Footpaths   *Also applies to Bircham Newton and Felixstowe

The airfields

Alconbury, Cambridgeshire

TL295795. By the A14 NW of Huntingdon

Apt that Alconbury should be the first airfield to be historically considered, for there seems little doubt that it was the first used satellite landing ground for a main base. Prior to 1939 it was usual to place aircraft in hangars at the end of the working day. Fear of air attack led to their being dispersed around airfields, where possible with some camouflaged surroundings. With perhaps 40 aircraft on an airfield, grass dispersal areas quickly became crowded, for airfields were quite small in 1939.

The best means of dispersal came about in 1938 when the satellite idea was born. Each operational station would be awarded a suitable site a few miles away where non-operating aircraft could be dispersed, brought back to parent stations for arming and fuelling for operations. By the summer of 1940 the system was evolved whereby squadrons could operate from satellites and be permanently based there. This required the provision of bomb dumps and operations rooms, but major overhaul was still done at parent stations. By mid-war satellites had been raised to full station status.

Land for this satellite was acquired in 1938 just north of Alconbury village on the hill top, a large grass field to which, on May 17-18 1938, Battles of 63 Squadron, Upwood, were dispersed, crews being accommodated under canvas in operational conditions whilst the first trials of the satellite system were undertaken. A Battle squadron was chosen because they were earmarked for the Advanced Air Striking Force and needed practice in mobility.

When war came Alconbury at once was used, but not for Upwood's squadrons since they were now non-operational. Instead, it became Wyton's satellite and Blenheims were dispersed there.

May 1940 brought fierce action for Wyton's squadrons, and XV Squadron used Alconbury as its dispersal base during those grim days. In the autumn Wellingtons replaced the Blenheims in XV Squadron and there was much movement between Alconbury and Wyton. In February 1941 XV Squadron was switched with 40 Squadron, also flying Wellingtons, for the former was to re-equip with Stirlings at Wyton. Briefing facilities and a weapons dump were now available at Alconbury. Three runways were laid there in 1941 for XV Squadron's Stirlings which used it for training and dispersal and, at the end of the year, for operations when runway laying commenced at Wyton.

Throughout 1941 3 Group administered Alconbury whose Wellingtons took part in many raids. In October 1941 much of 40 Squadron was hurriedly sent to the Middle East, leaving a home echelon to continue operations. This element — soon quite divorced from 40 Squadron — was re-numbered 156 Squadron on February 14 1942. Five days later they received their first Wellington III and first operated with this type on March 25. The squadron operated from Alconbury for the three '1,000 bomber' raids, carried out mining and gradually slipped into a marker role dropping flares and incendiaries during rudimentary target marking. There were many instances when extreme courage was called for. On July 23 Flight Sergeant T.E. Case had to take sudden evasive action when another Wellington closed upon him. Some of his incendiaries caught fire and Warrant Officer McLennan saved the aircraft by picking up burning bombs and pushing these and magazines through the aircraft's fabric even though he had no gloves on his hands. During a Bremen raid of July 27 a Wellington was coned by searchlights, anti-aircraft fire shooting away the port elevator and injuring some of the crew. The second pilot took over at the Dutch coast and the remainder of the crew decided to bale out, leaving the second pilot to land successfully at Coltishall, a very fine effort.

In August 1942 the Pathfinder Force formed and 156 Squadron moved on August 5-7 to nearby Warboys and into the marker force proper. There was another reason for the move; the Americans were coming, the station being held by 8 Group from August 12 1942.

Come they did in August 1942 and early in September the first B-24 Liberators to be based in Britain arrived, forming the 93rd Bomb Group. With their high aspect ratio wings the B-24s were immediately recognisable. The 93rd showed themselves off by flying low around the neighbourhood. The Americans were raring to go into action, and when one talked with them one sensed that they did not understand that it could be a dangerous activity, and knew nothing of the torture endured by Alconbury's Blenheim crews.

The 93rd entered combat on October 9. Five formations were laid on against Target Z183, the Fives-Lille steel works, including B-17s of the 301st Bomb Group leading followed by 12 of the 11th CCRG with 24 B-17s of the 306th. Then came 24 B-24s of the 93rd and bringing up the rear 24 B-17s of the 97th Bomb Group, so that the Liberators had rear cover in the largest American raid so far.

Take-off from Alconbury was around 0830 hours, on a fine, sunny autumn morning. Exciting it was to see the B-24s taking up battle stations over Cambridge against a sky crossed by countless vapour trails. Then they headed for Felixstowe where the entire force made rendezvous. They flew south meeting two squadrons of RAF Spitfire IXs, then three squadrons of USAAC P-38 Lightnings five miles east of Dunkirk. To the east was a group of Defiants of 515 Squadron which took up position to screen the force from enemy radar.

The bombers flew directly to Fives-Lille meeting three more squadrons of RAF Spitfire IXs giving target support and there primarily to ward off attacks on the 93rd and 306th Bomb Groups, both inexperienced. German reaction was fierce. A B-24 was shot down, ten were damaged and the bombing was poor. Only nine bombs fell within a quarter of a mile of the target, many homes being destroyed. When the evening news bulletin revealed the operation American claims of 48 enemy fighters shot down and 38 probables were unbelievable. Post-war research suggests that only one fighter was destroyed. One thing was certain, the B-24 crews discovered that combat was no joyride.

B-24 spares at Alconbury were in short supply, the aircraft needing many modifications, but operations continued with the bombing of La Pallice, Brest, St Nazaire and Lorient. A new task was soon set the 93rd. With convoys sailing for North-West Africa it was essential air cover be provided over Biscay. The 93rd left Alconbury to provide this, the Liberator being ideal for a maritime role.

In December 1942 the 93rd moved to the Middle East, but American personnel remained in strength at Alconbury and in January 1942 B-17s of the 92nd Bomb Group arrived. The visitor to the base was then rewarded by the sight of B-17s in training including some of the early B-17Es in unusual camouflage.

In mid-summer the 95th Bomb Group briefly lodged here, and on June 19 Alconbury became a full member of the US 8th AAF as Station 102. The 92nd later moved to Podington.

August 20 1943 saw the arrival of the 482nd Bomb Group, its task to provide pathfinding leadships for the offensive. Three squadrons flew B-17Fs, the fourth B-24s, all of which were fitted with blind bombing devices. These aircraft preceded bomber formations to mark targets when cloud covered, flying their first missions on September 27 1943 and leading the 1st and 3rd Air Divisions to Emden. Later, their aircraft were detached to other bases, to attack, for instance, factories at Gotha, Schweinfurt and Brunswick. The Group was awarded a Distinguished Unit Citation for their part in the action of January 11 1944 when they led deep into Germany despite bad weather and fighter attack.

In March 1944 the 482nd came off operations to operate a pathfinder school at Alconbury. They made radar photographs of enemy territory, tested radar and guided H2S into service. For this purpose they flew a few Mosquito PR XVIs which used to disperse in the south-west corner of the field with the Dominie, Norseman and Cessna Bobcat used for communications.

Sometimes the Group operated as on D-Day when they led attacks on enemy traffic. The mixture of trials and training with some operations continued to the end of the war, the 482nd leaving for America in May-June 1945. Alconbury then lay quiet, and was returned to the

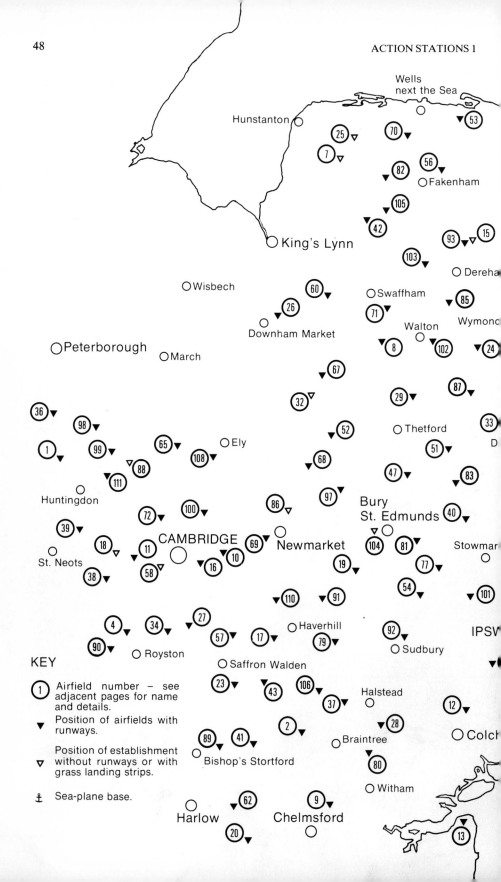

The Military Airfields of East Anglia

No	Name	County	O/S No
1	Alconbury	Cambs	142
2	Andrewsfield	Essex	167
3	Attlebridge	Norfolk	133
4	Bassingbourn	Cambs	154
5	Beccles (Ellough)	Suffolk	156
6	Bentwaters	Suffolk	156
7	Bircham Newton	Norfolk	132
8	Bodney	Norfolk	144
9	Boreham	Essex	167
10	Bottisham	Cambs	154
11	Bourn	Cambs	154
12	Boxted	Essex	168
13	Bradwell Bay	Essex	168
14	Bungay (Flixton)	Suffolk	156
15	Bylaugh Hall (camp only)	Norfolk	133
16	Cambridge	Cambs	154
17	Castle Camps	Cambs	154
18	Caxton Gibbett	Cambs	154
19	Chedburgh	Suffolk	155
20	Chipping Ongar	Essex	167
21	Coltishall	Norfolk	133
22	Debach	Suffolk	156
23	Debden	Essex	154
24	Deopham Green	Norfolk	144
25	Docking	Norfolk	132
26	Downham Market	Norfolk	143
27	Duxford	Cambs	154
28	Earl's Colne	Essex	168
29	East Wretham	Norfolk	144
30	Eye	Suffolk	144
31	Felixstowe	Suffolk	169
32	Feltwell	Norfolk	143
33	Fersfield	Norfolk	144
34	Fowlmere	Cambs	154
35	Framlingham	Suffolk	156
36	Glatton	Cambs	142
37	Gosfield	Essex	167
38	Gransden	Cambs	153
39	Graveley	Cambs	153
40	Gt Ashfield	Suffolk	155
41	Gt Dunmow	Essex	167
42	Gt Massingham	Norfolk	132
43	Gt Sampford	Essex	154
44	Halesworth	Suffolk	156
45	Hardwick	Norfolk	134
46	Hethel	Norfolk	144
47	Honington	Suffolk	144
48	Horham	Suffolk	156
49	Horsham St Faith	Norfolk	133
50	Ipswich	Suffolk	169
51	Knettishall	Suffolk	144
52	Lakenheath	Suffolk	143
53	Langham	Norfolk	132
54	Lavenham	Suffolk	155
55	Leiston	Suffolk	156
56	Lt Snoring	Norfolk	132
57	Lt Walden	Essex	154
58	Lord's Bridge	Cambs	154
59	Ludham	Norfolk	133

Map labels:
ngham
Cromer
North Walsham
(21)
(59)
(76)
NORWICH
Great Yarmouth
(84)
Beccles
Lowestoft
(14)
(75)
(5)
(66)
(44)
Halesworth
Southwold
(48)
Saxmundham
(55)
(35)
Aldeburgh
(22)
(6)
Woodbridge
(109)
(61)
50
Felixstowe
ch
(31)
acton on Sea

Scale 5 0 5 10 miles

60	Marham	Norfolk	143	88	Somersham	Cambs	142
61	Martlesham Heath	Suffolk	169	89	Stansted	Essex	167
62	Matching	Essex	167	90	Steeple Morden	Cambs	153
63	Matlaske	Norfolk	133	91	Stradishall	Suffolk	154
64	Mendlesham	Suffolk	155	92	Sudbury	Suffolk	155
65	Mepal	Cambs	143	93	Swanton Morley	Norfolk	133
66	Metfield	Suffolk	156	94	Swannington	Norfolk	133
67	Methwold	Norfolk	143	95	Thorpe Abbotts	Norfolk	156
68	Mildenhall	Suffolk	143	96	Tibenham	Norfolk	156
69	Newmarket Heath	Suffolk	154	97	Tuddenham	Suffolk	155
70	North Creake	Norfolk	132	98	Upwood	Cambs	142
71	North Pickenham	Norfolk	144	99	Warboys	Cambs	142
72	Oakington	Cambs	154	100	Waterbeach	Cambs	154
73	Old Buckenham	Norfolk	144	101	Wattisham	Suffolk	155
74	Oulton	Norfolk	133	102	Watton	Norfolk	144
75	Pulham	Norfolk	156	103	Wendling	Norfolk	132
76	Rackheath	Norfolk	133	104	Westley	Suffolk	155
77	Rattlesden	Suffolk	155	105	West Raynham	Norfolk	132
78	Raydon	Suffolk	155	106	Wethersfield	Essex	167
79	Ridgewell	Essex	155	107	Weybourne	Norfolk	133
80	Rivenhall	Essex	168	108	Witchford	Cambs	143
81	Rougham	Suffolk	132	109	Woodbridge	Suffolk	169
82	Sculthorpe	Norfolk	132	110	Wratting Common	Suffolk	154
83	Shepherd's Grove	Suffolk	155	111	Wyton	Cambs	142
84	Seething	Norfolk	134		Notes:		
85	Shipdham	Norfolk	144				
86	Snailwell	Cambs	154				
87	Snetterton Heath	Norfolk	144				

The O/S Sheet No gives the number of the relevant 1:50,000 (1st series) sheet of Ordnance Survey maps.

Above right: Wellington 1c R1331 R-Roger of 40 Squadron in 1941. Returning from Berlin on April 18 the crew baled out and the aircraft crashed at Combe Martin, Devon.
Below: *A view of the RF-4Cs of the 10th Tac Recon Wing at Alconbury (USAF).*

RAF on November 26 1945. It remained inactive until June 1 1953 when the Americans returned.

The 7523rd Squadron took up residence and in 1954 work came underway to extend the station to huge proportions and much lengthen the main runway. In March 1955 the 7560th Air Base Group was activated in the 3rd Air Force and on September 15 1955 the 85th Bomb Squadron arrived from Sculthorpe with B-45s, staying until August 1959 by which time they were flying B-66Bs. Between May and August 1959 the 53rd Weather Squadron was at Alconbury and flew WB-50Ds.

The departure of the 85th was the result of the French being unwilling to accommodate US forces, and a general rearrangement followed, the 10th Tactical Reconnaissance Wing arriving on August 25 1959 from Spangdahlem, Germany. They brought RB-66s, the 1st and 30th Squadrons taking up residence at Alconbury. In May 1965 the Wing began to equip with RF-4C Phantom IIs which the 1st TRS still flies from Alconbury. On April 1 1976 the 30th Squadron was deactivated, as the 527th Tactical Fighter Training Aggressor Squadron formed, to act as targets for many NATO organisations. They received their first Northrop F-5E Tiger IIs in May 1976 and became fully operational on January 1 1977.

Wartime Alconbury has been swallowed by the present sprawling complex. Such is equally true of all other active East Anglian airfields. In the case of Alconbury it is a strange twist of fate that the first satellite station, once a mere grass airfield by the old A1, should have blossomed to such stature.

Andrew's Field (previously Great Saling — re-named May 21 1943), Essex

TL695245. SW of Great Saling

Andrew's Field was the first airfield in England built by the US Pioneer Corps, and was named after the late Lieutenant-General F. M. Andrews. Construction began after the Americans arrived at Great Saling on July 4 1942, a very suitable day upon which to begin any American venture. But this is not the only niche in history the station holds, for it was the first airfield in East Anglia at which jet fighter squadrons were based.

The airfield opened on April 24 1943 and the US 95th Bomb Group arrived with B-17Fs in May. They moved to their permanent base, Snetterton Heath, on June 12 and their place was immediately taken by B-26 Marauders of the 322nd Bomb Group arriving from Rougham. Re-positioning placed them nearer the Continent, and thereafter all the Marauder bases were in Essex.

The 322nd had first operated in a low-level role for which the B-26 was unsuitable. More training now took place for medium level formation attack, the Group resuming operations on July 17 1943. Airfields were main targets, but in late 1943 a switch to attacking flying-bomb sites came, the Group being transferred from the 8th to the 9th Air Force on October 16 1943.

On most of their raids, which included attacks on shipyards and railway installations, the B-26s were escorted by RAF fighters, and the main losses came from flak against the 18-strong groups of bombers which usually operated in forces of 72 aircraft. During March 1944 the 322nd switched to the support of the invasion build-up and bombed tactical targets.

June 6 1944 found the B-26s attacking coastal defences and gun batteries before switching to fuel and ammunition dumps, bridges, railway junctions and troop defiles during the time the Allies were penned in around Caen. The 322nd supported the break-out at St Lô, then gave general field support to advancing forces. So rapid was the advance that the B-26s needed to move to France to be able to operate effectively, and the 322nd left for Beauvais/Tille in September.

Left: *Looking north across Attlebridge in 1978, with turkey farm broiler houses on the old runways.* Below: *Bassingbourn on June 6 1944. Trees top left hide Wimpole Park dispersals (USAF).* Right: *In 1951 Mosquitoes and others of 237 OCU replaced the Americans at Bassingbourn (E. Watts).*

The war now took on a new look, bases in the south-east being ideal for RAF fighters covering Lancaster and Halifax raids into Germany. Accordingly, escort fighters moved into Andrew's Field in strength. Indeed, more RAF Mustangs were based here than at any other station.

First to arrive was 129 Squadron which, on October 15 1944, supported 18 Lancasters raiding the famous Sorpe Dam. Three days later they came across an Me 163 rocket fighter near Arnhem, and were now busily flying *Ramrods*. They were joined in October by Nos 19, 65, 122, 315 and 316 Squadrons, all flying Mustang IIIs, there being about 100 Mustangs on the station.

Gradual re-arrangement of the squadrons came about, 309 (Polish) Mustang Squadron arriving in December and others moving out to Bentwaters, Peterhead and Banff, the latter to support Coastal Command's strike operations off Norway. Bomber escorts were flown deep into Germany and on February 28 a new

sound was heard over Andrew's Field when seven Meteor jet fighters of 616 Squadron arrived from Colerne for anti-diver patrols. They achieved no successes and moved via Manston to B77 on March 31 1945.

During March the Germans launched the last of their long-range flying-bombs across Essex towards London and the Mustangs at Andrew's Field rose to challenge the intruders. But it was mainly *Ramrod* operations which occupied them. On March 15 315 Squadron escorted Lancasters and Mosquitoes attacking the Bielefeld viaduct and, with 303 Squadron which arrived at this time bringing the first Mustang IVs to Andrew's Field, took part in the Lancaster raid on Berchtesgarden.

Mustangs remained here after the war, the last two squadrons to leave being 315 in August 1945 and 316 in November 1945. Andrew's Field then went into retirement. It is now used by light aircraft.

Attlebridge, Norfolk

TG105148. Turn S off A1067 at Morton, airfield ½ mile SW of Weston Longville

They were making their first bombing raid on their homeland, on the Dornier factory at Flushing, these Dutchmen of 320 Squadron. Intense flak greeted them and, as the formation headed back to Attlebridge, 'C-Charlie' was hit. The crew tried to keep going, but their aircraft fell behind. In mid-afternoon they ditched. Proficient in their dinghy drill and with intrepidity they sailed away from the sinking Mitchell. Luck was in for a couple of Mustangs circled and radioed for help. A Walrus amphibian from Coltishall appeared, Spitfire escorted. It landed then took the Dutchmen back to Norfolk.

Attlebridge opened as a grass field satellite of Swanton Morley in June 1941. Blenheims of 105 Squadron dispersed there. In July 1941 88 Squadron arrived at Swanton Morley from Northern Ireland. During August they gradually moved into Attlebridge. No 88 was an unusual squadron. Half the unit was in England flying Blenheim IVs, the remainder in Ireland trying out the Boston for 2 Group. Soon, this element also came to Swanton Morley to fully equip with Boston IIIs.

Meanwhile their companions worked up on Blenheims which went into action from Attlebridge in August 1941 aiding 2 Group's anti-shipping campaign. After a couple of low-level attacks on Rotterdam docks the squadron was detached to Manston for three weeks to take part in the fearsome *Channel Stop* campaign directed against German merchant ships supplying French ports.

Back at Attlebridge, 88 Squadron had a few more dangerous anti-shipping raids to undertake. When they flew their last Blenheim operation on October 26 1941 it was as fierce as any. A 4,000-ton motor vessel had been located off the Hague with four other merchant ships guarded by three flak ships. Squadron Leader Barr led his formation to the convoy. Low level, very low level, attack was ordered. It was Barr's task to photograph the attack. Pilot Officer Rowlinson roared in at masthead height, dropped his four 250lb bombs and then fire from the flak ships set ablaze his port engine. Soon he had crashed in the sea. The other two crews attacked one of the ships, then the race for home.

Compared with the Blenheim the Boston was utter luxury. Finely appointed, streamlined and so attractive to view,

it was ideal for low-level work. Bostons came to Attlebridge in November 1941. They took time to train, the nosewheel undercarriage taking some getting used to. In January 1942 they flew to Long Kesh for tactical work-up, to a place now the site of the notorious prison.

Barely were they back when the German battle cruisers sailed through the English Channel. Quickly armed, 88 Squadron took its Bostons somewhat prematurely into fruitless action. Committed to battle, they flew a few anti-shipping sorties then attempted a low-level raid on Poissy near Paris. It was abortive for, as they left Thorney Island there was trouble, and the formation never found their target.

Thereafter, Attlebridge's Bostons were out most days, usually fighter-escorted during *Circus* operations, attacking Continental targets. In suitable weather 88 Squadron mounted some fast, low-level attacks on power stations — hazardous, lonely ventures. Come August they took part in the Dieppe raid. After more *Circuses* they moved to Oulton on September 30 1942, after a busy year for Attlebridge.

They were moved because the Americans were coming. They arrived in September when the 319th Bomb Group moved in, to train for their part in the North-West Africa landings. To Attlebridge came a new and again very attractive-looking aeroplane, the Martin Marauder in early form. These were far from battle-ready and left in November amid great secrecy. Attlebridge continued as home for Americans, and runway laying carried on to bring the airfield to full station status.

In March 1943 2 Group was further expanding. New squadrons had to be accommodated as the RAF and USAAF clamoured for airfields. No 320 Royal Netherlands Navy Squadron was at Methwold, but when 3 Group won Feltwell the Venturas moved to Methwold and 320 was pushed out to Attlebridge.

Yet again, a new type was to work up here, for 320 was in the process of learning to use the North American Mitchell. It was being very temperamental, its armament very troublesome. Despite the wish to employ Mitchells on low-level work the aeroplane was unsuitable. In May 320 Squadron was ordered to stop low flying over Norfolk where B-24s needed to practice for the Ploesti raid.

Very frustrated, 320 Squadron was allowed, in June 1943, to undertake some deep air-sea rescue sweeps. The Dutch Prime Minister visited them on July 29 to keep their spirits up, but next day they fell when a Mitchell went missing from an ASR sortie.

The first bombing mission was flown on August 17 1943 when six crews attacked marshalling yards at Calais. On the 19th they bombed Poix airfield and on the 20th came the Flushing raid. Then, no more operations. The squadron moved to Dunsfold via Lasham on September 2 to be closer their scene of action. Attlebridge lay quiet again, closed for massive extension and modification. Typhoons of 247 Squadron had briefly used the station in August.

The Americans returned and in March 1944 B-24Hs of the 466th Bomb Group arrived. Work-up was rapid, the need urgent, and on their first raid, on March 22 1944, they went to Berlin. The morning of D-Day found them bombing gun emplacements on the Normandy shore and thereafter they acted in an interdictor role. They aided the break-out from St Lô and, when fuel was short in September 1944, ferried supplies to France. Since July the 784th Squadron had engaged in pathfinder duties.

Targets for the Liberators ranged widely across Europe and included marshalling yards at Liège and Saarbrucken, airfields such as St Trond and Chartres, aviation targets at Kempton and Eisenach, fuel targets and factories at Brunswick and Hamburg. They helped stem the Germans in the Ardennes offensive and bombed Nordhorn airfield in support of the Rhine crossing.

Their final operation came on April 25 1945, against a transformer station aiding German railways at Traunsten. Early in July the Americans began their exodus, riding home on the *Queen Mary* and with 232 operations behind them. Attlebridge was transferred to Maintenance Command on July 15 1945 and eventually disposed of on March 15 1959.

Visit Attlebridge now and one sees the unmistakable tall water tower, runways and the perimeter track. What is most distinctive, though, is the array of broiler houses on the runways, comprising a huge flourishing turkey farm. Such flying as now takes place is done by the feathered occupants. A very good view can be seen across the airfield site from the road passing it on the east, and a memorial window is to be placed nearby.

Bassingbourn, Cambridgeshire

TL330460. On A14 4 miles N of Royston, Herts

In the moonlight Wellingtons were about their business flying the usual round of circuits and bumps, or setting off on cross-country journeys. Bassingbourn was the home of the most easterly bomber Operational Training Unit, No 11, the

Top: *For 16 years 231 OCU was at Bassingbourn. WJ728, a Canberra B2, was the aircraft in which I was lucky enough to fly in May 1969.* Above: *The first F-101 Voodoos arrived for the 81st Fighter Bomber Wing in December 1958. F-101C 60004 is seen touching down here.* Below: *Bassingbourn from the air on June 24 1947, still in wartime state (DoE).*

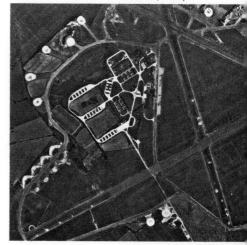

easiest within strike of the enemy who rightly assessed that, for his intruders, crews in training were the easiest game.

In from the Wash crept Leutnant Heinz Völker, flying Ju 88C2 '842', letters R4 + BL. He had set out from Gilze Rijen in Holland at a time when such operations by night over East Anglia were often being carried out by his formation, NJG 2. Wellington R1334 had just taken off when the '88' closed, and to the west of the airfield its pilot opened fire. The Wellington quickly swerved just as the German aircraft turned likewise and they collided. There was a tremendous explosion and a brilliant flash which lit the countryside for miles around. For the 11 men the end was all but instantaneous as the mangled wreckage fell near Ashwell station. That common sight of a low glow soared then faded. July 22 1941 was a night to remember.

Bassingbourn attracted several intruder attacks. On April 10 1941 a Wellington 1, L4253, was shot down near Ashwell and a fortnight later a further Wellington was shot down and crashed on to another of its tribe on a dispersal. On May 7 one was shot down on landing approach and in August yet another was destroyed northeast of Barrington — not far from Lord's Bridge and its huge bomb dump.

The station opened in March 1938 but before this date aircraft had landed and Hinds of 104 and 108 Squadrons moved in as part of 2 Group even before building of the four 'C' Type hangars was complete, let alone the mock Georgian buildings which typified the Expansion Scheme airfields. The hangars, in the early days, were left as bare concrete, disguised only by saplings alongside. Early in 1939 large brown nets were slung across the hangars, and camouflage painting followed when war came.

During May-June 1938 the two squadrons were equipped with Blenheim 1s. In September 1939 both became training units for 2 Group, and moved out to Bicester when war commenced. They were replaced on September 24 1939 by Wellingtons of 215 Squadron, likewise a training unit, now for 3 Group. There were severe drainage problems which made a quagmire of parts of the airfield. No 215 Squadron dissolved, becoming 11 OTU in April 1940, and Ansons in bomber camouflage were added in June 1940 for navigational training. The dispersals for these were built between the aged elms of Wimpole Park. As the Ansons went into hiding, traffic on the Old North Road halted to let them cross. Leaflet dropping by Wellingtons commenced on July 21/22. On November 5 1940 Whitleys of 10 and 78 Squadrons set off from Bassingbourn for Italy, and the first bombs fell on the station on November 28.

The most memorable bombing came on January 16 1941 when a huge bomb fell close to the main road not far from the water tower, leaving a giant crater 20 feet deep and 50 feet across. There was some thought that it might have been a mine, especially since the first such weapon dropped in the area had fallen in a garden by a Kneesworth cottage at this time.

Wellington Ics progressively replaced earlier variants. In December 1941 runway building commenced which caused 11 OTU to move temporarily into Steeple Morden satellite and to Tempsford. At this time 54 Wellingtons, 11 Ansons and two Lysanders were at 11 OTU. On April 24 1942 the first runway at Bassingbourn opened and 11 OTU filtered back, in time for the '1,000 bomber' raids. The Wellingtons participated in other Main Force operations, attacking Düsseldorf during the *Grand National* of July 31 and Bremen on September 13/14. Between September 28 and October 2 1942 11 OTU moved to Westcott.

In September news spread fast through adjacent villages: the Americans were coming. It could be that the rumour was founded by chance for the first American aircraft was C-47 '7820' ex-Chelveston which set down in a hurry on August 3. Flying over the Grantchester heavy gun battery it was not recognised, failed to fire the colour of the day and was fired upon, the crew hastening to safety at Bassingborn. It was, however, October 14 1942 when the Americans arrived in the B-17Fs of the 91st Bomb Group, some of the first '17Fs to arrive in Britain. They dispersed mainly in the northern areas of the station, and in Wimpole Park. Because of its comparative luxury the Americans soon came to know Bassingbourn as 'the country club'. Few US bases ever afforded such luxury.

On many ensuing days the B-17s could be seen in formations which ever increased in size, parading at the head of crisscrossing vapour trails. In November they commenced bombing missions. Submarine pens, shipyards, docks, airfields, factories and communications targets, all were attacked. The 91st Bomb Group took part in the first raid on Germany when, on January 27 1943, Wilhelmshaven was raided. A Distinguished Unit Citation was awarded for the attack on Hamm on March 3 1943 when the weather was bad, the fighting tough. From mid-1943 the targets had become mainly aircraft factories, airfields and oil installations, but deep penetration raids came, to Oranienburg, Peenemünde and Schweinfurt.

Schweinfurt. The very mention of this word at Bassingbourn at any time in the war evoked a silent response, and with good reason. The raid of August 17 1943 began badly, being delayed whilst the mist cleared. In all some 230 B-17s set off for the distant target, with the 91st leading, Colonel Warzbach at the helm. It was a year to the day since the 8th Air Force had commenced operations in Europe, during which time they had dropped 15,722 tons of bombs and claimed an impossible 1,728 enemy aircraft shot down, 871 probables and 817 damaged for the loss of 419 bombers.

It was mid-morning when 18 B-17s formed up over Cambridgeshire, far later than was customary. When they returned they were within a gaggle of 36 with nine trailing behind, two of which could be seen with engines out of action. They had, during almost the entire time over enemy territory, been engaged by fighters which concentrated upon the leaders.

During the late evening I recorded in my dairy that '3 B-17s have come home late.' Little wonder, Schweinfurt for the 91st had been a ghastly experience. At the final count ten of the 36 B-17s lost were from the 91st.

The evening 9 o'clock news bulletin gave news of the day's adventures, and by next morning it was common knowledge locally that the 91st had suffered badly. Indeed, on the dispersals at Bassingbourn only three B-17s were to be seen next day, the remainder having been shot down, or presumably taken into hangars for repairs.

Operations were soon resumed and the 91st went again to Schweinfurt, that dreaded place, on October 14 when only one of their 11 aircraft was shot down. They received a second Distinguished Unit Citation for action on January 11 1944 when, with inadequate fighter cover and in poor weather, they bombed their objective.

There were great names among their Fortresses — 'Jack the Ripper', 'Stric Nine', 'Oklahoma Okie' and, most famous of all, 'Memphis Belle'. To the end of hostilities the 91st was in action,

often leading the 8th AF to battle, wearing 'A in a triangle' marking and at a later period splashes of red on wings and tail.

A few weeks after VE-Day they were all gone, a never-to-be forgotten régime of peaches and ice-cream, interminable piles of peanut butter, Dodge trucks, cheery coloured faces and particularly of plates of food for rationed Britishers.

On June 26 1945 the RAF returned and 47 Group Transport Command took control on July 20. Nos 422 and 423 Canadian Squadrons arrived but soon disbanded. In August 1945 Liberators of 102 Squadron moved in, mostly in Coastal Command colours. They commenced trooping flights to the Far East in October 1945. No 466 Squadron also arrived in August 1945, disbanding in October. No 102 Squadron moved to Upwood on February 14 1946 a few days after 24 Squadron and 1359(VIP) Flight had arrived, the latter with Lancastrians. In March 1946 two of the Lancastrians flew a record flight to New Zealand. On June 3 1946 the two units were combined with a strength of five Lancastrian IIs, five Yorks and 12 Dakota 3s and 4s, some manned by Canadians. Among the aircraft were such famous Yorks as MW100 and Field Marshal Montgomery's LV633 containing a huge leather armchair for his personal comfort. In March-April 1947 the squadron was very busy during the Moscow Foreign Ministers' Conference and in 1948 they joined in the Berlin Airlift.

In June 1948 No 24 (Commonwealth) Squadron moved to Waterbeach and was promptly replaced by Yorks of 40, 51 and 59 Squadrons from Abingdon, which were employed on the Far East run. No 40 Squadron disbanded on February 20 1950 and Nos 51 and 59 on October 31 1950.

Korean conflict had brought the Americans back, their arrival being on August 25 1950. In April 1944 Bassingbourn's occupants had thrilled to a visit by a B-29 Superfortress, the first to visit Britain. Now the 353rd Bomb Squadron, 301st Bomb Group, brought B-29s in plenty. Soon the dispersals were again full and the Somerset Light Infantry mounted perimeter guard. Once more the Americans enriched the area.

Yorks ceased route flying on October 16 1950 and 38 Group controlling them moved out on November 1. The 301st had a prolonged stay due to the international situation. Rotation brought RB-50Bs of the 38th Squadron, 55th SRW, in January 1951 and they stayed until May 1951. The

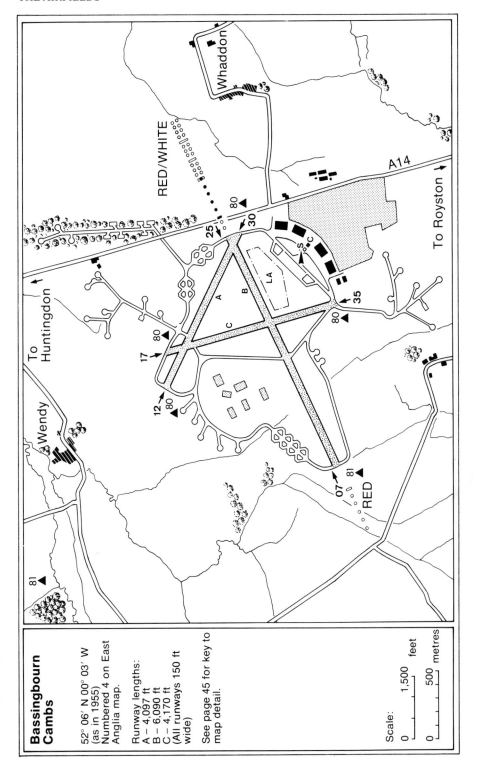

Bassingbourn Cambs

52° 06' N 00° 03' W (as in 1955) Numbered 4 on East Anglia map.

Runway lengths:
A – 4,097 ft
B – 6,090 ft
C – 4,170 ft
(All runways 150 ft wide)

See page 45 for key to map detail.

Scale:
0 — 1,500 feet
0 — 500 metres

97th Bomb Group was the first to fly B-50Ds here.

In September 1951 the Americans once more vacated the station. The RAF took over with the arrival of 12 Mosquito T3s, five PR34s, two Mosquito VIs, six Meteor T7s and four PR10s of 237 OCU. On December 1 1951 No 231 OCU reformed and absorbed them. Then to the thrill of all around, in February 1952 came the first Canberra 2s. Training with them commenced on May 27 and by June there were 14 Canberras at Bassingbourn. Later T4s were put into service here and by June 1953 the full strength of 26 Canberras was reached. Seven Canberra PR3s were received in November 1953 but it was June 1955 before the Meteor PR10s were retired. The PR element of 231 OCU moved to Merryfield soon after and in 1958 to Wyton where they reformed as 237 OCU. They returned to Bassingbourn on January 20 1958 and were absorbed by 231 OCU.

In 1959 training for the Low Approach Bombing System commenced and in April 1960 low-level PR work. Between March 1 1965 and November 1 1967 the station came under 3 Group, reverting to 1 Group thereafter for 3 Group had disbanded.

Flight Lieutenants R.L.E. Burton and D.H. Cannon hit world headlines when, on October 8-9 1953, they took WE139 (now preserved in the RAF Museum) to New Zealand in the Air Race. The visitor to Bassingbourn in June 1967 might hardly have believed his eyes. Six Caberras were painted in Russian markings for the film 'Billion Dollar Brain', an incident which prompted the Israelis to declare British collusion with their enemies during the Six Day war.

On May 8 1969 it was my privilege to fly on a practice for the last Canberra fly-past to mark the closure of Bassingbourn. It was an exhilarating experience as the 16 aircraft raced around the whole of southern East Anglia, ending in a fighter style peel-away. On May 19 1969 the Canberras left and flying virtually ceased.

One memorable sound would follow, to remain a cherished memory. This was a station where famed Glen Miller brought his music, almost for the last time. In the hangar he had used the Syd Lawrence big band re-created the Miller sound, thanks to the East Anglian Aviation Society, on a warm June evening in 1974. The ghosts of the B-17s were very clear and 'Moonlight Serenade' brought back that magic moment when I had climbed aboard 'General

Ike' in the same hangar and on the spot where the music was being made.

Now the Queen's Division reigns supreme. Superficially little has really changed, although only a portion of the main runway remains. The saplings are huge trees, the wartime control tower is a museum and the airfield holds a golf course and entertains land yachts. Many of the elms in Wimpole Park have died, but the memory of any who knew Bassingbourn in yesteryear cannot but be stirred upon passing.

Beccles (Ellough), Suffolk

TM450885. 2 miles SE of Beccles, Suffolk, on B1127 (crosses site)

There can be few who have not heard of 'The Dam Busters', No 617 Squadron, but less well known is its sister squadron, No 618, formed to sink the *Tirpitz* with 'Highball', a smaller edition of the 'Upkeep' bombs used against the German dams.

No 618 Squadron equipped with Mosquito IVs specially modified at Weybridge and Cambridge, each accommodating two of the spinning mines. Emphasis was placed upon the Dams raid and the intended simultaneous operation against the *Tirpitz* fell by the wayside. A lot of research and development went into 'Highball', but the perfected weapon was held back because any operation would be in daylight and the enemy would learn of the secret weapon. It was argued that he could easily produce similar weapons, and that targets available to him were numerous. Only in the Pacific would 'Highball' be used. No 618 Squadron formed and reformed, and in August 1944 moved to Beccles where training was undertaken with sashlite bulbs against a target marked on the runway. It would not have been possible for a viewer to see the technique of releasing 'Highball'.

British Airways helicopter base utilises one of the wartime T2 hangars.

Beccles, built in 1943 for the USAAF, was taken over by Bomber Command in mid-summer 1944. Then, on August 14 1944, 16 Group, Coastal Command, took over the station and 618 Squadron brought in their Mosquitoes. As at other Coastal Command stations the Royal Navy was ever near and on September 13 five Swordfish of 819 Squadron and five Albacores of 119 Squadron, RAF, arrived for operations that night, but only three aircraft operated. The Navy moved out to Swingfield next day and 119 Squadron soon after.

On October 11 1944 17 Barracudas of 827 Squadron, FAA, moved in from Crail, Fife, for anti-shipping operations and left for Langham on October 28, the day before 618 Squadron moved out. Their place was taken by Warwicks of 280 Squadron which operated both lifeboat-equipped and conventional aircraft. Most of the deep sea searches, commenced November 1 1944, were in support of the US 8th AAF. A detachment of Walruses of 278 Squadron also used the station from March 1945, staying until October 1945.

No 814 Squadron, FAA, had a detachment here from Thorney Island and in April 1945 Barracudas of 810 Squadron operated anti-midget submarine patrols from Beccles. Success came to 'L/810 Sqn' on April 13 when a small submarine was sunk. Another was attacked the same day and a spotting made of a third.

No 288 Anti-Aircraft Co-operation Squadron was briefly here in May 1945, then 810 Squadron withdrew to Machrihanish on June 3, leaving 280 Squadron's Warwicks as prime occupants. These continued patrols until the end of October 1945. It fell to 280 Squadron to give ASR cover when HM King George VI and the Queen visited the Channel Islands on June 6 1945. Some Warwicks were detached to Tiree during August 1945 to offer rescue facilities for any USAAF crew ditching in the Atlantic when flying home.

On September 3 1945 279 Squadron arrived with more Warwicks and Sea Otters from Thornaby, and the Mosquitoes of 248 and 254 Squadrons were briefly here in September 1945 to take part in the Battle of Britain flypast over London on September 15, flying on the day from North Weald.

No 280 Squadron moved to Langham on October 31, leaving 278 and 279 Squadrons and 15 Aircrew Holding Unit in residence. With 280 Squadron gone by the middle of the month and others

removed, 15 ACHU closed on November 16 and the station became non-operational on November 30 1945. It closed during December of that year.

A number of buildings remain, many among the Ellough Industrial Estate which uses a 'T' hangar. The helicopter depot of British Airways has another. The main runway is still *in situ*.

Bentwaters, Suffolk

TM350530. On A1152, 5 miles NE of Woodbridge, Suffolk

For close on 30 years the Americans have resided at Bentwaters. Little wonder, then, that the station has witnessed the great advance in weapons and aircraft since the closing of World War 2.

Construction began in 1942 and the station was intended for an American bomber Group. It was known at the time as Butley after a village to the southeast. From January 23 1943 the name became Bentwaters, after a house originally sited on the position of the main runway.

Bentwaters opened on April 17 1944 under Care & Maintenance in Bomber Command, the station being surplus to US needs. Building was slowed down and with the base almost complete construction work halted by June 1944. Whilst under Care & Maintenance the airfield was host to some emergency landings despite runway obstructions. First came a 96th Bomb Group B-17, on July 20, being severely damaged by those runway obstructions. Next was a P-51 of the 359th Fighter Group and on October 6 1944 another B-17, of the 95th Bomb Group, homed here.

Accordingly, the runways were cleared by October 10 and two weeks later three P-51s short of fuel put down on Bentwaters. The usefulness of a station so near to the coast was apparent. No 11 Group, ADGB, took the station over, it becoming the last station to take on an operational role for the RAF in Britain.

Bentwaters now became an RAF Mustang III base, the first unit to arrive being 129 Squadron on December 1 1944. During that month another five Mustang III squadrons moved in, Nos 64,118,126, 165 and 234. Their role was to offer escort to RAF bombers making daylight raids, a task commenced on December 23 when four squadrons escorted 150 Lancasters to Trier. Such operations continued until April 1945, and included participation by 64 and 126 Squadrons as escort during the

Mosquito day raid from Fersfield on the Gestapo HQ in Copenhagen. The final operation was flown on May 4 1945 when 64 and 126 Squadrons escorted Beaufighters attacking U-Boats in the Great Belt off Denmark, when five U-Boats were damaged.

After the war training in bomber escort continued, but in May 1945 Nos 129, 165 and 234 Squadrons moved out. The remainder had gone by September of that year. No 65 Squadron was at Bentwaters during May 1945, and Spitfire IXs of 234 Squadron moved in during August, leaving in February 1946 to re-equip with Meteor IIIs at Molesworth. The first jets to be based here were Meteor IIIs of 124 Squadron which arrived in October 1945. This squadron was re-numbered 56 on April 1 1946 and remained at Bentwaters until September. They had been joined by 245 Squadron in June, who were awaiting the opening of Wattisham to which they moved in October 1946.

On October 10 1946 226 Operational Conversion Unit moved in, staying until August 26 1949. Fighter pilots were trained here after initial fighter conversion at 61 OTU.

Bentwaters was inactive from September 1 1949 until July 1 1950 when again it was put on a Care & Maintenance basis before being transferred to the USAF on March 16 1951. The station hit the headlines when, on September 3 1951, F-86A Sabres arrived, the first in Europe and flying with the 81st Fighter Interceptor Group who based their 91st Squadron here. On April 1 1954 the unit was redesignated 81st Fighter Bomber Wing and began to receive F-84F Thunderstreaks in April 1954.

The Wing's name changed again, to 81st Tactical Fighter Wing on July 8 1958, and since January 1955 had been fully equipped with F-84Fs. In December 1958 F-101 Voodoos arrived, the first touching down on December 4 1948. Forty-one F-84Fs were then transferred to the West German Air Force. Operations became centralised in 1958, the 92nd Squadron having arrived from Manston in April. They were sited on the east side of Bentwaters opposite the 91st Squadron. Voodoos of the Wing had completed 100,000 flying hours by August 8 1963.

The first F-4C Phantom II for the 81st reached Bentwaters on October 4 1965 and conversion was completed by April 1966. In 1969 the Woodbridge squadron received F-4Ds completing conversion on June 18 1969. Bentwaters squadrons con-

verted in September 1973.

Bentwaters has also housed F-86Ds of the 87th FIS, 406th Fighter Interceptor Wing, armed with 'Mighty Mouse' rocket projectiles. Now it is the main European base for the A-10 'tank buster' which began to replace the Phantoms in autumn 1978.

Bircham Newton, Norfolk

TF790340. On B1153 S of Docking, Norfolk

Squadrons of Coastal Command operated in a manner totally different from those of any other Command. Often, their aircraft were detached to distant places and even other Groups. Sometimes, the point of departure differed from that of return — and frequently the site of take-off lay far from the parent base. The story of the Command and its operations is one of vast complexity and would take many volumes to relate.

A typical and eventful operation involving one of the Bircham Newton crews befell on May 29 1943. Flying Officer Sherwood and crew, on detachment at Davidstow Moor, Cornwall, left at dawn in Hudson 'K' of 279 Squadron. Their task, to assist in the rescue of 28 survivors from an action which took place 100 miles WSW of Land's End. Surprising, isn't it, that an East Anglian crew should be operating so far from their base? On Friday May 28 a Whitley of 10 OTU had crashed in the sea. Its crew clambered aboard their dinghy and were spotted by a Sunderland of 461 Squadron. The flying-boat attempted to alight but crashed in the process.

Next day another Sunderland of 461 Squadron reached the scene, found the dinghies and took their occupants aboard. Engine trouble then developed and the Sunderland was unable to take-off. The crew of K/279 arrived and made contact with a destroyer which they led to the scene. The crews of the Sunderlands and Whitley were taken aboard the ship, which then took a Sunderland in tow. Later, and with a skeleton crew, the other Sunderland took off and the Hudson returned home having much aided those in distress.

This was a busy period for the Hudsons of Bircham Newton. On July 25/26 1943 nine of them were despatched to search for the crew of a dinghy reported by the USAAF. They looked too for a ditched Lancaster later reported safe. A half-submerged dinghy was seen and a high-speed launch went to the spot. Reports of more dinghies turned out to be of Danish fishing vessels. In the afternoon after these fruitless sorties things really began to hot up. Wing Commander Corry, DFC, set off in W/279 after a dinghy reported 65 miles north of Ameland. About 35 miles north-east of Cromer he and Flight Lieutenant Penderson spotted a B-17 in the sea. At 1445 hours W/279 dropped an airborne lifeboat whilst the B-17 crew were climbing in their dinghies. Penderson then set off to look for the other reported dinghy. A second lifeboat was then dropped to the B-17 crew just before their bomber sank. The Americans boarded both lifeboats.

Meanwhile reports were received of a ditched RAF bomber and a Halifax was circling the spot. Some 60 miles NNE of Cromer two Hudson crews came upon two dinghies tied together and eight American airmen began firing Very cartridges. V/279 kept with them while U/279 headed for Ameland. Lindholme gear was dropped to the Americans. At 1845 hours a Walrus arrived and picked up survivors, and was followed by a second Walrus for the remainder. All were brought home safely.

U/279 had meanwhile resumed course and was working with an MTB. At 1835 hours they were led by a Halifax to five dinghies tied together and carrying US airmen to whom the Hudson dropped a lifeboat. Other aircraft homed in and joy was unbounded when the Americans set sail and started to row too. Three very successful operations had been completed in one day.

Perhaps more than any other station in East Anglia Bircham Newton certainly was an action station with a very long and varied history. It was closely associated during the war with Docking, the two being really inseparable with the satellite holding squadrons under full control of Bircham Newton.

Bircham Newton was built in 1916 and used as a training station. No 3 Fighter School formed here. Fame and importance did not come until the closing months of conflict in the First World War. The station became the first mobilising unit of No 27 Group, under Lieutenant Colonel R.H. Mulock, and began to prepare for long-range bombing attacks on Germany. It was indeed at Bircham Newton that the RAF concept of strategic bombing of Germany was forged. On June 13 1918 166 Squadron formed to carry out the task and was to be equipped with Handley-Page V/1500 four-engined

bombers with range sufficient to take them to Berlin. But by Armistice Day only three aircraft had arrived and no operations were flown, although preparations to attack the German capital were in hand. No 166 Squadron disbanded on May 31 1919. The back-up to 166 would have been 274 Squadron formed at Bircham Newton in April 1918. What huge aircraft the V/1500s were with a wingspan of 126 feet and a length of 64 feet.

Squadrons returned here after the war to disband, among them 56 Squadron, McCudden's old squadron, which arrived in December 1919 and disbanded in January 1920.

In those days another famous RFC station was nearby, at Seighford where 64 Squadron formed in August 1916, and where fighter pilots were trained until October 1917. DH5s were based there, but Bircham Newton, a larger airfield, took over from Seighford in 1917. The site of the smaller airfield was about a mile east of Seighford village, on the south side of the main road to Fakenham, and came into use in 1915. Little remains of this famous School of Air Fighting, but one can just make out roads, the site of the main gate and tarmac bases of the hangars.

Meanwhile Bircham Newton had been earmarked to be a heavy bomber station where, on June 1 1923, 7 Squadron formed and flew Vickers Vimys. No 99 Squadron, similarly equipped, joined them in May 1924 changing to Avro Aldershots later that year. On September 12 1924 Station HQ was established at Bircham Newton, command of the station being now held by Wing Commander L.J. Fiennes.

On April 7 1927 7 Squadron, commanded by the late Marshal of the Royal Air Force Lord Portal, and equipped with Virginias, moved to Worthy Down, followed three weeks later by 99 Squadron which moved to Upper Heyford. Since December 1925 they had been flying Handley-Page Hyderabads. Along with the heavies, 11 Squadron flying DH 9As had been at the station between September 1923 and May 1924. Another DH 9A squadron, No 39, arrived in January 1928 and left for India at the end of that year. Some of that squadron's DH 9As were passed to 101 Squadron after they formed at Bircham Newton on March 21 1928 then, in early 1929, they received the first examples of a newer type, the Boulton & Paul Sidestrand which was a product of that Norwich-based company. The Sidestrands left in October 1929.

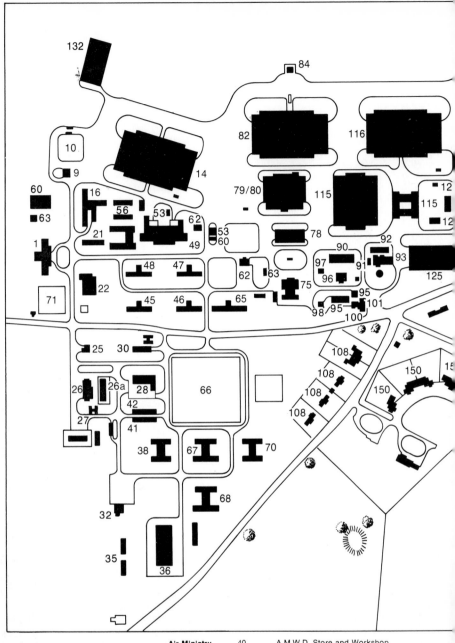

Building No		Air Ministry drawing no/ year
1	Station Head Quarters	1725/36
9	Petrol Tanker Shed	2773/34
10	72,000 gallon fuel installation	
14	Aircraft Shed Type C (Hipped)	2029/34, 6438/37
16	Sergeants' Mess	3484/36
21	Single Sergeants' Quarters	4526/36
22	Operations Block	7040/38
25	Ambulance Garage and Mortuary	5703/36
26	Sick Quarters and Annexe	7503/37
27	Sick Quarters Garage	
28	Gas Decontamination Block	6224/37
30	Disinfector	
32	Central Heating Station	2340/38
35	Sewage Compressor House	
36	F.F.M.T. Shed	3681/38
38	Barrack Block 8/56 'L'	11587/38
40	A.M.W.D. Store and Workshop	
41/42	Airmens' Garage	
43	Works Services Building	4195/35
44	Grocery Shop and Store	6271/38
45-48	Barrack Block Type 'C'	1100/28
49	Airmen's Mess and N.A.A.F.I.	1483/36
52	Vegetable Preparation Hut	
53	Cold Store	
55	Ready Use Pyrotechnics Store	
56	Quarters for N.A.A.F.I. Staff	
60	Petrol Tanker Shed	2773/34
62	Central Heating Station	5710/37
63	S.A.A. Store	
65	Barrack Block	2357/36
66	Parade Ground	
67, 68,		
70	Barrack Block 8/84 'L'	1132/38
71	Tennis Court	
75	Armoury and Photographic Section	7616/37
78	Main Stores (old)	752/28, 1568/28

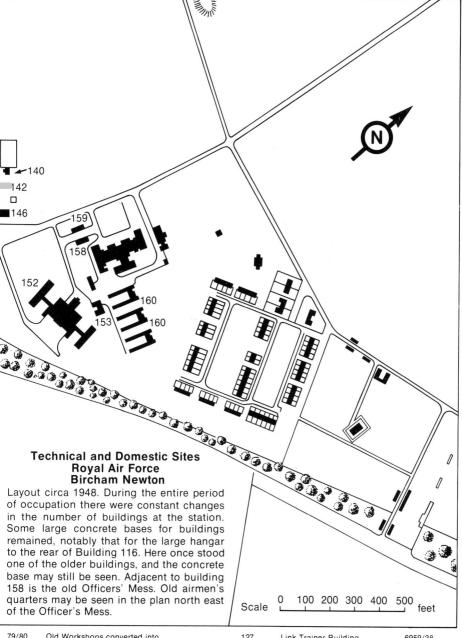

Technical and Domestic Sites
Royal Air Force
Bircham Newton

Layout circa 1948. During the entire period of occupation there were constant changes in the number of buildings at the station. Some large concrete bases for buildings remained, notably that for the large hangar to the rear of Building 116. Here once stood one of the older buildings, and the concrete base may still be seen. Adjacent to building 158 is the old Officers' Mess. Old airmen's quarters may be seen in the plan north east of the Officer's Mess.

Scale 0 100 200 300 400 500 feet

79/80	Old Workshops converted into Cinema and Information Room	
82	Aircraft Shed Type 'C' (Hipped)	
84	Watch Office with Tower	1959/34
90	Workshops (old)	1354/38
91	Latrine	AM/16/29
92	Parachute Store	
93	Power House (old)	694/23
94	High Level Water Tank (old)	
95	Booster House	1010/23
96	Reservoir (100,000 gallon)	704/23
97	S.A.A. Store	
98	Oil Store	
100	Fire Party House	
101	Guard House	166/23
108-112	Married Officers' Quarters	2414/37
115	Workshops	6958/37
116	Aircraft Shed Type 'C' (Hipped)	
121	Parachute Store	6351/37
122	Gas Defence Centre	9132/37
125	Fuel Compound	
126	R.C. Church	
127	Link Trainer Building	6959/38
128	Tailor's Shop	
129	Lubricant and Inflammables Store	1967/34
130	Main Stores	7064/37
131	Petrol Tanker Shed	2773/34
132-133	Aircraft Shed (Bellman)	
138	Gas Chamber and Practice Bomb Store	1144/37
139	Engine Test House	8800/37
140	Machine Gun Test Butt	3984/37
142	M.T. Shed	778/38
143	Detached M.T. Shed	6225/37
146	M.T. Shed	778/38
147	M.T. Office	
150	Married Quarters	395/21
152	Officers' Mess	2948/34
153	Squash Racquets Court	2078/18
158-159	Officers' Garage	
160	Married Airmen's Quarters	

Area to south of camp – bomb and pyrotechnics store.

In April 1929 No 35 Squadron formed at Bircham Newton flying DH 9As and later some Fairey IIIFs before, in the autumn of 1932, they re-equipped with Fairey Gordons, a type which stemmed from the famous IIIF. This unit had as companion No 207 Squadron which, commanded by the late Lord Tedder, formed here on February 1 1920 with DH 9As and left in the autumn of 1922 for Turkey and returned to Bircham Newton on November 7 1929. They, too, operated IIIFs before equipping with Gordons in September 1932.

During the early 1930s Bircham Newton's Gordons were a frequent sight in East Anglia, during exercises and at flying displays. They took part in the RAF Jubilee Review at Mildenhall then on October 3 1935 hurriedly moved to the Middle East because of the Abyssinian crisis. The move came as Bomber Command was being established. On October 1 1933 the Wessex Bombing Area had split into the Central Area (of which Bircham Newton, 33, 35 and 207 Squadrons were a part) and the Western Area. These two Areas were amalgamated to form 3 Group on May 1 1936.

Once the Gordons had left two new squadrons formed here on December 3 1935, Nos 21 and 34, both of which left in July 1936 for Abbotsinch there to form the nucleus of 2 Group. No 18 Squadron had arrived in January 1936 flying Hawker Hinds and, on February 10, 'C' Flight was detached to form the nucleus of 49 Squadron which moved to Worthy Down in August 1936.

This latter move ended a page of history for, on August 10 1936, the station was transferred from Bomber to Coastal Command and placed in 16 Group. At the end of July 206 Squadron had begun to bring in its Ansons from Manston and on August 17 220 Squadron formed here similarly equipped. 'C' Flight, 220 Squadron, was hived off to form 269 Squadron on December 7 1936, this new squadron leaving for Abbotsinch at the end of the year.

The expansion period was now much in evidence at Bircham Newton for under the new plan this would be a two-squadron Coastal Command base for which three 'C' Type hangars were now being built to replace the old 1916-type wooden sheds. Thus a station arose which looked like a new one, although the domestic site on the east side of the road through the camp retained, and still retains, buildings from the earlier stage.

No 220 Squadron took over the new No 1 Hangar on July 27 1937. They left in January 1939.

Meanwhile, another activity had commenced at Bircham Newton. Anti-aircraft firing ranges were brought into use on the north Norfolk coast in the summer of 1936 and for this reason 'B' Flight of No 1 Anti-Aircraft Co-operation Unit arrived with six Westland Wallaces for target towing. They returned to Biggin Hill in the autumn and the following May 'C' Flight arrived, staying until mid-September. This Flight returned after equipping with six Hawker Henleys and 'D' Flight, similarly equipped, joined them on April 28 1939 for the summer camp.

Commencement of hostilities found 206 Squadron at Bircham Newton using Ansons for inshore convoy protection, 42 Squadron which had arrived on August 18 flying aged Vildebeest torpedo bombers and the Flights of 1 AACU. Immediately war commenced the Ansons began watching over shipping from north Kent to Lincolnshire which brought one crew face-to-face with a Do 18 flying-boat on November 8 1939. That day the first U-Boat kill of the war was made by Pilot Officer Harper and crew of 206 Squadron in Anson K6184.

Reconnaissances were flown to the Elbe and off Holland then, in March 1940, 206 Squadron began to equip with Hudsons which came gradually into use in May 1940 during which month they made a bombing attack on Rotterdam. In June they operated Battle Flights over the Channel using all available aircraft to cover the Dunkirk evacuation. Reconnaissances were made and attacks by day and night on Dutch targets and shipping. The squadron left Bircham Newton for Aldergrove in August 1941.

Much had happened at Bircham by then. Concern had been expressed at the start of the war for the safety of the herring fleets operating in great numbers off East Anglia from Great Yarmouth and Lowestoft. Accordingly Blenheim Flight at Bircham Newton became 'D' Flight of 233 Squadron in January 1940, then 254 Squadron arrived on January 28 for trade defence operations. They took over the old Blenheim Flight which now became 'B' Flight of 254 Squadron flying Blenheim IVF fighters. Heinkel 111s operated against the ships and 254 Squadron engaged one on February 22. Some convoy escorts were now flown from Lympne and, when Norway was attacked,

254 Squadron was rushed north to Hatston on April 24 and partly detached to Lossiemouth, which led to a busy period of operations off Norway. No 235 Squadron replaced 254 at Bircham Newton. The Vildebeests left in mid-April 1940. The opening of the war against Holland brought 235 Squadron into action at once and they escorted Coastal Command aircraft operating over the North Sea and making sweeps off Holland. They took part in many engagements over the Channel using advanced bases at Detling and Thorney Island, and flew convoy patrols. Many sorties were to waters off Denmark. Thus, 235 Squadron found itself exceedingly busy and during the Battle of Britain had detachments at Thorney Island taking part in the fighting. Add to this the high pressure operations conducted by 206 Squadron and Bircham Newton can be seen to have been a very busy station, by day and night. No 229 Squadron maintained a detachment here from June to September 1940.

On November 21 1940 221 Squadron formed here, and equipped with 24 Wellington lc/VIIIs. They commenced East Coast patrols on February 23 1941 before joining their detachment at Limavady on May 2 1941. These were not the first Wellingtons based here for No 2 GRU formed on March 4 1940 with five Wellington DW1s for anti-magnetic mine

F-4C Phantom IIs replaced the Voodoos at Bentwaters. 40884 is seen, in 1967, with mixed weapons load.

activities before moving soon after to Manston.

Fighter reconnaissance operations by Blenheims continued throughout most of 1941, 500 Squadron arriving for this rôle on May 30, releasing 235 Squadron which moved to Sumburgh on June 3 after making much use of Docking. No 500 Squadron operated off the East Anglian coast with their detachment at Carew Cheriton patrolling off the French northwest coast and making shipping strikes. The squadron re-equipped with Hudsons which meant *Rovers* and shipping strikes being flown, often by night, off the Dutch coast.

No 248 Squadron arrived on June 15 and stayed until September 1941 operating Blenheim IVFs giving fighter protection to shipping and flying sweeps and

The Boulton & Paul Sidestrand entered service here in 1929, J9185 appearing in the photograph.

convoy escorts. Yet another squadron arrived on June 30 1941, No 608, to fly Blenheims until re-equipping with Hudsons in August 1941 and operating from Bircham Newton until December 1941.

At the start of 1942 the station was operating mainly Hudsons for anti-shipping operations. Additional strength was provided by the arrival of 407 Squadron on March 31 1942 and the Dutchmen of 320 Squadron on April 24. Hudsons of 320 and 407 Squadrons operated during the Bremen '1,000 bomber' raid. No 407 Squadron moved out on February 2 1943 and 320 left on March 15. The last Hudson strike had been flown on March 9.

Shipping escort and attack was not, however, the only task being carried out under the station's control. Target towers used the station throughout the war co-operating with the gunners on the Norfolk coast. 'K' Flight of 1 AACU had arrived with six Henleys on September 5 1940 and on January 1 1941 'M' Flight, similarly equipped, arrived at the station. Both stayed until the end of 1941 when they moved to Langham. Bircham Newton's share came again when 1611 and 1612 Flights were based there in 1942 until they were amalgamated into 695 Squadron on October 31 1942. This unit operated with the Weybourne Range gunners until the war ended, by which time Martinets and Vengeances were also in use.

Bircham Newton was very usefully sited for weather reconnaissance flying. No 403 Meteorological Reconnaissance Flight formed here in November 1940 equipped with three Blenheim IVs. In 1941 they received some Hudsons and became 1403 Flight on March 1 1941. They were joined by 1401 Meteorological Flight which arrived on October 29 1941 having risen from the pre-war Met Flight at Mildenhall. They brought along a few Blenheims but mainly Gladiators, which type flew from the Norfolk bases of Coastal Command to the end of the war, maintained by Marshall at Cambridge. In May 1942 Hudsons replaced their Blenheims and in July Spitfire 5s were added. A lot of their operational flights were flown from Docking.

These two Meterological Flights disbanded on July 31 1942 and arose next day as 521 Squadron equipped with Spitfires, Hudsons and Gladiators. But for operations over the Continent they held a handful of Mosquito IVs which remained in use until the squadron disbanded on

March 31 1943 when 1409 Flight took over the Mosquito role.

That one station could conduct such a wide assortment of operations seems almost impossible, but use of Docking and Langham helped reduce the pressure. It needed to for on November 16 1941 a further complete change of face commenced when No 279 Air-Sea Rescue Squadron formed and flew its first sortie using Hudsons on January 22 1942. The Hudsons conducted deep ASR search and sometimes did so under fighter watch off the Dutch coast. The number of aircraft ditching was ever increasing with the increase in operational activity. The Hudsons and the increasing skill of their crews in locating airmen down in the sea were in demand over a wide area and frequent detachments came about. Remember, too, that whilst the targets were being towed, the weather recorded and ASR Hudsons went about their tasks, Bircham Newton and its satellites were still despatching Hudsons on anti-shipping or convoy escort duties.

On June 28 1943 a large and new shape arrived at Bircham Newton. This was the Vickers-Armstrong Warwick. Intended as a bomber, its long development period rendered it of little value as such when it became available, and it slipped into the air-sea rescue role. In June 1943 the Warwick came into use at the Warwick Training Unit which flew from both Bircham Newton and Docking. This was a heavy aeroplane, and Bircham Newton had no runways. Although 279 Squadron certainly flew them it was not actually equipped until much later.

The Warwick Training Unit vacated the base on November 21 1943 leaving 279 Squadron busily operating with Hudsons which, since the spring of 1943, had been modified to carry the airborne lifeboat.

No 280 Squadron had departed to Thorney Island on September 23 1943. A major change in the station's war effort came with the arrival on November 15 1943, both here and at Docking, of 415 Squadron flying Wellington XIIIs and Albacores for night anti-shipping duties off the Dutch coast.

The early months of 1944 saw a relatively unchanged picture with 279 Squadron ever-active by day and 415 busily occupied at the satellite at night and using Bircham Newton as a maintenance base. No 2 Armament Practice Camp had a short spell here, moving to Docking on August 29 1944.

That month witnessed the opening of

the Coastal Command Preparation Pool at Bircham Newton. Here Mosquitoes, Beaufighters, Wellingtons and Albacores were fitted with the specialised equipment needed by Coastal Command squadrons, in the case of Mosquito VIs, for instance, rocket rails. This work continued to August 1945.

On September 6 1944 the Royal Navy arrived, 855 Squadron flying Avengers for night shipping raids mainly from Docking. They were followed at the end of the month by 819 and 119 Squadrons forming 157 Wing and equipped with Swordfishes and Albacores. They arrived principally to train for anti-submarine night operations to be conducted from Belgium, whence the Wing proceeded, Swordfish-equipped, in January 1945. No 855 Squadron left for Lee-on-Solent on October 17 1944.

At this time 279 Squadron was at last beginning to move, a Flight proceeding to Thornaby on October 14 and the remainder of the squadron at the start of November, there to convert at last to Warwicks. This left Bircham Newton somewhat depleted.

On February 27 1945 819 Squadron returned to disband, doing so on March 7 1945. Three days later a training flight for 119 Squadron formed here with Swordfishes. No 598 Squadron arrived on March 12 1945 from Peterhead for additional AAC duties, leaving for Ipswich and disbandment on May 3.

Bodney housed Blenheims of 82 Squadron in the autumn of 1940.

Bircham Newton is now the home of the Construction Industry Training centre and little changed as this recent photograph shows (CITB).

In 1940 Hudsons of 206 Squadron were based here (Flight International).

The end of the war brought closure of 119 Squadron training flight, but on June 8 1945 No 18 Aircrew Holding Unit for RCAF personnel awaiting return home was opened, disbanding on September 2 1945. No 695 Squadron had, on August 11 1945, moved to its post-war station at Horsham St Faith. August 14 brought 1693 Flight from Copenhagen for a brief stay. Between July 4 and September 14 the Coastal Command EBT School was at Bircham Newton.

After the war No 15 Air Beam Training Flight was based here until September 1948 using Ansons, but the lack of any runways limited the use of the station. Also present at that time was the Transport Initial Conversion Unit which disbanded in 1948. Fighter Command held the station from 1945 until October 1946 when 4 Group Transport Command took control. In October 1948 Technical Training Command took over the station from 38 Group and the Officers' Advanced Training School was transferred from Hornchurch.

On December 18 1962 the station closed, the Junior Command and Staff School moving to Ternhill and the Administrative Apprentices' Training School to Hereford. Although Bircham Newton's demise had come the station was used for some trials of the Kestrel in 1965.

Now the station houses the Construction Industry Training Centre. The two 'C' Type hangars remain, and many of the very old domestic buildings.

Bodney, Norfolk

TL850990. On B1108 SE of Hilborough, Norfolk

Take-off came before sunrise over Bodney on June 6 1944. On that momentous dawn a Mustang taking off in darkness careered into the control tower, demolishing it and causing a replacement, still there, to be built.

Grim though that moment was, Bodney had known worse for, from here, many a 2 Group Blenheim crew set out for a horrific finale in the fearsome actions of 1940 and 1941. But if Bodney needs a unique memory it must be of May 31 1942 when Bomber Command first took delivery of the unpopular Lockheed Vega Ventura at this station.

Bodney came to life in early 1940 as satellite to Watton. The careers of these two stations were inextricably bound. Blenheim IVs of 82 Squadron dispersed here from March 1940, and soon afterwards 21 Squadron, also based at Watton, used the satellite until Norway was violated which took the squadron to Lossiemouth in late June 1940. Thus the two squadrons were here, partly, during the invasion of France and Belgium.

Until April 1941 82 Squadron used Bodney for dispersal and operations, this famous squadron encountering all the problems which 2 Group knew. There were, too, the inevitable intruder forays as on February 11/12 1941 when a Ju 88 followed a Blenheim which, short of fuel, was forced to crash away from base. Then the enemy machine shot down another Blenheim on approach to Bodney. Such incidents were a hazard of life at all night bomber stations in East Anglia.

For a few days in May 1941 Bodney housed RAF Fortress 1s of 90 Squadron, dispersed from Watton. A detachment of 61 Squadron's Hampdens had operated from the airfield, making a few daylight cloud cover raids before returning to 5 Group on April 30.

No 105 Squadron arrived on May 21 1941 with Blenheim IVs but the stay was short for, in July, the squadron was detached to Malta and the Mediterranean anti-shipping campaign, a torturous, cruel conflict, fought by 2 Group with its customary bravery.

For much of 1941 82 Squadron operated from Bodney, or Watton, against shipping in the North Sea, or flying fighter-escorted day raids on the Occupied Countries. At the end of the year the squadron found itself thrown into an intensive night intruder campaign against enemy airfields. Truly, Bodney and the Blenheim became inseparable — until the Japanese entered the war. No 82 Squadron was quickly taken off operations, forgot its Blenheims, and hurried to the Far East.

Shortly before this, Watton adopted an unlikely role when No 17 (Pilots) Advanced Flying Unit formed there with Master IIs, some of which spasmodically flew from Bodney for nearly a year and a half.

On March 4 1942 21 Squadron reformed taking over 82's old Blenheims, and commenced to work up into an operational unit.

A Ventura servicing party arrived on April 25 1942 to train crews for the new type, the first two of which arrived on May 31. There were small, but irritating snags, as the squadron trained. Then, to the astonishment of all, another new type for the RAF appeared on July 16, for it was here that the Mitchell joined operational service. Two new types were just too much and the Mitchells left early in August for West Raynham. Fearing heavy losses if Venturas were used in daylight, 2 Group decided that they would be best employed to replace Blenheims in the night intruder campaign. The Venturas left Bodney on September 30 before operations commenced, which left the station free for Watton's Masters.

No 17(P)AFU left Watton for Calveley in early May 1943 and Bodney became quiet, but only for a few days because the Americans arrived late in the same month followed by the 352nd Fighter Group. They brought P-47D Thunderbolts and flew their first mission on September 9. They performed the usual round of escorts and patrols and in April 1944 the Group received its first P-51 Mustangs. Very soon these were in the thick of the battle, the Group receiving a Distinguished Unit Citation for its action of May 8 1944. Brunswick was the target for B-17s and the 352nd among the escort fought until their ammunition ran out and fuel ran low. Bomber escorts were the order of the day, for attacks on factories, submarine pens and V-weapon sites. D-Day found the Group covering the dawn assault. Strafing and dive bombing followed as the 352nd supported the Normandy invasion, the St Lô break-out and the operations around Arnhem. The December Ardennes offensive caused part of the 352nd to be rushed to Belgium to give close support, followed soon by the remainder of the Group which also took part in the Rhine crossing.

Bodney was quiet until April 1945 when the 352nd returned to fly a few more missions before the war ended. In November 1945 the Group returned to America. A few airmen arrived to close the station late in November 1945. There is little to be seen now apart from the replacement control tower.

Boreham, Essex
TL740120. 2 miles NW of the A12(T) at Boreham

The base was built in 1943-1944 and had one of the briefest operational careers of any. It became the home of the 394th Bomb Group flying B-26s between March and July 1944, when they moved to Holmsley South.

Operations commenced in March 1944 with *Ramrods* to France, Holland and Belgium. Targets included marshalling yards, airfields, gun emplacements, bridges and V-weapon sites. On D-Day they bombed gun emplacements in the Cherbourg peninsula, then switched to attacking communications and fuel dumps strong-points and troop concentrations. Thereafter Boreham remained in American hands, and although it was earmarked for 38 Group RAF, in the end they did not need the station and it closed in 1945.

Bottisham, Cambridgeshire
TL540595. S of the A45 about 5 miles E of Cambridge. New A45 road crosses the centre of the airfield

It was one of those hot, cloudless 1940 days. Life seemed even more precious, rather precarious. By chance I took the lane to Wilbraham that used to come off the main Cambridge-Newmarket road. A large expanse of grass followed a wheatfield. No fence, none of the customary barbed wire. Yet on the field, widely dispersed, a clutch of Tiger Moths diverted from their daily flying at Cambridge. Close inspection followed. Incredibly, they had 20 lb bombs hanging from fuselage racks. The situation was indeed alarming. These were attached to Training Command's anti-invasion force, their task to assault enemy troops should they step ashore — and irrespective of losses. Instructors would fly the aircraft.

Bottisham was quickly prepared in May 1940 as a satellite for Waterbeach. It never accepted any aircraft from that station. Instead the Tiger Moths and a few tents for living quarters tarried until September 1940 when the main scare receded, although it was, of course, very late in the war before invasion plans finally elapsed. There was always the fear of raiding parties, if nothing more.

Until the summer of 1941 22 EFTS used it for Tiger Moth training, until on July 15 1941 it was taken over by Army Co-operation Command. On to the station came Lysanders of 241 Squadron working closely with Eastern Command Army units and often having detachments at Snailwell. They undertook practice shoots for gunners, carried out patrols over Army convoys and generally supported Army exercises.

In August 1941 the sound at Bottisham changed when a few Allison-engined

Tomahawks, with their high-pitched rasping sound, supplemented the Lysanders. Their task was fighter-reconnaissance, and they were seen in pairs flying low on training sorties and often 'beating up' Army convoys. Serviceability was poor. There were ground loops and constant engine troubles. No operations were possible.

Soil revetments were now built along the A45 side of the field where a couple of blister hangars were provided for maintenance. A few huts were erected in the north-east corner and are still standing. On October 15 laying of two metal Sommerfeld track runways commenced. The first came into use in July 1942.

The next big change occurred on March 15 1942 when some of the RAF's first Mustang 1s arrived for 241 Squadron. Fast and manoeuvrable as it was, the Mustang, whose performance fell off rapidly above 15,000 feet, was a great initial disappointment. These very elegant aircraft quickly became a daily sight in the area.

On May 2 1942 241 Squadron moved to Ayr affording training to Army formations in Scotland. Their place was taken on June 15 by Tiger Moths of 652 AOP Squadron which moved to Westley on August 21.

The newly formed 168 Squadron had flown in from nearby Snailwell on July 13 and again the Tomahawk dominated the scene. Some brief excitement came to Bottisham on September 23 when a couple of Whitleys brought in two Horsa gliders. This was a prelude for things to come. On November 7 eight Mustangs arrived from Ayr for 168 Squadron. Eleven days later five Whitleys and Horsas arrived to transport 168 Squadron to Odiham for operational deployment.

On November 20 1942 Tiger Moths and a few Auster AOP 1 air observation posts arrived on the station to work up before being posted to North Africa, staying at Bottisham until late January and spotting for gunnery shoots off Hunstanton.

After they left the airfield was put on Care & Maintenance for it had been decided to extend the runways and facilities, which took place during most of 1943.

On December 3 1943 the unmistakable din of the Republic P-47 arrived overhead. The 361st Fighter Group, USAAF, was arriving and did so in full strength in a matter of days. By mid-December the letters 'E2' and 'B7' were being applied to the camouflaged fighters which commenced operation with the 8th Air Force on January 21 1944. Their role was twofold, bomber escort and ground strafing, and they were soon in the thick of the fight. Thus the daily sight now was of P-47s scampering off making an awful din before forming into their 'finger-four' battle sections.

During May 1944 the 361st began to receive P-51Ds, some of the first to arrive in Britain. At the time of D-Day when the Mustangs were dispersed along the airfield perimeter, and the runway now crossed the road where I had enjoyed the site of armed Tiger Moths, some of the P-51s were to be seen with their upper surfaces painted in a superb shade of deep blue. Indeed, that was to become my most vivid memory of the evening of D-Day when I managed a tour of the perimeter, notebook carefully tucked away! Among the Mustangs sat the inevitable Norseman and Bobcat.

Bottisham's Mustangs were extremely busy during that summer, operating mainly over France. As soon as the A-20 Group left Little Walden in September the 361st moved there, for it was a far better-equipped station. Bottisham then lay silent for all time. In 1945 some Belgian airmen training at Snailwell were billeted at Bottisham but the station closed on May 1 1946 and was sold on October 1 1958.

On a blustery afternoon, February 14 1958, I happened by chance to be passing Bottisham as bulldozers went into action. Within a few moments the control tower was a heap of rubble. Little remains now but the roadway leading to the guard-room, alongside a garage on the A45. The new dual carriageway races across the centre of the airfield. If you take that road you will have but a few moments in which to gaze across the fields which were once the lair of the Lysanders, Mustangs and Tomahawks.

Bourn, Cambridgeshire

TL340590. On A45 7 miles W of Cambridge

Few who frequent Bourn's Bank Holiday market have much idea of the importance the airfield once played in the bomber offensive. From here Mosquitoes of 105 Squadron, *Oboe*-equipped, spearheaded Bomber Command for a year.

Before them Stirlings and Lancasters set off for some of the most famous raids the Command mounted. No record seems to have survived to show just when Bourn

Left: *Mosquito B XXV KB458 'U' Uncle of 162 Squadron on dispersal at Bourn (R.F. Clark).* Right: *Bourn's wartime layout is shown in this photograph taken by a Canberra of 58 Squadron on April 20 1956 (DoE).*

Below: *P-51 Mustangs of the 361st Fighter Group at Bottisham in 1944 (USAF).* Above: *The only remaining buildings at Bottisham, in the north-east corner.*

first resounded to a landing, but Wellingtons of 101 Squadron and Stirlings of No 7 from Oakington used the landing ground by summer 1941. The airfield was bombed on April 9 1941, three bombs hitting a runway. It was to Bourn that two Stirlings homed on return from the memorable daylight raid on Best on December 18 1941, the battered form of one sitting at the end of the main runway throughout Christmas 1941. Bourn was at this time Oakington's satellite.

To relieve some pressure on the parent station, No 101 Squadron moved into Bourn with newly received Wellington IIIs on February 11 1942. They courageously waged the bomber war until August 12 1942 from Bourn, taking part in the '1,000 bomber' raids on Essen and Cologne, and had bombed Rostock and Lübeck in the 1942 fire raids. The squadron left for Stradishall in August, to make room for XV Squadron's Stirlings, manoeuvred out of Wyton when the Pathfinder Force took over that station.

The first Stirling raid, against Düsseldorf, came on August 15 and Stirlings participated in the long-distance and harrowing night raids on northern Italy in the autumn. At the end of 1942 XV Squadron was selected to introduce the refined Stirling III into squadron service and gradually introduced them to operations in February and March 1943.

Just as this was fully underway XV Squadron was ordered to Mildenhall to make way for 97 Squadron's Lancasters, an extension to the strength of the Pathfinders. No 97 Squadron arrived on April 18 and first operated, against Duisburg, on April 26 1943. During May a third Flight was added to the squadron. The squadron bombed distant Pilsen on May 13/14 and took part in the heavy raids on Wüppertal and Essen. A special raid was mounted by four crews flying from Scampton on June 16 who bombed Friedrichshafen, flew on to Maison Blanche in a shuttle operation, and attacked Spetzia on return.

The Straits Settlement Squadron, 97, played a marker role in the huge Hamburg raids, sent 16 aircraft to Peenemünde and then entered the Battle of Berlin. A Lancaster returning from 'The Big City' on August 23 was shot down by an intruder over Norfolk. There were hosts of eventful moments for the Lancaster crews, but one night came to be outstanding. Twenty-one Lancasters set off for Berlin on December 16 1943 and the opposition was strong. But it was the return to Bourn which proved quite disastrous, for bad visibility set in over the area and 28 aircrew were killed as aircraft short of fuel crashed. Eight crews landed safely at Bourn, three at Graveley. Flight Sergeant Coates had incendiaries from another aircraft fall on his, and flak put two engines out of action. He thought he would have to ditch, but managed to bring the crippled Lancaster into Downham. Two Lancasters crashed near Ely and Wyton and another was lost without trace. Flying Officer Thackway crashed near Bourn, two more crashed near Graveley and one near Gransden. Another, flown by Squadron Leader Mackenzie, could be seen next morning as a burnt wreck by the side of the main road. The night's disaster was the worst suffered by any East Anglian airfield in such circumstances.

The squadron operated as intensively as any. On March 18 1944 'C' Flight, 97 Squadron, moved to Downham to form the nucleus of 635 Squadron. At midday on April 18 1944 21 Lancasters left for Coningsby for 5 Group wanted back one of its 'crack' squadrons. Their last raid from Bourn came on April 11/12 with Aachen the target.

By chance runway building was about to commence at Marham and in the late morning of March 23 1944, No 105 Mosquito Squadron roared glamorously into Bourn. This was a squadron with a glittering war record, the premier Mosquito day bomber squadron. Some of the glamour of those days had been lost when they were switched to night bombing, but now Oboe-equipped and flying Mk IXs, they were to hold as important a place at night as any squadron. On the evening of the day of their arrival they operated marking Laon's marshalling yards. Next night they marked airfields during a Berlin raid, for the range of Oboe was limited. Their main task at this time was marking transport targets in occupied countries and airfields, then they placed their target indicators on gun batteries along the French coast, and spearheaded the bomber attacks on such targets as a prelude to the Normandy landings.

Then came a busy period when they operated by day and night against V-1 targets before finding oil refineries. By now they had some Mosquito XVIs with some cabin pressurisation. Their Mosquitoes carried out bombing raids in their own right too, and were able to place their loads with enviable accuracy. Things did not go all their own way though for, as they returned from Orleans and Le Mans on May 23, an intruder bombed and strafed Bourn damaging two aircraft on the ground and holding up landing by an hour.

By late 1944 the Mosquitoes' range was extended by modified *Oboe*, and continental stations permitted *Oboe* operations from Bourn deeper into enemy territory. They marked, too, for the Light Night Striking Force, whose sting was as great as many a Main Force raid and often more accurate.

On December 18 1944 a new squadron, No 162, formed at Bourn with Canadian-built Mosquito XXs and XXVs. A proportion of its aircraft were equipped with H_2S and they, too, adopted partly a marker role. They could mark for their own crews and soon began the nightly — even twice nightly — run to Berlin. What was even more important, these raids were almost without loss, and with accurate and heavy loads. Bourn was indeed a busy station, equipped with the most cost-effective warplane of all time.

A new shape came to Bourn in March 1945 when Spitfire Vs and Hurricane IIs of 1686 Bomber Defence Training Flight used the station giving training for 8 Group crews in fighter defence.

Stirlings were part of Bourn from 1941 to the end of the war. From the Sebro factory on Madingley Road, Cambridge, the bombers or transports were brought to Bourn for repair, erected in the T hangars still to be seen on the eastern side of the airfield, and partly occupied now by helicopters of Management Aviation, test-flown from Bourn.

By August 1945 the scene had changed. No 105 Squadron left in June 1945 and 162 moved to Blackbushe on July 10 to fly mail and courier flights to distant parts of Europe. Sebro began overhauling Transport Command Liberators, work continuing almost to the end of that year.

On January 1 1946 3 Group handed the station to 48 Group and on July 21 1947 it passed to Maintenance Command. It closed in 1948 and the land was sold in April 1961. Bourn lay dormant until 1947 when Pest Control moved in and later conducted crop spraying from here using helicopters. Management Aviation currently uses Bourn for a similar purpose. The dispersals have been torn up and much of the airfield is farmland. The old fire engine shed may still be seen on the west side near where the tower stood. Most of the living accommodation was around Bourn village. The Mosquitoes were mainly dispersed in the south-east corner near the trees.

Boxted, Essex

TM015305. 5 miles NE of Colchester, W of A12 (T)

When the Allies reached Berlin there was indeed a scramble for the spoils of war. The three major contestants grabbed as much of the Reich's archives as remained. Among those eagerly sought were the Luftwaffe's aircraft loss records. The British struck lucky — to a degree — retrieving the Luftwaffe Quartermaster General's master volumes for the period to the end of 1943. Beyond that — nothing complete. It has always been believed that the Russians found the remainder. Thus, it has not been possible to compile in the West such accurate listing of German losses as these documents revealed for earlier years. Unlikely it is that the USSR, with its obnoxious attitude to accurate history, will ever make available to us the extent and results of any research. So, the claims made by pilots beyond December 1943 remain, for verification, upon sources available to intelligence organisations.

It is generally accepted that to Boxted's 56th Fighter Group went the highest number of combat successes credited to any 8th AF Group during the war, a total of 674 enemy aircraft destroyed. Apt, then, that Boxted did not fade away as soon as the Americans left, but was transferred to RAF Fighter Command who used the station for a year or so. Thus, for all its anonymity to most people, Boxted certainly has some claims to fame, as well as a more involved history than most USAAF East Anglian bases.

Incomplete, the base opened in May 1943. Early in June the 386th Bomb Group arrived with B-26s which commenced operations in July. Principal targets were airfields in France although attacks were also made on marshalling yards and gun positions. Marauders were seen but briefly at Boxted, moving to the better site at Great Dunmow in September, by which time their bombing campaign was only just becoming effective.

Their place was taken by the 354th Fighter Group, 9th AF, which flew in from Greenham Common, and more importantly brought along some of the first USAAF P-51s. Furthermore they took them into action in December, and found themselves working up deep penetration fighter escort tactics with the Mustang. As early as January 11 1944 the Group was honoured with the award to Major James H. Howard of the Medal of Honour after his courage during a bomber escort. But the 9th AF was awaiting a chance to position its strength in the south and during April 1944 the 354th moved to Lachendon.

As soon as they had gone in came the dashing 56th with their P-47 Thunderbolts. They already had an enviable reputation and a long score list to their credit. Among their pilots were two who were outstanding on the Allied side. Francis S. Gabreski flew with the 56th between April 1943 and July 1944 until, on July 20, he crash-landed and was soon taken prisoner, but with the highest 8th AF fighter pilot's tally, for he was credited with 28 enemy aircraft shot down. His runner-up, whose score of 27 was later adjusted to 28, was also with the Group. He was Robert S. Johnson who flew his last mission in Europe on May 8 1944, then returned to the USA and later joined Republic Aviation.

The 56th was always in the thick of battle during escorts and ground strafing missions. They fought hard over Normandy and played a part in the airborne landings in Holland and the Ardennes battle, as well as flying protective patrols above the Remagen bridge over which the Americans crossed the Rhine into southern Germany. Their last patrols were flown on April 21 1045, and the 56th returned home in the autumn. For six months the 56th had as their companions at Boxted an air-sea rescue unit formed in May 1944 and equipped with P-47s. They moved out to Halesworth in January 1945.

Boxted took its place in late 1945 in Fighter Command. The primitive nature of wartime airfields would never have been long acceptable in peacetime. Accommodation was widely dispersed and primeval, heating arrangements in living accommodation usually a tortoise stove or two in the centre of the hut. Offices and the Operations Sections were little better, and the rough brown linoleum which served as floor covering over concrete or wood gave little or no comfort in cold conditions, although it lent itself to polishing on 'fatigues'. Engineering workshops were equally poor — when they existed — and most maintenance was done in the open on dispersals. Boxted served the RAF only on an interim basis

whilst pre-war permanent stations were redecorated and living standards and runways improved.

As Castle Camps closed in January 1946 25 Squadron's Mosquitoes moved to Boxted on the 11th. In March Meteor IIIs of 234 Squadron joined them and both squadrons stayed here until early September. They had as company two other Meteor III squadrons, Nos 222 and 263 which arrived in June 1946. No 222 left soon after and 263 in September. Meteor IIIs of 56 Squadron were here in the autumn of 1946. Boxted closed on November 3 1946, partly because the proximity of Colchester was likely to make jet flying unacceptable. The site of the airfield has now been given over mainly to orchards, the RAF having vacated the site in August 1947.

Bradwell Bay, Essex

TM000085. To E of end of B1020, E of village

Visit the site of Bradwell and there is little to see of this one-time busy airfield. One is, instead, confronted by a nuclear power station.

Bradwell came about rather by chance. Before the war an air-firing range existed on marshland known as Denghie Flats, which was used into the 1950s. A landing ground was set down for refuelling purposes, but because of its strategic siting by the coast it was developed into a fighter station.

Concrete and tarmac runway building commenced in February 1941, runways being twice lengthened that year. The station opened as an independent one in Hornchurch Sector on November 28 1941, previously having been merely a satellite landing ground. The intention was that it would be operational in January 1942, but winter weather delayed this until April 1942.

In the mid-morning of April 15 1942 Boston III intruders of 418 (Canadian) Squadron arrived from Debden and late on April 16 Pilot Officer Stabb left to intrude upon Gilze Rijen, thereby opening a highly successful type of operation, many sorties of like nature being flown from Bradwell. Almost nightly the Bostons operated against airfields on the Continent, or against transport targets, and played a part during the '1,000 bomber' raids. Other squadrons called at Bradwell to refuel during shoots at Denghie Flats.

Bradwell turned a new face on August

20 1942 when Spitfires of 402 Squadron landed to refuel after a Boston escort. Many times such an event would bring in fighters from famous squadrons. But it was as a night fighter/intruder base that Bradwell won its fame, and frequent visitors were 29 Squadron's Beaufighters.

In September 1942, 23 Squadron arrived with Mosquito IIs, and 418 Squadron was now leaflet dropping during its forays. The proximity of Bradwell to the coast brought along night bombers short of fuel or in damaged state. It became an extremely busy station, as on the night of January 17/18 1943. While German aircraft made a feeble attack on London, 418 Squadron was intruding upon Beauvais, Creil, Chièvres, Bretigny and Melun. Two Typhoons of 609 Squadron landed back after attacking a train and one overturned on landing. Three Lancasters of 106 Squadron and one of 57 landed from attacking Berlin, and a Hudson arrived back from a shipping sortie. Seven Mosquitoes of 85 Squadron put down, Wing Commander Raphael with a Ju 88 to his credit. In many respects the station did the work of Woodbridge in later years.

No 23 Squadron had left in December, and now 264 Squadron was placing detachments forward for intruder operations. No 418 Squadron left on March 14 1943.

Just after dawn on May 14 45 P-47s of the 4th FG landed and later set off to cover the return of US bombers from Antwerp. On May 20/21 the only *Ranger* flight that month took place when Flying Officer Crome of 29 Squadron, lately arrived here, claimed an He 111, his squadron's 50th victory. Patrols were flown that night off Dunkirk for expected FW 190 activity but the only event of substance came when a Mosquito crashed in the sea off Bradwell.

Between March and May 1943 157's Mosquitoes were here, then on June 1 1943 the station was transferred to North Weald Sector. Two days later Harrows brought ground crews of 247 Squadron to Bradwell, their Typhoons being based here in June-July 1943 to discourage FW 190 fighter-bomber attacks in the area. Nos 198 and 56 Squadrons held this commitment here in August. The Typhoons also mounted attacks on shipping off the Dutch coast.

July 13 was another busy night when three small-scale raids developed in the Newmarket, Colchester, Bradwell and York areas, 29 Squadron chasing a raider far out to sea.

Boston III intruders of 418 Squadron airborne from Bradwell.

Day fighter activity began to be greater at this time. On July 25, for example, the Ibsley Wing joined 341 and 485 Squadrons from Biggin Hill to cover 18 B-26s attacking Ghent. No 165 Squadron was 'bounced' out of the sun and next day it and 485 Squadron again used Bradwell. It was from here that 141 Squadron, normally based at Wittering, flew some of its bomber support *Serrate* sorties. Eight of its crews operated on July 30, among them the famous Wing Commander Bob Braham. On August 12 it was the turn of the RAF's top scorer, Wing Commander Johnnie Johnson, to lead Spitfires of 127 Airfield into Bradwell after escorting home B-17s from Antwerp. Late on August 23, 29 Squadron scrambled against bandits, Squadron Leader Arbon and Flight Lieutenant Goodman each bagging an Me 410, bringing 29's score now to 56. A Halifax of 76 Squadron back from a raid belly landed, badly shot up by fighters, on August 31. No 29 Squadron left for Ford on September 3 and 488 Squadron arrived from Drem to replace it. It was immediately joined by 605 Squadron, both units being based here until May 1944.

The accent again turned to day fighter activity as Spitfires flew from Bradwell during Operation *Starkey*. September 5 found 402 and 416 Squadrons here from Merston led by Wing Commander Chadburn, also the two Spitfire XII squadrons. There was an impressive rendezvous over the airfield with Bostons, then the 'beehive' set off for Woensdrecht. Supporting the raid were 72 B-26s, but all their bombs fell wide in the sea. September 9, the peak day of *Starkey*, proved an anti-climax for, apart from escorting 182 Squadron's Typhoons which had bombed Fort Rouge airfield, 56 Squadron had an uneventful time.

The first success achieved by 488 Squadron since arriving came on September 15/16 when Flight Lieutenant Watts claimed a Do 217 off the French coast. This squadron concentrated on defensive operations, leaving 605 to continue its very productive intruder campaign. Problems of controlling night fighters in busy airspace were highlighted on December 12 1943 when Mosquito XII HK227 was shot down by Beaufighter V8619 of 68 Squadron six miles west of Stowmarket. From well placed Bradwell some daylight photo-reconnaissance sorties were now being flown by Spitfires, whilst their armed contemporaries were still repeatedly arriving for escort duties. At night 488 Squadron stood by, ever ready for action. It arrived on January 21 1944 when the 'Baby Blitz' on London opened. On the first night of action Flight Lieutenant Hall and Flying Officer Karins returned after bagging a Ju 88 and a Do 217. The next most profitable night was February 24 when seven crews of 488 operated and a Ju 188 and a possible Do 217 were claimed.

Tempests of 3 Squadron arrived in March and stayed until late April. For night landings FIDO was now available. No 219 Squadron replaced 488 at the start of April and as companions it had Warwicks of 278 ASR Squadron based here. Warwicks and Hudsons were also staging at Bradwell, supporting daylight operations. The main activity, though, surrounded day fighters, and 124 Squadron made a brief stay.

July 21 1944 saw a new challenge to Bradwell's fighters for six V-1s passed over the station at night after air launching by He 111s at sea. No 219 Squadron, which had been making beach-head patrols, was switched to deal with them.

No 278 Squadron was very busy at this time and on July 24 dropped a lifeboat 30 miles south-west of Portland Bill and watched as airmen scrambled aboard. The local Walruses were also active.

The afternoon of August 30 was auspicious for, after so many months accepting passing squadrons, Bradwell Bay received its first fighter Wing, Nos 64, 126 and 611 Spitfire squadrons arriving to operate as Bradwell Bay Wing. A dozen Dakotas landed bringing their ground crews.

Next day the Wing went into action patrolling the Arras area and supporting a Bomber Command operation. No enemy fighters were seen so the Wing profitably indulged in ground strafing. No 126 Squadron swooped upon an airfield near Cambrai. Only as the aircraft pulled away did they realise it was a dummy!

September 1944 witnessed the start of the almost nightly V-1 attack against London, the weapons being fired from Heinkels about 50 miles out to sea. Their course often brought them in not far from Bradwell and the British response was to bring 501 Squadron in at dusk so that their Tempests could engage the intruders. Later in the month 501 Squadron moved in, staying here for the task until March 1945 and obtaining many successes. This released 219 Squadron, but Mosquitoes of 68 Squadron backed the Tempests in October, being detached here. The Warwicks of 278 Squadron moved to Martlesham Heath on September 24 1944.

Meanwhile the Bradwell Bay Wing Spitfires were flying many day escorts for Lancasters, but on September 17 made an anti-flak patrol over Holland ahead of the Arnhem armada. That evening they escorted Lancasters bombing a Dutch target. During the bad days at Arnhem the Wing made ground support sorties. Escort operations were usually devoid of enemy fighter interference but in December, when 64 Squadron was escorting Lancasters to Witten, they came across 50 Bf 109s near Recklinghausen. The Spitfire pilots jettisoned their drop tanks and gave chase through the clouds, but to no avail, and the enemy bagged two Lancasters.

A photograph of Bradwell Bay taken from a 540 Squadron Mosquito on February 5 1953 (DoE).

Bungay's Liberators on a mission on November 24 1944 (USAF).

At the end of December the Wing disbanded, then reformed when the Czech squadrons, Nos 310, 312 and 313, replaced the other Spitfires. No 278 ASR Squadron left in January.

With the war racing across Europe it made better sense to position the Spitfire Wing at Manston, so they moved there on February 28 1945. Their place was taken on March 1 by 151 Squadron's Mosquitoes, here initially to intercept V-1s and their carriers but soon switched to night bomber support, for which task they were joined by 456 Squadron mid-March. Both squadrons operated here to the end of hostilities and on April 25 the last operations were flown from Bradwell. Four Mosquitoes of each squadron flew *Night Rangers* in the Munich area and two of 151 Squadron operated from Juvincourt.

Squadron reduction was rapid, but not until they had both shown the flag over the Channel Islands on May 9, and raced across the islands at 1,000 feet. No 456 Squadron disbanded on May 31 and 151 on May 17. This did not mark the end of flying at Bradwell for 25 Squadron was here for a few weeks, also 19 Squadron. The Main Party of 2 APS staged through Bradwell on posting from Hawkinge to Spilsby in November and their Masters and Martinets were the last aircraft to use the station, which was closed in 1946.

Bungay (Flixton), Suffolk

TM325870. 9 miles SW Bungay, Suffolk, to S of B1062

It truly was an unforgettable sight, the tremendous roar quite deafening. Time 0820 hours, date June 6 1944. I was just about to leave home as I heard a distant grumble growing fast. Within moments a B-24 was nosing its way very low across the roof of the school opposite my home. Within seconds there was a sky full of Liberators, every one literally at roof top height, a sight never to be witnessed on any other occasion. All were heading north-east, in their bright Group markings. There were so many B-24s that single-handed it was impossible to record all the code letters although I did my best.

I was very late for school and the headmaster entertained me. He was a huge, powerful man and I decided it was best just to tell him my story.

'I just had to see them,' I said, to which he replied, 'Calm yourself, boy!'

'Sir, I've been waiting for the invasion for three days!' I told him. He was aptly speechless, probably with disbelief. Yet that it was about to take place was common knowledge at the start of June. Mr A.B. Mayne took a benevolent view of my antics, let me off and muttered 'I don't know what will become of you.' I thanked him and told him that for 30 minutes those B-24s back from Normandy had raced overhead, over 200 of them, adding that the leadship was from the 446th Bomb Group. The yellow- and black-tailed machine hailed from Bungay. I never pass a one-time Liberator base without thinking of that momentous day.

Work began at Bungay in mid-1942, the station opening late in the same year as a satellite of the American base at Hardwick where, in mid-December, the 329th Bomb Squadron arrived with B-24Ds. The remainder of their Group had gone overseas leaving the 329th to try their hand at cloud cover solo sorties over Germany. These commenced in January 1943, the Americans discovering, as the RAF had done in 1940, that cloud runs out when it is most needed. Nuisance raids were halted and the 329th joined B-24s of the 44th Bomb Group in formation bombing raids until mid-June, by which time the 93rd Bomb Group was back in Britain and ready to join with the odd man out. B-24s still used Bungay, but it was not until November 1943 with the arrival of the 446th Bomb Group that Bungay took a fully active part in the 2nd Air Division's activities. Four squadrons of B-24Hs were flown across the Atlantic to Bungay, ground crews travelling to Britain on the *Queen Mary*.

The 446th went into action on December 16 1943. Then their targets were to include U-Boat yards at Kiel, Bremen's port area, factories at Rostock, Berlin, Munich, marshalling yards at Koblenz, the motor factory at Ulm and oil refineries at Hamburg.

After their share in the dawn assault on D-Day the 446th Flew support missions to the Normandy invasion, aided the St Lô break-out, dropped supplies at Nijmegen in September 1944, operated during the Ardennes battle and dropped supplies during the Rhine crossing. Their final and 273rd operation came on April 25 1945, the bombing of a bridge near Salzburg, deep in Austria.

In June 1945 the Liberators began the journey to America and their companions again sailed away in the *Queen Mary*. In autumn 1945 Bungay closed down without accommodating further units.

Bury St Edmunds (Rougham), Suffolk

See Rougham

Bylaugh Hall, Norfolk

TF035158. 3 miles SW of Bawdeswell, off B1147, turn left immediately before crossing River Wensum

If you tour the airfields of Norfolk make a slight detour to Bylaugh Hall. Without doubt, this ruined mansion deserves the title of 'action station'. No aeroplanes flew from the site, but within its walls, and the huts still around the grounds, planning took place for many famous 2 Group operations, and then Bylaugh Hall became the headquarters of 100 Group.

In poor state, apart from its outside walls and ground floor, the mansion may be seen from the road which comes off the B1147 to Sparham, and follows the course of the picturesque River Wensum. Remaining is the clock tower, with a clock still functioning but with scant regard for BST or such triviality. Standing by the old entrance to the camp is the guardhouse in quite good condition, along with Nissen huts. How many times did the occupant call 'Pass please' to the famed?

The hall is privately owned, but can easily be viewed to good effect from the road. You will probably notice the delightful little church built by a one-time estate owner. The hall stands in extensive grounds, and is beautifully situated upon the brow of a hill overlooking the river and other delightful countryside.

Choose a lovely day for your visit and

Not an aerodrome but certainly an action station was Bylaugh Hall where 2 and then 100 Group raids were planned.

you will without doubt enjoy some fine scenery whilst you imagine the fascinating conferences which took place within these walls, the complex planning of 100 Group's night bomber support operations. For good measure you can imagine that day when 38 Douglas Bostons roared over at rooftop height bound for the naval stores at Rennes on a sunny afternoon in August 1943.

Cambridge (Teversham), Cambridgeshire

TL485585. E of Cambridge on A45. Good view across airfield from Coldham's Lane

'You're just the chap I want,' said a man carrying a huge plate camera. 'I want you to come with me for a few moments... Now, just stand there, by that propeller. You'll be the first schoolboy in England to be photographed by a Spitfire. Stand still, please, while I take some pictures.' Indeed, it was exciting — and flattering — to be with 19 Squadron's Spitfires and Squadron Leader Cozens on their public debut. Nevertheless I dreaded what my mother would say on finding me making such an exhibition of myself, at the opening of Cambridge Airport on October 8 1938.

Marshall's is an institution in Cambridge. Since 1929 that name has been synonymous with aviation here. Of the old aerodrome nothing remains, for it now supports Whitehill housing estate. When the expansion scheme of the 1930s came under way the present airfield sited by Teversham was acquired, and a large aerodrome opened to accommodate 22 E & RFTS whose Hart variants and Battles flew the circuit at weekends as the Volunteer Reserve trained. Whitleys of 7 Squadron were frequent pre-war visitors, dispersed along Teversham Lane. The Cambridge Aero Club flying Gipsy Moths became one of the first to use the attract-

Marshall modified the Hercules for Farnborough use producing the only W Mk 2, XV208.

Many airliners have been overhauled at Cambridge, among them the beautiful ex-BEA Elizabethans. G-ALZR is seen landing, the wartime Blister hangar in the background.

Sporting days at the old Cambridge airport. DH Gipsy Moths can be seen with a Klemm in the foreground (Marshall of Cambridge Ltd).

tive Moth Minor, but it was Tiger Moths — 'Marshall's Messerschmitts' as everyone soon called them — that from 1938 to 1951 were a daily sight. You could sometimes see 30 at one time during wartime, flying circuits in the hands of many a pilot who would soon be famous, Johnnie Johnson among them.

Come the war and the Gipsy Moths fled to Prestwick and soon Whitleys were arriving for overhaul and repair. Marshall's also became the Civilian Repair Organisation backing the Airspeed Oxford, a very large number of which passed through their hands.

On a windy day in late in June 1940 the local sky echoed to an unusual sound and sight, Lysanders of 16 Squadron were arriving back from a mauling in France, and they dispersed in the south-west corner where the gliding club now has its headquarters. Battered and worn by the fight in France, the Germans nevertheless soon found them and tried to bomb them. Detachments of Nos 2, 26, 239 and 268 Squadron were here in 1940. For security Newmarket Road was closed and traffic diverted through Fen Ditton until May 24, 1941, and Teversham Lane was also closed to civilian traffic since some Lysanders dispersed along the lane. At dusk and dawn every day, into 1941, two Lysanders would set off, to watch over East Coast beaches for any sign of invaders.

The enemy came again on December 30 1940 when one of those rare Dornier 215s raced across, machine-gunning the airfield and getting a few shots into dispersed aircraft, after calling on Waterbeach. 'The pilot was at the University before the war' the locals said. Goodness knows how they knew; but they repeated this line whenever the Luftwaffe appeared.

Battered Whitleys came, and left immaculate, for Marshall is a proud name whose standard of workmanship has always been second to none. In 1942 a 60-footer arrived carrying an Albemarle hurriedly placed in a shed on the north side of the main road. It turned out to be the first of many to arrive for repair until VE-Day when a pile of Albemarles was used by the local citizens for their end of war bonfire — cruel fate.

The aeroplane which would always be associated with Marshall's arrived first in February 1943, when two Mosquito IIs landed. Whipped into the large No 2 Hangar, their noses were soon off and centimetric radar in 'thimble noses' was added to produce the Mosquito XII, prin-cipal home defence night fighter from 1943 and into 1944. All Mk XIIs were produced at Cambridge, then all the Mk XVIIs with American radar. A multiplicity of Mosquitoes arrived for repair and modification, which work did not cease until the 1950s when Marshall also used Waterbeach. USAAF PR XVIs, Canadian-built Mk 25s and, most secret of all, those Mk IVs to deliver *Highball*, the anti-shipping version of Barnes Wallis's brainchild, came through Cambridge.

Early in the morning of September 18 1943 Stirling MZ260 was forced to land here during training, but it was B-17G 'LL-D' 237767, with wounded aboard from a raid in December 1943, and which skidded across the airfield, that was perhaps Cambridge's saddest sight.

There was no mistaking the powerful high-pitched roar of a Typhoon and from mid-1944 to the end of the war Marshall's repaired them, often with the dust of Normandy in their air intakes, and festooned with black and white invasion stripes and rocket rails. One of the first to arrive, though, was P5216, the second prototype.

Not content with this workload, Marshall's undertook work on Dakotas of 46 Group, overhauling them for rapid return to action.

Meanwhile the training school strength had risen to around 120 Tiger Moths, some of which are still flying today in civilian hands. Master 1s, Magisters and Tiger Moths were used by No 4 Flying Instruction School to train instructors, and part of 22 EFTS trained pilots on Auster AOP aircraft. Cambridge was, indeed, a busy place and most days attracted visiting aircraft such as a prototype Firebrand, a Flamingo, a Cygnet and even a FW 200 to mention but a few.

From time to time the factory work included caring for rare types such as Fortress 1s. Come the end of the war, during which Marshall's had working parties based in various parts of the country and even in Scotland, and the remaining rare Spitfire Xs were all broken up here. Plans to convert Hamilcar gliders into powered aircraft fell by the wayside after the first had arrived. Immediate post-war work was connected with Dakotas and Mosquitoes.

On January 1 1946 a major event took place when an aged Tiger Moth, G-ACDG flown by Lady Bragg, made the first post-war private civil flight in Britain. Marshall's soon had a couple of Rapides, one of which — G-AHED — is now in the

Aerial view of Marshall's late in the war. A variety of aircraft, including Albemarles in 'invasion stripes', can just be discerned (Marshall of Cambridge Ltd).

Rapide G-AHED, a common sight in Cambridge in the late 1940s, is now with the RAF Museum. Here it is seen alongside the Duty Pilot office adjacent to No 2 hangar.

hands of the RAF Museum. A new trade developed, still pursued, was that connected with racing and horse transport from Newmarket to many parts of the world.

The EFTS became 22RFS which was equipped with Chipmunks in 1951 and disbanded on April 30 1954. They followed in the footsteps of the Cambridge University Air Squadron, the second RAF unit to fly Chipmunks and equipped at the start of 1950. The CUAS now flies Bulldogs, received in March 1975, from Cambridge.

Like so many civil operators, Marshall's acquired an Autocrat, G-AHAW, and a rare immediate post-war visitor was often the Spitfire G-AHZI owned by Mr Bramson. One of the rarest and oldest aircraft ever to touch down here since the war was a Klemm KI 25a coupé, HB-ETU, from Switzerland on May 4 1947, advertising holidays in Arosa.

As re-armament picked up in the 1950s Marshall's maintained RAF Dakotas for the Berlin Airlift and modified Mosquito 35s into target towers. Then came Sea Hornets, which programme slipped into refurbishing and modifying Venom NF 2s whose fins needed changing, and the building of Venom fighter-bombers. After the war Marshall's drawing office and design department expanded and recently was responsible for the modifications leading to the Hercules W2. Earlier design work led to the conversions of Brigands into T4s and 5s, and the Valetta T4.

In the mid-1950s came that outstanding post-war aeroplane the Canberra, large numbers of which have passed through the works. For these heavier jet aircraft a runway was essential and Marshall had a long concrete one laid. It was strong enough to allow work to be undertaken on many Valiant V-bombers.

Britannias came here for overhaul and storage and a franchise was awarded for the overhaul of Gulfstream prop jets, extended in recent years to handling that rich man's magnificent joy, the Gulfstream 2.

In the early 1960s the flying school began to operate Cessnas in place of the worthy Tiger. Gone were the Rapides, their place taken by an Apache, a Queenair and lately a Cessna Citation for company business.

Without doubt the most exacting time came when the company acquired work on Concorde. They had been a partner in TSR-2 and the SR 177 rocket fighter. Concorde, though, must surely be worthy of any accolade for any aviation concern. Marshall's built noses for some Concordes on a very special jig, and used a tape-controlled miller to produce side

An aerial view of Marshall's today with Canberras and a Hercules in sight (Marshall of Cambridge Ltd).

panels for the engine nacelles. A Vulcan was modified to take the RB 199 engine for MRCA development work and the two Buccaneer instrumented aircraft were thus equipped here.

One cannot live long in Cambridge now without hearing the unmistakable sound of a Lockheed Hercules, for Marshall's look after those of the RAF and a number of civilian operators. On a dull February day in 1966 the first unpainted RAF Hercules arrived. The task of painting such large aircraft is highly specialised and Marshall's pioneered the use of polyurethane for such purposes, a Vampire 11 used for trials still being visible on the fire dump. A third very large hangar was now in use which has held VC-10s, Britannias and most of the RAF's Belfast fleet. Viscounts have been handled here in large numbers and Intra Airways still operate a summer scheduled service to the Channel Islands. By mid-1968 Marshall had undertaken work for 38 countries.

Charter operators, executive aircraft and private fliers call on most days, and a liaison service between Pye Radio and Phillips at Eindhoven is run by Dassault Falcons. Helicopters — civil and military — whirr in from time to time. When the Battle of Britain film was made Spitfires, '109s' and the Mitchell staged through on their way to the south of France, and Duxford's B-17 has called, a link with the old Fortress Is.

Since May 1972 Cambridge has had a longer runway to make the operation of large aircraft safer. The old Teversham Lane has become part of the airfield.

On a fair Sunday the Chipmunks and the sole Husky of 5 AEF flying Air Cadets are around, but the sight which must readily please most is that of a Tiger Moth, one of two operated by the private Flying Group. G-AOEI saw service in France in 1940, a fascinating thought surely if you stop to view the flying at what must be East Anglia's most interesting airfield.

Cambridge remains in the private hands of Marshall (Engineering) Ltd, a magnificent tribute to enterprise and tremendous hard effort. The firm's contribution to British aviation, largely unrecorded, has been truly great. At the helm remains Sir Arthur Marshall who has done so much to maintain the very highest standards of workmanship in aviation throughout the world. Little wonder the world's rich and famous have their aircraft maintained here. Little wonder, too, that the accolade has been awarded to a very great man.

Castle Camps, Cambridgeshire

TL630425. 3 miles NW of Steeple Bumpstead, to W of Camps Green

Windswept and bleak, Castle Camps sits atop the East Anglian Heights. A few ruined huts and fragments of perimeter track remain, otherwise prosperous farmland marks the spot where history really was made. Here, on January 26 1942, the magnificent Mosquito fighter (in dual control form) joined the first RAF squadron. One might have expected some visual token in memory of this great event; instead, open fields. Indeed, it is difficult for anyone who did not know Castle Camps in the flourishing days to even find its precise location.

Work on Castle Camps began in September 1939 and in mid-June 1940 it became Debden's satellite, an attachment which did not cease until Great Sampford became available in 1942. On June 27 1940 85 Squadron began to use the open field where tented accommodation was made available. Then 111 Squadron, pulled out of the front line on August 18 1940, rested at Castle Camps at the height of the Battle of Britain. Apart from East Coast scrambles, 'Treble One' had what they needed before returning south.

No 73 Squadron then arrived from Church Fenton and made Debden their home but were instantly transferred to Castle Camps, then known as F.1. Action was almost immediate. Some four hours after arriving on September 5 they engaged a raid over the Thames Estuary. The targets for the Luftwaffe were oil tanks at Thameshaven. It cost 73 Squadron one pilot killed, another wounded, three Hurricanes shot down and three damaged, in return for which an He 111 of KG53 had been damaged.

September 6 was a superb day as 73 Squadron was hurled into fierce action again over the Thames Estuary and North Kent, and Pilot Officer Marchand drew first blood, a Bf 109 of JG26. Next day the Luftwaffe launched its first heavy day raid on London and in the Billericay area 73 Squadron engaged Bf 110s, claiming three. Back at Castle Camps the pilots had to sleep in tents at the dispersals, and feed in a marquee set up in the woods, alongside which a hangar was later sited. Then they awaited the invasion, expected on September 8. On the 11th they went into action again with 17 Squadron, against He 111s over the Isle of Sheppey. All and every day 73 Squadron was ready for action and on September 15 it intercepted a mid-morning raid over Maidstone, claimed two Bf 109s and shot down another low over the Blackwater estuary. At 1445 hours the squadron was off again, the only six Hurricanes serviceable coming face to face with 100 German bombers over Maidstone, three of which they claimed to damage.

The exposed siting of the satellite field meant that it was highly susceptible to strong winds which made flying tricky. On September 21 73 Squadron began to be daily reinforced by 257 Squadron from Martlesham under Flight Lieutenant Stanford Tuck, which returned to its base at night. Two days later 17,73 and 257 Squadrons were 'bounced' over Kent and 73 Squadron lost five Hurricanes. A fierce encounter with Bf 110s came on September 27 and, into October, 17,72 and 257 Squadrons flew as a Wing. Then, on October 23, 73 Squadron received the news that it was to become a night fighter squadron and Castle Camps became vacant in early November.

During 1941 the airfield was extended, better accommodation provided and runways laid. Although SHQ opened in 1941 it was 1942 before the black Mosquitoes came. Amid great secrecy the squadron worked up, surrounded by many amazing stories about the secret wonderplane. One tale was that a notice in the cockpit reminded the pilot not to exceed 600 mph! The Mosquito for all its excellence was not a forgiving aeroplane and there were some unfortunate accidents. Worrying moments came when cowling panels were burnt through due to hot exhausts, but under Gordon Slade, later to become famous as a Fairey test-pilot, the bugs were worked out at an airfield loathed by its occupants. Why this wet place, which played havoc with the aircrafts' electrics, was ever chosen as the first Mosquito station remains a mystery. Its proximity to de Havilland at Hatfield was one possible reason, another its relative remoteness in those days.

On April 27 1942 crews of 157 Squadron were ordered on their first operational patrols, when a 'Baedeker raid' broke on Norwich. A few sightings were recorded, but little else resulted until May 30 when Squadron Leader Ashfield chased a Dornier 217, fired at it off Dover and claimed the first enemy aircraft to fall to 157 Squadron — but not to the Mosquito, for this prize went to 151 Squadron at Wittering. Confirmation of all these early claims is unlikely to be established now. Certainly four Do 217s were lost on May 30.

South coast radar lost trace of Ashfield's quarry, but a Do 217 came down off Holland and seems likely to have been his. No 157 Squadron was very unlucky for so many of their patrols and scrambles were fruitless. Not until August 22 did they have a proven success, a Do 217 which came down at Worlington, near Mildenhall.

On March 15 1943 No 157 Squadron moved to Bradwell Bay, their place being taken by No 605 (County of Warwick) Mosquito squadron. They had only just received Mosquitoes, and used them mainly in the intruder role in which they were adding to 23 Squadron's Mosquito knowledge. In July 1943 (when Castle Camps became a satellite of North Weald) they began to use Mk VI fighter-bombers for intruder operations, doing so very effectively and scoring a number of successes. They flew *Rangers* widely over Europe, but their greatest contribution was the introduction of the Mosquito to bomber support duties. Their first such operation came on August 31 when they supported a Berlin raid. Four nights later they began *Mahmouds*, operations on the flank of the bomber stream designed to intercept enemy night fighters. The squadron left Castle Camps in October 1943, after having had some support from Mosquitoes detached from 456 Squadron.

Replacement for the dashing Mosquitoes was of an unexpected type, for it came in the form of Blenheim IVs, Hurricanes and Hornet Moths of 527 Radar Calibration Squadron here until February 1944, and dispersed in the north-east corner of the airfield. A point of interest was that a few Blenheims wore the predominantly white scheme of Coastal Command, for the unit flew some operations over the sea.

February 1944 brought an unmistakable roar, that of the Griffon Spitfires of 91 Squadron. They arrived flying Mk XIIs but whilst at Castle Camps received the Mk XIV, the second squadron to equip, and left with 13 Mk XIVs and four Mk XIIs on March 17. Their immediate replacement was 486 Squadron flying Typhoons — but not for long. Early in April they began to re-arm with Tempest Vs and as part of 149 Airfield left on April 29.

Whilst these two squadrons were re-equipping, Castle Camps had again, since the end of December 1943, housed Mosquitoes, Mk XIIIs of 410 Squadron. This was primarily a night home defence squadron guarding the northern approaches to London. When, on January 21 1944, the enemy opened the 'Baby Blitz' with his fastest bombers and He 177s, No 410 Squadron was at once drawn into the night battle and very busily engaged, having notable successes. This Canadian squadron stayed here to the end of April 1944.

There was a brief quiet spell before, in July 1944, 68 Squadron brought their Mosquitoes along, and stayed until October 1944, during which time they made some night interceptions of V-1s. A five-week stay beginning on October 8 was made by other Mosquitoes of 151 Squadron, and on October 27 25 Squadron, also Mosquito-equipped, came for a sojourn which lasted until the station closed. Bomber support was their main activity and they were joined in this by 307 Squadron between the end of January 1945 and June. At the end of that month famed 85 Squadron came once more, now with Mosquito night fighters. On July 28 six of them escorted the Prime Minister to the Potsdam Conference. They moved to Tangmere in October 1945.

The rear party of Station HQ left Castle Camps for Boxted on January 17 1946 and the station rapidly wound down, was never again used for flying and closed in the summer. It was always a strange place. The main entrance was from the road leading beyond the village church, from which the airfield site can be viewed, although apart from a handful of huts there is nothing to see. Stand on the Steeple Bumpstead road just south of the village and you are in line with the old runway. Best to just imagine you can see a couple of Mossies of '605' jubilantly returning. Strange, it is, that a station so unpretentious should have known so much interesting history.

The site of wartime Castle Camps photographed from a Canberra of 58 Squadron flying at 40,000 feet on August 3 1961 (DoE).

Caxton Gibbet, Cambridgeshire

TL300653. At junction of A14(T) and A45(T) E of St Neots

Night flying took place at Caxton Gibbet by Tiger Moths of No 22 EFTS before any was undertaken during the war at Cambridge. In the early hours of July 16 1941 a Tiger Moth was floating around the circuit when an intruder opened fire. Some flashes, and the trainer burst into flames, falling to the ground. Easy game for sure. The Germans came for a repeat performance on August 6, and in style. The German crew circled, called up the control van — there was never any control tower — made two approaches, circled and then on the fourth run deposited a stick of ten bombs across the landing ground damaging five 'Tigers' as a parting gesture.

It was in the summer of 1940 that the Air Ministry requisitioned a large grass field, on the western apex of which still stands the inn by the hangman's gibbett at the junction of Ermine Street and the A45. The field was used from September as a Relief Landing Ground for 'circuit and bumping' Tiger Moths of 22 EFTS, thus relieving pressure on busy Cambridge. Then, in June 1941, 'F' Flight of the EFTS moved to Caxton, operating from there until well into 1942. It was a small field, but somehow a Wellington of 101 Squadron landed there on one occasion.

Huts along the northern end of the field are still there. In 1944 they were taken over to accommodate personnel of 105 Squadron then at Bourn. Evidently the squadron had a skilled artist who decorated the hut walls with murals which could be seen into the 1950s. They are gone now, and remaining huts contain farm equipment.

Chedburgh, Suffolk

TL792565. On the A143, S of the village of Chedburgh

Their uniforms were slightly different, and one looked upon these men as very brave. In many cases they had trod a tortuous journey here, over many, many miles. These people were, of course, the Poles. Following the outbreak of war many arrived at East Anglian airfields awaiting an uncertain future. When our countrymen were demobbed they left sizeable numbers of Poles manning fighter squadrons. At Chedburgh the Poles were found in two transport squadrons soon equipped with Halifax C VIIIs, a rare commodity in the RAF.

Chedburgh is most readily remembered for its Short Stirling bombers. The station opened on September 7 1942 as a second satellite for Stradishall and, in the first week of October 1942, 214 Squadron moved in. From here the Straits Settlement squadron operated until the Stirling was withdrawn from Main Force operations late in 1943. In the summer of 1943 a second squadron formed here, No 620, from 'C' Flight of 214 Squadron. They only stayed until late November when they moved to Leicester East to become part of 38 Group and fly transport Stirlings.

On November 21 1943 1653 Conversion Unit formed at Chedburgh with Stirlings. It had been decided in mid-summer 1943 that Stradishall — where 32 Base formed in May — would be a Stirling training base controlling Chedburgh and Wratting Common, these last two being sub-stations. All Stirling training for 3 Group would be carried out by the three stations, although it was some months before this became effective.

For a year 1653 Conversion Unit used Chedburgh then, in December 1944, the unit left for North Luffenham, its place being taken by 218 Squadron which arrived on December 5 flying Lancaster Is and IIIs. These participated in the 3 Group bomber offensive and at the end of hostilities dropped much needed food to the Dutch. They flew prisoner of war repatriation flights, but soon wound down and disbanded at Chedburgh on August 10 1945.

In the first week of September 1945 two Polish squadrons, Nos 301 and 304, arrived bringing with them examples of the rare Warwick III and, in the case of 304 Squadron, some Wellington GR XIVs still wearing Coastal Command colours. These they used for conversion training, then the Warwick IIIs settled down to route flying under Transport Command, going mainly to the Middle East. The Warwick had trod almost as difficult a path to success as had the Poles on their journeys, and was only an interim transport until the first Halifax VIIIs arrived for 301 Squadron at the start of 1946. These aircraft, with large belly panniers for freight, were able to make the run to India if needed, and had officially been looked upon as the ideal transport. In May 1946 304 Squadron also equipped with them and the two squadrons operated trunk routes overseas until both disbanded in December 1946. The site was sold in October 1952.

Thereafter for Chedburgh it was the usual story. Clearing the station took some months then, for a long time, it lay idle. The process to civilian use as elsewhere was quite protracted. Chedburgh still has hangars used for light industry, still a sorry collection of huts which once were so vibrant. It is not easy to view, but may be seen from the road to Rede which leads off the A143 just to the east of the village. Crop sprayers use the airfield in summer.

Chipping Ongar, Essex

TL055580. 2 miles NE of High Ongar

Chipping Ongar was built in 1942-1943, one of the earliest stations constructed by and for the Americans. It came into use late in June 1943 when the 387th Bomb Group arrived to operate B-26s. Such raids commenced in August 1943, the initial attacks being concentrated on airfields. Late in 1943 emphasis lay upon raiding V-sites, and during the famous 'Big Week' of February 1944 the 387th concentrated their attacks on Dutch airfields. Bridges were principal targets in May 1944, then came support to the invasion followed by general aid to ground forces. The 387th vacated Chipping Ongar on July 18 1944 and moved to Stoney Cross, Hants.

In their place came Waco CG-4 Hadrian gliders for storage in some numbers, many awaiting transfer to the RAF. This brought C-47s frequently to the station.

During April 1945 Chipping Ongar was returned to the RAF and it spent some time both in Army hands and those of RAF Technical Training Command. Little remains, apart from the Operations Block, for the airfield has reverted to agricultural use.

Coltishall, Norfolk

TG270225. 9 miles NNE Norwich on B1150

When war began Duxford was responsible for defending the northern half of East Anglia, Debden the southern. Their Sectors covered large areas. Ferocity of battle in May 1940 brought abrupt change.

Building of a bomber station at Coltishall commenced in February 1939 but in May 1940 it was decided instead to make it a fighter station. No 66 Squadron first used it as a forward base on May 29 and Sections were placed here for coastal shipping guard. Wing Commander W.K.

Beisiegle took command of Coltishall, which opened as fully operational at 0001 hours on June 23 1940. Three days earlier the remnants of 242 Squadron had arrived and Squadron Leader D.R.S. Bader was put in command to work up the squadron.

Enemy aircraft had already bombed the area around, but most of the action would for months be off the East Coast where, on July 10 1940, 66 Squadron drew first blood for Coltishall, a Do 17. The squadron had moved into Coltishall on July 4. Later on the 19th 242 Squadron also bagged an He 111. Another two Heinkels were claimed on July 29 and a Ju 88 by 242 Squadron on August 1. Action off the coast remained the occupation of both squadrons.

Through the clouds an He 111 appeared over Coltishall on August 19, dropping six bombs on an unfinished hangar. No. 66 Squadron scrambled and claimed the intruder from KG 27.

But the Battle of Britain was passing Coltishall by, until 12 Group's idea of the 'Big Wing' was born, an assembly of squadrons operating out of Duxford. Each day the required squadrons would assemble there, '242' among them. Action came on August 30 when the Wing scrambled and engaged a large enemy formation between Enfield and Hatfield and claimed seven Bf 110s and three He 111s without loss. No 66 Squadron, left to do shipping patrols, bagged a Do 17 off Happisburgh. Daily, 242 Squadron flew to Duxford, and was heavily engaged over North Weald on September 7 when Pilot Officer D. Crowley-Milling was shot down near Chelmsford. No 616 Squadron was briefly at Coltishall, then 74 Squadron replaced it and on September 9 began to participate in the 'Big Wing'. On September 11 the unit claimed six enemy aircraft over the London area. No 242 Squadron patrolled over London on September 14, on the day that Bader was awarded the DSO, and '74' claimed a probable Bf 110 and a Ju 88 off Happisburgh.

The Battle of Britain reached its climax when 242 Squadron flew to Duxford on September 15. Hectic battles came about, 242 Squadron claiming five Do 17s and a Bf 109. Later that day it claimed two Do 17s, a Do 215, an He 111 and two Bf 109s, and there was more action around Hornchurch on September 18. Post-war research corrected these figures, but they do indicate the intensity of the action.

Although 242 Squadron flew regularly to Duxford, more often than not there was no action due to the difficulty of placing the 'Big Wing' most effectively. Then, on October 20 1940, '242' left Coltishall to be based at Duxford, being replaced by 72 Squadron which wasted no time and damaged a Do 17 on the 27th. At dusk an He 111 bombed Coltishall and machine-gunned the station. Ground defences opened up, and the Heinkel came down in the sea off Lowestoft.

In October Matlaske opened as Coltishall's satellite, and began to accommodate Coltishall's squadrons, the two airfields really operating as one. Furniture was removed from Matlaske Hall, and the staircase and fireplaces were boxed in, so that air and ground crews could be accommodated there.

Eleven bombs fell on Coltishall on November 8, the watch office being damaged. Then 222 Squadron arrived on November 11, to replace 64 Squadron which had been here since October 15, while 72 Squadron, here since October 20, moved to Leuchars on November 29. Into Coltishall on December 15 came 257 Squadron with Hurricanes. This 'Burma' Squadron came to be looked upon as Coltishall's own for they stayed here for 11 months flying Hurricanes. By the end of 1940 Coltishall squadrons had claimed 83 enemy aircraft shot down.

Early 1941 action centred around enemy aircraft operating off the coast and there were a number of successes. Intruders frequented East Anglian skies on cloudy, rainy days and Coltishall's fighters did their best in difficult circumstances.

A new face was turned to the enemy on March 20 when 151 Defiant Squadron began placing detachments at Coltishall for night standbys. Previously such duty was carried out over the region by aircraft from Wittering. Nos 222 and 257 Squadrons handled daylight operations. Squadron Leader Stanford-Tuck of 257 Squadron claimed several enemy aircraft and, on May 12, Flight Lieutenant Blatchford, who became a well-known Coltishall figure, shot down an He 111 off Yarmouth. Greater success came to Squadron Leader Tuck on June 21 when, off Holland, he engaged three Bf 109s and shot down two. His damaged Hurricane went into the sea off the English coast and a trawler fished him out of the water 30 minutes later.

The RAF did not have it all their own way, for on April 26 the Ferry Inn at Horning was bombed and 22 people killed including three Coltishall pilots. A plaque can be seen in the bar recalling the event.

June 22 1941 marked a turning point in Coltishall's war for on this day 222 Squadron made their first offensive sweep over France, damaging a Bf 109F — a welcome change from 'Kipper patrols'. Coltishall's distance from France made such operations difficult unless the squadrons flew to advanced bases. Instead the fighters operated as escort to Blenheims of 2 Group and Coastal Command attacking targets off Holland.

Squadron Leader Stanford-Tuck ceased commanding 257 Squadron on July 4 1941, was promoted Wing Commander and had his place taken by Squadron Leader 'Cowboy' Blatchford as leader.

Coltishall has never been a full American base. Probably the nearest it ever came was when, on July 29 1941, the third Eagle Squadron, No 133, formed here.

Close proximity to the sea rendered Coltishall an ideal base for ASR units. No 5 ASR Flight formed here in July 1941, receiving its first two Walruses on July 19. In October the Flight became 278 Squadron at Matlaske and jockeyed between the two airfields until April 1944, contributing much to the ASR service, mainly by providing inshore search and rescue operations.

In August 604 Squadron's Beaufighters arrived after their main trade over the south ceased. Wing Commander John Cunningham and Pilot Officer C.F. Rawnsley shot down an He 111 35 miles north-west of Coltishall on August 22 1941, at a time when Coltishall's day fighters were still escorting Blenheim raids.

A night to remember for Norwich was September 16 1941. Just as 604 Squadron had run out of business so had No 93, equipped with aerial mining Havocs, a detachment of which moved into Coltishall. Mine laying in the area was difficult because there were so many RAF aircraft active at night. But on this occasion a minelayer was scrambled. Unfortunately the minefield was sown over the south-west corner of Norwich and 83 mines drifted down on to the residents. One landed on the roof of a house. Warned of the danger, the occupant astonished a policeman by telling him that they would vacate the bedroom over which the mine rested, and move into another. East Anglians are a tough lot!

No 604 Squadron moved out on September 21 1941 and were replaced by Merlin-Beaufighters of 255 Squadron from Hibaldstowe. Their task was the night defence of Norfolk.

In November 1941 257 Squadron left after their long stay, their place being taken by Whirlwinds of 137 Squadron which soon moved to Matlaske. Ludham opened as Coltishall's second satellite on November 19. An escort from Coltishall by 152 Squadron Spitfires on November 27 resulted in the sinking of a 1,200-ton ship off Holland by Beauforts of 217 Squadron. To the end of 1941 antishipping operations were supported by Coltishall's fighters, night fighters of 151 and 255 Squadron mounted night defence stand-bys and 278 Squadron was on hand for rescue duties.

Coltishall figured in the dash of the *Scharnhorst* and *Gneisenau* through the Channel on February 12 1942. Fourteen Beauforts of 42 Squadron were rushed in from Leuchars. Nine took off and six unsuccessfully released their torpedoes. Next day Beauforts of 86 Squadron arrived, but they were too late to be of use, as were Beauforts of 22 Squadron which stood by at Coltishall on the 15th.

In March 1942, 2 Group resumed its daylight offensive with Bostons, and the Coltishall Spitfires participated from advanced bases. Life was not, of course, one long round of action. On March 27 Coltishall's aircrew sat back near Winterton to watch a demonstration of Churchill tanks. One tank ran on to a land mine which exploded. To the delight of the

Mosquito NF 36s of 23 Squadron lined up at Coltishall in September 1951.

RAF watchers the tank suffered no visible damage, and the aircrew delighted in telling the Army that their land mines were not much good!

Operations within the clutch of Coltishall airfields — the main station, Ludham and Matlaske — were integrated, and squadrons moved forward daily from Duxford to take the place of any sent to other Sectors. The action at this time was typified on April 24. The day commenced with 137 Squadron patrolling off Yarmouth and Lowestoft. There were Sector and convoy patrols. A Lysander of 278 Squadron did an ASR search with 154 Squadron's Spitfires. Off Holland 610 Squadron flew a shipping sweep. There was a Wing sweep practice, 137 Squadron made an evening patrol around Hammond's Knoll light and 68 Squadron did a dusk Sector patrol.

In early March No 68 Squadron had fortuitously arrived, under the command of Wing Commander Max Aitken, son of Lord Beaverbrook. Shortly before midnight on April 27 a sizeable force of German bombers came in over Wells-next-the-Sea to make an hour-long raid on Norwich. Heavy incendiary loads soon fired the city then high explosives rained down. Among the many fires 53 people died, and nearly 200 had serious injuries. Coltishall's squadrons were scrambled, ten Spitfires of 610 Squadron, nine Beaufighters of No 68 and some of 151 Squadron. There were contacts but no enemy aircraft were claimed.

Two nights later the enemy returned to Norwich, inflicting more serious damage. Coltishall's sorties were once again fruitless. When, on April 30, the Luftwaffe made for more northerly targets, 68 Squadron found the bombers, claiming two He 111s and a Do 217.

Some surprise punctuated this period when, on May 7, six Defiants joined the circuit, arriving for 278 Squadron. Too bad, for the squadron had no fuel bowser carrying 100-octane fuel, let alone a 24-volt starter!

The Luftwaffe again tried for Norwich on May 8, but the raid was a failure, bombs falling widely around the outskirts of the town. No 68 Squadron patrolled unsuccessfully, but a Do 217 of KG 2 was brought down near Stoke Holy Cross either as a result of hitting a balloon cable or by AA fire. Three dead occupants were found, but of the other man there was no trace. By dawn rumour was rife and during the morning no less than two battalions of the Norfolk Division were scouring the countryside for the intrepid fellow and there were countless sightings reported.

Great Yarmouth came under attack on May 29 and 68 Squadron was luckier. Wing Commander Aitken claimed a Do 217 and a damaged Ju 88. Squadron Leader Howden and Flight Lieutenant Winward between them accounted for a Do 217 and a Ju 88.

Throughout the war Coltishall's closeness to the sea made it a ready spot for the arrival of 'cuckoos', bombers damaged or short of fuel putting down for safety. On the night of the Cologne '1,000 bomber' raid a Stirling landed — with fuel left for only five minutes' flying.

Norwich was yet again attacked on June 26 when more serious fires were started. This time 610 Squadron patrolled with success, destroying a Ju 88 — a rare event for fighters without airborne interception radar.

Commencement of shipping reconnaissances by Snailwell's 268 Squadron now began to bring Mustangs in for refuelling before or after *Lagoons*.

The night of July 23 1942 proved outstanding for 68 Squadron. Bombs were dropped on Yarmouth and King's Lynn and ten Beaufighter patrols were despatched. Wing Commander Aitken destroyed a Ju 88 and Do 217, Sergeant Truscott a Do 217, Warrant Officer Bebek a Do 217 and Squadron Leader Vesely another Do 217. Max Aitken was awarded the DSO on July 27.

July 1942 saw the introduction of the Spitfire IX at Hornchurch and on August 8 a practice B-17 escort brought some of the new Spitfires into Coltishall for the first time. Ten days later the 12 Group Wing was in action during the Dieppe raid, Nos 411, 485 and 610 Squadron led by Wing Commander Jameson claiming three FW 190s and two Bf 109s for the loss of five Spitfires.

Autumn 1942 found Duxford overflowing with aircraft and when USAAF P-39 squadrons arrived there, No 346 Squadron was detached to Coltishall to train, taking pressure off Duxford.

January 28 1943 was an auspicious day for Coltishall, HM King George VI visiting 68 and 118 Squadrons and personally giving 278 Squadron their badge signed by himself, the first occasion when he had handed over a badge in person.

A reminder of earlier days came on February 4 1943 when Wing Commander Blatchford was posted into Coltishall as Wing Commander Flying, at the time when Swordfish and Albacores of 841 Squadron, Fleet Air Arm, were here for night operations. Another unit currently operating small detachments was 515 Squadron, a special duty squadron flying Defiants from Hunsdon which flew ahead of bomber forces giving them *Mandrel* screening.

Then came the phase of Ventura day escorts by Coltishall's Spitfires which included the disastrous operation of May 3 1943 (see *Methwold*) when 118 and 504 Squadrons participated from here. Wing Commander Blatchford was shot down during the ambush of the operation.

Mid-1943 found the station extremely busy, particularly 278 Squadron. On June 13 a searching Walrus found a dinghy with eight men in it. A five-foot sea made landing difficult, although the pilot eventually put down. After the Americans had scrambled aboard, the Walrus pilot found he could not take-off, so taxied for ten miles in the stormy sea and then was able to transfer his precious load to a launch before taking off. A week later an Anson of 278 Squadron found the crew of a ditched Halifax off Yarmouth and a Walrus picked them up whilst 31 Spitfires of 118, 402 and 416 Squadrons set out to escort home B-17s which had been bombing the synthetic rubber plant at Huls. On June 14 141 Squadron flew their first bomber support *Serrate* operation from Coltishall.

What the American B-17 crews were enduring was forcibly brought home to Coltishall's occupants on June 25 as a badly damaged B-17 stooged around the airfield disgorging its crew until only the dead navigator and wounded pilot remained aboard. The pilot took the aircraft, impossible to land, to Waxham and then baled out. This meant a swim to the shore but when picked up he seemed none the worse physically for his grim landing. In the early hours of the following morning it was a Lancaster back from Gelsenkirchen and heavily damaged by flak which put down at Coltishall. It had been chased home by a FW 190 and the crew agreed that they had been lucky to survive. Aboard was Group Captain McKenna, Station Commander at Langar. Operations meanwhile continued unabated for 841 Squadron was now flying anti-E-Boat sorties at night.

July 6 1943 was a bad day for Coltishall Sector. Seven Typhoons led by Wing commander Rabagliati were sent on a shipping strike and left three small ships in a convoy damaged. When 60 miles

Javelins of the AWDS keep company with 141 Squadron Venoms on Coltishall's ASP.

from home the leader reported engine trouble. He climbed, streaming smoke, before crashing in the sea. He was thought to have scrambled clear, but the dinghy was empty during the time the others orbited before their fuel began to run short. A Walrus escorted by six Spitfires of 118 Squadron set out from Coltishall. The sea was getting rougher, it started raining and thunderstorms were met. Some 60 aircraft searched unsuccessfully for the Wing Commander.

The day's drama was not yet over for Coltishall scrambled four Typhoons to intercept FW 190s near Yarmouth. Soon the 190s were chasing the defenders and Flight Sergeant Clusas was shot into the sea. A Walrus searched, but in the awful weather nothing was seen. That was not the last of the bad moments, for a Spitfire which had taken off to escort the Walrus crashed soon after take-off. At this time 278 Squadron was using Ansons for search, and when the pilot of a PR Spitfire baled out not far from the coast an Anson crew directed a launch to the steamer *Cagny* which had fished him out of the water.

On July 17 it was 278 Squadron which was again to the fore. An Anson crew sighted two dinghies from a B-17 which had shot down two of four FW 190s following it home. Two Walruses were scrambled, and one landed and picked up the survivors. A heavy swell prevented it from taking off and an Anson and two launches went to the scene, picked up the men and took them aboard, leaving the Walrus guarded by 118 Squadron Spitfires to make a six-hour taxi journey back to Yarmouth harbour.

Better weather on July 25 took 611 Spitfire Squadron into action escorting day bombers to Holland and they mixed it with some German fighters. Thirty miles off the Dutch coast Squadron Leader Charles leading 611 Squadron went into the sea and his position was orbited by Flight Lieutenant Mansfield. A dozen pilots of 611 then went to watch over him, relieved by 416 Squadron led by Wing Commander Chadburn who had escorted a Walrus to the spot. It alighted and rescued Squadron Leader Charles despite his proximity to the enemy coast.

So busy was Coltishall that the runways were now lengthened with Sommerfeld tracking and extra D/F stations opened making 11 in all available to the base.

When Flying Officer Overton of 613 Squadron, back from a *Lagoon*, landed to refuel on August 20 he brought news of a dinghy 50 miles east of Lowestoft, and had circled it until his fuel ran low. A Walrus found the dinghy and alighted despite the rough sea, picking up four Dutchmen of 320 Squadron who had been returning from Flushing. Their port engine had been hit necessitating ditching. Yet again the swell prevented the Walrus from taking off, so Flying Officer Sims taxied until he found a sufficiently smooth patch. This was the 100th rescue by 278 Squadron.

About this time enemy activity over Britain increased as he made a somewhat weak attempt at intruding by night, often bombing from a considerable height and using the new Me 410s and Ju 188s. A Beaufighter of 68 Squadron had just landed at Coltishall on August 22 when three bombs fell parallel to the flare path, the first of a string starting in front of the control tower. Another such incident came on September 27. A Halifax back from Hanover and flying on two engines landed wheels-up at the main runway end. Almost immediately high explosives fell on the airfield and a load of the pernicious butterfly bombs which caused annoyance over many parts of East Anglia at this time. Intruders did not have it all their own way, though. On October 12 Flight Lieutenant Allen of 68 Squadron chased an Me 410 across Norfolk and, when it crossed the coast at Cromer, Flying Officer Boyle in a Mosquito of 151 Squadron attached to Coltishall was waiting. He caught up with the raider just as it turned east, and was being aided by Neatishead Radar. Boyle closed in, gave it a short burst and there was an explosion in its fuselage followed by an engine fire. The Messerschmitt went down, a mass of flames, into the sea. A welter of fragments hit the Mosquito which landed safely at Church Fenton.

February 5 1944 was a noteworthy day. No 68 Squadron, which had been here since March 8 1942, moved out, credited with a score of 70 enemy aircraft. No 25 Squadron arrived in its place, under Wing Commander Wight-Boycott, DSO. The squadron came at the time when the Luftwaffe was making raids in the 'Baby Blitz' series, but Coltishall was too far north to be much involved until March 19 1944 when the enemy entered the 12 Group area and 25 Squadron went after them. It proved to be a night to remember for five German bombers were shot down by 25 Squadron aircraft. They added two more Ju 188s to their score on March 21, No 25 Squadron having now claimed 11 since its arrival. The high spirits of the night fighters was reflected by charm on the airfield — LACW Swann was christened 'Miss Coltishall'.

Intruders were still sneaking up on Coltishall. About 12 followed our bombers home on April 12 and just as a 64 Squadron Spitfire was landing with navigation lights on it was attacked. The pilot felt a severe shock, opened up and climbed to 4,000 feet. His engine temperature rising, Flight Sergeant Maunders rolled over to bale out. Instead he found himself in the aircraft making a spin but managed to hurl himself out of the right side to parachute safely.

Three other long-serving squadrons left Coltishall in April 1944, '611' which had arrived on September 25 1943, and '64' which had been here since July 1 1943 going on the 29th. No 316 (Polish) Squadron now moved in and the month finally witnessed the removal of 278 Squadron to Bradwell Bay.

At this time Coltishall was being used by Mosquito squadrons setting out or returning from long-distance *Ranger* flights. On May 16 four crews of 418 Squadron set off in the afternoon and near Lübeck shot down an He 111. Near Zingst an FW 190 was destroyed and over Kubitzer Bay they shot down an He 177. Then they went to Stralsund and destroyed an He 111 on the ground and blew up a Bücker 131. Another success in Kubitzer Bay was a Do 18 and south of Stralsund they shot down a Ju 86. But Squadron Leader Cleveland's Mosquito was hit and he had to come down in Sweden.

Coltishall was not much involved with the Normandy landings, but on June 8 reports came in that enemy aircraft had attacked three night-flying B-24s. A Mosquito of 25 Squadron was vectored on to an Me 410 which was shot into the sea 40 miles east of Southwold.

The first alert for V-1 flying bombs came on July 1 when Mustangs of 316 Squadron destroyed a missile five miles off Lowestoft. These Mustangs, though, were primarily intended to give close support to Coastal Command Beaufighters.

Spitfire IXs of 229 Squadron arrived in the Sector in July 1944 and formed part of the screen covering the Arnhem landings, but the arrival of the first V2 rocket at 1630 hours on September 26 heralded an offensive role for the Coltishall Spitfires, as rockets began to fall around Norwich. The task now was to mount armed reconnaissances by Spitfire bombers to attack any evidence of V2 launchers around the Hague, a duty carried on well into 1945. Detached Mustangs of 26 Squadron scouted for the Spitfires.

Apart from Spitfires, the closing months of the war saw 307 Squadron's Mosquito 30s at Coltishall as well as Mustangs of 303 and 316 Squadrons. For this, the most active airfield in East Anglia, the end of the war brought no quiet period. There was great elation when, on July 27 1945, Group Captain Douglas Bader visited Coltishall. The station turned out to see the famous warrior fly a Spitfire again, for the first time since his capture.

There was the usual jockeying of Mosquito, Spitfire and Mustang squadrons until Coltishall settled to peacetime role as a night fighter base. From the wartime days the station held claims to 207 enemy aircraft destroyed, 48 probably destroyed and 100+ damaged.

Mosquito 36s of 23, 141 and 264 Squadrons settled for the immediate post

war years. No 23 Squadron arrived on January 23 1947, 141 Squadron was reformed here on June 17 1946 and 264 Squadron arrived here on January 13 1948. In November 1949 the Mosquito Wing temporarily moved to Church Fenton, returning to Coltishall in September 1950 after the station had been modified and attention given to the main runway. No 23 Squadron equipped with Vampire NF 10s in the autumn of 1951 and 141 Squadron received Meteor NF 11s. No 264 Squadron left for Linton-on-Ouse on August 24 1951. Venoms NF 2 and 3 replaced the initial jet equipment, 141 Squadron being the first to fly Venom NF 3s, and in 1957 these two squadrons were re-equipped with Javelin 4s to become the first Javelin Wing in Fighter Command. No 141 Squadron was re-numbered 41 Squadron on January 16 1958 and, after re-equipping with Javelin 8s, left in July 1960. No 23 Squadron, still at Coltishall, later received Javelin 7s then 9s, and stayed until March 1963.

In 1958 extensive alterations were made to the station and in 1959 the Air Fighting Development Squadron of the Central Fighter Establishment moved in to be the first RAF unit to receive Lightnings. Late in the afternoon of August 2 1960, No 74 Squadron, which had arrived flying Hunters in mid-1959, received its initial Lightning 1s, the first for an RAF squadron. April 1964 saw the arrival of No 226 Operational Conversion Unit equipped with an assortment of Lightnings and training pilots to fly them, replacing 74 Squadron which had left two months previously, and remained until September, 1974.

Amongst the fighters, 202 Squadron has been active flying Whirlwind HAR 10 helicopters and standing by 24 hours a

Lightnings of 226 OCU lined-up on the readiness platform by Coltishall's runway in September 1964.

day at 15 minute readiness, after having moved from Horsham when that station began to close. Whirlwinds remain, but the principal use of Coltishall is now as an operational base for the Jaguars of Nos 6, 41 and 54 Squadrons.

Coltishall occupies far more space in this book than any other station, simply because it has been for so long the most active station in East Anglia. For millions of people though, the name of Coltishall will be associated with the Battle of Britain Memorial Flight. Their Spitfires and Hurricanes, not to mention the Lancaster, must have given more enjoyment to the public than any other RAF aeroplanes.

Debach, Suffolk

TM240540. S of B1078, 17 miles W of Wickham Market

Built none too well by the US Army in 1943-1944, Debach was the last airfield to become a base for bombers of the US 8th AF, the 493rd Bomb Group arriving in April 1944 and equipping the following month with B-24s. These were replaced by B-17s in September 1944.

The Group's first operations came during the Normandy invasion and it then aided the break-out from St Lô. Apart from assisting during the airborne landings in Holland, the Ardennes offensive and Rhine crossing, the Group acted chiefly against industrial targets such as an ordnance depot at Magdeburg, oil plant at Merseburg and numerous factories. They bombed airfields, bridges and gun batteries, flying their last mission on April 20 1945 when they attacked marshalling yards at Nauen before returning to the USA in August 1945.

So poor was the runway state at Debach by the end of 1944 that the Group temporarily moved to Little Walden whilst repairs took place, returning to Debach in March 1945. After the war the base became a POW holding camp and later accommodated displaced persons. Parts of two runways remain, also the control tower.

Debden, Essex

TL565340. 3 miles SE Saffron Walden on A130

For those privileged to be at RAF Debden on April 25 1975 it was both a sad and significant day, for the occasion marked the formal closure of this historic station.

Broadly speaking, Debden's history can

be divided into four distinct periods. It originated as one of the Expansion Scheme stations during the late 1930s, its location largely determined by the chance forced-landing of a Bristol Bulldog in May 1934.

Construction began in 1935 and was still incomplete at the time of its official opening on April 22 1937, No 87 Squadron having the distinction of being the first unit to be based here, flying its newly acquired Gladiators. Accommodation was for three squadrons and soon Nos 80 and 73 arrived, also equipped with Gladiators. In November 1937 73 Squadron was replaced by 29 Squadron flying Hawker Demon two-seater fighters, but when 80 Squadron was ordered overseas in April 1938 No 85 Squadron was re-born at Debden and it was these three squadrons which saw out the final months of peace, Nos 85 and 87 flying Hurricanes and No 29 flying Blenheims. Before converting to Hurricanes No 87 Squadron won acclaim for aerobatics performed by three Gladiators tied together. They performed in various parts of England and visited France for the air display at Villacoublay on July 8 1938. Now it was back to France again, for the war was only a week old when Nos 85 and 87 were posted there. They were replaced at Debden by Nos 17 and 504 Squadrons, also flying Hurricanes.

As one of the important Sector stations within 11 Group, the southern half of East Anglia was under the watchful eye of Debden Operations Room. Construction work continued after the commencement of hostilities with runways and additional taxi-strips laid, the defences being strengthened by the addition of AA units. A satellite airfield at Castle Camps was also prepared, but the squadrons were frequently split into Flights to operate from Martlesham Heath, used as a forward base on a rotation basis.

With all three squadrons it was a case of routine patrols and practice interceptions — important, if unspectacular. Temporary detachments were made to other airfields, the Hurricanes being particularly busy during the evacuation from Dunkirk. Likewise, when such remnants of our valiant, decimated squadrons in France returned to Britain, Debden received No 85 Squadron back to remuster under its new Commanding Officer, Squadron Leader Peter Townsend, to fight the imminent Battle of Britain. The Blenheims of 29 Squadron were on frequent night patrols, working

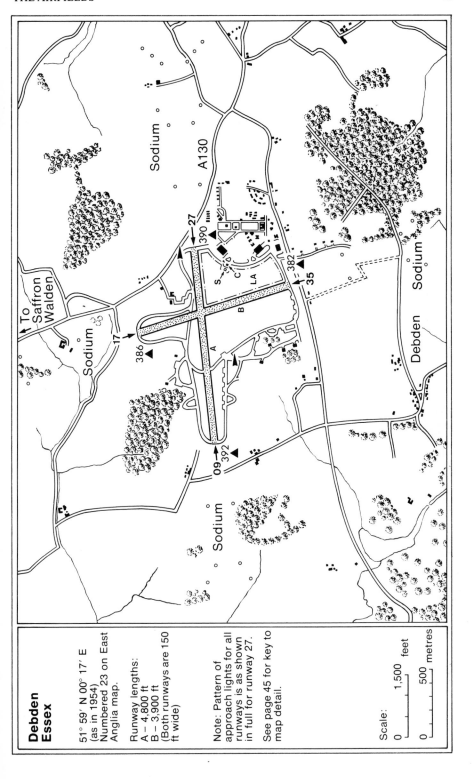

Debden
Essex

51° 59′ N 00° 17′ E
(as in 1954)
Numbered 23 on East
Anglia map.

Runway lengths:
A – 4,800 ft
B – 3,900 ft
(Both runways are 150
ft wide)

Note: Pattern of
approach lights for all
runways is as shown
in full for runway 27.

See page 45 for key to
map detail.

Scale:

0 — 1,500 feet

0 — 500 metres

up on the new AI radar. It was on June 25 1940 that bombs were first dropped at Debden, the raider using as its marker the flarepath which was switched on for a returning Blenheim. Damage was insignificant. Later No 29 Squadron moved to Digby and the tempo for the Hurricanes increased.

Castle Camps satellite became operational in July, but it was August which proved to be the hot month — both in terms of weather and enemy activity. The number of plots at Debden Operations Room increased, indicated from information supplied by RDF stations and the Observer Corps, and the number of interceptions increased rapidly. Both Nos 17 and 85 Squadrons moved south to be replaced by Nos 111 and 601 Squadrons which were immediately in action.

On August 24 the Luftwaffe mounted its concentrated effort to eliminate fighter stations. Debden soon figured within this phase of the Battle and suffered its first major attack on August 26 when, in mid-afternoon, a small force of Do 17s bombed the station, damaging the airfield, buildings and aircraft with some casualties. The leading Dornier was shot down nearby, and from its wreckage a map indicating the course to Debden was retrieved and proudly displayed for the rest of the war in the Officers' Mess.

Four days later, Debden received more attention when, early on August 31, a strong force of Dornier 17s, escorted by Bf 110s, attacked, again causing damage to buildings and aircraft with further casualties. The raiders were engaged by Spitfires of No 19 Squadron from nearby Duxford. Losses were suffered on both sides, but the enemy never again bombed Debden in such strength. Instead, attacks on Britain were now made mainly under cover of darkness and again Debden's squadrons were involved. The Beaufighter was being introduced to operational use and No 25 Squadron arrived in October, working up on this type to intercept the night bomber. No 85 Squadron had also returned to Debden with a mixture of Hurricanes and Defiants operating in night defence duties, with No 264 Squadron's Defiants replacing 25 Squadron by the end of the year.

So 1940 closed with the Battle of Britain a victory for the immortal 'Few', and Debden can boast of playing a vital part in the action. There was a price to pay, all participating squadrons at Debden losing valuable pilots. One such

Americans commenced their association with Debden when the Eagle squadrons arrived. Spitfires like AV-F: BM461 of the 335th Fighter Squadron became part of the 4th Fighter Group (Leroy Nitschke, via Keith Braybrooke).

A P-51B Mustang of the 334th Fighter Squadron, 4th Fighter Group, in a sand-bagged emplacement in June 1944 (Leroy Nitschke).

Hurricanes of 85 Squadron lined up at Debden.

The crew stand by Boston III intruder W8317 'Victoria' of 418 Squadron at Debden.

was Flight Lieutenant 'Dickie' Lee of 85 Squadron, whose skill was legendary at Debden long before the war. Action film required for a comedy starring George Formby involved flying an aircraft *through* No 3 Hangar — duly accomplished by 'Dickie'.

His Majesty King George VI and Queen Elizabeth were visitors at Debden on January 28 1941, but on February 14 the station received an unwelcome guest — an He 111 which landed and took off again before the airfield's guns could be used. In the next few months the airfield was busy with pilots undergoing final training on Hurricanes, for No 52 OTU was established here and also included Battles and Masters. The Havoc made its presence felt at Debden too, when No 85 Squadron began conversion, later moving to Hunsdon.

As 1941 progressed, new squadrons were formed at Debden. No 418 (Canadian) Squadron began its career in November, flying Douglas Boston III intruders, and the aesthetic Mosquito made its debut as a night fighter when 157 Squadron formed at Debden, equipping at Castle Camps.

Fighters were now on the offensive rather than the defensive and by the turn of the year the Debden Wing had formed. Thus 1942 could well be called 'Spitfire Year' at Debden, the first nine months' duties being undertaken by various RAF squadrons, operating mainly *Circus* operations. One squadron, No 65, was moved to the new satellite at Great Sampford in April and No 71 'Eagle' Squadron replaced it at Debden. This was a prelude for major change as, in September, the other two 'Eagle' Squadrons came to Debden to be officially transferred to the USAAF. Thus, the 4th Fighter Group was born, and with it the second chapter of Debden's history.

The three squadrons, now re-numbered 334, 335 and 336, carried on a similar pattern of operations, still flying Spitfire Vs but with American markings until the spring of 1943. After reluctant conversion to the P-47 Thunderbolt the initial mission with the new type was flown on March 10 — the first kill coming on April 13. US 8th AF bomber losses were worrying, deeper fighter cover was needed and Debden's P-47s created history by being the first to penetrate German airspace on July 28 1943, an achievement made possible by using newly introduced auxiliary tanks.

More success followed and, under the

Pilots of 87 Squadron race towards their Gladiators in a pre-war practice interception.

brilliant leadership of Colonel Don Blakeslee, 1944 at Debden was eventful. In February P-51 Mustangs replaced the Thunderbolts and with these Blakeslee led the 4th Fighter Group to Berlin on March 4 — another 'first'. With two underwing tanks the red-nosed Mustangs roamed far over Europe gaining a steadily mounting total of enemy aircraft destroyed. D-Day, June 6, had the squadrons flying three times, supporting ground operations, but it was on June 21 that Debden spearheaded another 'first' — this time a 'shuttle' escort to Poland and a landing in Russia. From Russia they flew to Italy, providing escort en route, returning to Debden on July 5, again providing escort. The Group was awarded the Distinguished Unit Citation, the US highest corporate military honour.

In October 1944 a new sound at Debden heralded the arrival of the jet fighter, for No 616 Squadron had sent a detachment of Meteors to develop tactics. The closing months of the war were not without incident, as on March 18 when a returning Mustang carried two pilots aboard, one landing in enemy territory to rescue his companion. Many dignitaries visited Debden during American tenure, and the station's popularity for parties led to many varied types of visiting aircraft,

British and American.

With the cessation of hostilities in Europe, the 4th Fighter Group emerged as the highest overall scoring unit with over 1,000 enemy aircraft destroyed.

The post-war years were with RAF Technical Training Command — firstly as the Empire Radio School. Amongst the varied aircraft used were the two prestigious 'Mercuries', a Halifax and later a Lincoln, both of which made global tours. The station's role continued as the Debden Division of RAF Technical College until 1960, the last types flown here being Varsities and Chipmunks.

The final chapter commenced in 1960 when Debden became the RAF Police Depot, a role fulfilled until 1975. Nostalgia had returned in 1968 when the Battle of Britain Film Unit used the airfield for varying periods and the sight of Spitfires and Hurricanes in circuit revived happy memories of yesteryear. A series of Gala Days was held between 1967 and 1970 and, on June 5 1973, HRH Princess Margaret conducted a Royal Review at Debden. A tenuous link with the past can still be seen when a Gliding School carries out Air Cadet training at weekends. No less than four books (three American and one British) have been written on the life and times at Debden — a sure indication of the affection held for this hallowed ground.

Deopham Green, Norfolk

TM030990. 2 Miles NE of Great Ellingham, off B1077

Turn off the B1108 at Hingham then right at the crossroads where there are remains of huts, and the wartime water tower can be seen on the domestic site a mile or so from the airfield. Soon you will find yourself in the middle of what used to be an airfield. You will probably discover that you have a wide expanse of cultivated land and a huge East Anglian sky all to yourself. How remote it must have seemed to the Americans.

Perhaps most moving of all, you can easily stand on the main runway, still much in evidence. How nostalgic to recall the sound of a Fortress straining under its bomb load, groaning and bumping along for Berlin or, in this case, even Russia. In the distance Nissen huts can be seen on the north side, and there are many remains of other runways and the perimeter track. Tarry awhile, and the station curiously seems to come alive, yet there is little tangible to see. If you try hard

enough you may think you can hear the B-17s coming home. Deopham is a 'must' if you enjoy nostalgia, and for best effect chose a day when the cumulus towers and showers produce the sort of magnificent cloudscape that only East Anglia provides for man's enjoyment.

Ponder now what was demanded of the American crews during daylight raids. It was patently obvious to any East Anglian between 1942 and the end of the war. A low-flying Fortress would often be seen with large chunks clearly shot away from its structure. All too often smoke would be trailing from an engine, and there would be the inevitable straggler in which the crew was making a superhuman effort to survive, often carrying in their midst the critically wounded and those who had paid the ultimate sacrifice. One could so often imagine the pathos and the tensions, as the bombers staggered home and, watching those forlorn formations, the sensitive among us prayed many times even if we never admitted it.

From the missing we could imagine just how horrific the battle was, especially in view of the comments of survivors, some of whom would honestly admit that they were terribly frightened. These men were foreign by birth, British by tongue, and although one chided them for their late entry into conflict, viewed their battle claims with suspicion and frankly disliked it when their tongues ran away with them, one admired their display of courage so far from home. Such sentiments surrounded the exploits of every American base, many of which had names unknown to most. Deopham Green might well stand for them all, and is an ideal place to pause and remember.

The special brand of American courage was well displayed on November 9 1944 when the 452nd Bomb Group set out for France. This time it was heavy flak which demanded the courage when a B-17 piloted by 1st Lieutenant Donald J. Gott and 2nd Lieutenant William E. Metzger was crippled beyond recovery. Maybe it took off from the runway on which you can still stand. Three engines were hit and flames spewed to the aft part of the bomber. A serious fire developed and others of the crew were badly wounded. In an effort to save their companions the pilots tried for a landing in friendly territory, and Metzger passed his parachute to a companion. Gott located a suitable landing place on which to put down to save the wounded, even though he had only one engine functioning. But as he came in for the crash landing the aircraft exploded and three of the men aboard, including the two pilots, were killed. To mark their courage the two pilots were posthumously awarded the Medal of Honour.

It was at the start of 1944 that the 452nd Bomb Group arrived at Deopham and the base came alive. Operations using B-17s commenced on February 5 1944 when the Group attacked an aircraft assembly plant near Brunswick. Primarily their targets would always be of a strategic nature, and the list included an aircraft components factory at Kassel, the ball bearing works at Schweinfurt, synthetic rubber plant at Hanover, oil installations at Bohlen, marshalling yards at Frankfurt, the aircraft assembly plant at Regensburg, etc.

On June 21 1944 the Group was part of the force of well over 1,000 bombers and 1,000 fighters which attacked Berlin. Flying in the lead of the 3rd Air Division, the 452nd carried on eastwards to land at Poltava in the USSR, after attacking an oil plant south of Berlin. This 12-hour flight took them through a harrowing ordeal, and the end was equally distressing. At night the Luftwaffe, having located the landing ground in Russia, despatched a strong force of bombers which made a crippling attack on the Fortresses which nullified their notion of assaulting the enemy on return. The Group survived and, undaunted, made yet another shuttle raid to Russia on September 11, bombing Chemnitz on the way.

Like so many others they gave tactical support to the Normandy landings and to the airborne venture around Arnhem. During the Ardennes offensive they attacked communications targets in the battle area, and bombed an airfield whilst the Rhine was crossed.

A Distinguished Unit Citation was awarded after the 452nd attacked the jet fighter base at Kaltnekirchen on April 7 1945, in the face of vigorous fighter defence. Before the war finished the Fortresses from Deopham dropped eagerly snatched supplies to the Dutch, having made their last bombing attack on April 21 against rail yards at Ingoldstadt.

During June 1945 the Americans began to pull out of Deopham and by August 1945 they had gone. RAF Maintenance Command retrieved the airfield on October 9 1945 and the site was sold in March 1959.

You can experience some of the feeling of former occupants of the old airfield, for the runway runs alongside a road which crosses the site, and, travelling at moderate speed along that stretch you could easily imagine yourself becoming airborne, heading deep into enemy territory.

B-17s of the 452nd Bomb Group set out from Deopham on January 10 1945 (USAF).

A group of Nissen huts still stands at Deopham.

Docking, Norfolk

TF770380. E of B1153 out of Docking

A satellite for Bircham Newton was selected at Docking in December 1939. Preparation resulted in a grass airfield which was probably first used in July 1940 by Blenheims of 235 Squadron. Hudsons of 206 Squadron were also using the airfield by September 1940, it then being principally a dispersal field for the parent station. Later in 1940 235 Squadron's Blenheims were generally placed here and later in full residence until the start of June 1941. A few weeks later 53 Squadron's Blenheims were based here. These Blenheim squadrons flew patrols to the Dutch coast and escorted convoys.

On December 25 1941 221 Squadron, flying Wellington VIIIs, arrived from Iceland and stayed but briefly for, in January, the squadron proceeded to the Middle East.

No 1401 Meteorological Reconnaissance Flight, prominent among the gatherers of weather forecast material, brought its Gladiators and Blenheims to Docking from Bircham Newton early in 1942. In May the Flight received Hudsons, and in July Spitfires for use on *Rhombus, Prata* and *Thum* flights. These aircraft were maintained at Bircham Newton where the Flight disbanded on July 31 1942.

The next residents were Beaufighter 1cs of 235 Squadron, here between May 31 and July 16 1942. Like so many stations Docking accommodated a BAT Flight, for the benefit of the Bircham Newton clutch, 1525 Flight arriving in July 1942 and staying until May 1945.

No 53 Squadron re-established itself here with Whitley VIIs in February 1943, during which month Hampden torpedo-bombers of 415 Squadron began using the station as an advanced base for operations off Norway. Such operations continued into May 1943. By then 53 Squadron had left and on April 2 304 Squadron's Wellingtons arrived and stayed until early June.

Bircham Newton had swung to playing the major part in Coastal Command's ASR operations. The Warwick bomber had been chosen to supplement their Hudsons. To Docking and Bircham Newton came the first Warwicks for Coastal Command and on June 25 1943 the Warwick Training Unit formed at Docking. The unit moved to Bircham Newton on July 3 1943 leaving a Ferry Training Unit here since Warwicks would

need to be flown to the Middle East.

No 1401 Meteorological Flight re-formed at Bircham Newton on April 1 1943 and straightaway moved to Docking where it operated Gladiators, Spitfires and Hudsons. In May the unit received a few Hampdens and it was very active from here until moving to Manston in September.

Any gaps which may appear in this outline history of Docking do not imply that the station was out of use for, with so many units using Bircham Newton, flying regularly took place by these from the satellite. Its position near the coast also attracted aircraft returning from operations and needing to land as soon as possible.

The meteorological reconnaissance role was almost continuous here until after the war. In late 1943 521 Squadron began 'met' flights from Docking using Venturas and Hudsons. These flew reconnaissances to Wick in north-east Scotland, returning the following day, whilst 519 Squadron at Wick did flights in the reverse direction so that their Ventura Vs were a common sight at Docking. No 521 Squadron moved to Langham on October 30 1944.

Possibly the busiest operational squadron to use the station was No 415 which, it will be recalled, had used it as an advanced base early in 1943. On November 15 1943 the squadron moved in with its Wellington XIIIs which flew many anti-shipping and E-Boat attacks by night off the Dutch coast until July 1944. They used Bircham Newton as their mainten-

An aerial view of the site of Docking. Little remains apart from the control tower by the trees and part of the perimeter road.

ance base, like 524 Squadron which replaced them, flying Wellington XIVs, and remained until November 1944 when they finally moved to Langham after detachments there.

Bircham Newton's target towers, of course, used Docking although they were not based here until No 2 APC arrived on August 1944. No 288 Squadron had a small detachment here in March 1945.

Nor was the Royal Navy absent from the station for on September 7 1944 855 Squadron arrived with Avengers, using this and the parent station for *Rovers* until mid-October.

Bircham Newton's operational days were now over and with the removal of 524 Squadron Docking assumed less importance, serving merely as a satellite to Bircham Newton and never again accommodating operational units. No 1693 ASR Training Unit was briefly here in June-July 1945.

Coastal Command relinquished use of the station on September 21 1945 when it passed to 54 Group. It was finally sold off surplus to needs in April 1958.

Downham Market, Norfolk

TL630045. 2 miles NE of town, on A10

Bombing raids on Italy from British bases were always unpleasant operations. As well as the distance involved there was that great barrier, the Alps, to cross or even thread one's way through — and in darkness. One such raid came on the night of August 12/13 1943, participants including Stirlings of 218 Squadron. Target for the squadron was the Fiat works at Turin and one aircraft was captained by Flight Sergeant Louis Aaron.

Over the target his Stirling was raked by machine-gun fire which put three of the four engines out of action, shattered the windscreen, caused damage to the elevator cables and put two of the three turrets out of use. Aaron suffered terrible wounds, his face and a lung being injured. His right arm too was broken. How anyone could have survived was miraculous. Aaron not only lived on, he persisted in continuing to help fly the crippled bomber.

Return across the Alps was clearly out of the question and instead the crew decided to head for North Africa, a long way off. Aaron's place at the controls was first taken by the bomb aimer, but the gallant skipper, after trying to fly the aircraft again, instead wrote instructions for the bomb aimer using his left hand, despite

A Stirling of 218 Squadron on dispersal at Downham Market (D. Thomas).

Many a large house was requisitioned for RAF use, this one serving as Downham Market's Officers' Mess (D. Thomas).

the tremendous pain he was suffering. After five hours' flying Bone airfield was sighted and the worst moment of the flight came, the landing. Four attempts were made trying for a belly landing with Aaron still assisting as best he could whilst on the point of collapse. The fifth attempt was successful. Nine hours later Aaron died, his death due more to his selfless devotion to his colleagues than to his wounds. Had he rested he might have recovered. He was posthumously awarded the Victoria Cross.

The site of Downham Market photographed by 58 Squadron on February 7 1964 (DoE).

Downham Market, just north of the town on a site now marked by a tall TV booster aerial and a few huts, opened in 1942 as Marham's satellite in place of Barton Bendish, which was unsuitable for Stirlings. When Marham passed to 2 Group in August 1942, 218 Squadron took its Stirlings to Downham, where previously some had dispersed, and commenced operations from the station. From Downham, taken over by 3 Group on December 1 1942, the squadron's Stirlings took part in the bombing and mining campaign until late 1943. To expand the strength of 3 Group, 'C' Flight of 218 Squadron became 623 Squadron on August 10 1943 and operated from Downham until it disbanded on December 6 1943. Since March 1943 Horsa gliders had been stored on the airfield and in March 1944 they were towed away for a part in the invasion.

Nudged out of Chedburgh when Stradishall Base switched to operational conversion, 214 Squadron arrived at Downham in December 1943. Its stay was brief. Between January 17 and 24 the unit relinquished its Stirling IIIs and moved to Sculthorpe to undertake training for special operations in 100 Group. Downham passed to the Pathfinders, 8 Group, a new squadron forming from elements of 35 and 97 Squadrons as 635 Squadron. It first operated against Frankfurt, on March 22/23.

Like other 8 Group stations, Downham fell into line by housing also a Mosquito bomber squadron when No 571 formed here on April 7 1944. This did not operate from Downham, but a detachment at Graveley flew two operations from there before the squadron moved to Oakington.

By now 635 Squadron was in the thick of battle. During July 1944 a rare item of equipment came its way, the Lancaster Mk VI. This was an interim bomber, produced to try out the new armour-plated annular-cowled Merlin intended for the Windsor and by now scheduled for the Lancaster IV which came into use as the Lincoln. To 635 Squadron came five of these unusual Lancasters and the squadron tried them out operationally between August and November 1944.

Downham's own Mosquito squadron, No 608, formed on August 1 1944 equipped with Canadian-built Mosquito XXs. These began operations on August 5 with an attack on the Wanne Eickel synthetic oil plant. Thereafter the squadron was busily engaged as part of the LNSF, flying the refined Mk XXV from October 1944. In March 1945 the Mosquito XVI with

two-stage Merlins was introduced for operations, this type entirely equipping the squadron before the war ended.

In August 1945 No 608 Squadron disbanded followed by 635 Squadron on September 1. All flying ceased in April 1946 and the station closed on October 24 1946. The land was sold in February 1957.

Duxford, Cambridgeshire

TL460460. 7 miles NE of Royston, Herts, on A505

One sound, one sight, one supreme shape, will forever be synonymous with Duxford. Of course, the Spitfire. Saturday, July 30 1938 was a fine summer's day. As customary then Duxford closed at noon for the weekend. Sad, in a way, because something which would change the course of history was to take place.

Around 4 pm, with few there to witness it, a Spitfire—the first for the RAF-whistled in as only a Spitfire could. A few fast aerobatics then K9792 landed. The pilot was entertained to tea in the Mess, one may assume in that gracious style of pre-war days. Before leaving he flew the Spitfire again, presenting a stunning display to the watching few. Then the precious aeroplane was pushed into a hangar and 19 Squadron had its first Spitfire.

During the autumn of 1938, as the country passed through the sobering ordeal of the Munich crisis, 19 Squadron explored its new mounts and in November 66 Squadron also began to equip. No 19 had become the RAF's premier fighter squadron and Duxford's place in history was assured.

Visit Duxford now and it is the hangars of World War 1 style which immediately greet the eye. But Duxford was not a 1914-1918 station, that distinction being held by nearby Fowlmere, a station much resembling Duxford except that its domestic site was adjacent to the technical site, whereas at Duxford a main road separated them.

Duxford opened in 1919 and in June 1920 became the home of the 15 aircraft of No 2 Flying Training School which flew Avro 504s, F2Bs, DH 9As and a few RE8s before moving to Digby in July 1924.

In 1923 a major review of the air defence of the United Kingdom had resulted in a dramatic change of role for Duxford, which became a fighter station charged with the defence of East Anglia and barring entry to the East Midlands.

To achieve this two squadrons, Nos 19 and 29, reformed on April 1 1923 equipped with Sopwith Snipes. At the end of the year they began to receive Gloster Grebes and in March-April 1928 Siskin IIIs. They had been joined by 111 Squadron which reformed here on October 1 1923 with Grebes and which, from June 1924, flew Siskin IIIs. 'Treble-One'

became the High Altitude Squadron in 1926 responsible for developing equipment for high altitude fighting. It received Siskin IIIAs in September 1926 and in 1927 command of the squadron fell to Squadron Leader Keith R. Park, later of Battle of Britain and Malta defence fame.

On April 1 1928 Nos 29 and 111 Squadrons vacated the station just after 19

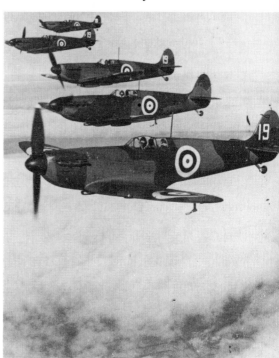

Left: *In July 1935 HM King George V took the salute when the RAF mounted its fly-past over Duxford (Flight International).* Right: *Duxford's most famed — the Spitfires of 19 Squadron in 1938 (IWM).* Below: *This Heinkel He 111 AW177 was for long seen flying from Duxford in the war years.*

Squadron had received Siskin IIIAs. In September 1931 19 Squadron re-equipped with Bulldogs. Since 1926 fighters here had been adorned with squadron colours, 19 adopting light blue in their markings because of its local associations.

In January 1935 19 Squadron became the first to equip with Gloster Gauntlets and, when 66 Squadron reformed on July 20 1936, it was similarly equipped.

At the time of the Munich crisis the Spitfires were armed and refuelled, for conflict seemed imminent. Once it had passed both squadrons reverted to air drill, exploring the possibilities of the Spitfire, tried some night flying and detached themselves to Sutton Bridge for armament training.

Since early 1926 Duxford had housed another unit, the Cambridge University Air Squadron, which had been formed on October 1 1925 to interest undergraduates in the RAF and was the first such organisation to have headquarters in the Engineering Laboratories on Cam Causeway. At Duxford the squadron commenced practice flying in Avro 504s on February 19 1926. It received a boost in 1933 when it was re-equipped with Avro Tutors whose yellow forms graced Duxford to the outbreak of war.

Duxford was also the home of the Meteorological Flight which used Bulldogs, then Gloster Gauntlets, between September and November 1936 when they moved to Mildenhall.

No 611 Squadron was here at the outbreak of war for summer camp. When it left on October 10 1939 its aircraft formed up in the squadron number as they impressively flew north.

Already a new squadron was at Duxford for No 222 had formed on October 5 1939 and equipped with Blenheim 1Fs in November for long-range fighting and escort duties. To this squadron, housed in the western hangar in early 1940, came Squadron Leader D.R.S. Bader, very much a Duxford figure. The station was far removed from the early war battles, but Flights were detached to forward stations and 19 Squadron had a spell at Catterick and operated off the East Coast without claims being made.

In March 1940 222 Squadron received Spitfires. The suddenness of the May 1940 Blitzkrieg caught the squadrons unready. Quickly Defiants of 264 Squadron were rushed to Duxford from Wittering and moved forward daily to operate from Horsham St Faith, the advanced SLG for Duxford, whence they fought their first battles. Nos 19 and 66 Squadron drew first blood, off Holland, and on May 25 moved to Hornchurch to help cover the Dunkirk withdrawal during which the units fought hard before returning to Duxford on June 5.

The new satellite at Fowlmere now came into use, 19 Squadron dispersing there. In June 1940 264 Squadron re-established itself after its hammering and moved to Fowlmere.

Come July and 19 Squadron found that it had been chosen to try the cannon-armed Spitfire 1B. From the start these aircraft were troublesome, the main problem being cartridge ejection after the guns had fired. The squadron was told to persevere.

The Battle of Britain opened and 19 Squadron was not yet equipped for action. Fortunately Duxford lay largely beyond the range of the daylight onslaught. There were many scrambles and 19 Squadron fought off the East Coast. For Duxford July 11 was an auspicious day as the Czech pilots for 310 Squadron arrived, their Hurricanes coming on July 18. They made their first patrol on August 18 and first engaged in combat on August 26. But it was August 31 1940 which became the most memorable day at Duxford during the great Battle.

It was a glorious hot summer's day when, at 0800 hours, the local air raid warning sounded. Could the Luftwaffe be coming at last? I for one was soon without doubt when there was a tremendous noise as 3.7-inch guns opened fire. This sent the large work force at Pye Radio in Cambridge, near my home, scurrying to the shelters, for mingled with the gunfire was the sound of bursting bombs. A force of Do 17Zs was heading for Duxford, but the raid developed too fast for its squadrons to intercept. Instead, 111 Squadron from Debden accepted the challenge and shot down a Do 17 of KG 2 and a Bf 110. Much disorganised, the bomber force began jettisoning its load near Shelford and finally released the rest of its bombs between Harston and Shepreth. Meanwhile a second force of Do 17s made for Debden and 19 Squadron was scrambled from Fowlmere. Stoppages wrecked their firing but three claims were laid.

By now a second Czech squadron had formed at Duxford, No 312, but left in September. That month saw the introduction here of the 'Big Wing'. In the belief that large formations were best met by a host of fighters in one formation, 12 Group pressed the idea which brought

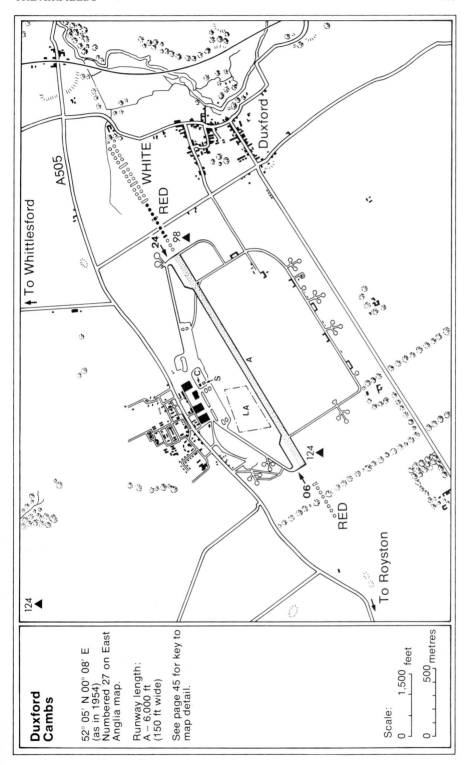

Duxford
Cambs

52° 05′ N 00° 08′ E
(as in 1954)
Numbered 27 on East
Anglia map.

Runway length:
A – 6,000 ft
(150 ft wide)

See page 45 for key to
map detail.

Scale:

0 _____ 1,500 feet

0 _____ 500 metres

To Whittlesford

A505

WHITE

RED

Duxford

24

98

124

06

RED

To Royston

124

The Typhoon entered squadron service at Duxford. R7847, a Mk 1b, joined 266 Squadron, the first to equip with this type (IWM).

many squadrons daily to Duxford for operations in which Douglas Bader and 242 Squadron took a leading part. The resident squadrons participated with mixed success, fighting mainly to the north and west of London into October.

As the battle died down Duxford's value was assessed. It was too far from France for offensive operations and so 310 and 19 Squadrons were assigned to Sector Patrols over mid-Anglia.

December saw a major change at Duxford. To free Northolt for offensive duties the Air Fighting Development Unit moved to Duxford joining 310. No 19 Squadron was soon based at Fowlmere. AFDU held some Spitfires and Hurricanes for tactical developments but its main role was the tactical assessment of new types of aircraft, sometimes borrowed from new squadrons. This brought the newly received American types, and the Royal Navy established a counterpart to assess the Fulmar, Martlet and Skua which gave Duxford a cosmopolitan look. The procession of types made Duxford a spotter's paradise where one could gaze

upon such rarities as the Maryland, Fiat CR 42, Halifax 1 and Mohawk, among many others.

On June 26 1941 310's Hurricanes moved out and at once 56 Squadron's replaced them. The squadron flew a few offensive sorties, but it had come primarily to receive a new fighter, the Typhoon. In September 1941 it began to re-arm on a long torturous path to operation, for the Typhoon was a troublesome aeroplane at this period.

Meanwhile, more of interest was to be seen for 601 Squadron arrived in mid-August 1941 at the time when it was taking delivery of the Bell Airacobra, with which it fully equipped in October 1941. It was a strange aircraft for the engine was behind the pilot and the cannon fired through the propeller hub. Firing upset the compass so badly that the Airacobra had to be rejected and very few sorties, from Manston, were flown before the squadron left in January 1942.

In the south-east corner of Duxford and along the southern perimeter road were presently dispersed the Blenheims

Right: A P-47 Thunderbolt of the 78th Fighter Group undergoing servicing at Duxford (USAF). Left: Javelin 7s of 64 Squadron lined up on the ASP at Duxford (Flight International).

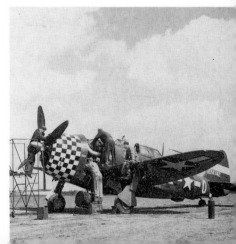

and some Cierva C 30a autogiros of 74 Signals Wing whose task was radar calibration. The autogiros had arrived in the summer of 1940 and stayed until late 1942. Frequently they were away, settling at some radar station whilst carrying out their duties.

In September 1941 much excitement was aroused when an He 111, a Ju 88, a Bf 109 and a Bf 110 arrived for tactical evaluation from Farnborough. At the end of 1941 these aircraft were placed in No 1426 Enemy Aircraft Flight and dispersed in the south-west corner. Their job was to display the 'circus' at many other operational stations.

The main task in 1942 was to work the Typhoon into operational service and 56 Squadron was joined by 266 in January, followed by 609 in March, both of which equipped with Typhoons to create the Duxford Wing led by Wing Commander John Grandy. The Typhoons first went into action in June and, flying from West Malling, were busy during the Dieppe landings. Gradually they moved to operational stations then, in the autumn, 181 Squadron formed at Duxford to try out the 'Bomphoon' before moving to the second satellite at Snailwell. The 'Hurribomber' too had been first tried at Duxford where AFDU was still busy evaluating new types such as the Mitchell, Marauder and Ventura.

Activity dropped away in early 1943 and in February-March AFDU moved to Wittering to make way for very new arrivals, the P-47s of the 78th Fighter Group which came in April. Already Duxford had accommodated US P-38s and P-39s on tactical trials and had briefly handled the Merlin Mustang AM203, judged as a winner.

The 78th flew its first sorties on April 8 and by summer 1943 was using long-range tanks which much improved their aircrafts' performance. The numbers of aircraft held seemed unbelievable, a stream landing by the Group being something ever to remember. They took a very active part in operations for the rest of the war and in late 1944 re-armed with P-51s. The Americans worked up great affection for 'the Duckpond' and endeared themselves enormously to the neighbourhood.

They flew their initial operation from Duxford on April 12 1943 and made their first claim, two FW 190s, on May 14. Long-range ranks began to be carried on July 30 which enabled them to reach Germany. In January 1944 they began strafing operations and gave beach-head cover on D-Day, and then forward support for the Arnhem landings.

Their first P-51 operation took place on December 29 1944, their mounts formerly having been teardrop-cockpit P-47Ds. A PSP runway was laid at Duxford in November-December 1944 whilst the 78th operated from Bassingbourn. By April 1945 the unit was operating over Czechoslovakia and its final operation came on April 25 when it supported the RAF raid on Berchtesgaden.

The Americans left Duxford in August 1945 and the station was put on to Care & Maintenance until the end of 1945 when Spitfire IXs of 165 Squadron arrived. In April 1946 they were joined by Mk XXIs of 91 Squadron which stayed until November, 165 having gone in August.

February 1947 saw the arrival of the first jet squadron, No 92, whose Meteor IIIs were joined by those of 56 Squadron on April 16 1947 and stayed until October 1949. Then a concrete runway was laid and Duxford re-opened in August 1951 when Nos 64 and 65 Squadrons arrived with Meteor 8s. In July 1953 the station housed Sabres here from Germany to take part in the massive Coronation fly past.

In September 1956 No 64 Squadron switched to a night fighter role, equipping with Meteor 12s and 14s housed in a new 'T' Type hangar at the eastern end of the airfield, which now had a number of concrete walled revetments against intruder attack. No 65 Squadron received Hunter 6s in March 1957 and Javelin 7s replaced 64's Meteors in September 1958. The squadron was using Mk 9s when, in August 1961, it vacated Duxford. No 65 Squadron had disbanded on March 31 1961.

The general state of Duxford gave concern, for its buildings were nothing short of antique. No runway extension for modern jets was feasible, indeed it was considered insufficiently strong to even take one Lightning.

On July 31 1961 Air Vice-Marshal R.N. Bateson took off in a Meteor T7, ceremoniously ending Duxford's days as an RAF station, and it was supposed that flying had ceased here. Not so, for in 1968 the aerodrome resounded again to a host of Merlins for it had become the main base for the filming of the *Battle of Britain*. Now the sight was of Spitfires and Hurricanes once more together with 'Me 109s' and 'He 111s' and the photographic Mitchell.

This use of Duxford awoke tremendous desire that it should stay alive, most so in the minds of a group of young enthusiasts who banded themselves together to form the East Anglian Aviation Society, and who aroused the interest of the Imperial War Museum. Gradually more and more aircraft found their way here, and Mr Haydon Baillie based his T-33s and Sea Fury here until his tragic death.

The news that the Science Museum wanted to place the first British Concorde at Duxford was greeted with mixed feelings. To some this was quite incongruous. Tragically, it brought the culmination of differing outlooks between the enthusiasts and the museum. The East Anglian Aviation Society, which had done so much to save Duxford, departed from the scene and in its place the Imperial War Museum formed its own society here.

Now the Cambridge Western bypass has hacked its way across Duxford and its runway. It remains a place of great interest, the home of many old aeroplanes, and is regularly open to visitors. The Shuttleworth Collection's Spitfire is a reminder of great days past.

Earl's Colne, Essex

TL850270. By B1024 S of Earl's Colne

This was one of the first bases built by the US Army in Britain. The station came alive under the RAF's 3 Group and Stradishall control on August 26 1942, although building was only just under way. It became an active airfield in May 1943 when the 94th Bomb Group arrived with B-17s, staying only into June. Their place was immediately taken by B-26s of the 323rd Bomb Group which commenced operations from here on July 16 1943 under 8th AF control. Its round of operations was as for other B-26 Groups as outlined under Great Dunmow. Some of their attacks on airfields in 1944 were particularly successful when they employed carpet bombing techniques. The Group came under 9th AF control on October 16 1943.

The 323rd's part in supporting the Normandy invasion was briefly interrupted when, on July 21, they left Earl's Colne for Beaulieu, Hants.

The station lay unused until late September 1944 when Nos 296 and 297 Squadrons of 38 Group arrived. Although commencing to fly Halifax IIIs, they reached Earl's Colne still using Albemarles. Conversion to Halifaxes occupied the next few weeks and SOE operations took place from December 1944. Horsas arrived in strength and both squadrons

A Javelin of 64 Squadron leads two Hunters of 65 Squadron over Duxford. The domestic site layout is evident above the line of the road through the camp.

Duxford was rejuvenated in summer 1968 when part of the film The Battle of Britain *was made here. Mock Messerschmitts line the apron.*

Duxford photographed on July 9 1946 (DoE).

participated in Operation *Varsity* from Earl's Colne.

In February 1946 the Halifaxes left and next month the station was put under Care & Maintenance. The site was given up in the 1960s and is now agricultural land although the control tower still stands, converted into a private dwelling.

East Wretham, Norfolk

TL910810. A1075 5 miles NE Thetford

Some 200 Czechs escaped from France in the 1940 collapse. They gathered on the French west coast and sailed in the *Appapa*. After a lengthy voyage the ship docked at Liverpool on July 9 and the Czechs were taken to Beeston Castle, Cheshire. Next day Air Ministry officials hurried to interview them, then posted them to Innsworth Lane, Gloucestershire, where many were grouped to form 311 (Czech) Bomber Squadron. On July 17 they proceeded to Cosford, were sworn in and the 43 officers given British commissions. Wing Commander Griffiths took over the squadron which moved to Honington on July 29, having as its Czech commanding officer Wing Commander Toman.

The task of teaching the crews to fly Wellington lcs was undertaken by the famous Flight Lieutenant P.C. Pickard. Three weeks later the Czechs began to fly from Honington's grass satellite, East Wretham, where previously some of Honington's Wellingtons had resided since about March 1940. The Czechs made their first operational sorties on September 10 with Brussels the target.

On September 16 the ground echelon of 311 Squadron moved into the satellite for better dispersal. They found the accommodation very primitive. Tents housed the airmen, a brick building the officers. Just as the ground parties arrived a Dornier 17 came out of the clouds and circled. Airfield defences opened up, so the German crew decided to unload their eight delayed action bombs at Honington. There the reception was even more fierce and accurate, and the Dornier came down near Bury St Edmunds.

Three days later the Wellingtons of '311' flew into Wretham and the same afternoon five were flown back to Honington for that night's operation. It was cancelled, the first operation taking place against Calais on September 21. Return was scheduled to be to Wretham, but fog descended and only Flight Lieutenant Ocelca was able to land — and he damaged his aircraft in the process.

On September 23/24 three crews set off for Berlin, one returning early. The second reached the target but the third, in KX-E:L7778, forced-landed intact in Holland. On September 26 the Dutch radio gave news of the arrival of the Wellington, whose crew had escaped. An offer of £60 was made to anyone who could give news of the crew.

Thereafter the squadron took part in many 3 Group night raids from Wretham or Honington, a number of incidents punctuating the action. Three crews were despatched on December 16 to Mannheim. As the third Wellington, P2577:Q, took off it circled low trying to land again. Instead, it crashed on the Wretham-Wretham Hall road and burst into flames, then the bombs exploded.

Pilot Officer Nedved scrambled clear, then, in spite of the exploding bombs, went back to rescue his colleagues. Fire tenders had come fast on the scene to rescue Pilot Officer Taul who was critically injured.

During the winter of 1940-1941 enemy intruders were often active in the Wretham area. On February 3 1941 20 bombs were dropped, 13 on the airfield, and a Wellington damaged. Another attack came on March 3/4 when 311 Squadron was carrying out night flying. A Ju 88 followed a Wellington into Wretham, dropping ten bombs in the process, and on April 8/9 another Ju 88 shot down 'X-Xray' making a training flight.

Until April 1942 311 Squadron operated from East Wretham against a wide variety of targets, flying Wellington lcs. On May 1 1942 the squadron was transferred to Aldergrove, joining Coastal Command. Backing '311' had been the Czech Training Unit which became 1429 Flight in January 1942 and held 12 Wellingtons and three Airspeed Oxfords at Wretham. When Bomber Command demanded maximum effort for the '1,000 bomber' raids, 1429 Flight despatched six Wellingtons for the Cologne and Essen attacks and two to Bremen on June 25 1942. The Flight moved to Woolfox Lodge on July 1 1942 and in August East Wretham was switched to Care & Maintenance pending transfer to the USAAF.

Plans had already been made to build runways at Mildenhall where 115 Squadron was operating. In November the runway work commenced and a new home was needed for 115 Squadron. As a temporary measure the squadron moved to East Wretham which became the third satellite for Mildenhall. Wellington IIIs moved into East Wretham on November 21.

In February 1943 the first Lancaster IIs suitable for operations became available. They were placed in 3 Group because that Group had experience of the Hercules engine which powered the Mk II. Thus in March 1943 the Mk II, best of the Lancasters, entered service at this little-known airfield, the last Wellington III operation from Wretham occurring on March 12 1943. To train crews for the Lancasters a Lancaster Conversion Flight formed in March with eight Mk IIs, becoming 1678 Conversion Unit on March 25. No 115 Squadron took its new type into action on March 20 for mine laying, and made its first bombing raid — against St Nazaire —

on March 22. The first major raid, against Berlin, came on March 29. Thereafter the squadron engaged in Main Force operations until moving out on August 7 to Little Snoring, again to make way for the Americans.

In mid-October 1943 the 359th Fighter Group moved in flying P-47D Thunderbolts, commencing operations on December 13. In April 1944 it equipped with P-51s, using them for escorts, patrols, strafing, dive-bombing and weather reconnaissance. At first the Group flew escorts covering raids on French airfields. In May 1944 they switched to escorting bombers raiding rail targets in Germany and oil plants in Poland, very deep penetration. They supported the invasion, patrolled over the Channel, escorted bombers to France and made dive-bombing and strafing attacks on the battle area perimeter.

A highlight came on July 28 when the Group made the 8th AF's first sighting of Me 163 rocket fighters. Between July 1944 and February 1945 the 359th concentrated on bomber escort and on September 11 was awarded a Distinguished Unit Citation for the close protection it gave to B-17s bombing Chemnitz en route for a shuttle raid to Russia. Thereafter the unit participated in the Arnhem operation, the Battle of the Bulge and the Rhine crossing.

On November 10 1945 the Group was de-activated and Wretham bid farewell to the Americans. On November 1 1945 Fighter Command took over the station and it came under Hethel's control within 12 Group. It passed to Bomber Command on May 21 1946 and on July 10 1946 to RAF Technical Training Command, subsequently becoming a Polish Re-Settlement Camp. Although much of the land was sold in October 1954 the airfield still has a T2 hangar. It stands on the fringe of the Stanford Battle Area and some accommodation is still used by the Army. The PSP runway has gone but some hardstandings are still in existence.

Ellough (Beccles), Suffolk
See Beccles

Eye, Suffolk
TM130750. 1 mile SW Brome, on A140, NW of Eye

To have one of the lowest loss rates in 8th AF operations was a welcome distinction brought about partly because the 490th Bomb Group joined the conflict relatively late. The Americans arrived at Eye, built by British and American organisations, in February 1944. The 490th Bomb Group moved in during April, commencing operations on May 31. It took part in attacks on airfields and supported the Normandy invasion. Rail targets were bombed, vehicle concentrations, bridges, and the Group was active in the Caen area in July 1944. The Liberators flew their 40th and final operation on August 6 1944 after which the Group switched to flying B-17s in keeping with other 3rd Air Division units. Gone their 'T in a square' identity in favour of red and white tails with curious '—' or '+' signs ahead of the individual letter on the fin which seemed so unusual at the time.

September found them helping to reduce Brest prior to its capture. Then they switched to the strategic offensive, bombing oil plants, tank factories, marshalling yards, aircraft plants and airfields. Berlin, Hamburg, Merseburg, Munster, Kassel, Hanover, Cologne — all were on target manifestos. They took part in the Ardennes offensive in bad weather which had allowed von Rundstedt to make his surprise offensive. Then they switched to further interdiction attacking rail and military targets to support the advance which ended the war. In the closing days of hostilities they dropped food supplies to the Dutch, retrieved prisoners of war and flew refugees and troops back to their home countries. The 490th left Eye in August 1945. It was allowed to run down and Eye is now the scene of light industry and agriculture.

Felixstowe, Suffolk
TM280330. Now the Port of Felixstowe, S of town. Car park, for Felixstowe-Harwich Ferry, may have now closed.

It was September 1940. An urgent call came to Britain. Four Dutchmen were at risk, and they had to be snatched from Holland. But how? A few Fokker T8-W Dutch naval seaplanes had escaped in May; what better than to use one to rescue these freedom fighters? Flying was unsafe at Felixstowe at this time, for Harwich had a balloon barrage. Nevertheless, a Fokker was made available. Would such a landing be possible? Not on a moonlight night, but perhaps when the night was not too dark. Three nights in October 1940 were earmarked. On the 14th there was a

Left: *An aerial view in the late 1950s shows the slipways gone (Felixstowe Dock Co).*
Right: *A 1978 photograph of the giant container dock at Felixstowe. It quite dwarfs the old hangars (Nigel Ruffles).*

heavy rain storm but, late the following day, and in great secrecy, the Fokker left Felixstowe for Vlieland. Visibility was good — except over the chosen lake. No accepting lights were flashed and the Fokker returned, landing on the Stour at 0430 hours. At midnight on the 16th it again foamed its way along the river, and flew to Lake Tjeuke where the welcoming 'K' was flashed. The seaplane landed and a small boat came towards the Fokker. Some 30 yards off, someone in the boat opened fire and the seaplane's gunner replied. Searchlights swept the surface of the lake, but the worthy old aircraft made it on to a straight course for Felixstowe where it landed at 0500 hours. But to keep up the worry, as it came in for landing, some trigger-happy Home Guards opened up, and the crew made quickly for the shore. Forty bullet holes were found in the T8-W, whose tanks were now empty. Years later it was discovered that the Germans had arrested those agents on the second night and on the third arranged an ambush. It was a narrow escape for the seaplane's crew.

The growth of Felixstowe as a ferry and commercial port in recent years has been truly phenomenal and has physically changed the face of East Anglia. The terrifying floods of February 1953 battered the old flying boat slipways, then the building of a quayside by deep water over the area where once Singapores crept ashore put an end to such activities. For a time the huge crane, more accustomed to lifting a Scapa or two, hoisted road tankers aboard coasters. That massive memorial of great days has now gone. Not so the huge black sheds erected during World War 1 which are the home of peaceful merchandise. The Officers' Mess is now a Customs HQ, and juggernauts accost the parade ground. What would the SWO of yesteryear say?

Felixstowe in pre-war days was always a hive of exotic activity. Almost every type of British seaplane from early World War 1 onwards passed its way, although 209

Felixstowe photographed from the air on October 16 1945 (DoE).

Squadron operated mainly Singapore IIIs from the base between May 1 1935 and August 12 1939. All the beautiful boats knew its waters — Perths, Irises, Stranraers, Londons and Scapas — as their performance and seaworthiness were investigated; and, of course, the first Sunderlands. That huge six-engined Sarafand was once there, but no sight was more enthralling than the few times when 'Maia' and 'Mercury' separated over the estuary.

Come the war and Felixstowe was too exposed for experimental flying. The Marine Aircraft Experimental Establishment at once fled to Rhu, near Helensburgh on the Clyde. Training Command took over and the huge concrete apron echoed to the sound of the boots of recruits of 7 RTC. Coastal Command retrieved their station on May 17 1940 and on the 29th Dutch personnel arrived with their Fokkers. But it was a dangerous place for flying and at least two Hampdens clouted the balloon cables.

The hangars were largely vacant until March 1942 when Sunderlands, Lerwicks

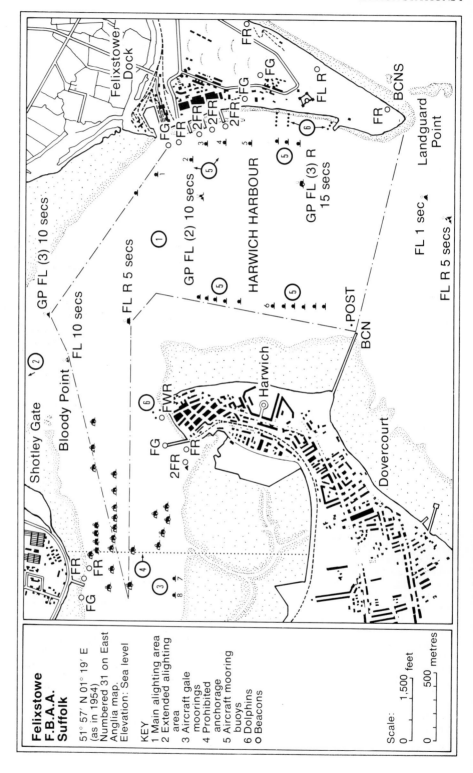

**Felixstowe
F.B.A.A.
Suffolk**

51° 57′ N 01° 19′ E
(as in 1954)
Numbered 31 on East
Anglia map.
Elevation: Sea level

KEY
1 Main alighting area
2 Extended alighting
  area
3 Aircraft gale
  moorings
4 Prohibited
  anchorage
5 Aircraft mooring
  buoys
6 Dolphins
○ Beacons

Scale:
0   1,500 feet
0   500 metres

and Londons started coming here for major overhauls. Late in August 1942 the first Catalinas came and the task was soon the attaching of Leigh Light airborne searchlights under the Catalinas' wings. Such work continued until the end of the war. Almost the only flying-boats over East Anglia during the conflict were flying to or from Felixstowe from west coast bases. The Norwegian Government also stored a Northrop N-3PB here from January 1944.

In May 1945 the MAEE returned to its palatial home, but it was never again to be very active. Magic post-war moments came when captured German flying-boats arrived — a couple of those peculiar Bv 138Bs, two Do 24s and briefly some Ju 52 floatplanes. The giant Bv 222 also tarried a while. A Sunderland or two arrived for hull research, as did the nippy little Saro Shrimp whose hull and tail unit were modified for research connected with the Shetland flying-boat programme. The coming of that huge aircraft gave a tremendous boost to MAEE, but its life here was shortlived. Before performance testing was complete sudden disaster overtook it. Early in the morning of January 28 1946 an air duct overheated and very quickly parts of the hull caught fire. Before anything could be done to save the Shetland it was burnt out and sank at its mooring. A huge pall of smoke drifted out to sea, virtually marking the end of the British military flying-boat. As if to rub salt in the wound a few Solents retired here after BOAC use for storage, and the two Seafords, here for tests, were abandoned for MAEE disbanded on July 31 1950.

There was a brief re-acquaintance with boats, the USAF using the waterlane for water training with their SA-16 rescue Albatrosses. The station closed on August 20 1962.

Visit Felixstowe now and one sees a vast container depot and a long quayside along the tideway. The area east of the port, once partly grassed and where some of the experimental sheds were built, has now become a concreted area for container vehicles. The largest of the three hangars is used for storage. Set in the roof still are large gantry cranes once used for lifting engines from the boats. One of the massive hooks can still be seen. The central, smaller hangar has for some time housed giant rolls of paper, for Felixstowe has been the entry port for most of the country's newsprint. Remains can be seen within the hangar of the old workshops

site. This hangar has been dismantled and replaced by a new passenger terminal. An addition has been built on to the control tower, which otherwise remains in excellent condition although it is now well back from the waterfront.

The dock basin, the old harbour — once the lair of MTBs and ASR launches — is still much in use. From 1956 to 1961 a detachment of two Whirlwind HAR 2 helicopters of 'B' Flight, 22 Squadron, was stationed in the large hangar.

What a magnificent sight, 'Mercury' on the back of 'Maia'. The central hangar was dismantled in July 1978 to make way for a new passenger terminal, sad to say (IWM).

In April 1946 my lifelong friend Alan Wright and I made our first post-war spotting sortie to Felixstowe — to swoon over those Bv 13s close by the now gone metal fence. I had another desire. In 1935, in my destructive youth, I had managed to contrive my peephole in the high fence which led by the rear of the big black hangar, behind which towered a magnificent Blackburn Perth. Was that peephole still there, one which had brought such magic moments? Indeed, it was — but there was no flying boat to view. All that was left were the memories of long ago.

Feltwell, Norfolk

TL710900. To left of B1112 at Feltwell village

Feltwell, which lies on the edge of the Fens, certainly has been an 'action station'. Early on July 8 1941, Squadron Leader Widdowson of 75 Squadron was returning from Münster over the Ijsselmeer when a Bf 110 attacked. The rear gunner of Wellington L7818, hit in the foot, fired at the fighter, sending it off out of control. Fire broke out near the bomber's starboard engine and, fed by fuel from a fractured pipe, threatened the entire wing. Sergeant J.A. Ward left his co-pilot's seat and made aft. The crew made a hole amidships in the fuselage and tried to douse the fire, even emptying the coffee in their Thermos flask. They were warned to prepare to abandon the aircraft, at which point Sergeant Ward offered to try to smother the flames with an engine cover left by chance in the Wellington.

He was reluctant to wear his parachute for fear its bulk tore him from the aircraft, but accepted it and then was tied by a cord to the geodetic frame. He had decided to slide out on to the wing to put out the blaze. Ward squeezed through the astro hatch, then attached his parachute before making foot holes in the fabric for the perilous journey. By supreme effort he succeeded in smothering part of the wing fire. He was unsuccessful in putting out the blaze in the pipe line, but since most of the fabric was burnt away from it the future was brighter for them all. Satisfied that he had done his best, he made his way back into the aircraft.

For the crew anxiety would remain, brought to a climax later when petrol in the wing again ignited. Widdowson landed at Feltwell, and for his selfless courage Sergeant Ward received the Victoria Cross.

Feltwell, its bold 'C' Type hangars still very evident across the Fens, opened in April 1937, as part of 3 Group. On April 19 1937 Harrows of 214 Squadron arrived form Scampton. On April 26 'B' Flight detached itself to become 37 Squadron, also Harrow-equipped, as an interim measure before both squadrons received their first Wellington 1s on May 6 1939.

On August 27 1939 37 Squadron mobilised and 214, a reserve squadron, moved

One of 75 Squadron's Wellingtons in the cold winter of 1940/41 (via Chris Ashworth).

to Methwold. The war was six hours old when six crews of 37 Squadron left to attack warships off Heligoland. Bad light and approaching darkness defeated them. Although they flew sweeps over the North Sea, it was December 15 before they tried again. The sorties were fruitless. On December 22 they tried once more. The enemy, aware of the Wellingtons' undefended beam, had fighters waiting. For 80 miles they pestered the bombers and only one of the six crews returned.

On April 4 1940 the RNZAF Heavy Bomber Flight, flying Wellingtons, became 75 Squadron. As soon as Norway was violated 37 and 75 Squadrons went into action, trying to locate the *Scharnhorst*, operating off Norway and bombing the Danish airfield at Aalborg. Late on the afternoon of April 30 two pairs of Wellingtons from 37 Squadron set off to bomb Stavanger. The first pair dived in and raced away followed by enemy fighters. The second two then zoomed to the target, getting away at sea level pursued by Bf 109s, one of which was claimed. The other bomber climbed into cloud chased by Bf 110s which ten times made quarter attacks, and did not give up the chase until 70 miles from home shore. Amazingly it was not hit, but two crews

Venturas occupied Feltwell late 1942. 'K' King of 464 Squadron is seen in 1943 with 15 sorties to her credit (via R. Kitching).

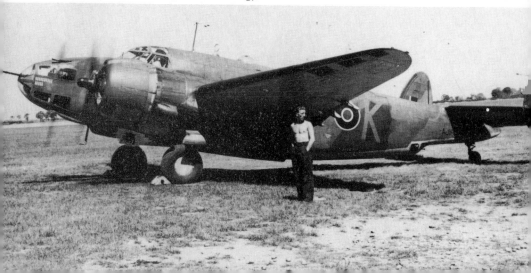

were missing.

On the night of May 10 Waalhaven was bombed by Feltwell's Wellingtons and general support to the Allies was given at night. On June 11 six crews were ordered to Salon in France, but never allowed to bomb Italy as was intended. A hectic round of difficult operations followed.

In June Feltwell's Wellingtons were among those which dropped phosphorus strips into the Black Forest area hoping to start large fires — or tempt a German into pocketing a souvenir which would burst into flames and singe his person. For the Dutch they had better offerings, small bags of tea and sweets for the children. But there was little merriment on most operations carried out at great risk and well into the Fatherland.

L7781 was being bombed-up on August 3 1940 when a fuse ignited in a photo flash in an aircraft with 600 gallons of fuel aboard plus six 500 lb bombs. Four of the latter exploded and splinters rained on N2937 which burst into flames.

During the autumn the enemy mounted intruder patrols in earnest and on October 27 set ablaze one of Feltwell's hangars and secured hits on an air raid shelter.

To increase Middle East strength 37 Squadron flew to Malta between November 8 and 13. Their place was taken by 57 Squadron which arrived on November 18, despatched its earliest Wellington sorties on January 13, and first went to Berlin on March 23 1941. Based at Feltwell, the squadron dispersed its aircraft at Methwold.

Meanwhile, the enemy had again been attracted to the station, dropping a bomb near the bomb dump on February 3 and attacking again, by flare light, on March 1/2. Five days later a Dornier raced across the aerodrome strafing as it went, and after an attack on the next night 22 craters dotted the flying ground. A few moments after midnight on May 11 incendiaries rained down on No 1 Hangar which was set on fire. Unexploded high explosives were later found, and there were three craters to fill on the tarmac.

Wellington raids continued at a fast pace and in July a DSO was awarded to Flying Officer Pritchard whose badly damaged Wellington skidded to a wheels-up landing. Both squadrons participated in many major raids of the period and, in January 1942, began to re-equip with Wellington IIIs, taking them into action during the 'Channel Dash' on February 12. Then came Lübeck, Rostock, and the 'Thousand Plan' raids when Feltwell's

two squadrons won the honour of despatching 37 Wellingtons, the highest number of aircraft operated by any one station on May 30, and managed 39 for the Essen raid. As a sideline, 75 Squadron maintained its ability to deliver gas attack, the only squadron in the Group so trained.

Summer 1942 saw the arrival in quantity of the Lockheed Vega Ventura, a bomber based on the Hudson and one forced upon 2 Group as a Blenheim replacement. On August 15 No 2 Group took over Feltwell, 75 Squadron moving to Mildenhall. Then, on September 4, 57 Squadron also left Methwold. Long the home of New Zealanders, this link would be retained when 487 Squadron formed here on August 15 1942, and then came Australians manning 464 Squadron which formed in September.

These squadrons took four months to work up, but when they went into action they did so spectacularly, on Sunday December 6. In mid-morning the station launched a fleet of 30 Venturas all carrying incendiaries and bound for the Philips works at Eindhoven. In immaculate formation they crossed Feltwell and flew low over the sea to avoid radar detection. Exactly on time they went into the attack, leaving the factory a mass of flames.

Thereafter these unwanted bombers were used for *Circus* daylight operations over Occupied territories until April 1943. There had been a brief interlude when Dutchmen of 320 Squadron had been stationed here and at Methwold, but 3 Group, forced out of stations needed for 8 Group, again obtained Feltwell. No 192 (Special Duty) Squadron and the BDU arrived form Gransden. Mosquitoes and Wellington Xs of 192 Squadron began snooping on enemy radio transmissions during bomber raids and the BDU continued to develop bombing aids, equipment and techniques. Among the unusual aircraft they tested were a Vengeance, a Liberator and a Marauder, all rare sights in RAF hands at this time in Britain. On September 14 1943, 1473 RCM Flight, 80 Wing, arrived for operations under 3 Group.

Upon deciding 3 Group should have Lancasters, No 3 Lancaster Finishing School was established at Feltwell at the turn of the year after 192 Squadron, the BDU and 1473 Flight had moved out. Lancaster training commenced in December and, with sufficient crews trained, ended in January 1945. This freed Feltwell again for the BDU which, before the war ended, had begun testing the Lincoln bomber, produced the black and white scheme for bombers of Tiger Force and initiated RAF trials of in-flight refuelling, testing one of the saddle tank Lancasters in the process.

After the closure of BDU the station was thoroughly cleaned for post-war use, 1688 BDTF, which arrived on February 26 1945, leaving for Wyton on March 19 1946. Then No 3 Flying Training School arrived with Tiger Moths and Harvards, the latter soon being replaced by Prentices. In 1949 the Tiger Moths withdrew. At the end of 1954 Provosts began to replace Prentices and served until the school closed in April 1958.

On May 1 1958 two groups of six Provosts left Feltwell. A farewell beat-up by a Valetta virtually brought flying to an end. Feltwell was later used as a Thor base for 77 Strategic Missile Squadron, until their missiles' vulnerability forced these to be discarded. It has served for WRAF training and been used for signals purposes, and remains an RAF station.

Fersfield, Suffolk

TM080850. 4 miles NE South Lopham on A1066

Fersfield is well tucked away. Maybe this had something to do with its choice as a base for personnel involved in Operation *Aphrodite*. It was at Fersfield that the USAAF and US Navy worked upon a joint scheme to employ 'war weary' bombers, radio controlled by escorting fighters. The heavily laden, aged bombers could thus be directed against heavily defended precision targets by the fighters. Operations were limited, partly because such targets were relatively few and could better be attacked conventionally. When word leaked out to those living around about what was going on it caused no mean alarm, and a lengthy flight path to the coast was also in evidence.

The Americans moved out late in 1944. Then the station was taken over by 2 Group TAF, RAF, becoming a training and holding camp for its crews. No 2 Group Support Unit arrived in mid-December 1944 and flew a few operations from here using Mitchells before resuming their primary role.

Fersfield came into prominence in March 1945. To avoid flying over Germany on a spectacular daylight raid Mosquitoes of 21, 464 and 487 Squadrons arrived. Escorted from here by Mustangs of 64 and 126 Squadrons, they made the famous low-level attack on the Shell House, Gestapo HQ in Copenhagen, on March 21 1945.

After the war squadrons of 2 Group began arriving for armament training, No 180 in June 1945 and Nos 605, 140 and 613 in July. Then, on August 1 1945, No 2 Group Disbandment Centre formed from the GSU and through the unit squadrons of 2 Group passed to wind down. No 2 Group Training Flight was also in residence at this time and when it closed in December 1945 Fersfield ended its active days.

Flixton, Suffolk
See Bungay

Foulsham, Norfolk
TG029265. E of Foulsham village, off A1067

This was an unconventional operation. Whatever else, the Mitchell was not a low-level strike aircraft, it was too slow and clumsy. Yet when 98 and 180 Squadrons entered battle on January 11 1943, they did so with a roof height attack on Ghent/Terneuzen, from Foulsham. Flak was heavy and, as the bombers and their unusual escort of Mustangs, best at low level, retired, FW 190s raced in. Three Mitchells out of 12 were shot down.

Foulsham opened in May 1942, joining 2 Group the following month. It was far from ready to receive its squadrons and not until October did 98 and 180 Squadrons bring their aircraft in from Massingham. Foulsham would always be remembered as the first Mitchell operational station, for here the squadrons worked up, plagued with gun and turret problems. Indeed, these were so bad that the squadrons had to be withdrawn from a share in the December Philips raid, although 180 Squadron managed ASR patrols on December 8, the first operational sorties by RAF Mitchells.

Turret and gun troubles retarded Mitchell operations until May. Training had been hindered, too, by the poor state of the muddy airfield where accommodation was primitive. This did not prevent Horsa gliders arriving for storage, where No 12 Glider MU was situated for a year.

By May 1943 both Mitchell squadrons were training to fly in box formations and on the 11th six crews of 180 Squadron set off for Boulogne, but were thwarted by bad weather. Next day 98 Squadron successfully raided the same target. On May 15 and 16 they bombed Caen airfield, 180

Squadron flying its first *Circus* on May 16 and attacking Tricqueville. A large number of enemy fighters rose to give battle, but the Mitchells all returned safely to Foulsham. Thereafter both squadrons flew *Circuses* and *Ramrods* when the weather permitted. By mid-August 180 Squadron had flown 17 operations. The long haul to the south was time- and nerve-consuming, and to be better placed for operations running up to D-Day both squadrons flew out, aircraft going singly for security reasons, to Dunsfold on August 18/19, having flown their first large scale 24-aircraft operation on August 12. The feeling in July had been that the Mitchell might be better in the Middle East. Indeed, 98 Squadron flew to Honiley in July for range trials, but the idea was abandoned.

Vacant Foulsham was taken over by 3 Group on September 1. On the same day No 514, the second Lancaster I squadron in the Group, formed here. Providing crews for Stirling-orientated 3 Group had caused 1678 Flight to form, and this moved to Foulsham on September 16 to be on hand to supply crews for 514 Squadron. It took them two months to reach operational status and, on November 3/4 1943, six Lancasters commenced operations, two going to Düsseldorf and four mining. Not for long did they operate out of Foulsham for, in a general shake up, both units moved to Waterbeach on November 23.

The need to base 3 Group Lancaster Finishing School at Feltwell meant it must lose its operational commitment. So, on November 25, No 192 Squadron left for Foulsham. This highly specialised squadron was flying Halifaxes, Mosquito IVs and Wellington Xs all specially fitted out with listening equipment to snoop on German radio and radar transmission. On December 7 100 Group took over Foulsham and snatched 192 Squadron in the process, the unit being enlarged on December 12 when 1473 Flight, which had been similarly employed, arrived from Little Snoring to become its 'C' Flight. Backing the squadron, the Special Duty Radar Development Unit arrived in mid-April 1944 and became the Bomber Support Development Unit on May 1. It stayed until December 23 1944, and used Mosquitoes. The Americans needed similar intelligence material and, from August 1944 to early 1945, a detachment of two-seater P-38s was stationed at Foulsham.

Once BSDU had left the station Halifax IIIs of 462 Squadron RAAF arrived from 4 Group on December 27 1944, trained in the use of special equipment, and commenced operations on March 13 1945.

No 192 Squadron played a vital part in the bomber offensive from 1943. Operating widely over occupied territory and Germany, its crews listened to enemy radio chatter and discovered frequencies of these and radar equipment. They snooped upon the airborne radar of night fighters, jammed VHF transmissions and afforded RAF control of German fighters. By summer 1944 they were operating by day and night, and the squadron was, on April 9 1945, the last to fly the Mosquito IV operationally when Mosquitoes jammed enemy R/T.

Foulsham's value was greatly extended when, in 1944, the main NE/SW runway was fitted with FIDO equipment to allow operations in misty weather.

The war over, both squadrons disbanded, 192 on August 22 1945 and 462 on September 24, then the station passed to Care & Maintenance under 40 Group in 1945. The RAF soon vacated it, but the station was not sold off. In 1954-1955 the USAF based a special signals unit there.

Runways, 'T' Type hangars, the perimeter track and the water tower all remain among the farm land. Flying has not ceased, for often a crop-spraying Piper Pawnee can be seen about its business in the summer months.

An aerial view of Foulsham taken on January 31 1946 (DoE).

Fowlmere, Cambridgeshire

TL415440. By B1368

It is memory now, the airfield — or should it be airfields? — at Fowlmere. The first opened as a training establishment in 1918, ending its days as a store place for hefty HP 0/400s in hangars like those still seen at Duxford but which were demolished in 1923.

The second airfield was on a different site, and quickly developed in the spring of 1940. Possibly the Germans had rapid knowledge of it, for in mid-June 1940 they rained incendiaries on to a field at nearby Thriplow in the first bombing of Cambridgeshire.

Strange what one's personal recollections of such places as Fowlmere hold. It is the rare sight, one afternoon in July 1943, of one of those beautiful DH 90 Dragonflies in RAF markings taking off across the Royston road that I always recall when passing the site of the airfield.

It was originally known as G.1 (each fighter airfield having a letter and number allocated for its satellite at this time) and opened in June 1940. Spitfires of 19 Squadron, Duxford, began to disperse here on July 1. Apart from tents nothing else marked it out as an airfield at this time. Exciting Spitfires these were, each armed with two 20 mm cannon. But they were there only three days before 19 Squadron returned to Duxford to make way for Defiants of 264 Squadron, also being dispersed. Recovering from its recent mauling, '264' was working back to operational state, detaching Sections for convoy patrols out of Martlesham and standing by for action before leaving for Kirton-in-Lindsay on July 23 1940.

On July 25 19 Squadron resumed using Fowlmere, sending Sections to Coltishall for East Coast patrols.

During August, 19 Squadron was partly dispersed at Fowlmere where the Spitfire IBs stood ready for the action which came on August 19, when Green Section claimed three Bf 110s. The squadron engaged Bf 109s on the 24th and on August 31 rose to protect Debden and Duxford during large-scale enemy activity in the area.

Through September and October Spitfires of 19 Squadron flew as part of the 'Big Wing', usually staying away from the parent station during the day because so many aircraft daily assembled at Duxford. One cannot segregate '19' from Duxford. In those days it was synonymous with the station, whence it fully returned in November 1940. Hurricanes of 310 Squadron as well as 19's Spitfires now dispersed at Fowlmere (now known as WA1), but it soon became the permanent base of 19 Squadron which moved in on February 6 1941 as AFDU needed more space at Duxford.

Standbys, interception patrols, sector patrols, reinforcement flights into 11 Group to replace fighters operating daily over France, these were the daily routine for the squadron that defended Cambridgeshire.

In May 1941 it ventured south to commence sweeps across the Channel, taking part in a *Circus* for the first time on May 21. Enemy reaction was spasmodic and it was not until June 23 that, during a day away at West Malling, the Fowlmere Spitfires tangled with Bf 109s, claiming two destroyed. Thereafter action became more intense, 19 Squadron being engaged in battle against Bf 109s near St Omer on June 27. Then, as ever, back to Fowlmere in the evening, to a strange sensation, surely, for the peaceful home with few huts and now some blister hangars was so remote from the day's swift battle.

Offensive operations continued through July and August 1941. On August 12 the squadron had an early call. It flew to Ipswich, whence it departed to meet, off Holland, returning Blenheims which had ventured to Cologne in daylight. A quick, fierce battle ensued off Schouwen. Then, on August 16, 19 Squadron took off from Fowlmere for the last time, flying to a new home at Matlaske.

No 19's place was taken by the third US Eagle squadron whose Hurricane IIBs arrived at Duxford in August and moved almost immediately to Fowlmere. Here the Americans saw little activity and spent a brief time at Wittering before moving to Eglinton, Northern Ireland, on October 4.

A new squadron, No 154, formed at Fowlmere on November 17 1941, flying Spitfire IIs. It, too, flew forward base patrols from Coltishall and Swanton Morley, having made its first scramble from Fowlmere in February 1942. It moved to Church Stanton on May 7. A vacancy was followed by 174 Squadron at Fowlmere in July.

Then 'Treble One' arrived with their Spitfires on September 27 1942 and almost immediately went on leave. On their return the squadron personnel were given tropical kit, said goodbye to their

Spitfires and left by train to their port of embarkation for North Africa.

Auster 1s of 655 Squadron were briefly based here in February-March 1943 having arrived from Gatwick. Then came Fowlmere's part in Exercise *Spartan* testing the mobility of the tactical element of Fighter Command. This brought 411 Squadron's Spitfire VBs to Fowlmere for a brief stay in March 1943.

Their place was taken on March 19 by 2 Squadron's Mustang 1s from Bottisham. Ten days later they commenced *Lagoons* off Texel, operating quite intensively during April, in pairs, before returning to their native Sawbridgeworth on April 27.

The task now was to extend the airfield, adding two Sommerfeld track runways and a 'T' hangar to the blister hangars still here, in order for Fowlmere to become Station 378 USAAF.

Early in April 1944 the Americans arrived with P-51Bs and the 339th Fighter Group flew its first sweep on April 30. Five weeks of fighter escorts were followed by mixed operations including heavy and medium bomber escorts, interdictor operations and ground strafing. On September 10 the Group was awarded a Distinguished Unit Citation for, whilst primarily engaged in protecting bombers, it had made a noteworthy strike on Erding airfield. Next day the Group was astonishingly awarded a second Distinguished Unit Citation for providing bomber escort during a Munich raid, and strafing an airfield near Karlsruhe. It provided fighter cover over Normandy's beaches and strafed during the St Lô break-out. The Group's P-51Ds gave cover during the airborne landings in Holland as well as flying offensive patrols during the Ardennes battle and also during the Rhine crossing. Final sorties were flown on April 21 1945.

This Fighter Group, the 339th, made very heavy claims of over 200 enemy aircraft shot down and 400 destroyed on the ground during 264 operations.

After the war the green-nosed P-51s were still a common sight, but by August 1945 the unit was winding down fast and eventually left for America in October that year. Fowlmere withered away by the end of 1945 and was soon farmland again, being sold in 1957.

Framlingham, Suffolk

TM330605. 1 mile SW Great Glenham, off B1190 E of Framlingham

Mighty was the explosion. It rocked the countryside around, damaging every house in Parham. Heavily laden with bombs and fuel, the B-17 of the 390th ('J in a square') struggled to get airborne. December 27 1944 had unfolded as an icy day when, shortly before 9 am, the B-17 was forced down, possibly due to ice accretion on take-off. The bomber careered into the village centre, the entire crew dying in the holocaust. Miraculously, not one of the inhabitants suffered beyond minor injuries, but every house was damaged. Mercifully, such disasters were comparatively few.

Framlingham was built during 1942-1943, the 95th Bomb Group ('B in a square') arriving here in May 1943. Barely had they entered action when disaster struck. On June 13 1943 the 8th AF despatched two forces of bombers, one to Bremen and the other — led by the 95th — to Kiel. As the 95th led into the attack enemy fighters pounced upon the Fortresses and only half the force survived. Indeed, this meant that the Group had, within a few days, lost half its aircrew

Bombs in plenty ready to be loaded on B-17s at Framlingham (USAF).

Framlingham's deserted tower sits amid a wheat field.

Many domestic buildings remain at Framlingham as this photograph shows.

strength. Two days after this operation the 95th left for Horham in part to re-establish itself and also because Framlingham was still incomplete.

A month passed, then the 390th Bomb Group arrived, again with B-17s. They flew the first of some 300 operations on August 12 1943 and on the 17th, as part of the 4th Combat Wing, took part in the first shuttle raid on Regensburg, after which they flew on to North Africa. A brave endeavour indeed so soon after entering operations. Soon they were taking part in the general run of attacks on strategic targets, the second highlight coming on October 14 1943 when the Schweinfurt ball bearing works was the target. This was a two-pronged attack with the B-17s of the 3rd Air Division flying a westerly course which brought them into contact with enemy fighters later than was the case with the others of the force. Photographs of the raid showed the 390th's bombing to have been the most accurate, but then came the big fight for, as they flew homewards, German fighters switched their main onslaught on

to B-17s of the 3rd Air Division, pressing home their attacks back to the English Channel. The 390th only lost one of their 15 aircraft, good fortune indeed, for Mission 115 cost 60 B-17s. For their part the 390th were awarded a Distinguished Unit Citation.

Thereafter, often aided by pathfinders, the 390th attacked such targets as marshalling yards at Frankfurt, oil facilities at Zeitz, factories at Mannheim, naval installations at Bremen, and the synthetic oil plant at Merseburg. They gave tactical support to the invasion and, as the war ended, dropped food supplies to the Dutch, having made their final bombing raid on April 20 1945.

In August 1945 the Americans left for home and flying ceased at Framlingham. The nearby village is attractive thanks to its impressive castle. The tower still stands on the airfield site which was finally sold off in 1964. A T2 hangar remains and a number of huts. The perimeter track is available for light aircraft.

Glatton, Cambridgeshire

TL185870. Off A1 11 miles N of Huntingdon, on B660 to E

Built by US Army engineers during 1943 and having two T2 hangars, unobtrusively sited away from the A1, Glatton was taken over by the USAAF at the end of that year. The 457th Bomb Group arrived late in January 1944 flying B-17Gs, mostly unpainted, and soon identified by the 'U in a triangle' on their fins. Their first operation took place during the 'Big Week' on February 21 1944, when they attacked German aircraft factories.

Thereafter the Group concentrated on strategic targets until June 1944 when they participated in the softening up raids immediately prior to the Normandy landings, and bombed defences along the Cherbourg peninsula. During June 1944 they attacked airfields, roads and railways, before returning to strategic bombing in July 1944. Such raids continued until the final operation, the 237th, on April 20 1945. The Group then took part in Operation *Exodus*, the repatriation of POWs from France and Austria, before leaving for the USA in June.

On July 5 the base passed from the 1st Air Division Substitution Unit (which occupied vacant US bases after the Groups left) to 3 Group RAF Bomber Command, to be prepared for the trooping of personnel between Glatton and the Middle East. It was planned to handle

20,000 personnel a month both on leave and duty.

Late in August 1945 Liberators and Lancasters began to use the station, but not at the forecast rate for, by the end of December, only 1,149 personnel had been flown out, 174 in. The station passed to Care & Maintenance on April 30 1946 and was closed soon after.

Now it is known as Conington Airport and use is made of part of the main runway for light aircraft. A memorial to the 457th can be seen in Conington churchyard.

An aerial photograph of the site of Glatton taken on June 14 1967 (DoE).

Gosfield, Essex

TL770315. W of A1017 at Gosfield

The cheek of it! On the very day that Gosfield opened in autumn 1943 an enemy raider dropped a stick of bombs across the airfield. Such raids, usually by Me 410s or Ju 188s, directed against East Anglian airfields, had little more than nuisance value. Only two bombs landed on Gosfield.

Americans of the 9th AF arrived on October 22 and the 365th Fighter Group late in December. They trained with P-47s commencing tactical operations over France in February 1944. They gave fighter support to the B-26 Groups and carried out strafing and dive-bombing against targets in France before moving to Beaulieu, Hampshire, in March 1944. The 397th Bomb Group spent ten days here in April 1944 before proceeding to Rivenhall.

Their place was quickly taken by the 410th Bomb Group which brought along

A-20s, employing them in tactical bombing, but not in the ideal way to employ the A-20. The 9th AF flew them in formations of 12 and multiples of that number, or in boxes of six stepped up in 2 Group fashion. Operations commenced in May 1944, French and Belgian targets being attacked in the invasion build up. Coastal defences, V-sites and marshalling yards were often targets when the A-20s slotted into huge *Ramrod* operations, taking part with B-26s, and RAF Bostons and Mitchells, all heavily fighter-escorted.

Then came direct tactical support to Allied forces in France with attacks on reinforcements, railways, bridges and roads, especially to assist the break-outs from Caen and St Lô. Such duties continued ahead of the advance until, by September 1944, the ground forces were beyond the effective range of the A-20s. The 410th then took its aircraft to Coulommiers, France.

Gosfield, like other 9th AF bases, became clear of aircraft. Some such stations were soon housing squadrons of the RAF's 38 Group but there were more than needed, and some were, in any case, unsuitable. Gosfield was used briefly by Wethersfield's Stirlings and Martinets of 1677 Target Towing Flight in January 1945, then became a base for part of the mounting of one big operation, the last large-scale airborne assault in Europe. This was Operation *Varsity*. Dakotas of 46 Group were still based well back from the front and so three squadrons of Dakotas, Nos 271, 512 and 575, were briefly sited at Gosfield for *Varsity*, a swarm of these transports taking-off early on March 24 1945 carrying paratroopers for the massive Rhine crossing. After that Gosfield was quiet again, soon redundant, and closed late in 1945.

An A-20G airborne from Gosfield in 1944 (USAF).

Gransden Lodge, Cambridgeshire

TL293555. SE of Little Gransden on B1946 W of A14

Relatively few Canadian squadrons flew from East Anglian airfields. An exception was No 405 (Vancouver) Squadron which for two years operated from Gransden, a typical wartime station in appearance, well dispersed and tucked away in the countryside.

It opened as satellite to Tempsford early in 1942, No 1418 Flight arriving from the parent station (where it had been based since March 1) on April 8 1942 as the first unit to use Gransden. At almost the same time the Wireless Investigation Flight, detached from 109 Squadron, arrived, becoming 1474 Flight on July 4 1942. Both units flew Wellingtons, the former conducting trials of *Gee,* the navigation aid. No 1474 Flight became 192 Squadron on January 4 1943 shortly after first receiving Wellington Xs and a few Mosquito IVs.

No 1418 Flight conducted various trials with bombers and on July 20 1942 was absorbed by the Bombing Development Unit which then formed with four heavy bombers (two Stirlings and two Halifaxes), six Wellington IIIs and a Proctor. Trials of a technical nature were conducted by BDU, including a lot of work with H2S radar and radar for fighter defence in bombers, so the station played an important part in the bomber campaign. This unit and 192 Squadron moved to Feltwell early in April 1943, Gransden then switching from 3 to 8 Group and becoming the second satellite of Oakington on April 15.

On April 19 the Pathfinder Navigational Training Unit formed at Gransden equipped with Halifax IIs and moved to Upwood and Warboys between June 11 and 19 1943, the transfer being brought about because 405 Squadron had arrived with 20 Halifax IIs in April 1943, joining the Pathfinder Force. They flew their first operation from Gransden, against Duisburg, on April 26. In August 1943 the squadron began to operate Lancasters then, from the start of September, flew only Lancaster operations. The most famous Canadian-built Lancaster, KB700 'Ruhr Express', flew 50 sorties from Gransden.

Whilst runway work was undertaken at Bourn, 'B' Flight of 97 Squadron lodged at Gransden in August-September 1943, then left the station to the Canadians who intensively operated in the 'backer-up'

role to the end of hostilities. No 1517 BAT Flight also used Gransden until December 1943.

On October 25 1944 142 Squadron reformed equipped with Mosquito XVIs as part of the LNSF. As the war was ending the unit took delivery of the first Mosquito 35s to enter service but their stay was brief for 142 Squadron disbanded on September 28 1945.

To group the Mosquitoes 692 Squadron moved in from Graveley on June 4 1945, replacing 405 Squadron which left for Linton-on-Ouse on May 26 1945. No 602 Squadron disbanded on September 20 1945. In December 1945 No 53 Squadron Liberators arrived, but moved to Upwood in February 1946. The station then lay vacant. The main runway, 04/22, 2,000 yards long and 50 yards wide, remained in use for emergency landings into the 1950s.

In 1947 a small air display was held at the airfield. It brought to light the existence of a strange form dumped by the approach road. This was the last mortal remnant of the Lancaster II prototype DT 810. It has still not quite disappeared since I kept a small piece for posterity.

Graveley, Cambridgeshire

TL238645. W of Graveley village off A14 4 miles S of Huntingdon

It still seems unbelievable that such a small aeroplane as the Mosquito could have carried such a large bomb as a 4,000 lb 'cookie', which represented one fifth of the all-up weight of the combination. But carry that load Mosquitoes did, and many times. It was from Graveley that this heavy load was first taken into battle.

De Havilland had suggested modifying the Mosquito's weapons bay for the 4,000 pounder in April 1943. Within an astonishing seven weeks the trial installation was ready for tests, and very soon 30 conversion sets for the Mosquito IV had been produced.

The original intention was that 627 Squadron should pioneer the new Mosquito, but after a short time, on February 2 1944, the first two examples arrived at Graveley where, on January 1 1944, 692 Squadron had formed as part of the new Light Night Striking Force of 8 Group.

Shake-down was rapid. On February 23 three Mosquitoes set off for Düsseldorf each carrying one of the large bombs. The rest is history for, from that time henceforth, the Mosquito did not merely sting, it bit hard and with keen accuracy. Many a German city felt the punch of Graveley's Mosquitoes, progressively from the converted Mk IVs and, from March 1944, from Mk XVIs. By day and night they later operated, sometimes when the rest of Bomber Command was grounded.

Graveley had FIDO which 8 Group made good use of when fog descended over the 8 Group stations. Almost to the final day of conflict 692 Squadron operated.

Graveley came into use as a satellite of Tempsford when 161 (Special Duties) Squadron arrived from Newmarket on March 1 1942, 'A' Flight equipped with Lysanders and 'B' Flight with Whitley Vs. The latter operated from here and Tempsford and the Lysanders from forward bases, until the squadron moved to Tempsford in April 1942. On August 4 1942 Graveley came under the control of Wyton and the Pathfinder Force, 1504 BAT Flight bringing its Oxfords in for a week's stay before moving to Honington on August 14, the day before No 35 Squadron's Halifax IIs began to move into the station from Linton-on-Ouse and 4 Group. Wyton had lost Alconbury to 8 Group on August 12 and the new station therefore took its place.

The Halifaxes came to form part of the backer-up and target marking flare force. On August 18/19 ten Halifaxes began such operations, raiding Flensburg, and thereafter operated in increasing strength. The squadron was only too well aware of the limitations of the early Halifax. In the spring of 1943, it received some of the first Halifaxes with modified tails and noses, the Mk II srs i 'Z' Type being used first before the Mk II srs ia with clear nose came into use. The squadron took part in the Ruhr raids, attacked Peenemünde then went into the Battle of Berlin. Station HQ opened at Graveley in June 1943 when it was divorced from Wyton.

On October 4 1943 35 Squadron received its first Halifax III and introduced this mark to operations on December 20, eventfully. Twenty-one Halifaxes (four Mk IIIs) were despatched to Frankfurt. On circling prior to landing, Squadron Leader J. Sale, DSO, had a target indicator explode. He climbed and five of the crew baled out, the mid-upper gunner being unable to do so since his parachute had been destroyed by fire. Sale landed the burning aircraft and taxied off the runway, then the occupants left it rapidly. When they were 200 yards away it exploded.

Mk IIs and IIIs operated alongside each other until, on March 6 1944, re-equip-

ment with Lancaster IIIs commenced, aircraft flying in from Wyton, and 97 Squadron. Conversion was rapid, the last Halifax operation being flown on March 1/2 and the first all-Lancaster raid, on Stuttgart, was mounted on March 15/16 1944.

By June 1944 35 Squadron was providing Master Bombers leading attacks and on June 25 flew its first daylight raid, against Motorgueil. Thereafter day and night raids were mixed to the end of the war, the final operation coming against guns at Wangerooge on the afternoon of April 1945. The squadron then switched to Operations *Manna* and *Exodus*.

No 692 Squadron had meanwhile flown intensively on operations, making its last attack on May 2 1945. It moved to Gransden on June 4 1945, leaving 35 Squadron to settle to a peacetime routine whilst expecting to be part of Tiger Force. In June 1945 227 Squadron moved in with Lancasters and disbanded here on September 5. No 115 Squadron flying Lancasters arrived in September 1945.

During spring 1946 35 Squadron re-equipped with black and white Lancaster B 1 (FE)s originally intended for the Far East but now replacing older aircraft. An overseas commitment remained part of the squadron's role. In the summer of 1946 35 Squadron was often seen flying in formation for it was soon to engage upon a prestigious tour. In July-August 1946 the unit visited the USA, the first RAF Goodwill Mission there. Their stay at Graveley on return was brief. In September 1946 the station closed and 35 and 115 Squadrons moved to Stradishall.

Graveley was put on Care & Maintenance and held thus for a considerable time. In the mid-1950s it came back into use as a Relief Landing Ground for the Vampires of 5 FTS, Oakington, for which purpose it remained available until the late 1950s. It closed on December 1 1968 and has now been returned to agricultural use.

A 4,000 lb 'cookie' awaits loading on to a Mosquito of 692 Squadron, part of the Light Night Striking Force.

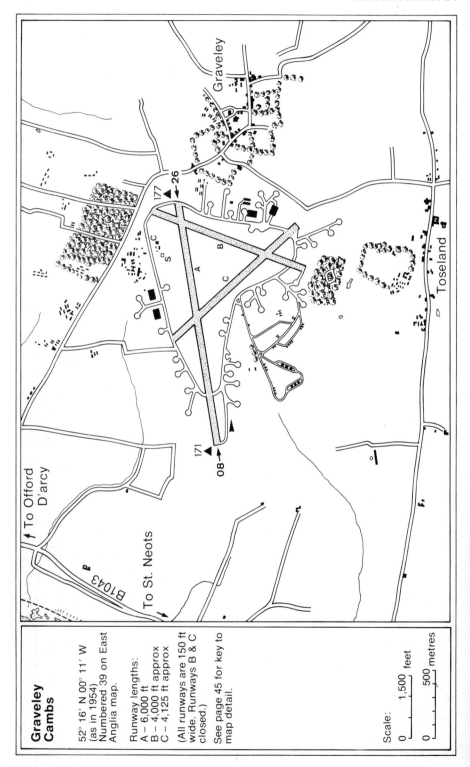

**Graveley
Cambs**

52° 16' N 00° 11' W
(as in 1954)
Numbered 39 on East
Anglia map.

Runway lengths:
A – 6,000 ft
B – 4,000 ft approx
C – 4,125 ft approx

(All runways are 150 ft
wide. Runways B & C
closed.)

See page 45 for key to
map detail.

Scale:

0   1,500   feet

0   500 metres

Great Ashfield, Suffolk

TM010665. 2½ miles NE Elmswell, N of A45(T)

Great Ashfield opened in March 1943, the intention being that a flight of 1665 Conversion Unit would form here in April 1943, nucleus of this new unit. It would remain until the rest of the unit formed here or elsewhere, then leave. In the event 1665 CU did not form here, although the first aircraft to touch down on the runways were Stirlings, of 1651 Conversion Unit, which used the airfield for circuits before the Americans arrived in June 1943.

The occupants between then and August 1945 were B-17s of the 385th Bomb Group ('G in a square'), the Group commencing operations with a raid on Germany on July 17 1943. A month later it was part of the shuttle raid force which bombed Regensburg.

Thereafter the Group's targets lay in Germany, France, Holland, Belgium, Norway and Poland. A number of raids were made on Berlin, and other targets included an aircraft factory at Oschergleben, Marienburg, battery works at Stuttgart, airfields at Beauvais and Chartres, an oil refinery at Ludwigshaven and rail targets at Munich and Oranienburg. The B-17s attacked coastal targets prior to D-Day and choke points on the day of the invasion. They aided the St Lô break-out and took part in repelling the Ardennes offensive.

The Group's second Distinguished Unit Citation was awarded for an operation on May 12 1944 when, leading the 4th Combat Wing, through heavy fighter opposition, it proceeded to bomb an aircraft repair plant at Zwickau where the aim proved very accurate. Coming home the B-17s endured further enemy attacks.

The Group held one distinction, it was the only B-17 Group to lose an aircraft to German bombs in Britain. An intruder bombed Ashfield on May 22/23 1944, hitting a hangar inside which a B-17 was destroyed.

The airfield was returned to the RAF who subsequently had a bomb store here. It was sold for agricultural purposes in 1959-1960. The runways remain fairly intact, and a memorial to the 385th can be found at Great Ashfield church.

Great Dunmow, Essex

TL590255. By Little Easton village

Under overall control of RAF Stradishall,

US Army personnel arrived to build the airfield here, also known as Great Easton, on July 4 1942. It was completed in almost a year to the day, July 1 1943. What was most memorable though was that in the autumn a host of B-26s arrived to be stored alongside roads leading to the airfield. The place seemed to swarm with Marauders, apparently held here for other stations.

The 386th Bomb Group arrived from Boxted on September 24 1943 and almost at once was operating from Dunmow. On October 16 the station passed to the 9th AF. The B-26s often operated within *Ramrods* — attacks planned against precise targets and intended primarily as bombing raids as opposed to fighter-attracting ventures — which often included RAF participation. A *Ramrod* might comprise as many as six parts. Part one was often a Typhoon fighter-bomber raid to put out of action AA guns and fighter bases, or perhaps attack radar stations. Other parts might be formations of RAF Bostons and Mitchells attacking a particular target — bridge, airfield, V-1 site or sites. The B-26s would comprise one or more parts, their basic formation consisting of 18 aircraft often flying in groups of 36 so that common B-26 formations comprised 72 or 108 aircraft. With such numbers involved the operational career of the B-26 bases falls into a similar pattern. Up to November 1943 the targets were mixed — harbours, airfields, some industrial sites. Then the emphasis switched to V-1 sites and supply depots. In February 1943 airfields were prime targets, then came attacks on coastal targets leading up to D-Day. During the Normandy invasion the B-26s gave close battlefield support, then began to attack bridges over the Seine and Loire to make enemy retreat difficult. POL (petrol, oil, lubricants) depots were then attacked and all manner of depots and communications. The B-26 Groups took part in the Falaise battle and in September lent a hand in the reduction of Brest. Next for them came the big upheaval. They moved to France to be nearer the scene of battle. All this was as true of Dunmow's B-26s as of others, the 386th moving to Beaumont-sur-Oise on October 2 1944.

Just as the Marauders were needed nearer the battle scene so it was with the transport and supply squadrons of RAF 38 Group. They were clustered in the south Midlands, which had been a disadvantage when the Arnhem operation was mounted and damaged aircraft — of which there were many — were nursed home far across England. As soon as the terrible wounds of Arnhem were licked the Stirling squadrons were moved to Essex, to be ready for the next venture.

This brought 190 Squadron to Great Dunmow (never Great Easton to the RAF) on October 14 1944 and 620 a few days later. These squadrons were virtually unemployed now, although they flew some supply dropping missions. To give them some operational service the squadrons suddenly found themselves undertaking bombing training, for there was no reason why the Stirling IV could not carry bombs instead of containers. In February they began night bombing of towns fairly close to the front line, so that their role of army support was not removed. Lacking sophisticated radar bombing aids they probably achieved very little. When they were not operating they were training, and by February this involved long flights towing Horsa gliders, as from Dunmow. These flights took them north, and over the sea, long trains of tugs and gliders making an indelible image for many an East Anglian.

The training led to the last big airborne venture, Operation *Varsity*, by which 38 Group and the US 9th AF would assist in the crossing of the Rhine near Wesel. Every aircraft and every available glider was involved, most stations despatching about 60 combinations on what broke as a beautiful sunny, warm March day. During the Arnhem operation the transports had traversed East Anglia, but this time the force was even greater as some US formations took their place in the seemingly never-ending procession to the coast. Losses were minimal and no resupply was required. Instead, the transport squadrons resumed a few dropping operations and had only to transport occupation forces to Norway. From Dunmow the passengers included a group of nurses needed badly in Norway. The operation was not easy for the weather was bad and snowstorms in Norway brought disastrous events.

The Dunmow squadrons then resumed training with some Horsas, took mail to the forces abroad and generally made themselves useful. No 190 Squadron re-equipped with Halifax A VIIs in June 1945 and left for Tarrant Rushton late in November 1945. No 620 Squadron converted to Halifaxes about the same time and late in 1945 left Dunmow posted to Palestine.

For many years Dunmow lay on Care &

Maintenance and in excellent condition, a public road utilising the perimeter track affording an excellent view. It was sold for agricultural use in April 1958.

Great Massingham, Norfolk

TF805235. E of Great Massingham, by road to Rudham

'This afternoon, Blenheims of Bomber Command attacked the German naval base at Heligoland. From this operation, one of our aircraft is missing.'

So often one heard such a simple line on the BBC's evening news bulletin. Unless one had first-hand experience of such an operation one could scarcely imagine just what was involved. But the crews of 107 Squadron at Massingham knew only too well.

Newly arrived at this bleak airfield set alongside one of Norfolk's most idyllic villages, 107 Squadron sent out 12 crews to bomb Heligoland on May 13 1941. Approaching at sea level, they attacked from 300 feet in line abreast, avoiding enemy fire until their withdrawal. Such low-level work was fraught with risk and Sergeant Charney, on his first operation with 107, flew momentarily too low. His port propeller touched the sea and was ripped off, but he made it back to base.

On May 21 the squadron was ordered again to Heligoland. One can imagine the tenseness with which the Blenheims roared off in threes from the grass airfield. Visibility was up to 15 miles in the target area and the enemy, ready for a return match, opened up with AA guns as the formation raced in. Almost half the force of nine was hit and the observer with Sergeant Kenneth Wolstenholme — best known now as a television commentator — was killed outright. Moments after, Sergeant Ratcliffe's Blenheim, its starboard engine burning, came down in the sea. The squadron had gone into the attack at 40-60 feet, dropped four tons of bombs and gained some satisfaction from seeing German football players scatter in all directions. Direct hits were claimed on some guns on the west side of the island. Such operations, so typical of 2 Group's, could have little effect on the outcome of the war, but they kept the enemy on his toes.

Massingham came into use, for 2 Group, in the summer of 1940 as a satellite of West Raynham and No 18 Squadron moved here from the parent station in early September. From here the squadron flew cloud cover raids and night intruders against enemy airfields. Massingham at this time was merely a grass field with a few blister hangars and huts supplemented, like so many satellite airfields, with tented accommodation when needed. On April 2 1941 the squadron moved to the equally primitive airfield at Oulton, satellite to Horsham.

On May 11 1941, 107 Squadron flew its Blenheims into Massingham and an intensive operational phase followed, mainly by day and against shipping and fringe targets. In September most of the squadron was sent to the Middle East where it busied itself whilst leaving Massingham out of the front line.

It was to Massingham that, on May 15 1941, No 90 Squadron brought its Fortress 1s. They were only here, under West Raynham's control, until the end of June.

At the start of 1942, 107 Squadron re-armed with Boston IIIs at Massingham. The squadron's first operation came on March 8 when, in what was to become traditional style, six Bostons led by Squadron Leader Lynn formed up in two stepped boxes of three and, fighter-escorted, made a medium-level raid on Abbeville's marshalling yards. Such raids and night intruding during the Bremen '1,000 bomber' raid on June 25 summarise the effort, 107 Squadron mounting escorted day operations to the end of June 1942. The squadron had a special role in that it was trained for gas spray operations.

July witnessed some very low-level attacks by single aircraft against power stations. In mid-August the squadron was briefly based at Ford to participate in the Dieppe raid when it bombed guns and AFVs. Massingham was the station from which 107 Squadron continued fighter-escorted day operations into late autumn 1942. Then came that 2 Group spectacular, the raid on the Philips works at Eindhoven in which 12 crews participated.

Circuses and *Ramrods* characterised 1943 — plus continued training for possible gas laying. Immediately ahead of 487's disastrous Amsterdam raid of May 3, 107 Squadron attacked the steel works at Ijmuiden. The main concern on all these day raids was the risk of being hit by flak, for enemy fighters rarely reached the bombers as they were screened by large numbers of fighters.

Low-level solo operations requiring skill and courage were again mounted against power stations in July 1943, and on August 8 a large-scale low attack was delivered on the naval stores at Rennes, an all-Boston operation in which rôle the aircraft was ideal. So low had they flown that their commanding officer, the intrepid 'Dicky' England, came home with cable picked up over France streaming from his aircraft. On August 20 107 Squadron flew out of Massingham for the last time, and made for Hartford Bridge.

Frenchmen manning Bostons of 342 Squadron were also at Massingham, having arrived in July 1943, and operated from here until September, when they followed 107 Squadron to Hartford Bridge. This left behind elements of 2 Group's fighter affiliation and gunnery training unit, No 1482 B&G Flight which, from its base at West Raynham, used Massingham for varying purposes at this time. Among the Flight's aircraft were some Mitchells. These were not the first of their type to fly from the station for, when 180 Squadron was forming at West Raynham in October 1942, some of the flying took place from Massingham, whence the squadron eventually moved to Foulsham on October 19 1942.

As soon as the Bostons left in September 1943 the airfield had a facelift. Runways were laid down, the airfield extended and better accommodation was built. It re-opened on April 17 1944 and 1694 Target Towing Flight (later Bomber Defence Training Flight) arrived from Raynham while 1692 Bomber Support Training Flight, using Beaufighters, moved in on May 22 from Little Snoring.

Then, with the Normandy invasion about to begin, 169 Squadron arrived flying Mosquito II night fighters. Within days the squadron was switching to the Mk VI for night operations under 100 Group. It at once proved a very efficient unit and on July 20 1944 was responsible for 100 Group's 100th claim in combat. The squadron flew an intensive night support campaign to the end of the war, equipping with Mosquito 19s in January 1945 whilst retaining some VIs for special purposes. At the end of the war they were dropping napalm bombs on German airfields having lately concentrated on such low-level raids.

The fighting over, 1629 Bomber Support Training Unit disbanded on June 15 1945 and 169 Squadron followed suit on August 10. Massingham passed to 12 Group on August 25 1945 and in October the Central Fighter Establishment arrived, staying here until December 1946. For the next four years the station was available for the use of West Raynham. It was sold in April 1958. There is little to see here now, although the site still has the appearance of once having been an aerodrome.

Great Saling, Essex

See Andrew's Field

Great Sampford, Essex

TL630360. W of village, off B1053

April 17 1942 was a bright, breezy day. Soon after 11.30 am 11 Spitfire VBs of 65 Squadron took off from Sampford, joined 'Treble One' Squadron from Debden, formated with 71 (Eagle) Squadron over Bradwell and flew to Manston. There they made rendezvous with six Bostons which bombed Calais. It was an uneventful operation like so many of 65's whilst they were at Debden's new satellite. There was a somewhat surprising return for, once in Sampford's circuit, following Squadron Leader H.T. Gilbert, the formation inverted their Spitfires and lowered their undercarriages, a curious and memorable sight.

Great Sampford opened in April 1942. On the 4th laying of the metal Sommerfeld runway commenced, 400 men putting down 1,000 yards of tracking in a creditable 12 hours. No 65 Squadron arrived from Debden in the early evening of April 14 after an operational flight.

Thereafter operations came at a pace, usually without interference from the foe. *Ramrod 26* on April 25 brought more action than most. Six Bostons were bombing Dunkirk and 40 FW 190s bore down upon them out of the sun. No 65 went into action, driving some off. Later that day they caught sight of more '190s, but there was no engagement. *Circus 142*, flown on April 27, was more memorable. Over St Omer 50 or 60 FW 190s gave combat and a mêlée resulted, during which two '190s collided. Pilot Officer T.A. Burk, a Rhodesian, claimed two FW 190s as he fought his way home, and Flight Lieutenant Bartley damaged one over the Channel.

In May trouble developed with the runway. The top layer at an intersection had to be removed, although 65 Squadron continued sweeps and escorts throughout the month.

The most eventful operation during 65's stay at Sampford came on June 1. Wing Commander J.A. Gordon led 11 Spitfires to take part in *Circus 177*. South of Bruges a dozen or so enemy aircraft

were spotted and the Debden Wing faced them. The enemy raced off and 65 Squadron turned for home. Near the French coast they were bounced and within minutes Wing Commander Gordon called 'm'aidez', while Sergeant Parak was also shot down. Over the coast an FW 190 shot down Pilot Officer Richards, who was lucky to be picked up 2½ hours later by a naval launch. Sergeant Kopocek, a Czech, was fired upon by anti-aircraft guns, and being wounded was forced to land at Manston. The FW 190s were more than a match for 65's Spitfire VBS.

Between June 15 and 22 1942 Sampford was quiet, with 65 away at Martlesham on a tactical exercise. Then the battle was resumed with *Rodeos, Ramrods* and *Circuses* until June 30 when 65 flew to Hawkinge on another exercise. Next day the ground crews were taken south in two Handley-Page Sparrows. Returning to Sampford on July 7, the squadron was ordered to prepare for overseas, but the order was countermanded and on July 20 they resumed operations. Next day it participated in a mass *Rhubarb* by the Debden Wing, which turned out to be the squadron's last fling from Sampford. It moved out to Gravesend, its place being taken by Spitfire VBs of 616 Squadron which stayed until September 23.

Immediately, 133 (Eagle) Squadron arrived from Biggin Hill and on September 29 paraded at Debden. On that auspicious day the three Eagle squadrons became part of the USAAC's 4th Fighter Group, 133 Squadron being re-designated 336 (Pursuit) Squadron. They left Sampford for Gravesend on October 2, returning on the 19th. At the end of the month the squadron moved into Debden. The 335th Squadron arrived from Martlesham with its 15 Spitfires on November 6 and remained until December 1 when it too went to Debden. Detachments of American personnel remained at Sampford which periodically received Spitfires.

During February 1943 the 4th Fighter Group received its first P-47 Thunderbolts and these from time to time visited Sampford or were dispersed here, but by March 1943 it was being used only for emergency landings. Its days as an operational station were over and in 1943 the RAF Regiment Battle School took over the camp, the station closing at the end of August 1944.

Hadstock, Essex

See Little Walden

Halesworth, Suffolk

TM400795. 2 miles NE Halesworth, off A144. Minor road to Upper Holton runs along perimeter track

As the song goes, 'I remember it well'. Date, March 29 1945, and the huge white amphibian circled low. Catalina flying-boats were always rare in our eastern sky, amphibian versions hitherto unknown. Its lair was Halesworth when, in January 1945, the USAAF began to station OA-10A Amphibian Catalinas for ASR purposes. Lucky, indeed, was the inland viewer to see such an exotic sight, for their theatre of operations was over the sea where the work of RAF ASR squadrons was supplemented.

Halesworth had become an American base in May 1943 and early in July the 56th Fighter Group, already one of the prime fighting units, arrived from Horsham where it had been ousted by B-24s. For ten months the P-47s fought valiantly over Europe, mainly giving bomber escort. During the latter period of their stay at Halesworth the 56th had learnt how profitable it was to attack the enemy on his airfields. In mid-April 1944 the unit left for Boxted.

In its place at Halesworth came the green- and white-tailed B-24s of the 489th Bomb Group which arrived at the start of May and flew its first mission on May 30 1944 against a pre-invasion target. Action came fast for the Group and on June 5 1944 the courage of Lieutenant Colonel Leon R. Vance, Jnr, won him the Medal of Honour. Vance, the Deputy Group Commander, was seriously wounded, and his right foot almost severed. Nevertheless he continued the attack then brought his B-24 back to the English coast where the crew baled out. Vance believed a crewman was still aboard and carefully ditched the crippled bomber to save the other man. Good fortune was with Vance for he was rescued and survived despite his horrific wounds.

Next day was D-Day and the 489th took part in the dawn assault on Normandy, then attacked airfields, railways, V-1 sites, bridges and rail targets.

In July 1944 the Group switched to the strategic offensive, bombing factories, oil refineries and marshalling yards, and took part in the St Lô action. Ludwigs-haven, Magdeburg, Brunswick, Saarbrucken — all had been attacked when, in November 1944, the Group ceased operations and was ordered back to the USA for the Pacific War.

In January 1945 the 5th Emergency Rescue Squadron arrived from Boxted flying 'war weary' P-47s and the rare OA-10As. P-47s carried dinghies and smoke markers with which to mark crews found at sea. It was customary for most USAAF units to hold 'war weary' aircraft, the letters 'WW' being carried on the tails of the aircraft alongside the serial numbers.

In March the unit began to receive a few B-17s fitted to carry an airborne lifeboat slung under their bellies, operating these aircraft to the end of hostilities. The first successsful drop was to a crew off Denmark on March 31 1945.

Additionally, Halesworth housed the 496th Fighter Training Group which arrived here from Goxhill (which, since 1942, had been the base to which crews went for indoctrination in the European theatre). The two squadrons flew P-51s here until the end of the war.

Halesworth was taken over by the RAF in June 1945 and on August 5 was handed over to the Royal Navy. In November 1945 798 Squadron Fleet Air Arm arrived, its Barracudas and Oxfords offering an advanced flying course. The unit was joined a few weeks later by 762 Squadron whose Oxfords and Beauforts were used

An aerial view of Halesworth taken by a 39 Squadron Canberra on August 6 1974 (DoE).

P-47Ds taxi out at Halesworth in 1944 (Merle Olmsted).

for twin-engined conversion training, the squadron having been an earlier off-shoot of 798 which left in January 1946. No 762 Squadron moved to Ford in February 1946, soon after which the station closed to flying. It is now the site of a turkey farm.

Hardwick, Norfolk

TM250900. 4½ miles NW Harleston

After they had gone, and the peace which they had done so much to secure had arrived, what would one remember most about the 8th Air Force? There were the men whose charm was so great that one could not keep a girlfriend for long, and others who upset many with their 'biggest and best' claims. There seemed few 'grays' among these characters.

Then there were the garish paintings which adorned so many Fortresses and Liberators — the RAF would never be allowed to display such emotions. There were the interminable convoys of men and materials that ever seemed to throng the narrow East Anglian lanes. Whenever one visited an American base friendship — sincere and voluminous — was showered upon one in a sea of food the like of which never then penetrated the British airman's Mess nor the local home.

If an outward sign of the operational side must be recalled, surely it must be of those mornings when the sun obliged and the icing level was low. As the Forts and Libs milled, taking up battle stations, the sky would seem covered by a mass of brilliant white vapour trails. Then, the glory. Positions attained, the formations — sometimes totalling hundreds — would proceed in superb battle array, spewing masses of vapour in long streams leading towards the battle.

Hardwick came into the American

B-24 Liberator 'Shoot Luke' had flown 27 sorties when it was photographed at Hardwick (USAF).

world in September 1942 when the 310th Bomb Group arrived with B-25 Mitchells, one squadron of which was sited at the satellite, Bungay. The Group's stay was brief for it left in November. These grey and green B-25Cs were few in number, incidentally, and one was lucky to see them.

Their place at Hardwick was taken, in December 1942, by B-24Ds of the 93rd Bomb Group whose identity was much concealed because their white stars were painted out. They had not been here long before they flew to North Africa to make attacks on shipping until inadequate maintenance facilities forced them back to Hardwick. A few B-24s had remained here throughout the period for special operations employing *Gee*.

Operations were resumed on March 18 and in May some crews undertook night flying training whilst others operated against the Continent, the East Anglian sky acquiring once more the long white trails as the Liberators set out for the East coast exit points near Yarmouth or Orfordness. Engine repair works, power plants and harbours were all targets. Then, abruptly, the Liberators began low-level training and in June 1943 flew once more to the sunshine, this time to support the Sicilian landings.

Their purpose in flying south, though, had been well disguised, even if the roar of low-level Liberators in practice had been exhilarating. On August 1 they set off on one of the great adventures of the war, to destroy much of the Ploesti oil field in Roumania. This required accurate low-level flying, no easy task. For the 93rd the operation went badly wrong as the Group followed others only to find itself running up on the wrong target. Opposition was intense and disaster really struck when the lead crew of the 93rd encountered serious trouble. The two pilots, Lieutenant Colonel Addison E. Baker and Major John L. Jerstad, pressed on when an abortive sortie might have saved their lives. Instead, they attacked the target presented to them, only to crash in the target area. For their example both were awarded the Medal of Honour.

The 93rd then came back to Hardwick, but after only two operations they were sent again to North Africa, this time to support the Fifth Army in its invasion of Italy, returning to Britain for the rest of the war in October 1943.

From Hardwick the 93rd took a prominent part in the war and with a total of 396 operations, flew more operations than any other 8th AF Bomb Group. The Group's pattern of operations was as for others — attacking targets widely spaced across Europe, participating in the lead up to and support of the invasion, Arnhem, the St Lô break-out and the Rhine crossing. When the Americans became short of fuel in the summer of 1944 the 93rd hauled petrol cans to France, an unenviable task for certain.

Of Hardwick not much remains, but runways are evident and crop sprayers use them. The RAF took back the airfield in June 1945, and the site was finally disposed of in June 1962. One might suppose that the tail of a B-24 suitably mounted might mark the spot, veritable home of the Liberator. Instead, one is left only to remember those days, to stare and imagine. Easier, if memory is long enough.

Hethel, Norfolk

TL150000. 4 miles SE of Wymondham, NE of Wreningham

The Poles fought courageously during World War 2. Tragic that, in victory, many lost all. When the war ended they found it impossible to return to the country they adored, for most would have suffered piteously. Little could be done to atone for this. Some Poles elected to stay in the RAF, and two squadrons flying Mustang fighters were stationed at Hethel whilst their future was decided. Ironically they were stationed at an airfield which had housed those who had also known bitter battle and for whom ultimate victory meant a return to the richest country of Earth.

Hethel was built between 1941 and 1942. In mid-September 1942 its first occupants arrived, Americans forming the ground echelon of the 320th Bomb Group (Medium) training for action in north-west Africa. They had worked up on Marauders, the aircraft being diverted to Africa where the ground echelon joined them in December 1942, leaving a few Americans to run Station 114. In June 1943 the 389th Bomb Group arrived, the third to fly B-24Ds. Like so many others, the Group had prepared in the USA for high-level bombing. Barely had they settled at Hethel when they were ordered to train in low-level attack. Quite suddenly the B-24s left East Anglia. They had also flown to North Africa, the 389th settling at Benghazi, which name so often figured in the fighting there. From Benghazi Hethel's B-24s attacked targets in Sicily, Italy and Crete, operations culmi-

nating on August 1 1943 in the hazardous long distance low-level attack on Roumanian oil fields around Ploesti.

This brought to 2nd Lieutenant Lloyd H. Hughes a Medal of Honour. Although his B-24 was hit and petrol streamed forth, he pressed on, making a low-level attack on the distant target. Before he could land the aircraft it crashed. His high courage and that of all who took part in the Ploesti raid was memorable.

On August 13 the 389th struck deep into Austria, at the Messerschmitt factory at Wienar Neustadt, before returning to Britain late in August 1943. The first operation from Hethel came on September 7 1943 as Operation *Starkey* was unfolding. Barely was the unit operational than it flew to Tunisia, the intention being that it should weigh in at Salerno. The Group was not really needed there and instead made raids on Italy, Corsica and again on Wienar Neustadt.

When the 389th returned to Hethel it was for more permanence, the Group beginning a long, intensive campaign of day bombing that continued until April 21 1945. Targets varied and included Berlin, supporting the Normandy landings and break-out at St Lô, supply dropping during the Nijmegen landing and again during the Rhine assault. When the last landing was made the Group had flown 351 operations. On May 30 1945 the 389th began the long trek home to America.

Many stations vacated by the Americans were quickly run down, but not so Hethel which passed to Fighter Command on June 25 1945. Here, on September 6 1945, Spitfire XVIs of 65 Squadron arrived when 12 Group took over the station. This squadron remained until September 1946, having been joined in September 1945 by Mustang IIIs of 126 Squadron which disbanded here on April 26 1946.

Late in March 1946 Mustang IIIs and IVs of 303 and 316 Squadrons and a few Harvards had arrived, but there was comparatively little flying. The Poles dispersed, leaving Hethel to run down in the early months of 1947.

In 1964 Lotus Cars established a base here and use two runways for high speed testing.

Honington, Suffolk

TL890755. 3 miles E of A134 S of Thetford

It was mid-afternoon on September 4 1939. Six Wellington crews of 9 Squadron

One of 199 Squadron's Honington based Valiants.

set off from Honington on the first bombing raid of the war, to attack warships off Brunsbüttel. Leading was Squadron Leader Lamb, whose section was met by nine Bf 109s which shot down his wing men. This represented the beginning of the end for it was the only time when pre-war Wellington 1s with fixed turrets operated from Honington.

Building of the station commenced in 1935. It opened in 3 Group on May 3 1937. The first occupant was 77 Squadron with Audaxes and Wellesleys which arrived in July 1937, and 102 Squadron which came in the same month flying Heyfords. They stayed a year. No 75 Squadron moved in during July 1938 with Harrows, received Wellingtons in March 1939 and moved to Stradishall in July. No 215 Squadron also arrived in July 1938 with Harrows, re-equipped with Wellingtons in July 1939 and moved to Bassingbourn in September. No 75 Squadron was swopped with 9 Squadron from Stradishall, and the newcomers spent three years at Honington, leaving in September 1942.

Their Wellington operations were a microcosm of Bomber Command's. They took part in the costly action of December 18 1939 against enemy shipping when four crews were lost, having re-armed with Wellington 1as at the outbreak of war. In April 1940 they joined 115 Squadron to form a detachment at Lossiemouth to operate over Scandinavia for two weeks of hectic action. Then from Honington they supported maritime operations off Norway until May 10 1940 when the Germans attacked in the West. No 9 Squadron had received its first Wellington 1cs in March and operated this type until late 1941. During the summer of 1940 the Wellingtons attacked industrial targets in Germany, always by night.

Just what a catastrophe had befallen the squadrons in France was brought home to the Honington residents when the remnants of 103 and 105 Squadrons gathered at Honington in June-July 1940. Then a new set of faces appeared, those of Czech airmen who came via France to fight with the Allies. They were formed into 311 Squadron at Honington on July 29 1940 and, after working up, left for the satellite at East Wretham in September 1940. Nos 9 and 311 Squadrons operated alongside, both using the two airfields. In December 1940 9 Squadron made the long journey to Venice and in January 1941 to Turin. In March 1941 two Wellington IIs (able to carry 4,000 lb bombs) joined 9 Squadron, but they were never popular in 3 Group. No 9 Squadron dropped its first 'cookie' on Cologne on May 3 1941. Attacks on Germany were now interspersed with raids on the *Scharnhorst* and *Gneisenau* at Brest.

In August 1941 9 Squadron was the first to receive the Hercules-powered

A Wellington 1c of 9 Squadron on dispersal at Honington in 1941.

Until late 1978 Honington was the shore base for the Buccaneers of 809 Squadron, Royal Navy.

Wellington III. The Commanding Officer, Wing Commander Wasse, was soon demonstrating this version's superior take-off to another pilot and gave the 'thumbs up'. The other pilot misunderstood and retracted his undercarriage, ending up in an awkward position in the corner of the airfield. The Mk III went into action on September 12 1941. Operations using this aircraft continued to the end of the year then tailed off whilst aircraft were fitted with *Gee* and navigation training took place.

Operations were resumed in a big way in March 1942 with concentrated attacks on Essen, Lübeck and Rostock, which revitalised Bomber Command's effort. For the Cologne '1,000 bomber' raid 14 of 9 Squadron's Wellingtons operated from Honington and two went missing. Another 14 took part in the Essen raid and 16 against Bremen in June, the largest number of Wellingtons ever despatched by the squadron. Operations, some employing the 4,000 lb bomb using Mk III Type 423 Wellingtons, continued until August 1 1942 when the last of 2,458 Wellington sorties from Honington were completed. On August 8 1942 No 9 Squadron moved to Waddington. The only other squadron here in 1942 was No 214 briefly in January. Nos 1504 and 1505 BAT Flights used the station too.

In September 1942 Honington passed to the Americans who had in mind developing a depot for their fighters here. Instead, it was the B-17s of the 3rd Air Division which were attended to in 1943.

A return to operational status came in February 1944 when the 364th Fighter Group flying P-38Js arrived and first operated on March 3. Their duty was long-range escort and ground support, and they re-equipped with P-51Ds in July 1944. The Group returned to the USA in November 1945. Honington won distinction by being the last USAAF wartime base to be returned to the RAF, which came about on February 26 1946.

Transport Command moved in two days later and the station became a maintenance base, No 1 TAMU, mainly for Dakotas, being especially useful during the Berlin Air Lift. It was transferred to Bomber Command in 1949, then to Maintenance Command as a home for 94 MU between 1950 and 1956. During this period the present long runway was built to replace the metal runway laid in 1943.

The new expansion period of Bomber Command then brought along Canberra 2s of XV, 44 and 57 Squadrons in February 1955, and 10 Squadron from Scampton in May 1955. A chance spotting of an albino pheasant nearby gave the Canberra squadrons an ideal tail badge, each squadron outlining a white pheasant motif in a chosen colour. The Canberra squadrons were detached to the Middle East in 1956 for Operation *Musketeer*. It was 10 Squadron which, on October 26 1956, opened the bombing of Egypt. No 57 Squadron left in November 1956, 19 Squadron disbanded in January 1956, XV in April 1957 and 44 in July.

The next major change came at the time of the Suez Campaign when 7 Squadron arrived in November 1956 to fly Valiant V-bombers. Honington soon became a vital station for the V-Force, 90 Squadron reforming here on January 1 1957, also to fly Valiants. They were further strengthened by the arrival of 199 Squadron with more Valiants and Canberras, a squadron which specialised in electronic warfare. The final stage in the V-bomber period was completed when 57 Squadron reformed on January 1 1959 and 55 Squadron on September 1 1966. Both flew Victor 1as.

The political decision to switch the nuclear deterrent to the Navy brought the removal of 55 and 57 Squadrons to Marham in 1965-1966, well after the Valiant squadrons had gone.

Honington went on to Care & Maintenance between 1965 and 1969, during which period it was brought up to date to become the base for Buccaneer maritime attack squadrons of Strike Command. No 12 Squadron arrived in October 1969 and 237 OCU formed to train crews for the new RAF type. Honington became the shore base for the Navy's 809 Buccaneer squadron. Other Buccaneer squadrons were trained here and, in October 1974, 208 Squadron reformed to become the second operational Buccaneer squadron at Honington. During the Buccaneer period an unusual sound was heard in the area when 204 Squadron reformed on April 1 1971 and equipped with Shackelton 2s before moving to Lossiemouth to become 8 Squadron in 1972. Honington remains very much a front line station, with the ability to launch attacks with TV-guided Martel missiles. It is, rightly, not a station for public viewing.

Horham, Suffolk

TM210730. By B117 at Horham, 8 miles E of Eye

For several weeks after the Japanese

attacked Pearl Harbour the 47th Bomb Group patrolled the west coast of America. Then they trained for overseas duties and moved to Horham in October 1942, equipped with A-20s. By January 1943 the Group had moved to North Africa. During May 1943 the 323rd Bomb Group moved in for a short stay, flying B-26s before moving to Earl's Colne in June 1943.

Mid-June 1943 witnessed the arrival of the 95th Bomb Group at Horham, the Group having come from incomplete Framlingham. Operations were resumed and by July 1943 the Group was fully engaged in the strategic bombing offensive. For maintaining tight formation in the face of sustained enemy fighter attack, the Group received a Distinguished Unit Citation after their participation in the Regensburg operation of August 17 1943. It received its second such citation for a similar courageous action against Munster on October 10 1943.

On March 4 1944, when many other formations engaged upon operations were forced back, mainly due to unsuitable weather, the 95th pressed on to become the first US 8th AAF Group to bomb Berlin. This it did in spite of snowstorms, dense clouds and severe enemy attack. Like so many others it took part in the Normandy assault and the break-out from 'St Lô and, on September 18, 1944, made the long flight to Warsaw to support Polish troops during the uprising there. After supporting the Ardennes counter-attack and the Rhine crossing the Group flew its final bombing mission on April 20 1945, attacking marshalling yards at Oranienburg. Then they dropped food to the Dutch and retrieved displaced persons from Austria.

The 95th went back to the USA in June-August 1945. The station returned to the RAF in October 1945 as a satellite for Nos 25 and 262 Maintenance Units. It closed in October 1948, but later saw use as a site for Bloodhounds positioned to defend the East Anglian V-bomber bases. It was sold for private purposes in the early 1960s.

Horsham St Faith, Norfolk

TG220138. E of A140 leaving N of Norwich

Time, 0400 hours, date May 31 1942. Across Horsham's grass two Merlin engines roar into maximum power. Squadron Leader Oakeshott is away, to him the honour of taking the brilliant

Mosquito bomber into action for the first time. Target: Cologne, not long after the 1,000 bombers had laid waste the city. Task: to run across at 24,000 feet taking photographs ... Impossible; smoke blots out the area, so bombs are aimed into the inferno as accurately as possible. Tremendous secrecy surrounds the Mosquito and only eight are in 105 Squadron's hands. What a distinction for any airfield, to be operationally first with the most outstanding bomber of all time, the trendsetter so ahead of its day.

Horsham was commenced in 1939 and placed very close to Norwich. It started out as a bomber airfield and, at the end of 1939, long before completion, 21 Squadron's Blenheims were dispersed here for fear of sudden attack on Watton. Horsham, generally known thus or as 'St Faiths', then lay dormant until May 10 1940. The effectiveness of the German attack on Holland was met at Duxford by the immediate forward placing of much of 264 Squadron, which operated the Defiant for the first time on May 12 from Horsham. Station HQ opened here on June 1 1940.

In France 114 Squadron was quickly decimated, its remnants joining Wattisham's intrepid crews until June 10 when Horsham was quickly made ready to take them. There the squadron re-equipped with Blenheim IVs before moving to Oulton for operations in August 1940. With them had been 139 Squadron, also badly mauled in France and which again received Blenheims at Horsham whilst its companions flew from its satellite. For over a year Blenheims waged war from Horsham, making cloud cover raids, and gradually switched, via night intruder sorties, into the day *Circus* campaign and anti-shipping raids in 1941 before moving to Oulton on July 13 1941.

The unit's place was taken by another Blenheim IV squadron, No 18, also part of 2 Group, and flying similar operations. This was the squadron which delivered a new metal leg to Wing Commander Douglas Bader after he was shot down. In August the squadron had a detachment at Manston for *Channel Stop* and soon went to Malta for operations before moving to Oulton on November 5 1941. Meanwhile, No 139 had, on September 7, taken up space at Horsham before returning to the satellite to re-equip with Hudsons for Far East service. In its place on December 9 1941 came 105 Squadron with Mosquito IVs.

At first the Mosquitoes operated high,

B-24s of the 458th Bomb Group taxi out for take-off on December 24 1944 (USAF).

lone nuisance and armed reconnaissance raids. It was soon decided to employ them in small forces as fast low-level strike aircraft, relying upon speed for immunity. From Horsham they raced across the sea to Denmark making very famous attacks. No 139 reformed on June 8 1942 to operate Mosquitoes when sufficient numbers were available. Meanwhile the squadron also trained on Blenheim Vs in case they were needed in north-west Africa. Suddenly, an abrupt change of policy took the Mosquitoes to Marham when that station passed to 2 Group in September 1942

Almost at once the Stars and Stripes fluttered over Horsham. The Americans came in the form of the 319th Bomb Group. Not long after, a handful of B-26 Marauders arrived, staying briefly and leaving for Africa in November 1942. Horsham was clear of aircraft until early April 1943 when the 56th Fighter Group moved in, bringing bulky, noisy P-47Cs, some of the first in Europe. Their first operation, a fighter sweep, came on April 8 1943 and the Group worked closely with the experienced pilots of the 4th FG at Debden. It flew its first bomber escort from Horsham on May 4 and during the next two months took part in similar operations before moving to Halesworth on July 9 1943 to allow the building of three runways at Horsham.

The base re-opened in January 1944 when B-24s of the 458th Bomb Group moved in. Already trained, they commenced operations on February 24, making a diversionary sweep. The first bombing raid took place on March 2, then the Group took their part in operations leading to the Normandy invasion, supported the field forces and delivered fuel to France in September. As an interesting sideline they had, in May 1944, tried out

Hunters of 74 Squadron being rearmed during rapid turn round at Horsham.

radio-controlled bombs against tactical targets in France. The B-24s operated until April 25 1945 when they flew their 240th operation. Deployment home was fast and RAF Fighter Command took over the station on July 19 1945.

It was then that the station took on its final military role as a fighter station. On August 8 307 (Polish) Squadron brought in its Mosquito 30s. Two days later 695 Squadron, providing target facilities, arrived, flying Spitfire 16s, Oxfords and Vengeance IVs. On August 18 Mustang 3s of 64 Squadron came from Bentwaters and on September 8 Spitfires of 118 Squadron. Horsham was tightly packed.

Its association with de Havilland was further renewed on February 16 1946 when the first Hornet 1 for an RAF squadron arrived, for 64 Squadron. On March 14 No 65 Squadron moved in, and took delivery of its first Hornet on June 17 1946. A busy time followed as these squadrons with few aircraft began to work out the new fighter, then suffering teething troubles which brought some pernicious accidents. No 118 Squadron had disbanded on March 19 1946.

In August the two Hornet squadrons left for Linton-on-Ouse, and within a week Meteor IIIs of 74 and 245 Squadrons arrived from Colerne, the Wing being

A general view of Horsham taken at the 1955 Battle of Britain display.

An aerial view of Horsham taken by 231 OCU on July 23 1963 (DoE).

completed by the arrival of 263 Squadron in September 1946 and later by 257 Squadron. Still much in evidence was 695 Squadron which, in November 1946, began to have Vengeances replaced by Martinets.

During 1947 the Horsham Wing began, on December 21, to fly Meteor 4s, each squadron on this day receiving one aircraft.

On February 11 1949, 695 Squadron was renumbered 34 Squadron at a time when it was getting Beaufighter TT 10s, Martinets being phased out in August. In Feburary 1949, when 695 Squadron was re-numbered, 266 Squadron at Tangmere became No 43, 266's number-plate being now added to 245/266 Squadron at Horsham.

In July 1950 245 Squadron began to receive Meteor 8s and some of them, like the 4s, were fitted with flight refuelling probes at the close of the year for trials. These commenced in May 1951 with in-flight refuelling Lincoln tankers to extend duration. Before that happened another re-arrangement of squadrons took place; 257 Squadron moving to Wattisham in October 1950 and 263 on November 22. In August 1951 1 CAACU at Little Snoring took over the Spitfire commitment from 34 Squadron.

December 1951 saw the establishment of the station change to two day and one night fighter squadrons, which became general on fighter stations. No 23 Squadron arrived on January 15 1952 with Mosquito NF 36s leaving 74 and 245 to provide the day force with Meteor 8s.

In March 1952 34 Squadron disbanded. Its Beaufighters joined 2 CAACU at Cambridge whilst awaiting Langham's suitability to receive them. No 23 Squadron returned to Coltishall on July 4 1952. Throughout 1953-1955 Meteor 8s of Horsham Wing were part of the air defence of East Anglia. In mid-1955 245

Squadron moved to a new Wing at Stradishall. No 23 Squadron returned to Horsham and 275 ASR Squadron arrived flying Sycamore helicopters. In March 1957 74 Squadron re-armed with Hunter 4s, these being replaced by Mk 6s in November 1957. The tiger-marked Hunters moved to Coltishall in June 1959 during runway re-surfacing, then returned in January 1960, moving out in August to receive the first Lightnings. No 23 Squadron had, since 1957, been flying Javelins, which also left the station now. No 275 Squadron, which became a Flight of 228 Squadron on September 1 1959, also moved to Coltishall in 1960. Horsham was now devoid of aircraft, which much pleased local residents.

What should be done with the excellent airfield? Opinions varied. Part of it passed to the new University of East Anglia, industrial interest took others. But it was the arrival of East Anglian Flying Services which brought the airfield back to life. From that organisation, with much enterprise, came the present fleet of Air Anglia which has progressed from aged Dakotas to F27 and F28 Friendships, and is much involved with the North Sea oil trade, linking Norwich with Aberdeen and Norway. Passenger services are also run to Amsterdam. Norwich Airport has become an active airfield and movements may be watched from an enclosure. It is one of the few airfields in East Anglia where watchers are encouraged.

Ipswich, Suffolk
TM190415. SE of Ipswich

A day before the war was declared Blenheims of 110 Squadron dispersed to Ipswich Airport. They never operated from here at this time, a legend which has died hard. Throughout the war, however, Ipswich was an active aerodrome.

It was officially opened by HRH the Prince of Wales on June 26 1930, becoming the home of the Suffolk Aero Club. Management was taken over by the Whitney Straight Corporation in February 1936, civilians co-operating with the Army and Observer Corps in 1938. In October of that year the Civil Air Guard began flying from here and in 1939 No 45 Elementary & Reserve Flying Training School was established to train Volunteer Reserve pilots.

Before the war Ipswich was earmarked as satellite station for Wattisham. Thus on September 2 1939 Blenheim IVs dispersed here, returning to their base for operations. Through to March 1942 Ipswich served Wattisham's Blenheim squadrons, which spent periods at the airfield. Mainly these were 107 and 110 Squadrons, the latter flying some operational sorties from Ipswich in February-March 1941. No 1517 Blind Approach Training Flight stationed at Wattisham also used Ipswich.

A memorable day in its history was August 12 1941, the date of 2 Group's brave daylight attack on two power stations near Cologne. Three Spitfire squadrons arrived at Ipswich beforehand, Nos 19, 65 and 266 and, from here, led by a Blenheim of 226 Squadron, they set off to escort the Blenheim squadrons home from the Dutch coast, tangling with enemy fighters in the process.

When the Blenheim squadrons vacated Wattisham in March 1942 Ipswich was transferred to Martlesham Heath as its satellite and came under 12 Group control. Thus, a succession of detachments and dispersals by aircraft of famous fighter squadrons came here, 340 Squadron being based at the station in July 1942. In the main Spitfires merely called at Ipswich, together with a few Typhoons. No 1517 BAT Flight also flew Oxfords from here at this period.

On March 1 1943 Ipswich was raised to RAF Station status and on the 12th 1616 Flight arrived from Martlesham flying Henley target tugs, an advance guard of a succession of such units which spent their time towing targets for naval gunners at Harwich, No 3 Anti-Aircraft Target Towing Flight arrived in April 1943. On June 19 No 1499 Gunnery Flight, formed at Wyton on May 24 1943, began lodging at the station using Martinets. The Flight disbanded on February 15 1944.

Army Co-operation Command, which had controlled the target towers, was disbanded on June 1 1943 and during that month 3 AATT Flight was absorbed into 1627 Flight which had arrived at Ipswich in July 1943.

Summer 1943 found a detachment of Martlesham's ASR squadron at Ipswich and in October another detachment, of 7 Anti-aircraft Co-operation Unit, flew from the station. November 6 saw the arrival of Auster IIIs of 652 Squadron which remained here, with detachments, until March 1944, moving out then to make room for a naval servicing unit.

Meanwhile 1616 and 1627 Flights had been dissolved into a new squadron, No 679, on December 1 1943, and were now flying Martinets and Oxfords for anti-aircraft and searchlight co-operation duties. Rare in RAF hands, two Barracudas joined 679 Squadron on March 18 1944. No 658 (Air Observation Post) Squadron flew Austers here in detachments before D-Day.

For the remainder of the war 679 Squadron flew from Ipswich providing target facilities for the Navy at Harwich. Live targets became available for them and other gunners in the area when, in September 1944, Heinkel 111s began air-launching V-1s over East Anglia. Many crossed the coast around Felixstowe and on September 1 a V-1 fell just outside the boundary of Ipswich aerodrome, demolishing a requisitioned house and killing an NCO and injuring three more men. On September 18 another landed in a residential area 400 yards from the airfield causing many civilian casualties.

No 1696 Bomber Defence Training Flight had arrived in March 1944 flying Hurricanes, Spitfires and Martinets, and stayed until 1945, then moving to Gransden Lodge and Wyton. Among the rarer visitors to Ipswich were Cierva C30a autogiros of 529 Squadron which, in November 1944, used the station as a base from which to carry out calibration flights for radar stations and gunners defending the East Coast against V-1 attacks.

The operational commitment of 679 Squadron passed to 695 Squadron, Bircham Newton, on June 30 1945 upon disbandment of the former unit, and Ipswich was placed on Care & Maintenance on August 1 1945.

Civil flying was resumed in 1946 at Ipswich Airport and continues to this day.

Knettishall, Suffolk

TL970795. Off A1066 2 miles W of Garboldisham. Road crosses site. Turn right after Coney Weston to pass west side of airfield

One year had passed since the 8th AF launched its first bombing raid on Europe. August 17 1943 was an apt day for celebration. Dawn brought the mist of a lovely summer's day and a sniff of disaster.

Elaborate was the plan. For the first time B-17s would attack a distant target then fly on to North Africa, to return bombing another target. Meanwhile, others would head for the all-important ball bearing works at Schweinfurt, a name never to be forgotten in American history. Knettishall's Fortresses, though, were to make for Regensburg then for the sun.

That accursed mist brought late take-off making assembly over East Anglia, as was so often the case in the early hours, tiresome and fuel consuming. Eventually they set off with a Thunderbolt escort through the exit area between Yarmouth and Lowestoft, the 96th from Snetterton leading with the 388th Bomb Group from Knettishall behind them, followed by the 390th, 94th, 95th, 385th and 100th Bomb Groups, all flying B-17s with additional tankage.

Had the Schweinfurt force proceeded at the same time then the enemy fighter force would have been split. Instead, it exacted punishment on one force at a time. Over Belgium the Germans began persistent attacks, picking off bombers in the rear. These attacks continued almost to distant Regensburg where the Messerschmitt factory was soon to produce Me 262s, although this was not known at the time. Seventeen B-17s had been lost when the enemy gave up the fight and the Fortresses effectively bombed the complex. Then, surely surprising the enemy, they flew across the Alps and to North Africa. After ten hours' flying they landed, with 24 of their number missing.

The problem now was how to prepare for the return journey with limited maintenance facilities. After a week half the remaining force, about 60 bombers, made the journey back via the convoy raiders' base at Bordeaux/Merignac. One can imagine the joy of returning to home bases, for some this being Knettishall. For its part in the Regensburg operation the 388th received a Distinguished Unit Citation. The Group won another for a trio of raids on a rubber factory at Hanover, synthetic oil plant at Brux and another shuttle raid, this time to the USSR.

Knettishall opened on January 6 1943 in 3 Group as a satellite to Honington. It was in June of that year that the 388th reached the station. The unit commenced operations on July 17, bombing an aircraft factory at Amsterdam. Thereafter it was in the thick of battle, Kassel, Brunswick, Berlin, La Pallice, Emden and Ludwigshaven all figuring on target manifestos before, like so many others, it gave tactical support to the invasion, landings in Holland and the advance into Germany. On the way to victory the 388th also had hit at Schweinfurt, and later dropped food to the Dutch.

Knettishall was set on a plateau on the edge of heathland which, with gorse and heather, is a sandy outlier of the Breckland and in surprising contrast to other

A B-17 with extended radome airborne from Knettishall.

land around. The best approach to the airfield site is from the north. This road to Coney Weston crosses the airfield, fragments of runway appearing. A large slice of the main runway remains, and a few buildings near a ruined church and to the south. There is a hangar in good state on the western side. A grass runway is used by light aircraft and you may find a Cessna here and a windsock to remind you of more active days. The site was given up by the Ministry of Defence in February 1957.

Lakenheath, Suffolk

TL740820. On A1065 4 miles SW of Brandon

Wartime Lakenheath bore virtually no resemblance to the sprawling NATO base which now covers a vastly increased area of sand and heather set in the middle of the Breckland, the 'broken land' which, before the war, was a sandy waste owned by a huge rabbit population and bordered by twisted pine trees. They had been planted to prevent sand from blowing over the surrounding fenland and ruining agriculture in the area. Such a flat, sandy waste made an ideal site for an airfield. Over the centre of the present airfield ran the Brandon road. Wartime Lakenheath was a desolate place, with a few 'T' hangars and huts but, curiously, had no fencing and little barbed wire so that one could virtually roam at will for a look at the occupants.

In May 1944 it all began to change. Lakenheath had been chosen for development as a heavy bomber base. Had the war progressed long enough, doubtless the occupants might have been B-29s or even projected large British bombers such as the Windsor or Lincoln which were reckoned likely to need frighteningly long runs at around 80,000 lb all-up weight.

The 'locals' had other ideas, claiming that this would be the site of a large international airport, once the fighting was over. Then came a fascinating new device, the Calvert bar landing light system which is featured by so many airports now. Trials with this under the watchful eyes of Farnborough's scientists came in 1945-1946. At every self-respecting airfield in the world there is truly a little piece of Lakenheath.

Lakenheath came into being in mid-1941 and in January 1942 Stirlings of 149 Squadron began dispersing there and, indeed, flew some of their earliest operations from the three-runway station, although as Mildenhall's satellite the station was generally used by the Conversion Flight of 149 Squadron between January and October 1942. Also here between November 24 1941 and January 12 1942 were Wellingtons of No 20 OTU, Lossiemouth, due to the poor state of their airfield. Lakenheath at this time had a role akin to Woodbridge in later years for many a damaged bomber found sanctuary here in 1942.

In April 1942 149 Squadron fully moved into Lakenheath and for two years operated entirely from the station. After bombing on so many occasions 149 Squadron gradually took a greater part in mine laying and by the end of 1943 this was the primary task. Dangerous and taxing as these operations were, many crews felt they were being cheated out of their main role. Not so, really, because their mining effort proved very effective. In early 1944 the squadron flew a lot of supply drops to the Resistance forces on the Continent.

Of all the courage exhibited by 149 Squadron, none surely eclipsed that of Sergeant R.H. Middleton, an Australian,

Many SAC bombers have been based here, like the B-29s of the 2nd Bomb Group.

and one of quite a number who made Lakenheath their home. Middleton was detailed to attack the Fiat works at Turin on November 28/28 1942. The Alpine crossing and the painful climb to get over the peaks consumed fuel rapidly on this dark night. The bombers reached Turin and flew low to identify the target, facing intense flak. One shot created a large hole in the wing, then a shell burst in the cockpit, wounding both pilots. A piece of shrapnel hit Middleton in the face and he lost the sight of his right eye. The second pilot was seriously injured too. The Stirling fell out of control, but the second pilot managed to right it. Enemy fire was still striking the bomber.

Middleton ordered the second pilot aft for treatment whilst he flew the aircraft. The two pilots set course for the awful journey home, praying that they had sufficient fuel. Crossing the French coast the aircraft was hit again then, over the Channel and with scarcely any fuel left, Middleton ordered the crew to bale out.

Five of the crew did so, leaving two to assist Middleton. The Stirling soon crashed in the Channel and all were lost.

Great relief, another operation from Lakenheath for 199 Squadron is over (S. Smith).

The body of Middleton, who was post-humously awarded the Victoria Cross, was recovered and taken to the church-yard at Beck Row, near Mildenhall, where Middleton was buried.

In December 1942 the station became part of 31 Base, Mildenhall. A second Stirling squadron was established at Lakenheath in July 1943 after No 199 arrived with Wellington Xs, flew a few sorties then set about conversion. The unit participated in the bombing and min-ing campaigns. In January 1944 it was taken off operations for training in a special radar jamming role using *Mandrel* equipment.

On May 1 1944 '199' moved to North Creake and 100 Group, and soon 149 Squadron moved to Methwold, Laken-heath being set aside for its expansion programme.

Not until July 1948 did it become active again when the USAAF flew in B-29s of the 2nd Bomb Group in answer to Rus-sian intransigence over Berlin. Over the next eight years the USAAF positioned over 30 Bomb Groups or Wings during Temporary Duty stays at Lakenheath, usually for about 90 days per unit. At first B-29s came until August 1949 when the 65th Bomb Squadron, 43rd Bomb Group, was here with B-50As supported by KB-29M tankers, the first in-flight refuel-ling aircraft to be based here. Supporting transports included C-97s and C-74 Globemasters, curious machines on account of their twin cockpit canopies. In January 1951 the 93rd Bomb Group became the first to fly B-50Ds and KB-29P boom refuellers from the base.

Within days came the unmistakable giants, the first B-36s briefly visiting. Impressive because of their huge size, they could never be missed because they soun-ded like a fleet of motor cycles. With the seven visitors came some of the first Globemaster IIs, C-124s, to arrive in Bri-tain. Three more B-36Ds arrived for a short stay in June 1951 and on July 1 made a memorable flypast at the Paris Aero Show.

The early months of 1952 saw a drama-tic change at Lakenheath. When the Americans arrived the entire airfield was open, then later barbed wire gave them their only protection. But with the arrival of weapons of vast potency the whole area acquired a high wire net fence, looked upon as quite an achievement of Ameri-can proportions at the time.

It was on April 13 1953 that the first B-47s visited Lakenheath, at a time when the base was used by reconnaissance RB-36s and RB-50s. Far greater secrecy than that which even enveloped these air-craft was that surrounding the antics of a far more elegant type. There was no mis-taking its identity as it flew so finely in the neighbourhood, although at the time the Lockheed U-2 was as secret as any aero-plane has ever been.

In 1954 KC-97 tankers were first based at Lakenheath and in June the first B-47s to be based here arrived on Group rota-tion. B-47 Stratojets dominated the scene until 1956 when the base became vacant, for the Americans placed their strategic bombers in the Midlands thereafter. A visit to a B-47 Wing was indeed memor-able for these unusual-looking aircraft lined up were a sight of such staggering might. On one occasion I was invited to Lakenheath to photograph the 1,000th B-47 built, behind which was a line of no less than 30 aircraft of the same type.

It was American forced withdrawal from France which brought Lakenheath its present occupants, the 48th Wing, which began to arrive early in January 1960. Hard to accept, isn't it, that the 48th has been here so long? When they came they brought along F-100D Super Sabres which in turn gave way to F-4s and two years ago the F-111s which presently occupy the base. It is now an astonishing 30 years since the Americans arrived at Lakenheath.

Langham, Norfolk

TF990420. On B1388 between Binham and Langham

Time 1100 hours, date May 14 1944. Ground crews were busy putting last minute touches to the Beaufighter Xs. Within moments the crew wagon arrived, dropping off a pilot and observer at each. Hercules engines burst into life. Soon the Beaufighters — 12 of 455 Squadron armed with rockets, six of 489 Squadron carrying torpedoes and another six armed for an anti-flak role — began trundling around the perimeter track. Near the run-way threshold they halted for final checks and engine runs. At 1130 hours the leader rolled and within ten minutes Langham Strike Wing had formed up and raced away to meet its Mustang escort.

Reconnaissance earlier had located four medium-sized merchant vessels off the Dutch coast, accompanied by 16 escort ships, all heavily armed, along with nine minesweepers to clear a path free from the efforts of bomber stations in East Anglia.

A Beaufighter TF X of 489 Squadron armed ready for action.

The sea was very rough. Langham Strike Wing entered rainstorms, and visibility below the 300-foot cloud base was very poor. Nevertheless, the convoy was located and the Beaufighter formation broke for the attack, facing a tremendous hail of fire from the escorting flak ships. A torpedo from 489 Squadron whammed into a 3,000-tonner which was left blazing. Another large ship was hit and began to sink. Meanwhile the rockets of 455 Squadron smashed into mine-sweepers and escort vessels, some of which suffered serious damage. Balloons flying at around 250 feet had to be watched, since one cable hit would bring instant disaster. Tremendous action was packed into moments. It was soon over and the Beaufighters regrouped for Langham shortly before 1330 hours.

One would never make it: 'B Beer' of 489 Squadron had been seen to dive into the sea. Six others were in trouble from the merciless flak, and 'M Mother' of 455 Squadron ended the sortie by sliding across Langham on its belly. 'C Charlie' and 'B Beer' had their wings well peppered and 'X' and 'K', also of 455 Squadron, sustained damage but brought their crews safely home. As it taxied back to dispersal 'Y Yoke' of 489 Squadron could be seen to have been hit in the wings and nacelles. Just another shipping strike from Langham was over.

And now? Well, it is not quiet at Langham for a large turkey farm sprawls across the field, leaving a runway clear for the occasional visiting light aircraft. The wartime watch office is in good form, now housing offices. One of those curious star domes, of which very few remain, can still be seen.

Langham opened in 1940 and Bircham Newton sent some of its aircraft there for dispersal. It was the arrival of 'M' and 'K' Flights of No 1 Anti-Aircraft Co-operation Unit with Henley target tugs on December 1941 that really made it come alive. Langham achieved independent status on July 16 1942 when it opened as a full station under Group Captain T.H. Carr, AFC, DFC. Next day its first arrivals were not RAF, but a detachment of six Swordfish of 819 Squadron here from distant Machrihanish under the command of Lieutenant Commander Davenport for night anti-shipping operations with 16 Group. Three days later they flew to Thorney Island, there to pick up torpedoes and, via Docking, came back to Langham.

In August 'M' Flight of 1 AACU began to equip with Defiant target tugs, but it was the general arrangement of Bircham Newton's huge commitment which was more important for 280 Squadron arrived on August 5. This unit's task was to seek and assist aircrew who had ditched in the North Sea off East Anglia. On August

Langham's control tower. The additional office on top is a post-war feature.

Langham's extended runway can be seen in this 1978 photograph.

6, No 819 Squadron left to operate from Bircham Newton. There followed a busy period for 280's Ansons until they moved out in October. 'M' and 'K' Flights returned to Bircham Newton to reform on November 3 1942, and Langham was put on Care & Maintenance for expansion and runway building.

The station re-opened in 16 Group on February 22 1944 and in April two Beaufighter squadrons arrived from Leuchars, Fife, No 455 manned by Australians and 489 staffed by New Zealanders. Between them they formed Langham Strike Wing, under 16 Group.

On April 19 the first *Rovers* were flown and ships attacked off Holland. Thereafter it was such action whenever the weather permitted it. The first big anti-shipping strike came on May 6. Fifteen of 455 Squadron's aircraft, six torpedo carriers from '489' and five anti-flak Beaufighters found five escort vessels shielding a large convoy of seven merchant ships. Hits were claimed on a number of ships but one Beaufighter was shot down; however, Flight Sergeant R. Walker came home despite jammed ailerons, hits in the starboard fuel tank and with his brakes out of use.

Rovers, reconnaissances and sea sweeps followed with a few very large shipping strikes, and often Langham Wing joined the North Coates Wing making formations of around 50 Beaufighters with sizeable fighter support from Norfolk bases.

On D-Day a detachment from Langham operated over the Channel out of Manston. Gradually the emphasis switched to operations against E-Boats.

A major Strike Wing attack came on June 15 aided by North Coates. A large ship of around 8,000 tons was being covered by 16 escort vessels and balloons, but the Beaufighters struck hard, securing two hits with torpedoes on the large ship, two damaging attacks on a naval auxiliary, blowing up a minesweeper and getting a torpedo in the leading merchant ship. On July 21 a similar heavy onslaught left a motor vessel sinking, another damaged by a torpedo, a third blazing and a fourth on fire and settling in the water. Two escorts and three other ships were burning when the Beaufighters left. After landing 'X' of 489 Squadron was found to have 50 yards of cable dangling from a wing leading edge and its rudder damaged. Two aircraft returned on one engine and five of '455' had flak damage.

During August 1944 some night strikes were attempted by the light of flares

dropped by Wellingtons, the first such attack being delivered off Le Havre. In September 1944 Intelligence sources reckoned that the Langham Wing had sunk 36 ships, damaged a further 61 and sunk four U-Boats. The last shipping operation, an armed reconnaissance, came on October 19 after which the Beaufighters left for Dallachy and trade off Norway.

Their place was taken by 280 ASR Squadron which returned on September 6 flying Warwick 1s for operations over the North Sea which took them far beyond the range possible with Ansons.

A more offensive period recommenced when, on October 18, Wellingtons of 524 Squadron arrived from waterlogged Docking for a temporary stay which became a long one. Bombing by flare light, their crews operated at night off the Dutch coast, E-Boats being the main prey. They were supplemented on November 1 when more Wellingtons of 524 Squadron arrived. No 280 Squadron then vacated the station, being replaced by Barracudas of 827 Squadron, Fleet Air Arm.

Another and portentious change occurred when 521 Meteorological Reconnaissance Squadron came in from Bircham Newton on October 30, bringing Hudsons, Gladiators and Hurricanes for daily sorties.

Barracudas of 827 Squadron first went into action on November 20 when three crews on a *Rover* attacked two ships. On the 25th the squadron went into action once more against E-Boats and other ships, and from time to time flew similar operations before leaving on December 13. Then 612 Squadron completely moved in.

Langham was now the base of 521 Squadron, which arrived on October 30 1944, two Wellington XIV squadrons and an Armament Practice Camp which had been here since the autumn. No 519 Squadron began flying *Rhombus* meteorological flights from here and 521 Squadron, which still had a few ancient Gladiators, soon received its first Fortress IIs.

Daylight meteorological reconnaissance flights and night operations by Wellingtons remained the order of events in 1945, 407 Squadron adding its Wellingtons to the force whilst on detachment from Chivenor between April 14 and May 9 1945. Shortly after the war a Meteorological Conversion Unit was established, then the Wellington squadrons disbanded. By August 1945 only 521 Squadron remained fully active, using mainly

Fortresses.

Langham was now the main base for weather reporting, its strength swollen by the addition of 1402 Flight. New Meteorological Flights formed here, some for overseas, and Hurricanes were made available for them in 1946. In January of that year the old strike role was resurrected when 254 Squadron came for a four-month stay.

This was one of the wartime stations for which there was no immediate post-war use, and it closed to flying on May 15 1946. A Royal Netherlands Air Force Technical Training School arrived in July and then the station was put on Care & Maintenance in September 1947. With the increase in RAF strength in the 1950s Langham came alive again, having a refurbished runway for use by Beaufighter 10s and Mosquito 35 target towers of No 2 Civil Anti-Aircraft Co-operation Unit, for nearly six years. The CAACU was present from March 23 1953 until November 1 1958, latterly using Vampire T 11s controlled by 61 Group. After this it became an Emergency Landing Ground for Sculthorpe. It was sold on October 3 1961.

Lavenham, Suffolk

TL895525. 3 miles NW of Lavenham, between the A1141 and A134 NE of Alpheton

Most people visit Lavenham to enjoy its old buildings and ancient Cloth Hall. If you have an aeronautical interest head for the bar of the Swan Hotel, a beautiful place to tarry. Therein, along with your ale, you can gaze upon a collection of signatures gathered during the war, donated by such famous RAF figures as Sir Basil Embry and Oswald Gayford, of long-distance flying fame, not to mention many others famous in 2 Group who called at The Swan when stationed at Wattisham.

Of Lavenham airfield there is much to see. Take the A1141 and, after a short distance, turn up the narrow road signposted 'Smithwood Green only'. It leads to the plateau upon which the airfield stands. The road leads directly on to the perimeter track and the runways may be seen intact. To the south you will see the control tower which has been turned into a private residence. The whole area is privately owned so you *must* have permission if you wish to take a closer look. In summer, crop-spraying aircraft operate

By Lavenham's tower, now a private dwelling, is the old fire station.

from the airfield. The area around the tower contains many wartime buildings in very good condition, and there is a large dispersal area still intact.

Lavenham was built during 1943-1944 and B-24s of the 487th Bomb Group arrived during April 1944. They began their operations with attacks on French airfields before switching to targets in support of the Normandy landings. Then they supported the British break-out from Caen. During July 1944 the Group (identity 'P in a square') converted to B-17Gs, switching from the 2nd to the 3rd Air Division and resuming operations on August 1 1944. It was soon attacking troops and fortifications around Brest, helping pave the way for the Allied take-over of this notorious port. It supported the airborne invasion of Holland in September.

So far most operations from Lavenham had a tactical bias, but between August 1944 and March 1945 strategic targets were bombed. These included oil refineries at Dulmen, Mannheim and Merseburg, factories at Nuremburg, Berlin and Hanover and marshalling yards at Cologne, Hamm and Munster. Like other Groups the 487th played a part in the Ardennes battle and assisted during the Rhine crossing.

The occupants of the tower surely will never witness a sight like this seen in 1944 from this tower (USAF).

Return to America came in August-September 1945. Lavenham was passed to RAF Transport Command on October 12 1945 and to Maintenance Command on July 31 1946. Bomber Command took control of the station on August 20 1946. It became inactive from October 26 1948 and was sold in April 1958.

Leiston, Suffolk

TM430645. Off B1119 W of Leiston. Turn first right, first left on to road along perimeter track

The one thing which saved the US 8th AF bombing campaign was fighter support to very distant targets. Only the long-range P-51 Mustang could provide this, and it did it well thanks to that greatest of all aero engines, the Rolls-Royce Merlin. The base which was the first 8th AF home for the Mustang surely has a special place in history — and that station was Leiston.

The first P-51s to arrive in Britain were delivered to the 9th AF, a strange situation although it seems that the importance of the P-51 was not fully apparent when the type began to trickle into the UK late in 1943. Understandably, the 8th AF, which had taken such a hammering in 1943, was eager to have Mustangs. The question was — how to acquire them? The answer was relatively simple, transfer them from the 9th AF.

In November 1943 Leiston had opened as an active station with the arrival of a new P-47 Group, the 358th, from Goxhill. Already trained, it commenced escort duties on December 20 1943, but in little over a month it was switched to Roydon, whence the 357th Fighter Group flying P-51Bs came to take its place as the 8th AF's first P-51 Group. The 357th commenced operations from Leiston on February 11 1944 with a fighter sweep over the Rouen area. Such short-range missions soon changed to deep penetration flights, to bomber escorts and to target and withdrawal cover for B-17s and B-24s. A single-engined fighter able to reach Berlin and back was no mean invention, and when the US heavies first raided that city in daylight Leiston's Mustangs went to give them target support. On June 29 they penetrated to Leipzig and in recognition of all that was called for in such long duration flights the unit received its first Distinguished Unit Citation.

Over France and the Low Countries P-51s flew sweeps. During the Normandy landings they flew fighter patrols and

Rarin' to go, a P-51B warms up prior to taking part in the 357th Fighter Group's first mission (Merle Olmsted).

soon they were dive-bombing and strafing airfields, marshalling yards, locomotives, ammunition dumps, barges and tugs, later combining such ventures with bomber escorts.

The 357th's second Distinguished Unit Citation was awarded for its part in a raid on Derben on January 14 1945 when the P-51s successfully broke up an onslaught on the bombers they were escorting.

The 357th ended the war as the second highest scoring Group in the 8th AF and flew its last operational sorties on April 25 1945. In July 1945 it moved to Neibiberg in Germany, and Leiston was returned to the RAF in October. Here the RAF set up No 18 Recruit Centre which closed in 1946. The site was sold off in the mid-1950s and is now mainly farming land.

Little Snoring, Norfolk

TF960335. 4 miles NE Fakenham, off A148

Ekwell's 'English Place Names' states that the names of Great and Little Snoring derive from the first wave of Saxon invaders in 450 AD as the Romans withdrew, and shows that they were settlements of Snear's people (Snear being a Saxon invader nicknamed 'Swift', 'Bright' or 'Alert'), hence the curious name of these parishes.

For the present day surveyor of the Norfolk airfield the centre of attraction may well be not the field itself, now used for private flying, but Little Snoring Church. Distinctive it is, with a slender round tower as featured by a number of East Anglian churches. It stands close to the airfield site (not open to the public) on the Great Snoring Road.

It is an unusual church, and not only for its shape. With an aeronautical interest, however, you will surely find the four Memorial Boards, three listing enemy aircraft destroyed and damaged and a record of awards and decorations whilst Little Snoring was in 100 Group, of special interest.

Respect the church for its religious purpose. It is surely a good place in which to tarry awhile and remember that airfields were places for people, places where people flew and from which, sadly, many thousands set out on life's last journey. Here Squadron Leader 'Micky' Margin of Dam Busters fame served for six months with 515 Squadron, and that intrepid intruder pilot Wing Commander Alan 'Sticky' Murphy with 23 Squadron who, with his navigator, Flight Sergeant D. Darbon, was killed on December 2 1944 when intruding upon Gutersloh.

Little Snoring opened in July 1943, a satellite for Foulsham in 3 Group, then was quickly raised to full station status. Early in August 1943 115 Squadron flying Lancaster IIs along with a small Conversion Unit, No 1678 supplying Lancaster II crews, arrived.

Operations by 115 Squadron soon commenced and continued until November 1943. When Foulsham became vacant 1678 Conversion Unit moved here on September 16 1943, to expand and supply crews to 3 Group as they converted to Lancaster IIs. Things did not, however, work out quite like that, for Lancaster II production tailed off as Hercules engines were diverted to improve the Halifax. The likely demise of the Windsor freed Merlin production for Lancasters and 1678 CU became redundant at Waterbeach in 1944.

During 1943 the policy of Group siring in East Anglia was radically reviewed. The 3 Group squadrons would be centrally placed. Pathfinding 8 Group would be further inland and the new bomber support Group, No 100, which formed at the end of 1943, would occupy a clutch of airfields in north Norfolk.

Little Snoring was chosen as one such station and 115 Squadron left for Witchford having flown its last operation from Little Snoring on November 26, target Berlin. When they left the Lancasters were crammed full of personal belongings including seven bicycles on one aircraft during the Berlin raid. What did the Germans make of the wreckage of DS680 when they shot it down that night? 'Stupid English, hoping to bike back to England.'

The station was transferred to 100 Group on December 7 1943 as 169 Squad-

Little Snoring photographed in 1946 (Airviews [Manchester] Ltd):

The control tower still stands. Strangely it was first painted red and after the war black.

The crew stand by one of 515 Squadron's Mosquitoes at Little Snoring (via M.G. Williams).

ron arrived, first equipped with a few Beaufighter VIs for training under Wing Commander E.J. Gracie, DFC. They were soon joined by more Beaufighter VIs and a few Defiant IIs of 1692 Flight which arrived from Drem in December, received a few Mosquito IIs and continued training crews to operate the radar with which 100 Group Mosquitoes were equipped, and in the tactics to employ.

Little Snoring then received 515 Squadron from Hunsdon. This unit arrived on December 15 1943 bringing Beaufighter IIs and a few Blenheim Vs, but in February 1944 began to equip with Mosquito IIs. This squadron, since 1942, had dabbled in radio and radar warfare and had been responsible for trying out the possibilities of *Mandrel* jamming to screen assembly and advance of bomber streams, British and American, by day and night. Now it would train to operate in the manner of 169 Squadron.

No 169 Squadron commenced operations on January 20 1944 during a Berlin raid, its task to prevent enemy fighters attacking our bombers. Squadron Leader J. Cooper and Flying Officer R. Connally scored the first success on January 30, a Bf 110. In February they flew 28 sorties, then 59 in March, during which month 515 Squadron flew its first operations. This squadron had, at that time, a detachment at Bradwell Bay and used some of 605 Squadron's aircraft in one of which, during the first sortie, the commanding officer, Wing Commander F.F. Lambert flying with Flight Lieutenant E.W.M. Morgan, downed an He 177.

During April 1944 515 Squadron continued to operate from Bradwell until, on April 7, the first operations were flown from Little Snoring. On April 19/20 some enemy intruders sneaked in among our returning bombers and put Little Snoring out of action by distributing antipersonnel bombs on the runway.

More successes came to 169 Squadron during April when the unit claimed four enemy aircraft. On May 15 Pilot Officer W.H. Miller with Pilot Officer F.C. Bone claimed three German aircraft when giving bomber support to mine laying in Kiel Bay. The squadron was still using Mosquito IIs.

Under Group Captain R.B.O'B.Hoare, a distinguished intruder pilot, the squadrons had begun a very successful night support campaign. Then came an abrupt change, for 23 Squadron, the 'No 1' intruder squadron, newly home from the Mediterranean, was ordered into 100 Group. To learn the new style of operations it replaced 169 Squadron and 1692 Flight both of which moved to Great Massingham.

Thereafter the fortunes of Little Snoring were akin to those of other 100 Group Mosquito stations, No 23 Squadron, after a lot of exciting low flying, resumed operations on July 5/6 attacking enemy airfields. Its first claim was of a Ju 88 damaged on July 26. Then both squadrons briefly flew daylight escorts of Lancasters bombing Bordeaux for which they operated from advanced bases. *Day*

Rangers were flown to intrude upon enemy aircraft during their training flights, and in September 1944 23 Squadron escorted Fortresses trying to discover whether V2s were radio-controlled.

October 29 1944 was a red letter day when, during a *Day Ranger*, Flight Lieutenant F.T.L'Amie and Flying Officer R.A. Smith, and Flying Officer T.A. Groves and Flight Sergeant R.B. Dockeray destroyed nine and damaged five enemy aircraft between them.

At the end of 1944 training began in the use of ASH radar, better for low level attack on airfields, the first success with the new equipment coming for Squadron Leader C.V. Bennett, DFC with Flight Lieutenant R.A. Smith on December 31 1944, a Ju 88 shot down at Ahlhorn. By April 1945 both squadrons were taking part in spoof attacks on German airfields and towns, supplying Master Bombers to control the raids. At the end of the war they flew *Firebash* sorties designed to set ablaze with incendiaries and napalm German airfield installations. The final sorties were flown from Little Snoring on May 2/3 1945 when Squadron Leader G. Griffiths acted as Master Bomber for an attack on Hohn.

The scores of enemy aircraft, still open to confirmation, were:

	Destroyed	Damaged
169 Squadron	13	1
515 Squadron	44	42
23 Squadron	9	32
Totals	66	75

On June 10 1945 515 Squadron disbanded followed by No 23 on September 25. Little Snoring closed to general flying on October 25 after 141 Squadron had been briefly based here.

Then, in December 1945 274 MU moved in, its purpose to look after Mosquitoes, in the hands of No 112 Sub Storage Unit until 1947 when the airfield was put under Care & Maintenance. This was not the first time aircraft had been stored here, for Horsas were placed at Little Snoring in 1944.

It was used again between June 1950 and September 1952 when Spitfire 16s of No 2 CAACU were here. Vampire T11s were later based here, the unit closing in October 1958.

In recent years Little Snoring has hosted the British Aerobatic Championships in spring time, and it has been possible to see some of our finest aerobatic pilots performing their art for the McAully Trophy in memory of a superb Norfolk aerobatic pilot.

After you have visited the airfield, should you want some light enjoyment move along to Cushing's display of steam engines and organs at Thursford, for a wealth of nostalgia. You still will not be far from the aviation scene for Little Snoring is now in the hands of the Cushing family.

Little Walden (Hadstock), Essex

TL550435. B1052 Saffron Walden-Linton crosses airfield

When driving from Saffron Walden to Linton on the B1052 the location of this former airfield becomes immediately obvious, for hangars and control tower are still extant 34 years after the cessation of hostilities. Indeed, the road, closed to civilian traffic in the lifespan of the aerodrome, was re-sited along the line of the north-south runway.

Little Walden began its career when construction commenced in 1943 on a plateau, and was opened for operational use on March 6 1944 as Station 165 under the aegis of the US 9th Air Force. In mid-March the first units arrived, comprising four squadrons of the 409th(L) Bomb Group flying A-20 Havocs. The 409th, under Colonel Preston P. Pender, was part of the 97th Combat Wing, the other two units in the Wing being at Wethersfield and Gosfield.

Their first mission was flown on April 13 1944 and set the pattern for operations for the next six months, namely operating in a tactical role against targets which were part of the pre-D-Day build up. Fierce German resistance was frequently encountered as on May 27 1944 when the Group suffered heavy casualties in an attack on the marshalling yards at Amiens.

One evening in May a Havoc crashed soon after take-off near the village of Ashdon and a lady from that village was tragically killed in attempting to rescue the crew when the aircraft exploded. For this action she was subsequently awarded a posthumous decoration by the USAAF.

After June 6 the pattern of operations continued with the selection of targets ahead of the advancing armies. This soon caused problems of range, and in September the 409th, in company with other units of the 9th AF, moved to newly liberated Continental airfields.

This meant changes at Little Walden, the airfield now coming under the control of the 8th AF and on September 26 the yellow-nosed Mustangs of the 361st

Little Walden's control tower stands not far from the road crossing the site.

Fighter Group moved in from nearby Bottisham. The three squadrons which comprised the Group, Nos 374, 375 and 376, continued their operations of escort and ground support until the early part of 1945 when they, too, were posted to France to operate from there until April, when they returned to Little Walden.

During their absence, the station saw a distinct change of type for B-17s of the 493rd Bomb Group arrived from Debach whilst their former home underwent repairs. So now it was the turn of the heavies to roll down Little Walden's runways, participating in the heavy daylight operations during the last few months of the war in Europe.

In April, however, with the return of the 361st Fighter Group from France, Little Walden reverted to its role as a fighter station and saw the war out as such. The famous 56th Fighter Group, 'the Wolfpack', joined the 361st during late summer, and both units returned home in November. Little Walden closed in January 1946.

Lord's Bridge, Cambridgeshire

TL385545. N of A603, from Barton village

It all looks highly secret, with its weird array of aerials and dishes which look like something Doctor Who would enjoy. Of course, these 'radar dishes' are really radio telescopes, where discoveries of pulsars and such stellar wonders take place. To the east of the present buildings lies an area which remains out of bounds, where during the war gas bombs were stored for 2 and 3 Groups of Bomber Command.

It is odd that, with such objects in store and then surrounded by a huge bomb dump supplying many airfields around, the authorities requisitioned a large grass field to the north of the road for use as a Relief Landing Ground. Of course, bombs were stored in most unlikely places during the war, sometimes being found in Nissen huts lining public roads and at times completely unguarded!

In the case of Lord's Bridge it was even more surprising that the RLG users were trainee pilots of 22 EFTS, Cambridge. That unit held as many as 120 Tiger Moths for pilot training and Cambridge could not cope with the amount of flying needed. Here and at Caxton Gibbet two fields were sited where, when the weather was fine, the Tigers would be active. At Lord's Bridge they would suddenly rise from behind a high hedge and sometimes fly right over that bomb dump. To be fair, the RLG was usually used when the wind was in the south-west so that flying took place well away from the gas bombs.

This was not the only time when grass fields were put to good use in Cambridgeshire. Incredible as it now seems, Alan Cobham's Circus flew on one occasion from a field on the Cambridge boundary to the north of the present Barton Road. What *would* today's residents say if such an enjoyable event took place?

Ludham, Norfolk

TG395195. Immediately N of Ludham village

Alfred Hitchcock could not have done better, and never could have achieved such casting. To Ludham shortly after 3 pm HM King George VI and Queen Elizabeth were coming. As they set out for the airfield, so did a Ju 88 of KG 6 leave Soesterburg to annoy mariners off the East Anglian coast, on the afternoon of January 28 1943.

Just as their Majesties were due to arrive, Pilot Officer Code and Sergeant Nash were scrambled. Nine minutes later the two pilots of 167 Squadron returned, and Code had scored his first victim, that Ju 88. Their landing coincided with the arrival of the Royal guests. Code was elated and the King made no attempt to conceal his delight at the present his Air Force had given him. This was a unique event.

Ludham, second satellite of Coltishall, came into use in the last quarter of 1941 as a forward base for fighter squadrons operating under Coltishall control. Its proximity to the coast made it an ideal base for maritime operations, escorting bombers raiding the Continent and for scrambles against raiders. In mid-November 1941 152 Squadron was sending Sections forward from Swanton Morley for convoy escorts and attacks on E-Boats. Then, on December 1 1941, 19 Squadron moved in and stayed until April 4 1942, carrying out convoy patrols, shipping reconnaissances, *Circuses* and sweeps under 12 Group, using Spitfire Vs. The squadron's place was taken by 610 Squadron from Hutton Cranswick, which stayed until September 1942. It quickly drew first blood at dawn on April 27 1942 by shooting down a black Ju 88 of 3/122 off Lowestoft.

Convoy patrols represented a considerable proportion of the effort, and there were a number of engagements such as during the evening of May 16 when a Ju 88 was damaged. During the night attacks on Norwich detachments from Ludham operated *Fighter Night* patrols, but unsuccessfully. When it was not patrolling, 610 was operating over Europe flying *Rhubarbs*, sweeps and escorts, and during the Dieppe raid the Ludham squadron moved forward to West Malling to take part with 485 and 411 Squadrons under Wing Commander Jameson.

An unusual arrival occurred on May 12. Warrant Officer Matte, a Free Frenchman of 253 Squadron, Hibaldstowe, had been ordered to make a Sector reconnaissance and evidently finding this not very exciting, skimmed off on his own initiative to Holland where he shot up a

An aerial view of Ludham taken by 58 Squadron on August 28 1958 (DoE).

gasometer at the Hague, setting it ablaze before firing at a nearby barge during his private *Rhubarb*. He was suitably greeted on his return — the authorities were far from amused.

Three days later Squadron Leader Haywood and Flight Sergeant Maren of 610 Squadron were off Yarmouth when they came upon a Do 217E. They swiftly attacked, then their Yellow Section had a go. The port engine burst into flames, parts fell off the tail, the cockpit area was hit and the Dornier sank leaving three bodies in the sea. A Walrus from Coltishall found them, one barely alive, then a launch from Yarmouth took the injured man and the other two bodies to Yarmouth.

At dawn on May 31 1942 Spitfires of 610 Squadron left to give rear cover to bombers returning from the '1,000 bomber' raid on Cologne.

On October 14 167 Squadron arrived in Spitfires and two Harrows after a long journey from Castletown near the northeast tip of Scotland. The squadron was at this time the only Dutch fighter squadron and destined for a seven-month active stay at Ludham. Its role, more offensive than defensive, reflected the current employment of Fighter Command. Much of their work related to escorting Venturas of 2 Group making day raids, escorting Coastal Command Beaufighters, giving rear cover to returning US B-17s, shipping reconnaissances off Holland and escorting Walruses of 278 Squadron making ASR sorties. Additionally they flew *Rhubarbs* to the Continent, losing Squadron Leader Lane in the process to a FW190 on December 13 1942. Such sorties were becoming increasingly dangerous now that the FW 190 was about in plenty, and the next day these operations were suspended whilst tactics were reviewed, before they were reinstated on December 22.

Activity for 167 Squadron reached a memorable peak in May 1943. Shortly before 5 pm on the 3rd 167 Squadron took off and joined 118 Squadron, the Coltishall Wing being led by Wing Commander Blatchford. They rendezvoused with 487 Squadron's Venturas and set course for Holland. Soon after entering Dutch airspace over 20 enemy fighters swooped upon them from ahead, dived below the Spitfires and set upon the Venturas which were cut off from their escort. In vain the Spitfires tried to shield the bombers but each Section was repeatedly 'jumped' upon by groups of enemy

fighters until eventually the whole fighter force mingled. The RAF Spitfires were badly mauled and 167 Squadron claimed only one success.

That morning a sudden sharp raid was made on Lowestoft by FW 190 fighter-bombers which raked the town and fled before the defenders could attack them. Spitfire Vs were no match for this sort of thing and they withdrew. No 195 Squadron was rushed in from Woodvale with its Typhoons. There were more such raids on the coast, but never was the warning early enough to give the Typhoons a chance to turn them back. Instead, the Typhoons undertook convoy and Beaufighter escorts before making way for Spitfire VBs of 611 Squadron which arrived in July from Matlaske. Whilst here they worked up for low-level operations.

The fighters vacated Ludham on August 4 and the base passed to Air Ministry Works on August 13. It had been decided to hand the station over to the Americans, but no flying units ever moved in.

Ludham lay virtually unused until August 1944 when the Royal Navy began using the station. Plans to extend the runways in May 1944 had come to little.

RAF fighters returned on February 22 1945. No 229 Squadron had been renumbered 603 Squadron at Coltishall on January 7, then resumed its attacks on V2 launching sites, undertook armed reconnaissances and escorted Beaufighters, which duties were continued from Ludham and shared with 602 Squadron using Spitfire XVIs.

Early in April 1945 a new sound was to be heard, for 91 Squadron arrived on the 8th bringing the latest version of the Spitfire, the Mk XXI. On April 10 the first operational sorties were flown by the new mark from Ludham when the Mk XXIs set off on scrambles, armed reconnaissances and showed a new operational face by seeking midget submarines. The first two sorties on the morning of April 26 by LA 252 and LA 223 were the most rewarding for during their course a midget submarine was destroyed. The Spitfire XXIs flew their 152nd and final sortie from Ludham on May 1 1945.

Maintenance problems brought the two operational Mk XXI squadrons together when No 1 Squadron arrived at Ludham on May 14. Both stayed until July 14 1945 after which Ludham lay quiet. It was handed to 60 Group in September 1945 and wound down during succeeding months in 1945.

Marham became the home of the RAF's B-29 Washingtons, the first of which is here being handed over to the RAF in 1950.

Marham's might reached an all-time high when Valiants of the V-Force were based here. Following them came the Victor tankers. XH616 is of 57 Squadron.

Marham, Norfolk

TL730685. By A1122 10 miles E of Downham Market

Marham meant Mosquitoes. From a wide expanse of grass, when the airfield was much smaller, Nos 105 and 139 Squadrons waged the most precise and inspiring bomber offensive of the war. They would form up in Flights — sometimes squadrons — and race across the grass, then fly faster than any other bombers deep into enemy territory to deliver a fierce, accurate sting, returning faster than the pursuing fighters. Truly, these unarmed bombers wove one of the most exciting tapestries in RAF history. Operating from Marham, they never bettered their morale-boosting performance of January 30 1943.

It was Hitler's birthday, and 2 Group was determined to give him a present, twice over. In the morning Goering would address a Nazi rally in Berlin and, after a sumptuous lunch, Herr Goebbels would burst forth. The news that they would broadcast was seized upon by the RAF. What better accompaniment could there be than the background noise of Mosquito bombs?

Shortly before 9 am three crews of 105

Squadron led by Squadron Leader R.W. Reynolds set off on their dog-legged course for the 'Big City'. Over Holland they came down low to delight those down-trodden people, while in Germany they spread a track of fear before climbing to 25,000 feet. All went well and exactly at 11 am they released their bombs in long sticks across the city. The Germans had located the raiders but could not intercept them. A confused announcement on German radio, greeted with delight in Britain, spoke of an hour's postponement of the speech. The Mosquitoes returned safely, as Geoffrey de Havilland and Charles Walker had said they would.

Already three crews of 139 Squadron had left Marham by another route. Just before 1600 hours they arrived above the city — as Goebbels was about to start his boasting. What anger the Mosquitoes must have provoked! But this time Luftwaffe fighters were ready and Squadron Leader Darling was shot down.

There was a by-product to all this. An accurate measure of Mosquito fuel consumption had been achieved, and from the evidence it was clear the aircraft could reach Berlin easily, knowledge which was put to good use later.

Marham's name is synonymous with bombers. The airfield has a long history and remains a very active station. It opened as Narborough, in August 1915, an Admiralty landing ground for night operations against zeppelins. In April 1916 the RFC took it over and it became a training station for Vickers fighters and FE 2Bs which arrived from Thetford in June 1916. In August, 59 Squadron formed at Narborough with RE7s and BEs. Thereafter squadrons worked up here for France and Narborough became a training and depot station. After the war squadrons disbanded here, on a site still marked by a wooden hangar about 1½ miles north-east of the present airfield.

Marham re-opened on April 1 1937 as a two-squadron heavy bomber station under Wing Commander A.P.V. Daly, AFC, and at 0930 hours on May 5 No 38 Squadron moved in equipped with Fairey Hendons, the only examples in the RAF. In November 1938 they began re-arming with Wellingtons, the second squadron to do so. No 115 Squadron, an offshoot of 38, was inaugurated on June 15 1937. It was equipped with Harrows and began to fly Wellingtons in April 1939. On June 1 1939 No 1 RNZAF Unit began forming to

A line-up of 139 Squadron's Mosquitoes at Marham (F.E. Hay).

fly Wellingtons as well. It had been decided in early 1937 that the New Zealanders would receive 30 Wellingtons, of which six would be ready to leave for New Zealand in August 1939. When war broke out the unit was put at the disposal of the RAF and they moved to Harwell.

Long-distance flying had taken place in July 1939 and upon the outbreak of war some Wellingtons were dispersed at a rudimentary satellite at nearby Barton Bendish. Soon after there was a spy scare; a man calling himself Flight Lieutenant Weston had been driving around RAF airfields asking about AA defences, but he was never found.

Dispersals to and from the satellite continued, with the fear of an enemy attack on Armistice Day. So far there had only been armed patrols over the North Sea, but things came to a climax in December. Bright winter weather on the 3rd resulted in 24 Wellingtons of 38, 115 and 149 Squadrons setting off for Heligoland. Despite cloud they managed to sink a minesweeper and drop a few bombs on defences. Fighters engaged them and an air gunner of a 38 Squadron aircraft, LAC J. Copley, had a bullet lodge in his parachute harness buckle. He returned the fire shooting down a fighter, and the Wellingtons came home without loss.

Crews stood by but there were no more raids until the night offensive opened in February 1940 when propaganda leaflets were unloaded over Germany by crews mainly engaged in training flights.

After the attack on Norway, activity rapidly increased with day and night raids on Stavanger and other targets. A brief resumption of patrols to inhibit enemy minelayers was abruptly halted when the Germans invaded the West. Marham's Wellingtons first bombed inland targets in Germany on May 15/16 claiming to drop bombs on Homberg, Duisburg and Gelsenkirchen.

On June 22 1940 the air raid warning sounded on the station, for a number of enemy aircraft were in the area. The following day at 0600 hours bombs fell around the station, the first of a considerable number of light attacks. RAF night bombing was now in full swing and on August 28 the Wellingtons made their first call on Berlin. Channel ports were then attacked before the offensive swung back to Germany.

In November 1940 38 Squadron was posted to the Middle East, their place being taken on November 25 by 218 Squadron which began operations with

Early occupants of Marham were Fairey Hendons of 38 Squadron.

Wellingtons on December 20 1940.

Throughout 1941 both squadrons went on a large number of sorties, suffering accidents attributable to battle damage and enemy intruders. On April 8/9, for instance, Pilot Officer Lambert of 218 Squadron was despatched to Kiel. Flak hit his port engine and it was difficult to stay aloft. Heading for the Frisians all removable equipment was jettisoned and an enemy fighter then picked the aircraft out. The crew flashed an Aldis lamp at it and to their surprise it flew away. Course was set by guesswork as they headed home at 80 mph; then the port engine seized and boost pressure fell on the starboard. Yet they made England on one poor engine and no navigational equipment for a belly landing at Horsham. There were many such hair-raising moments for Marham's crews.

Intruders, too, were a menace. On April 4 a Wellington of 115 Squadron was shot down near King's Lynn and the same night unexploded bombs fell on a hangar at Marham. In May 1941 there were five attacks on Marham. A heavy bomb fell by the Sergeants' Mess and equipment stores were set on fire.

On July 24 nine Wellingtons took part in the daylight raid on Brest facing flak and fighters in profusion. Later, on August 28, five aircraft were lost landing back at base, for Drem Lights and the runway had been damaged by enemy bombs. Operations were carried out throughout 1941 and at the end of the year 115 Squadron began to equip with Wellington IIIs for the 1942 offensive. The new radio aid *Gee* was being fitted into the aircraft and on January 6 1942 1418 Flight formed to test it using four Wellington IIIs, later moving to Tempsford on March 1. Early 1942 218 Squadron re-armed with Stirlings.

Both Marham squadrons took part in the '1,000-bomber' raids, and 218 Squadron had the distinction of carrying the AOC 3 Group, Air-Vice Marshal Baldwin, to Cologne. Marham's crews were in the thick of battle whilst Downham Market airfield was prepared as the new satellite, whence 218 Squadron moved in July 1942. No 1483 Flight arrived from Newmarket on July 14 returning there on June 20 1943.

In August 1942 it was decided to place Marham in 2 Group during a wide-ranging repositioning of squadrons, and 105 Squadron moved in on September 29, 115 going to Mildenhall. No 105 was already operating Mosquitoes, but the second squadron to arrive that day, No 139, had to content themselves for the present with Blenheim Vs and borrow Mosquitoes from 105. In June 1942 139 Squadron became operational with Mosquitoes and then came that impressive campaign which resulted in some of the most spectacular raids of the war.

On June 1 1943 the picture fundamentally changed when much of the 2 Group was placed under Fighter Command and the two Mosquito squadrons were switched to 8 Group, which proved very unpopular. For a time they made night nuisance raids, for Bomber Command had little time for these specialised aircraft. The Mosquitoes' immunity soon led to their being used as route markers and, as soon as *Oboe* showed its worth, 105's aircraft were fitted with this remarkable bombing aid. No 139 Squadron left in July and 109 replaced them. Thereafter both squadrons specialised in pathfinding and special night operations which continued until March-April 1944 when both squadrons moved out for runway building to commence.

In the early war years Marham had housed the 3 Group Fighter Affiliation Flight with Battles, etc. When it re-opened it was non-operational, housing the Central Bomber Establishment, which used Lancasters to train bombing and gunnery leaders and developed new techniques and aircraft from February 1946 to April 1949. Lincolns were added after the war, and a few Mosquitoes. Also work was carried out with remotely controlled guns.

In June 1947 Marham hosted a courtesy visit by nine American B-29s of the 97th Bomb Group. The long runway ideally suited the visitors and was one reason why Marham became a Master Airfield.

During 1947, three B-29s were based here for bombing trials against the Farge U-Boat pens and among the weapons tested were rocket bombs, for B-29s could not carry such large weapons as the Lancasters.

An affinity with the B-29 seemed forged, for in April 1950 the RAF, which accepted its first B-29 Washingtons here, set up the Washington Conversion Unit and trained crews initially for 35 Squadron. Others followed, Marham becoming home for Nos XV, 44, 35, 90, 115, 149 and 207 Squadrons for varying periods. Meanwhile, the USAF had based B-29s and B-50s at the station from 1948 to 1950.

The Washington interlude was brief,

until sufficient Canberras were available in 1954 to re-arm Nos 35, 90, 115 and 207 Squadrons which formed a Wing.

In 1956 the striking power of Marham expanded enormously. No 214 Squadron reformed here in March equipped with Valiant V-bombers, 207 Squadron in April and 148 in July. The station progressed to a high state of readiness within the V-Force and had the ability to release, at short notice, weapons of colossal power. Then, with astonishing suddenness this ability vanished with the discovery of fatigue problems in the Valiants after they had been switched to a low-level attack profile.

Yet the Valiant's useful life was not entirely over for some were modified into tanker aircraft and these operated from Marham until re-equipment came in the form of Victor 1/1A tankers used here by Nos 55, 57 and 214 Squadrons.

The Victor tanker fleet remains today, somewhat shrunken, and presently equipped with Victor 2s. Marham is also the home of Canberra training units — 231 OCU which arrived in February 1976 and trains crews, and 100 Squadron which provides target facilities. It has the longest history of any station still active in East Anglia, and is really the most distinguished too, for it is to Marham that Her Majesty Queen Elizabeth and Prince Philip fly for visits to Sandringham. The Americans still come periodically, using the spacious runways and dispersals as sitings for their B-52s for bombing competitions.

Martlesham Heath, Suffolk
TM245455. A1093 crosses site

It was the flat heathland to the east of Ipswich that offered a suitable site for a base from which to operate the Aeroplane Experimental Unit. This was required to move from Upavon and work commenced in 1916 with the official opening taking place in January 1917.

As the name implied, the all-important work of testing new ideas and aeroplanes was to be carried out from this site, Martlesham Heath, for the next 22 years. The Royal Flying Corps was responsible for operating the unit until the end of hostilities, and included captured enemy aircraft in addition to British machines.

The general run-down of the Services following World War 1 had its effect at Martlesham and the smaller force of pilots indulged in some aspects of early civilian flying, such as air races and air speed record attempts.

On the night of October 5/6 1922, a serious fire caused great damage at Martlesham and a hangar and its contents of aircraft and equipment was completely destroyed. Rebuilding took place on a larger site, with additional hangars and living accommodation transforming the original layout.

In 1924 Martlesham was given the title of Aeroplane & Armament Experimental Establishment. Each section was given a separate identity — the Armament Unit becoming XV Squadron and the Aeroplane Unit, No 22 Squadron. Under the new arrangement both military and civil aircraft were tested, No 22 Squadron being split into three Flights with separate responsibilities. Much of XV Squadron's tests were carried out with DH 9s.

Another all-important aspect of aviation safety figured in Martlesham's tests at the time, for the Parachute Section came under A&AEE until moved to RAF Henlow.

As the 1920s progressed into the '30s the tempo of testing increased, for the recession was being overcome and the growing popularity of aviation led to the introduction of many, varied prototype aircraft at Martlesham. It was in 1936 that the RAF introduced 'Empire Air Day' — a flag-waver to allow the public to see its men and machines at close quarters. Accordingly, on May 25 1936, Martlesham was one of the stations chosen. Later visitors in 1936 were HRH Duke of York and the Prince of Wales and they were able to inspect some of the prototypes intended for the expanding RAF, such as the Wellesley, Battle, Hurricane, Spitfire, Lysander and Blenheim. The expansion of the RAF was making its presence felt particularly in East Anglia, and at Martlesham an operational fighter Squadron, No 64, flying Hawker Demons, was posted in during 1937. The unit remained here until the following year when it moved to Church Fenton.

The tension created by the Munich crisis of 1938 called for much greater security at RAF stations and at Martlesham, with its highly secret activities, this was especially so. However, by the spring of 1939 things had relaxed enough to allow the public admittance once again for Empire Air Day on May 20. Nevertheless, the situation deteriorated and war seemed inevitable. Behind the scenes much activity was afoot as Martlesham delved into the true performance of the Spitfire, Hurricane and the new bombers. Top secret

A few of the old red brick barrack blocks remain at Martlesham, this one by the main road crossing the one-time airfield.

Against the heathland, one of those curious aeroplanes of the 1920s, a dual-control Blackburn Blackburn N9589.

All the famous British aircraft of the early war years were tested here, including K9787, the first production Spitfire, which arrived in July 1938.

work involved such unconventional activities as the laying of aerial minefields and the validity of cannon armament.

When war came it was prudent to move A&AEE to a safer venue, and on September 1 1939 the Establishment was transferred to Boscombe Down where it resides today.

Martlesham's proximity to the coast made it an ideal base for early interception of raiders and so units from stations further inland sent detachments on a rota-

tion basis. Early arrivals included Nos 17, 29 and 504 Squadrons from Debden, ground personnel being ferried daily in a lumbering Bristol Bombay. It was No 264 Squadron's hapless Defiants which provided the first fully resident unit and worked up to operational status here.

By summer 1940 the tempo increased and Nos 17, 85 and 151 Squadrons all claimed successes mainly against raiders attacking the convoys moving along the east coast. On the afternoon of August 15 the airfield itself was attacked, and although 17 Squadron gave chase they did not catch the raiders. Considerable damage was caused to buildings but casualties were light. Five days later, the station was attacked again, but little damage was done this time. Nos 56, 111 and 257 Squadrons, all flying Hurricanes, were busy at Martlesham during August and they were later joined by 25 Squadron's Blenheims detached from North Weald. It was on November 11 1940 that the Italians made a pathetic attempt to attack Britain. Their target was Harwich harbour, only a short distance from Martlesham, and No 257 based here, together with 11 Group squadrons, treated the visitors with the contempt they deserved. 257 alone claimed seven destroyed and four damaged without loss — a great day for Squadron Leader Stanford-Tuck's men.

With the Luftwaffe resorting to raiding after dark, the night fighters came into action, and No 3 Squadron which was equipped with Hurricane IIs operated from Martlesham during early 1941. However, the daylight fighter squadrons began to take part in offensive operations and during the spring of 1941 Hurricanes of 242 Squadron set the trend at Martlesham. There was still the important job of convoy protection, but an added task in which Martlesham played a part from the start was air-sea rescue. Patrols of this nature were flown by Lysanders of 277 Squadron, and Defiants, Walruses, Sea Otters and Spitfires were later used.

Increased activity in the offensive operations led to frequent squadron changes, with Spitfire units gradually assuming the major proportion, and by 1942 the onslaught was in full swing. As a coastal location Martlesham provided a haven for many aircraft returning in crippled condition, and both bombers and fighters could be seen in a sorry state. The proximity of the sea afforded squadrons useful facility for firing practice, and supporting aircraft in the role of target tugs included

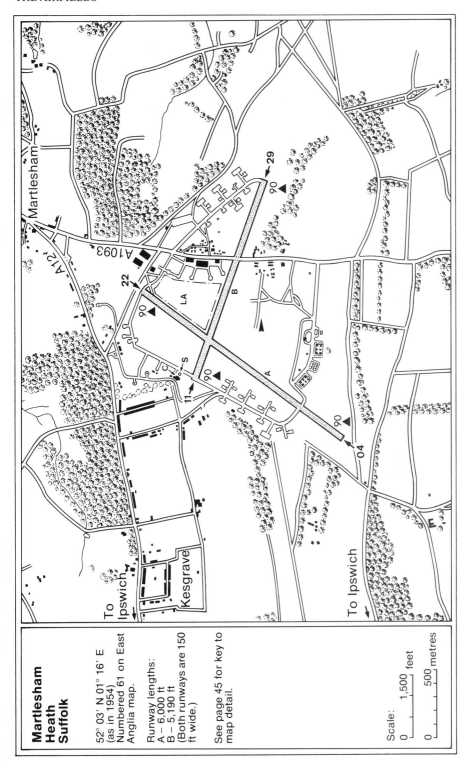

**Martlesham
Heath
Suffolk**

52° 03′ N 01° 16′ E
(as in 1954)
Numbered 61 on East
Anglia map.

Runway lengths:
A – 6,000 ft
B – 5,190 ft
(Both runways are 150
ft wide.)

See page 45 for key to
map detail.

Scale:

0   1,500   feet

0   500 metres

Henleys and Lysanders. Added punch was given to Martlesham when No 182 Squadron's Typhoons arrived in late 1942, but significantly there was an increasing number of USAAF aircraft dropping in. Not that the Americans were new to Martlesham, for No 71 (Eagle) Squadron operated there from as early as April 1941, with a second residence in the spring of 1942 before moving to the Debden Wing in May.

As the American presence grew, bases were gradually constructed or handed over by the RAF, and in the autumn of 1943 runways were laid and general preparations made for the arrival of the 356th Fighter Group, 8th Air Force, flying P-47s. Their first operation took place on October 15.

For two years the 356th FG was resident at Martlesham, operating both in the escort and ground-attack roles. In November 1944 the unit re-equipped with P-51s with which they carried out operations with increased range. Interestingly, the RAF's ASR duties at Martlesham continued alongside their American colleagues and, apart from the ubiquitous Walrus, other types operating included Ansons, Warwicks and Sea Otters.

A Distinguished Unit Citation was awarded to the 356th FG in September 1944, and the Group's Mustangs, recognised by their distinctive red nose panel with blue diamonds, flew their last mission on May 7 1945. However it was a misfortune that the Group had the highest loss rate in proportion to enemy aircraft destroyed of all the 8th Air Force Fighter Groups.

One of the first units to operate from Martlesham after the war was the Blind Landing Experimental Unit, which was based here until 1957. Alongside them was the Bomb Ballistic Unit, until it merged with BLEU in 1950 when it was renamed the Armament and Instrument Experimental Unit.

Not unusual for Martlesham was the immensely varied selection of aircraft operating at one time, just as in the pre-war days of A&AEE. The transition from propeller to jet was much in evidence, as Lincolns (one powered by two Merlins and two Avon jet engines) operated alongside such unusual types as the Short Sperrin and Avro Ashton, together with the more familiar Valiant, Canberra and Meteor. These were all involved with electrical and ballistics trials in conjunction with the long-established research station on Orfordness, where a landing strip was available. The other mainstream of development was in the instrument flying field, particularly concerned with landing procedures. Again, the composite range of aircraft varied from the Dakota to the Avro 707 delta wing.

After the departure of the A&IEU the station took on another role, for the arrival of No 22 Squadron in 1955 meant that search and rescue operations were once again to be carried out at Martlesham, the unit using Whirlwind helicopters. Another nostalgic note sounded at Martlesham in 1959 when the Battle of Britain Memorial Flight moved in with its mixture of Hurricanes and Spitfires, and the station held them until the Flight moved to Coltishall.

After their departure, activities decreased although an ATC Gliding School provided week-end training but they, too, moved away in 1963. There followed a period of speculation regarding Martlesham's future but it seemed that its flying days were over. Shortly after the RAF departed, commercial interests took over, some using the airfield facilities for light aircraft.

On January 16 1967 a celebration was held to mark the 50th anniversary of the opening of Martlesham Heath, and those attending included representatives from all the many chapters of its history. In 1968 the Post Office announced that Martlesham was to be the home for their research centre, and during the 1970s their large, new buildings have come into prominence including the very tall research tower. Also at Martlesham are the new Suffolk Police Headquarters — so Martlesham lives on, albeit in a new sphere of operations. Five of the old hangars remain as well as sections of the runway and some of the old domestic buildings. Many of the buildings have formed the nucleus of an industrial trading estate. A dual-carriageway now crosses the airfield giving good views of the old buildings.

Matching, Essex

TL550110. 1 mile E of Matching Green

Built by the US Army, Matching opened in September 1943. In January and February 1944 B-26s of the 391st Bomb Group moved in, commencing operations on February 15 1944. They attacked airfields, marshalling yards and 'V' sites in France and the Low Countries. They attacked coastal defences on June 6 and 7 1944, continuing cross-Channel operations between June and September, attacking in particular fuel and ammunition dumps, troop concentrations and giving support to the Allied advance. After the St Lô break-out they attacked the rear of the retreating enemy forces.

In common with other 9th AF Groups the 391st moved out to France on September 19 1944, to a new base at Roye/Amy.

Late in 1944 the station was taken over by 38 Group, RAF, and then the Operational & Refresher Training Unit moved in. Its task was to offer practice to crews of 38 Group held in readiness to replace any lost in action, and they had an operational commitment too. Stirling IVs, which formed the main equipment of ORTU, towed 14 Horsas as their part in Operation *Varsity*, the Rhine crossing.

In April 1945 ORTU mainly re-equipped with Halifax IIIs, leaving only one Flight of Stirlings. The unit moved to Wethersfield on October 15 1945 and Matching was run down.

Some of Matlaske's few remaining buildings.

ber of sweeps and escorts, sometimes to Short Stirling bombers. A strange sight appeared over Matlaske on August 13 1941, a Bell Airacobra, for 601 had been chosen to try out this type. But before that happened the unit moved, their place being taken by 19 Squadron which stayed until December 1941.

By then Matlaske housed some of the most talked of, most curious and always fascinating aeroplanes, the twin-engined Westland Whirlwind fighters. Only two squadrons ever used them and the second, No 137, moved into Matlaske at the end of November 1941. The Whirlwinds patrolled East Coast convoys mainly off Yarmouth, encountering several enemy aircraft without success. As companions at Matlaske at this time the unit had some Lysanders of 278 Squadron whose base was Coltishall. This ASR squadron formed here from No 5 ASR Flight on October 1 1941 with two Walruses and three Lysanders. The squadron used Matlaske spasmodically until August 1943.

Horsa gliders of the ORTU at Matching (M. Flack).

Matlaske, Norfolk

TG158345. E of village

Matlaske was prepared during the summer of 1940 as a satellite for Coltishall. It came into use during October 1940, 72 Squadron's Spitfires dispersing there. On October 29, five enemy aircraft bombed and strafed the grass field causing little damage and few casualties. Incendiaries fell there on May 12 1941, a few days before 222 Squadron took up residence. They used Spitfire VBs for sweeps and convoy patrols until July 1 when 601 (County of London) Squadron under Squadron Leader Gracie replaced it and flew Hurricanes. They made a num-

A day always to be remembered was February 12 1942. Soon after noon 137 Squadron was brought to readiness and at 1310 hours four pilots were ordered off, to patrol British destroyers racing to intercept the *Scharnhorst, Gneisenau* and *Prinz Eugen* which were daringly passing through the English Channel. The weather was very poor, but as the Whirlwinds swept round they caught sight of the German convoy 20 miles off the Belgian coast. They dived to investigate and immediately about 20 Bf 109s were on the scene and a fierce dogfight developed. Just as Flight Sergeant Mercer had a

B-26 Marauders taxi out at Matching (USAF).

Messerschmitt lined up in his sights his cannon developed a stoppage and another Bf 109 raked his aircraft. Pilot Officer de Houx fired all his ammunition without success. The other two Whirlwinds were shot down.

A second detail left Matlaske at 1340 hours. Nothing more was heard of them. This left Pilot Officer Bryan and Sergeant Ashton to keep watch over the British destroyers for 30 minutes, after which they returned. A sobering day indeed.

Whirlwinds were soon engaged in the constant battle against E-boats off the East Coast. During the raids on Norwich the squadron flew some fighter night patrols from Coltishall. It was at this time that one of the most distressing incidents of its kind took place. Two Whirlwinds latched on to what they identified as a Ju 88. In fact, it was really a Blenheim they fired at and one Whirlwind never returned.

First victory came to the Whirlwinds on June 25 1942. Pilot Officer McClure and Warrant Officer Smith were on patrol east of Smiths Knoll when they spotted a Ju 88. Two bursts from McClure put the raider into the sea.

While much of Fighter Command was operating during the Dieppe raid in August 137 Squadron went into action again off the coast. Flying Officer J.M. Bryan and Sergeant Roberts were scrambled during the morning and 50 miles off Happisburgh dived upon a Do 217 from which the crew baled out as the bomber was burning.

So far it had been mainly defensive action, but on September 3 No 137 Squadron took part in their first *Rodeo*. Eleven Whirlwinds with 24 Spitfires of 411 and 485 Squadrons mounted a feint on Lille. Hope was that enemy aircraft would come in to attack, but the Luftwaffe was not so easily caught. Within days the Whirlwinds left for Manston to carry on their offensive.

It is still just possible to make out Matlaske from the air. The main camp site was in the bottom left of the photograph.

The earlier months of 1942 had found sections of Coltishall's squadron dispersing to Matlaske and in the middle of the year Lysanders of 1489 Flight joined them together with the Walruses of 278 Squadron. Activity had picked up in August when 266 Squadron was here whilst 137 was away at Drem for training. On August 24 56 Squadron's Typhoons replaced 266's, and under Squadron Leader Dundas they stayed until July 22 1943. These were soon busy days for 56. On November 17, for instance, three Typhoons flew a *Rhubarb* to Flushing airfield damaging two Bf 109s on the ground. One pilot flew so low that his wing tip hit a German soldier! Daily *Rhubarbs* were now being flown to Belgium and Holland.

Thirteen FW 190s made a low-level attack on Lowestoft on May 12 1943, six Typhoons of 56 Squadron being scrambled to intercept them. They were too late, but one raider was shot down by anti-aircraft guns, whilst bombs fell on the town and harbour causing minor damage. Another attack came in the evening, and again the 190s withdrew before fighters could catch them. A gas holder at Lowestoft was set on fire and other smaller fires started. Twenty-three people were killed and 29 seriously wounded.

The British reaction was swift, for next day Typhoons of 245 Squadron were rushed from Gravesend into Matlaske and 195 Squadron came from Woodvale into Ludham, the other station under Coltishall. Sector patrols and standbys were now the order of the day, but the Typhoon squadrons soon resumed offensive operations flying *Rhubarbs, Roadsteads* and concentrating on anti-shipping operations. Spitfire IXs of 611 Squadron spent two weeks here in July 1943, then passed their aircraft to 19 Squadron and accepted their inferior Mk Vs, 56 Squadron having gone to Manston on July 22.

Before they left, 56 Squadron lost their commanding officer during a shipping strike mounted from Ludham. It was a bad day for the squadron. In the evening four FW 190s attempted an attack on Yarmouth, but the Typhoons reached them in time. In the action Flight Sergeant Clusas was shot down in the sea. In atrocious weather a Walrus of 278 Squadron searched for him in vain. Pilot Officer Libby had set out in a Spitfire to escort the Walrus, only to have his engine cut soon after take-off, causing him to crash in a cornfield.

Matlaske was placed under Care &

Maintenance on August 24 1943, the fighter squadrons having gone south to be nearer the current scene of activity, or withdrawn to the Sector station. Some bombing training took place and between March and April 1944 the 3rd Aviation Engineer Battalion, USAAF, practised here for duty in France. Thus, 1944 was a quiet year — until the autumn came. Bomber Command was now operating in daylight, and support was needed for the airborne landings in Holland. Tempest Vs of 150 Wing, comprising Nos 3, 56 and 486 Squadrons, spent a few days at Matlaske before proceeding to Grimbergen. Their place was taken by a Mustang Wing, Nos 19, 65 and 122 Squadrons, which operated from Matlaske in September-October 1944.

Matlaske was unsuitable for Mosquitoes and thus the station was not able to mount night operations against V-1s now attacking East Anglia. However, by October V-2 rockets were falling in Norfolk and the only effective defence against them was to find and destroy their launching sites. Since these were mobile it was no easy task. Into Matlaske in the third week of October 1944 came three squadrons with Spitfire IXs and these soon began flying some of the then new Mk XVIs with American-built Merlin engines. Then the field became waterlogged which meant that 229, 453 and 602 Squadrons had to operate from Swannington until the surface improved. No 229 Squadron flew against the V-2 sites for a month and 602 operated from Matlaske until February 1945, also flying armed reconnaissance patrols over Holland. It was 453 Squadron that proved to be Matlaske's final occupants, for they did not leave until April 1945. The aerodrome was finally vacated by the RAF in October 1945.

Some of the buildings and the control tower survive, and one other tangible item from Matlaske's wartime days. This is the Spitfire XVI TB863 whose remains, in poor health, have travelled around the country since being used by film studios. It has resided in recent years, in poor state, at Duxford.

Mendlesham, Suffolk

TM120635. By A140 N of Stowmarket

Mention Mendlesham and most East Anglians will know it as the site of a TV transmitter mast which has been erected on the one-time airfield. There is another reminder of past days for by the A140 is a stone memorial. The cost of erecting such items at each disused airfield in East Anglia would not amount to very much. Perhaps instead of building themselves grandiose surroundings in which to preach, some more feeling councillors might one day give thought to those who won them the freedom by which their chatter may be exercised — and the many who died to allow it to proceed.

The RAF moved into Mendlesham at the end of 1943. On February 19 1944 three Czech Spitfire IX squadrons arrived, 310, 312 and 313. Here they worked up a fighter-bomber role and were to be seen busily low flying over East Anglia in the process. One at a time the squadrons were detached to Southend for shallow dive bombing training. Otherwise they all took an active part in *Ramrod* operations, giving escort and cover to Mitchells, B-26s and Bostons. No 310 was the most operationally active since its training detachment did not come until the end of its stay at Mendlesham. The squadron participated in eight *Ramrods*. On March 26 the three Spitfire squadrons took part in *Ramrod 689* when a large force of B-26s attacked Ijmuiden. At the start of April 1944 the Czechs moved to Appledram and the Americans then moved in.

Late in April the 34th Bomb Group arrived, the oldest such formation to join the 8th AF. It was to be based here until July 1945, and had already seen active service patrolling the west coast of America looking for enemy naval activity. In 1942-1943 it had served as a training unit in the USA, then equipped with B-24s which it brought to Britain. The 34th began operations on May 23 1944 when airfields and ground defences were principal targets during the run-up to D-Day. It participated in the attacks on coastal defences on June 6 then, as they were landing back from operations on June 7, Me 410s attacked the Liberators, shooting down four. Flying-bomb targets were subsequently attacked, gun emplacements too, and there were repeated attacks on supply lines leading to the front.

During August the Group re-equipped with B-17s after flying 62 raids with B-24s, and took its Fortresses into action from mid-September. Tactical targets were still mainly under attack but in October 1944 to February 1945 the Group participated in strategic operations. This period took it to marshalling yards at Ludwigshaven, Hamm and Osnabruck, oil targets at Bielefeld, Merseburg, Hamburg and Misburg, to factories at Berlin, Dalteln, Hanover and to airfields at Munster, Neumunster and Frankfurt. From March 1945 the targets were mainly communications and by VE-Day the Group was dropping food to the Dutch. The 34th returned to the USA in July 1945 after which the station passed to 94 MU and was used as an ammunition store. The site became inactive in June 1954 but is busy now, the home of light industry set amid farmland.

Mepal, Cambridgeshire

TL449795. 7 miles W of Ely, on A142. Road crosses site

Waterbeach became the central station in 33 Base, 3 Group, in 1943. The initial intention was that Mepal, then with two runways, would form the second station, housing 1665 Conversion Unit which formed at Waterbeach. The third airfield of the Base was Witchford.

Whilst Mepal had final touches put to it in the spring of 1943, 1665 CU made use of Great Ashfield. When the time came to move the unit to Mepal it had been decided that Waterbeach would again become an operational station. To use Mepal for training was illogical, and it became a sub-station of Waterbeach to accommodate 24 aircraft on June 25 1943. Newmarket was unsuitable for heavily laden Lancasters and, in the general re-arrangement of bomber stations, 75(RNZAF) Squadron left Newmarket on June 28 1943 and brought its Stirlings to Mepal. No 75 was a three-Flight squadron and busily operating at the time, mounting its first operation from the new station on July 3 against Cologne. Thereafter the Stirlings took part in many 3 Group operations, flew a large number of mining sorties and dropped supplies to the French. During March 1944 the squadron re-equipped with Lancaster I/IIIs, first operating them in April whilst Stirlings were still in use. Main Force raids followed and at the end of the war 75 Squadron dropped food to the Dutch.

Hurried movement of 74 Squadron to Spilsby in July 1945 was partly brought about by the arrival of Transport Command at Oakington, and rapid wind down of other squadrons and bases. In July 1945 44 Squadron's Lancasters arrived from 5 Group and 7 Squadron from Oakington, forming part of Tiger Force for the Far East. No 44 left in August, replaced by 49 Squadron, the former having gone to Mildenhall to continue Lincoln trials. Nos

7 and 49 remained at Mepal until July 1946 when the station was put on Care & Maintenance.

To all intents and purpose Mepal passed away until 1958 when the site, still in official hands, took on a completely new look. Buildings were placed in the centre of the airfield, which had only been the site of two 'T' hangars and a few huts

One of 75 Squadron's Stirlings at Mepal.

close to Mepal village. Now, by the Chatteris road which opened after the war, a high fence was erected within which was placed three launching sites and associated buildings for 113 Squadron's Thor missiles. The Thors under 3 Group remained here until 1963, having been brought to high readiness during the Cuban missile crisis.

After the Thors were withdrawn Mepal fell into decay and reverted to farming. Jardin's have converted a hangar into their corrugated paper factory. The taxi track largely remains, the control tower and some blast walls. The airfield is best viewed from the road which crosses it.

Mepal photographed from 16,000 feet by 58 Squadron on March 29 1965 (DoE).

Metfield, Suffolk

TM310790. Off B1123 6 miles SE Metfield. Carry on, turn left, by-road crosses site

Transport aircraft were largely absent from East Anglian skies until the last year of the war. True, C-47s of the 9th AF became a frequent sight in 1943-1944, and the assembly of Horsa gliders on bomber bases had brought their tugs in plenty. At Metfield it was different for to this base the Americans brought urgently needed supplies of men and materials from the USA.

Metfield came into use as a base for the 353rd Fighter Group flying P-47s in August 1943. It entered operations under the watchful eyes of the 56th Fighter Group at nearby Halesworth on August 9 1943, flying bomber escorts and sweeps thereafter. During March 1944 tactical trials were undertaken at Metfield resulting in US fighters supporting bomber operations by strafing enemy bases after the manner of RAF operations for many months.

A re-arrangement of P-47 bases led to the 353rd moving out in April 1944, its place being taken by B-24s of the 491st Bomb Group which had spent a short time at North Pickenham. There, only the ground elements had assembled, but to Metfield came the B-24s. The Group commenced operations on June 2 1944 taking part in a prelude to Normandy, after which came army support before a switch was made to strategic bombing. On July 15 1944 a serious incident occurred when the station's bomb dump exploded.

Losses sustained by the 492nd Bomb Group at Pickenham had been heavy and when the Americans needed a supply base

Metfield photographed from a Mosquito on October 16 1946 (DoE).

in Suffolk they decided to move the 491st to Pickenham and use Metfield for this other purpose.

Thus from mid-August 1944 the occupants at this airfield varied and included visiting C-47s and C-54 Skymasters and many smaller transports. Liberators, too, were based here for hush-hush trips to Sweden.

At 0137 hours on March 2 1945, during a final burst of intruder activity against the UK, a Ju 88G-6 of 5/NJG 4 joined the Metfield circuit, attacking a B-24 from the lower starboard quarter. The Liberator pilot turned into the attacker without his crew opening fire. Meanwhile, the Ju 88 had been picked up by a Mosquito and, after being attacked, dived into the airfield perimeter.

Although Metfield returned to the RAF later in 1945 it saw no more active use.

Methwold, Suffolk

TL735935. By B1106 north of Brandon

It was just another *Circus*, to divert enemy attention whilst Bostons attacked the steel works at Ijmuiden. No 487 Squadron would bomb Amsterdam's power station, giving the Dutch Resistance some support. At 1643 hours on May 3 1943 12 Venturas took off from Methwold, one soon returning with trouble. Calamity; the fighter support had arrived off Flushing too early and, by ill fortune, stirred a hornet's nest. The German Governor of Holland was visiting Haarlem, and the Germans feared he might be under attack. A collection of skilled Luftwaffe pilots, already assembled at Schiphol to give him cover, was alerted.

At 1735 hours the Venturas crossed the Dutch coast at 12,000 feet. Within moments they were ambushed by the Luftwaffe. One, seriously damaged, made for home. The remainder were gradually picked off. Squadron Leader L.H. Trent pressed on, bombed the target and was then shot down. His story did not fully emerge until after the war and then, back from POW camp, he was awarded the Victoria Cross, the second to go to the Feltwell base.

Methwold was prepared before the war as Feltwell's satellite, one of the first such stations. After mobilisation 37 Squadron dispersed here in September 1939. Wellingtons became a common sight on the grass field, surrounded on much of its perimeter by trees. In September 1939 214 Squadron moved out of Feltwell to Methwold and was here until February 1940, leaving 37 and 75 Squadrons to disperse at Methwold whilst operations were flown from Feltwell.

When 57 Squadron reached Feltwell in November 1940 it soon used it and by 1942 operations were mounted from Methwold.

In September 1942 57 Squadron moved north and Methwold passed to 2 Group. On September 30 21 Squadron arrived with its Venturas, taking the type into action for the first time on November 3. The squadron operated from here for the Eindhoven raid in December, thereafter flying *Circus* operations with fighter escort. When 3 Group took over Feltwell in April 1943, 21 Squadron moved to Oulton making way for the two Feltwell squadrons, Nos 464 and 487, both Dominion squadrons — which meant the accents of Australians and New Zealanders abounded here. Day bombing operations continued.

At this time the solution to a difficult problem was being resolved. Production of Horsa gliders was embarrassingly large, posing problems of storage prior to use in forthcoming airborne assaults. The answer was to site them in groups of 32, dispersed on bomber airfields. One of the first to accept delivery was Methwold. By chance I was on the station when the first Horsas arrived. Hoards turned out to watch and two Horsas detached themselves from Albemarle tug ropes and amazed we onlookers with their astonishingly steep glide paths. Then the aircrews raced over for a close look before setting off for Ostend.

By August 1943, with the Horsas picketed and control surfaces removed to avoid gale damage, Methwold thrilled to the news that the squadrons would leave for Sculthorpe and Mosquitoes. Everyone was pleased to be rid of 'the pig'.

Methwold lay quiet although some of Feltwell's new occupants occasionally dispersed here. In March 1944 the Horsas were prepared for action and towed away south, some to be used in the Arnhem landings.

Lakenheath's closure to flying in May 1944 brought 149 Squadron to the station for its final months with Stirlings. In August 218 Squadron, flying Lancaster I/IIIs, arrived, and soon both Lancaster-equipped squadrons were operating by day and night in 3 Group's offensive, which continued until hostilities ended, 218 Squadron moving out in December when 149 Squadron was raised to three-

A wartime aerial view of Methwold.

Flight strength.

Post-war wind-down reduced the strength of the squadron, which was joined by a reduced 207 Squadron in October 1945. In April, both units moved to Tuddenham to equip with new aircraft, and Methwold was placed under Care & Maintenance in September 1946. Flying had not yet ceased for in 1955 elements of CSE Watton moved here whilst their runway was attended to. The station had been under Flying Training Command control since December 7 1946 and was then a satellite for Feltwell until June 1958.

A visit to Methwold brings the 'T' Type hangars into view, and across the B 1106 to the east among the trees are remains of living quarters and Messes. The airfield is now intensively farmed and recently two houses have been built on the site.

Ventura 'O' Orange of 487 Squadron being bombed up at Methwold in 1943 (R. Kitching).

Mildenhall, Suffolk

TL685768. By A1101 NW out of Milden-hall town

Line-upon-line, squadrons of silver biplanes, were there. Harts, Bulldogs, Furies, 356 of their like, to parade before HM King George V upon the Silver Jubilee Review by 'the Sailor King' on July 6 1935. About half the field—so much smaller than now—was covered by row upon row of aircraft floodlit at night. Upon the firing of a Very cartridge, swarms of aircraft roared off, taking an hour to do so before setting off in train for the Duxford fly-by. This memorable event is recalled by a memorial on the front of Building 562, the present WHQ of the 513th TAW.

Mildenhall, locally known as Beck Row, had opened on October 16 1943 under Wing Commander F.J. Linnell who became, at the height of the war, Controller of Research and Development at MAP, a most important post to hold. At the opening of Mildenhall came another event of great historic importance, the Mildenhall-Melbourne MacRobertson Air Race won by the beautiful de Havilland Comet racer which is now being lovingly restored at Old Warden.

The first squadron to occupy Mildenhall was No 99 which arrived on November 14 1934 when their nine Heyfords winged their way in. Mildenhall was rapidly immersed in the Expansion period and in September 1935 99 Squadron detached its 'B' Flight to become 38 Squadron, also Heyford-equipped. Late in 1936 this squadron received a few Fairey Hendons. The Hendon monoplane was an underpowered anachronism. Its deep wing section accommodated bomb cells. A huge trousered undercarriage reduced its speed. It had a turret, wrongly positioned in the nose, whilst rear defence was a gun mounted on a Scarff ring.

In January 1937 HQ 3 Group arrived at Mildenhall, here until the move to Exning when war broke out. Headquarters 4 Group formed here on April 1 1937 and 5 Group in July.

On April 12 1937 No 99 Squadron again detached its 'B' Flight, this time to form 149 Squadron, also Heyford-equipped. May 5 1937 saw the Hendons fly away to Marham. Then on June 14 1937 211 Squadron formed here, leaving for Grantham on September 2. During the Munich crisis in 1938 the Heyfords stood ready, armed and bombed up, for what would have been suicide operations. But

No 44 Squadron held a few Lincolns at Mildenhall for trials in 1946 (M. Drackett).

replacement was near.

Great excitement surrounded the arrival on October 10 1928 of the first Wellington 1 for 99 Squadron. The Wellington looked very beautiful, so modern and seemed so fast, and on January 18 1939 No 149 Squadron began to re-arm with them. These aircraft were soon to be seen flying around East Anglia in formation and then made some long distance trips over France, training and allowing range assessment to take place.

Mobilisation came on August 27 1939 and on Friday, September 1, when Poland was violated, 99 Squadron quickly moved to Newmarket Heath, its war station. Around the perimeter at Mildenhall 149 Squadron's Wellingtons were then dispersed, bombs at hand. On the Sunday afternoon after war was declared the airfield ostensibly was a scene of silence, belying what was going on behind the scenes. At 1825 hours three crews of 149 Squadron took off, but this came too late and because of poor weather their sortie against the German Fleet was nullified and they landed home at 2200 hours.

All next day 149 Squadron was at stand-by and at 1345 hours was warned to be ready for take-off to attack the enemy fleet near the Kiel Canal, at the entrance to Brunsbuttel. Shortly before 1500 hours

HM King George V arrives for the July 1935 Jubilee Review at Mildenhall (Flight International).

Mid-war Mildenhall was base for 149 Squadron's Stirlings (Flight International).

eight Wellingtons took off, but their formation was broken up by bad weather and five crews aborted. Of the other three one mistook the Eder for the Kiel Canal and one dropped bombs near Esbjerg. The third received hits in a fuel tank and the crew was lucky to reach Honington.

Already the refined Wellington 1a with power-operated turrets had arrived at Mildenhall. No 149 Squadron worked up with them, then came North Sea sweeps flown on a rotational basis by 3 Group crews. Also at Mildenhall at this time were Gladiators of the Meteorological Flight which had arrived from Duxford in April 1939. In November 1940 it became 401 Flight and moved to Bricham Newton on October 29 1941.

During February 1940 149 Squadron participated in night armed reconnaissance flights over Germany, which proved the difficulty of night operations. With the invasion of Norway the station was brought to a high state of readiness, further increased when the Blitzkrieg in the West broke. In June 1940, after night bombing had commenced, 149 Squadron was partly ordered to Salon for the bombing of Italy. French awkwardness made operations well nigh impossible, although 149 Squadron flew some sorties against Italy.

Dejected but home again, 149 Squadron threw itself into the night bomber offensive, conducted intensively from Mildenhall to the end of 1942. In 1941 its Wellington 1cs acquired national fame when the film *Target for Tonight* was made here, featuring Wing Commander P.C. Pickard and P2517 'F for Freddie'. The machine selected was as obscure as any, and there is no confirmation to suggest that it ever flew a bombing sortie. More portentous for the enemy was the night of March 31 1941 when two Wel-

lington IIs of the squadron were the first RAF bombers to drop 4,000 lb bombs. Only one could be carried in the Wellington, for which the centre doors had to be removed from the bomb cells. At this time only six Wellington IIs suitably modified were available, two going each to 9, 99 and 149 Squadrons. For the rest the mount remained the trusty Wellington 1c, reliable and popular but which, by 1941, was becoming out-dated. In October 1941 Stirlings began to arrive at Mildenhall and were introduced to operations in December 1941. Most of the operational flying now took place from Lakenheath, whence 149 Squadron moved in April 1942.

No 419 (Canadian) Squadron formed at Mildenhall on December 18 1941 and left for Leeming on August 14 1942, after a busy bombing campaign. It was replaced on August 15 by 75 New Zealand Squadron, here until November 1942. In the summer of 1942 No 1503 BAT Flight trained from Mildenhall, being replaced by 1505 BAT Flight on September 5 which itself moved to Upper Heyford, taking its Oxfords, on December 17 1942. Another arrival had been 115 Squadron's Wellington IIIs which moved in on September 24 when 2 Group took over their base at Marham, and 1403 Meteorological Flight reformed at Mildenhall in November 1942

C-130 Hercules now rotate through Mildenhall.

before going overseas. All this time Mildenhall had been a grass surfaced aerodrome, and it closed on November 7 for runway building. Three were laid down in customary pattern, which caused 115 Squadron to leave the station.

Marking the re-opening, an impressive formation of Stirlings of XV Squadron arrived on April 15 1943, quickly settling down to operational routine. XV detached its 'C' Flight to form 622 Squadron on August 10 and both squadrons carried on operations. In December 1943 they both converted to Lancaster I/IIIs and participated to the end of the war in day and night operations. Perchance, Lancaster R5508 joined XV Squadron as LS:C. This famous Lancaster was that in which Squadron Leader J.D. Nettleton had won the VC during the 1942 daylight Augsburg raid. Its dispersal was near the spot where the USAF now has a passenger terminal. From December 1942 to the end of the war Mildenhall was the headquarters station for 31 Base, the first such organisation to form. Over 8,000 bombing sorties were despatched from Mildenhall during the war, 23,000 tons of bombs were dropped and over 200 aircraft failed to return.

No 622 Squadron disbanded on August 15 1945 and was replaced at once by 44 Squadron, here until August 1946. Its task was to work out snags with the Lincoln whilst XV Squadron armed with some Lancaster B1 (Specials) which 617 Squadron had operated, carried out bombing trials with large bombs against the U-Boat pens at Farge and on Heligoland. Several USAAF B-17s joined in these trials. Those Fortresses were a pointer to the future, for the Americans would come to know Mildenhall well. Not yet, though, for in February 1949 four squadrons of Lancaster B1(FE)s arrived, Nos 35, 115, 149 and 207 which, later that year, re-armed with Lincolns. That bomber was already outdated so in February-March 1950 the four squadrons disbanded, their crews being mainly posted to Marham to train for the forthcoming Washington squadrons.

A few months of silence were followed by an astonishing burst of activity — the Americans arrived. Up went a high security fence, and anti-aircraft guns encircled the airfield. In July 1950 came B-50Ds of the 329th Bomb Squadron, 93rd Bomb Group(M), which stayed until February 1951. The Korean War had brought about this sudden move. In February 1951 the 509th Bomb Group arrived, replaced by the 2nd in May 1951 and later by the 22nd. On October 1 1951 Strategic Air Command took control of the station and Bomb Wings rotated on Temporary Duty stays. In August 1953 KC-97E tankers were first based at Mildenhall and thereafter it became a base for similar aircraft. Late in 1957 B-47s were first based here.

During January 1959 the base took over Burtonwood's role as a transport centre and the first C-124 touched down. Mildenhall was now the home of the 322 Air Division.

In 1966 the 513th Troop Carrier Wing arrived from Evreux, France, and the same year European Command's airborne command post function (Silk Purse Control) moved here. On July 1 1958 the controlling unit was redesignated 513th Tactical Airlift Wing and remains responsible for the care of the base, all aircraft maintenance, and provides for the four EC-135s of the airborne command post. Mildenhall became a staging post for flights to Britain and Germany, being host to C-124s, C-118s, C-133s, the even larger Starlifters and more recently gigantic Galaxy transports. C-130 Hercules Wings rotate here usually bringing about 16 aircraft on a bi-monthly basis, aircraft and crews being assigned to the 435th Tactical Airlift Group, a Military Airlift Command unit, whilst at Mildenhall. About 100,000 passengers a year are handled at the base, and much freight.

The European Tanker Task Force provided by Strategic Air Command operates from Mildenhall under the guidance of Detachment 1, 306th Strategic Wing. In 1977 alone some 2,100 KC-135 sorties were despatched from Mildenhall for inflight refuelling. There are normally 14 to 16 KC-135 tankers here from bases in America, on a six-week stay.

A naval air facility is stationed here with two aircraft, and in 1962 the US Third Air Division HQ moved to Mildenhall.

RAF Mildenhall now covers 1,042 acres, has a 9,240-foot runway and over 500 buildings located on its premises. The base population averages about 2,740 US military personnel, 100 Department of the Air Force civilians and 330 British employees. Nearly 5,000 dependants live in the area around.

Of all the activities here surely none would amaze the pilots of the Heyfords as much as the sight of an SR-71 Blackbird reconnaissance jet. Unless ... unless it be the public viewing enclosure which the Americans have provided and which, on a fine summer's day, is usually equipped with an ice-cream vendor. It certainly is a strange world.

Newmarket Heath (Rowley Mile), Suffolk

TL620630. Heath is W of the town

East Anglia's nearest approach to a motorway so far is the Newmarket bypass which cuts through the Devil's Dyke and curves past two wartime 'T' Type hangars, once occupied by Wellington Xs and Martinets of 1483 Flight. A splendid view of the Heath, still used for flying on race days, may be obtained from a layby on the bypass.

Few who race along the carriageway know they thunder by the spot where a Stirling mine-layer ended its days in one of the mightiest explosions heard in the area. The bomber, R9245, was taking off for the Bordeaux area from the Heath, whose 3,000-yard grass runway was the longest in the country at that time. Heavily laden, it lifted off a fraction too late. A mainwheel clipped the top of the Dyke and the oil tank was pierced. An engine seized and the giant bomber spun in, two mines then exploding.

Newmarket was one of the most interesting wartime airfields in East Anglia. It has known great pageantry as the titled and wealthy have flown in on race days since long before the war. Indeed, HRH the Prince of Wales landed here on his way to the 1935 Jubilee Review at Mildenhall.

Two days before the war began Wellingtons of 99 Squadron arrived from Mildenhall, crews and ground personnel being accommodated in the Grandstand in great discomfort, where thousands now stand to cheer on race days. No real action came until December 14 1939 when a dozen Wellingtons took off to attack German warships off Heligoland in daylight. Enemy radar alerted the fighters and the Messerschmitts waded in, found the Wellingtons easy game during beam attacks, shooting down five and causing a sixth to crash before it reached home. One crashed into trees, the crew having to be cut from the wreckage. This operation more than any other caused Bomber Command to switch to the night campaign, and ultimately led to bombers having beam defence.

Throughout 1940 the Wellingtons operated, and were detached at one time to the south of France to bomb Italy in the quaintly named Operation *Haddock*. But now they were operating at night.

On a grey afternoon in February 1941 a Dornier Do 17Z came out of the clouds over the Norwich road. The area swarmed with troops who opened fire on the raider which, as it flew low over the main street, unleashed its load. The bombs bashed into the shops along the entire street wrecking the White Hart Hotel, killing those unlucky enough to be in the old post office and leaving shattered glass along the entire length of the town.

Soon after 99 Squadron moved to Waterbeach, Stirlings of 7 Squadron arrived as their home base, Oakington, was water-logged. Stirlings made their first raid on Germany from Newmarket. No 3 Group Flight arrived with Wellingtons in May 1941.

Other new shapes came, Whitleys of 138 (Special Duty) Squadron. Working their cloak and dagger task some of them reached as far as Poland, using Newmarket as the advanced base for their parent station, Stradishall. Lysanders, too, operated to France from Newmarket, also in great secrecy. A little-known fact is that the squadron was so short of Lysanders that it even employed aircraft from the local 3 Group Gunnery Flight — still in target towing markings. As 1483 Flight these moved to Marham on July 14 1942 after having contributed to the '1,000 bomber' raids.

Wellingtons of 75 Squadron moved here for Main Force operations under Mildenhall control. But it was the arrival of the second prototype of the tank-carrying Hamilcar glider in 1942 that evoked more interest. This huge glider was towed aloft by a Halifax, the long run judged ideal for load carrying trials. These ended when the glider's undercarriage was damaged in a heavy landing, but shortly before this an unusual event had occurred. The large combination had just been towed aloft when warning was received that a Ju 86R high-flying raider was approaching from Clacton. The tug pilot, unhappy to be caught in a compromising situation, was ordered to release his glider and land, leaving the cumbersome Hamilcar to land luckily in safety.

Stirlings replaced 75's Wellingtons in the autumn. Newmarket became part of 31 Base in December 1942 and then came an even more exciting period. surrounded by great secrecy a Gloster F9/40, forerunner of the Meteor jet fighter, was brought to the Heath and assembled for flight trials. Low engine power, helped by the long grass run and good approaches, made Newmarket seem suitable for trials. They had to be conducted very secretly, and when the machine began its short duration flights it usually did so in the calm conditions of early morning. Evidently the MAP did not trust the RAF Police for, astonishingly, the machine was guarded by Army policemen who steadfastly ordered passing RAF personnel to 'look the other way'! Even so, the whole area around quickly buzzed with rumours about the strange craft which, one Sunday morning, soared aloft to make the first jet cross-country flight to its new base at Barford St John. To save you wondering — yes, I did have a good view of it!

Soon Newmarket was housing the secret work of the Bombing Development Unit which arrived on September 13 1943 to conduct trials of new bombing aids, develop medium level mine laying (a great advance) and then train crews to use H2S and other radar and radio aids. It was here, too, that the final form of belly defence for bombers was developed. Trials were conducted of the Vultee Vengeance dive-bomber which officials tried to dump on 2 Group, fortunately without success.

The Bombing Development Unit moved back to Feltwell in 1945, leaving 1483 Gunnery Training Flight which had returned on June 30 1943 and was now occupying the station, using 11 Wellington Xs and nine Martinets. Their place was taken by six Spitfire Vs, 12 Hurricanes and eight Martinets. The Flight became 1688 Bomber Defence Training Flight and moved to Feltwell on February 26 1945. A Flight of 3 LFS used the station briefly in 1945 before, on March 1, No 54 Maintenance Unit, in the area since September 1939, took up residence. Flying had ceased in February 1945 and by summer the RAF had gone. Long since abandoned too had been the idea that Side Hill might be a suitable site for glider training.

The end of the war brought a space in flying at Newmarket, but by 1946 racegoers were arriving from Europe and of the exotic aircraft which brought them in those days surely pride of place goest to the immaculate Grumman Mallard amphibian of M. Boussac. If you visit Newmarket on any race day you are bound to see a clutch of light aircraft here for the sport of Kings. Apt that, in 1942, the King's Flight changed form here into No 161 (Special Duties) Squadron for famed operations later from Tempsford.

North Creake, Norfolk

TF895385. E of village by Walsingham-Wells road

This airfield opened mid-war, built to accommodate RAF squadrons forced out of stations as the American forces enlarged. The site had long been acquired. In 1941 it served as a decoy field for Docking. Development took place in 1942-1943 when North Creake was completed as a sub-station of Foulsham.

It opened on November 23 1943 under 3 Group, passing to 100 Group on December 7 1943. The Windsor was a possible future type for Bomber Command as well as a revised, heavier Lancaster. There was also the possibility of larger American bombers, and all needed longer runways. Accordingly it was decided to lengthen those at North Creake. The station went on to Care & Maintenance pending extensions, a signals unit meanwhile encamping. During early 1944 the decision was made to extend Lakenheath into a Very Heavy Bomber station. North Creake was not extended and re-opened in April 1944. Lakenheath's 199 Squadron arrived at the start of May 1944 to continue using *Mandrel* jamming equipment. Its Stirling IIIs preceded many Main Force attacks and sometimes dropped *Window* to confuse defenders.

On September 7 their 'C' Flight was detached becoming the nucleus of a new Stirling RCM squadron, No 171. They operated with *Window*, commencing duties on September 15.

No 171 almost at once began to re-equip with Halifax IIIs and was soon assisting in placing the *Mandrel* screen. No 199 Squadron commenced operating Halifax IIIs in March 1945, being the last squadron in Bomber Command to fly Stirlings operationally. By this time both squadrons were also dropping bombs as well as *Window*. Final sorties were flown

Stirling III LJ543 'J' of 199 Squadron at North Creake (Frank F. Smith).

A 1978 photograph of North Creake.

North Creake photographed by a 58 Squadron Canberra on March 11 1965 (DoE).

on May 2 1945, then 171 Squadron disbanded on July 27 and 199 Squadron two days later.

North Creake was put on to Care & Maintenance on September 30 1945 and became a store for Mosquitoes in the hands of 274 MU. The Mosquitoes were gradually reduced to scrap at 274 MU and the station closed in September 1947.

North Pickenham, Norfolk

TL850070. By B1077 NW from South Pickenham. Road also along N side by ex-Thor site

Here was a site selected in 1958 to accommodate a trio of Thor IRBMs. Unlike the presence of Liberators during the war, the placing of Thors caused some misguided opposition; the older generation had shown more wisdom.

Early in January 1944 the 491st Bomb Group sailed for Britain with few personnel and little equipment. The air echelon was absent, continuing to train in the USA. It arrived in May 1944. Group HQ had been established at Pickenham in

February 1944 but soon moved to Metfield.

Its place had been taken by B-24s of the 492nd Bomb Group in mid-April 1944, the initial operation coming on May 11. Attacks were concentrated upon Germany at a high loss rate. During the first week of June 1944 the Group switched to airfields and V-1 sites in France, preluding invasion. Early on the morning of D-Day Pickenham's Liberators helped pound coastal defences, then flew interdiction sorties aiding troops holding the bridgehead. In mid-June 1944 strategic attacks on Germany were resumed, interrupted when support was given for the breakout from St Lô on July 25. Such support was continued into August 1944 when a sudden change came about.

The Allies wished to make maximum use of the Resistance Movement in Europe, but supply forces were limited. The lion's share of this work had fallen upon 3 Group, Bomber Command, using Stirling bombers and two special duty squadrons at Tempsford. Stirling squadrons had recently been reduced in number and by August 1944 none was available for supply duty. The Americans made their contribution by switching the 492nd Bomb Group — less personnel and equipment — to Harrington, in Northamptonshire, whence special duty operations were soon flown.

The absence of an operational formation at Pickenham was remedied by moving the 491st back from Metfield in August 1944, allowing that base to develop as a transport centre for the 8th AF. On September 18 the 491st took part in supplying the airborne forces in Holland, but a more momentous day was November 26 when the target was Misburg. Enemy fighter opposition was fierce and half the force of B-24s despatched from Pickenham was lost. Nevertheless, the Group pressed on to bomb the target, for which effort it was awarded a Distinguished Unit Citation.

During the winter Ardennes offensive the B-24s attacked enemy fortifications and supply lines, and attacked an airfield to prevent opposition to the Rhine crossing operation. Subsequently the Group's main effort was directed against communications as the Allies drove into Germany.

After the Americans left, North Pickenham became a sub-site for 258 MU at Shipdam. It was transferred to Bomber Command in October 1948, returning to Maintenance Command a year later, being unsuitable for development as a heavy bomber base for the Americans, although they took it over again in August 1954. Late in 1958 Bomber Command took command for 220 Squadron's Thors which remained until 1963, the station closing in October. A brief resumption of life came between October 1964 and November 1965 when Kestrels of the Evaluation Squadron at West Raynham did some flying here.

North Pickenham in 1978. Thor launch pads can be seen at centre left.

Pickenham is best viewed from the road along the north side. From here can be seen a hangar, now part of the Crane Freuhof works. To the west a TV booster mast towers high. A tall fence surrounds the area where the Thors were sited, inside which stand two blast walls and some concrete remainders. Pickenham has one of those tall water towers which were such an obvious wartime airfield land mark. This can be seen closely from the road to the industrial site.

Oakington, Cambridgeshire

TL409655. 2 miles N of A604, 6 miles NW of Cambridge

Stirling. The very name is synonymous with Oakington. It also means 7 Squadron which, from late 1940 to the end of the war, fought valiantly from the station by night and day. The present airfield is not the first at Oakington for in 1913 a monoplane was built and flown here, but no military use was made of the flying strip.

Building of RAF Oakington commenced in 1939, hence the two Type 'J' hangars. The unfinished station opened on July 1 1940, Wing Commander L.B. Duggen taking command at a time when many personnel were accommodated in tents. No 218 Squadron's Blenheim IVs

moved in on July 14 1940 and were dispersed on the south side. They commenced daylight operations against Dutch airfields on August 19.

The most memorable event of summer 1940 came on September 19. Blenheims were making mock attacks on the airfield for the benefit of army defenders. Suddenly a 'Blenheim' unexpectedly made an approach and belly landed, whilst two Hurricanes of 17 Squadron zoomed overhead. In fact it was not a Blenheim, it was Ju 88a 7A + FM, Werk Nr 0362, of 4(F)/121, packed with cameras and which had engine trouble. Leutnant Helmut Knab and his crew were captured.

The arrival of the Ju 88 was fortuitous. It contained excellent cameras which the stations soon made use of. On November 16 1940 No 3 Photographic Reconnaissance Unit formed here under Bomber Command for damage assessment duties. It brought in some astonishing Spitfires specially modified for the task and painted in a variety of colours including the customary grey-blue but also white, and even pink to tone with evening skies at high altitudes. Those German cameras proved very useful now. The first Spitfire operation was flown on November 29 1940, to photograph Cologne, after which 3 PRU flew many sorties and acquired some Wellingtons for night photography by the aid of high-powered flash bulbs.

It was the arrival of 7 Squadron on October 29 1940 that heralded the Stirling era. The squadron took some time fully to move in. Such was the state of the Stirling programme that in November they had only two aircraft here. There was nothing basically wrong with the aircraft apart from low-powered engines, but an assortment of small faults added up to give it a protracted teething period. It brought chagrin to the squadron to find that the aircraft would easily fit the hangars, yet span had been reduced in the project stage to allow indoor servicing.

No 5 Flying Training School post-war equipped with Varsities and ran twin-conversion courses at Oakington.

Oakington, primary home of the Stirling. Behind 7 Squadron's 'G' George can be seen Wellingtons of 101 Squadron (RCAF).

In January 1941 Oakington's surface fell into a terrible state, a mass of mud on the days when the ice thawed, a slippery morass when water froze; and it snowed often. Indeed, it was so cold that there was a rum ration 'to approved personnel'. Occasionally a Stirling made a flight, to the delight of the locals. On January 16 1941 King George VI took a look at the new bomber whilst behind the scenes pressure was being put strongly for operations to commence. On February 19, long before the aircraft was ready to fight, three Stirlings made the first raid, against Rotterdam.

Oakington already had its satellite at Bourn and on February 7 1941 personnel were sent there for ground defence duties, although precisely when the SLG opened remains unknown. Equipment had already arrived at Oakington for the handling of 2,000 lb bombs, the largest weapons the Stirling could carry.

The airfield had been declared unsuitable for Spitfires on January 22 and operations were at once switched to Alconbury, Wellingtons flying their first night sorties from Newmarket on February 5 and 6. On February 25 the 50th Spitfire sortie was flown. On March 14 Spitfire X4712 flew to Horsham St Faith and there took on an extra 20 gallons of fuel. It took off at 1020 hours and at 1225 hours was over Berlin, the first RAF aircraft to fly over the capital in daylight. It secured 95 photographs through the mist and landed at Alconbury with only 20 gallons of fuel left. No 3 PRU usually held about six Spitfires and flew a large number of sorties with them before disbanding late in July 1941.

By then Oakington's Stirlings were hitting the headlines, particularly with their daylight raids, but throughout 1941 the aircraft remained few in number. Oakington's runways were completed in the spring. The highlight of the year was a day raid on Brest on December 18. The squadron commander at this time was Wing Commander H.R. Graham who later commanded 5 FTS and became AOC 23 Group.

On May 30 1942 word passed around among the villagers at Oakington that 1,000 bombers would operate that night, against Cologne. It seemed impossible. This was 7 Squadron's biggest raid yet and in addition to its 19 Stirlings, 12 Wellingtons of 101 Squadron operated from Bourn under Oakington's control. That squadron had arrived at Oakington in June 1941 flying Wellington 1cs and moved to Bourn on February 11 1942. No 23 OTU placed five Wellington 1cs at each of these stations for the '1,000 bomber' raids. Of the whole force of 41 aircraft, 33 claimed successful attacks.

In August 1942 7 Squadron switched to the pathfinding role, and 101 Squadron vacated the SLG to allow XV Squadron to move in and come under Oakington's control. Now, the Stirlings often carried flare loads mixed with some high explosive, and backed up primary markers. A gradual switch to flares/target indicators and large incendiary loads came, particularly during the Battle of the Ruhr in 1943. On May 11 1943, 7 Squadron began to re-equip with Lancasters which took over the operational role completely on August 12 1943. Bomb loads immediately increased. No 7 Squadron made a great contribution to the bomber offensive, being a three-Flight squadron. It was busy during the Battle of Berlin, and sustained a constant campaign including marking gun batteries on June 5/6 1944.

Early in 1943 some additional Bellman hangars were erected. Their purpose was to provide a home for an entirely different phase in Oakington's history for here, on April 1 1943, No 1409 Meteorological Flight formed with eight Mosquito IVs from 521 Squadron. Its task was to seek out weather patterns for the whole of Bomber Command, PAMPA flights beginning on April 2. In May 1943 it began to use Mosquito IXs and by the time it moved to Wyton on January 8 1944 was fully equipped with that type.

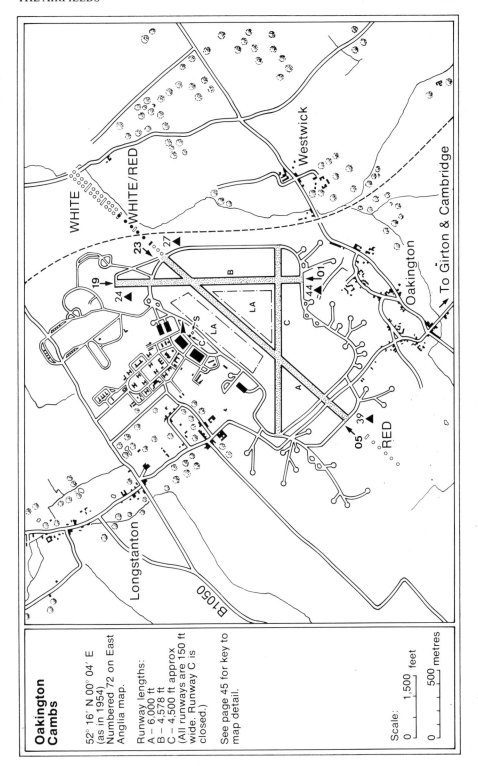

Oakington
Cambs

52° 16' N 00° 04' E
(as in 1954)
Numbered 72 on East
Anglia map.

Runway lengths:
A – 6,000 ft
B – 4,578 ft
C – 4,500 ft approx
(All runways are 150 ft
wide. Runway C is
closed.)

See page 45 for key to
map detail.

Scale:

0   1,500   feet

0   500 metres

In November 1943 No 627 Squadron formed at Oakington for bomber operations, leaving for 5 Group and a specialised role on April 15 1944. Its place was taken by Mosquitoes of 571 Squadron which arrived on April 24 1944 and stayed until July 29 1945. During that time the squadron operated 2,520 sorties, almost all by night, and within the Main Force of LNSF. Oakington's combination of Mosquito and Lancaster was unbeatable and continued to the end of European hostilities.

Termination of Bomber Command's stay at Oakington was abrupt. On July 24 1945 Transport Command took over the station and the first Liberator of 206 Squadron arrived, resplendent still in Coastal Command colours. So rapid was the change-over that next day two Liberators, KK226 and KK260, left for India on a training flight, even before the squadron's Liberators had all arrived from Leuchars. On August 1 the advance party of 86 Squadron moved in and both squadrons were in position by mid-August 1945. Next month trunk route flying to India carrying troops and cargo was underway, and continued until late in 1945 when the services were reduced. In April 1946 the squadrons disbanded.

Avro Yorks of 242 Squadron then replaced them on May 7 1946 to take part in Far and Middle East trunk route flying of passengers and freight. The squadron stayed here until November 1947. August saw the arrival of 238 Squadron, followed by 27 Squadron reformed here on November 24 1947, during which month 30 and 46 Squadrons also arrived. As part of the airborne assault force they had Horsa gliders with them. Between June 1948 and May 1949 these squadrons were much involved in the Berlin Air Lift. No 238 Squadron was re-numbered 10 Squadron on November 5 1948 and immediately moved to Lübeck, returning to Oakington in September 1949 and disbanding there on February 20 1950. No 18 Squadron was briefly here in 1949, leaving for Waterbeach in October. No 46 disbanded on February 20 1950 and 27 Squadron left in November of that year.

During February-March 1950 No 24 Squadron arrived bringing its VIP Yorks, Valettas and Dakotas. It was based here until October 1950.

During November 1950 Transport Command relinquished its hold on Oakington which passed to 23 Group, Training Command, who brought No 1 Flying Training School to the station with Har-

vards. Their noisy stay extended to October 1951 then No 206 Advanced Flying School took over on the 29th. It initially began using aged Meteor IIIs as well as new Mk 7s, Meteor IVs replacing the old aircraft in 1953. On June 1 1954 the unit was re-designated 5 FTS. Vampire 5s and 9s were now added to the unit's strength and Meteors phased out. In September 1959 5 FTS became fully equipped with Vampire T 11s. This was in keeping with the then-current scheme of Provost-Vampire training for RAF pilots inaugurated at 5 FTS. Advanced flying training was now afforded to pilots who began their RAF flying on Provosts.

Some trouble was being experienced by long-legged pilots when flying Vampire T11s and late in 1959 the Meteor Flight was formed to solve this problem, flying Meteor T 7s. During 1959 71 pilots received their wings at Oakington, 81 in 1960 and 73 in 1961.

The jets were completely replaced in 1963 by Varsities as 5 FTS switched to training pilots for multi-engined aircraft. The Varsities were intensively flown, and it proved most economical to start their engines as the day's flying commenced and run them until flying ceased. The noise of the Varsities brought local complaints, generally from newcomers to the area. One vociferous lady took up flying to solve the station's problems, an act which brought great merriment to 5 FTS when, on a cross-country flight, she became hopelessly lost!

Jetstreams began to replace the Varsities in late summer 1974, this offering much better training for airway flying. Ironically this required the building of a new fuel depot, at a time when the station was due for closure. No 5 FTS ended its days late in 1974, the Varsities being retired some after as many as 30,000 landings. The Jetstreams although popular with 5 FTS, had proven troublesome, and were put into storage.

A Wessex, XT606, seemingly made the final flight from Oakington on May 7 1975. Early in 1979, however, the station came to life again when 657 Squadron moved here to train using the Lynx.

Old Buckenham, Norfolk
TG085940. 2 miles NE of village, off B1077 S of Wymondham

Old Buckenham was a place of tragedy and glamour. On the one hand there were often horrific moments when a B-24 set down carrying those awfully wounded, and perhaps an undercarriage malfunction would produce that terrifying moment when a giant bomber slid along a runway in a shower of sparks which, at any moment, could erupt into a fireball. Then, the sound of ambulances and fire crews racing across to retrieve the wounded was a spectacle ever unforgettable. The courage the Americans displayed on day raids was outstanding, and the current glamourised view of the 8th AF is diluted for any who, like myself, witnessed scenes almost beyond one's worst imagination.

In off-duty moments there certainly was glamour, for Americans seemed such attractive personalities, who ate so well and lived fast. Surely none could portray the glamorous side of the 8th more than James Stewart who became such a popular film star and who in 1944 was Group Executive Officer at Old Buckenham. One would not readily associate him with the carnage, more with the officer in his 'pinks', for in those days the USAAF was still much an Army organisaton which dressed its men like soldiers and saw to it that their off-duty uniforms were as appealing as any.

Old Buckenham lay well within the territory of the 2nd Air Division which controlled the Liberators. From the end of 1943 it was home for the 453rd Bomb Group which operated from here to the end of the war. There is little to see now, beyond the remnants of the main runway and the perimeter track, marked sometimes by an ugly container vehicle. History seems far from the minds of people who park these monstrosities in sacred places! Over 250 operations were flown from here by the 453rd, whose first was against Tours airfield on February 5 1944.

Like other B-24 Groups, its history passed through the stages of attacking strategic targets supporting the invasion and airborne ventures and, finally, attacks on communications targets at the end of the war. The Group's list of targets included the fuel depot at Dulmen, rail yards at Hamm, I.G. Farben chemical works at Leverkusen, Gelsenkirchen's synthetic oil refinery, the aircraft assembly plant at Gotha and specialised targets like the viaduct at Altenbeken and Neumünster airfield. From Old Buckenham fuel supplies were flown to France in the summer of 1944, along with food, medical supplies and blankets, for which purpose the capacious fuselage of the B-24 rendered it useful.

During May and June 1945 the 453rd left for America, leaving Old Buckenham to run down. The sight of one of these airfields resting silent in the summer of 1945 was one to recall visions of a greater past when the field was alive. One wished so much that the pounding noise of engines running would return, like the sight of the bombers formating in the dawn. What a pity such magic moments could not come without the horror and the pathos.

Oulton, Norfolk
TG145275. At Oulton Street, on Cawston road

Reconnaissance photographs revealed a 490-foot long oil tanker in well-defended Brest. Blockade runners were often targets for day bomber operations, and on April 4 1943 No 21 Squadron, just arrived at Oulton, was briefed to attack. Twelve Venturas took off led by Flight Lieutenant Dennis and headed for their advanced base. Refuelled, they took off, to be screened by 10 Group's Spitfires.

On final approach to Brest a swarm of FW 190s ambushed them. A fierce battle ensued. Intrepid Luftwaffe pilots were little worried by the heavy anti-aircraft fire which always welcomed the RAF to Brest, and soon downed a Ventura. The others pressed on, their bombs falling alongside the ship. A large explosion was seen. Then came the return journey.

The '190s held off over the docks but were ready to pounce again, British fighters having been placed too high to protect the bombers. As the Venturas headed home one was ablaze and came down in the water. Although evasive action was good the Venturas could not escape, many shots entering their skinning. Forty miles from the Lizard another crashed into the sea and a fourth, flown by Pilot Officer Hicks, came down off Portreath. His crew were luckily rescued. Eight Venturas touched down that evening at Oulton.

Oulton opened as Horsham's satellite on July 31 1940. First to use the airfield was No 114 Squadron which arrived from Horsham in August and whose initial operations consisted of cloud cover day raids, attacks on airfields and some PR duties. It then took part in raids upon barges in the Channel ports, undertook roving commission flights and, in the winter of 1940-1941, participated in night Main Force raids on industrial targets, difficult for the crews. The squadron sent a detachment to Hornchurch at the start of 1941 and it fell to the squadron to take

part in *Circus No 1* on January 10 1941. It
flew several more *Circuses*, then in February was switched to an anti-shipping role
under Coastal Command, moving to
Thornaby on March 2 1941.

It was replaced by 18 Squadron with
Blenheim IVs at the start of April, which
flew its first sortie from Oulton, an anti-
shipping raid, on April 7. Operations continued until the squadron left in mid-July
1941. It came back in November, staying
a month whilst some crews were in Malta.

On December 9 1941 No 139 Squadron
arrived. It had been rapidly earmarked
for the Far East where it would fly Hudson IIIs. Crews trained here first with
1428 Hudson Conversion Flight, formed
on December 29 1941, then sailed for the
Far East in February 1942. The Hudson
Flight disbanded on May 29 1942, the
Ferry Training Section becoming 1444
Flight at Horsham St Faith before disbanding on June 20 1942. Between July 7
and September 19 1942, No 236 Squadron
was here flying Beaufighter 1cs under
Coastal command.

Oulton then lay relatively quiet until
later in September when it became a satellite for Swanton Morley and No 88
Squadron flying Bostons settled and
stayed until March 1943. This was a high-
spirited squadron, whose crews were bil-
letted in the delectable surroundings of
Blickling Hall where precious treasures
had been tucked out of sight and parts
boarded up to prevent any damage during
boisterous moments. Legend has it that
Anne Boleyn spent some time here and
the squadron commander was most satisfied to occupy her supposed bedroom.
Visit Blickling Hall now and you will see
the dining room much as the crews knew
it — apart from the paintings now on the
wall.

A 1978 aerial view of Oulton.

No 88 Squadron took a major part in 2
Group's Boston campaign by day, which
culminated in the Eindhoven raid of
December 1942, led by '88'. The Boston
squadrons in East Anglia suffered a
major blow when their aircraft were suddenly taken for the Middle East. The
squadron was virtually out of action until
the Mk IIIAs arrived in 1943, by which
time '88' was on the move from Oulton.

It was quickly replaced by 21 Squadron
which arrived at the start of April 1943
and flew its first bombing operation
against Brest on April 3. Similar day raids
followed on targets in France and Holland. In June 1943 the squadron had some
Mitchells here for training. Its operations
with Venturas ended in September 1943
during Operation *Starkey*, then it left for
Sculthorpe.

On September 10 1943 the station
passed to 3 Group, becoming the second
satellite for Foulsham. Oulton then
underwent major surgery for runways,
hangars and accommodation were built,
to prepare it for 100 Group.

It re-opened on May 16 1944 and
almost at once 214 Squadron, flying Fortresses, moved in together with 803 RCM
Squadron, USAAF. They were joined by
1699 Flight. The Americans were engaged
upon *Mandrels* and *Carpet* operations
when, after becoming the 36th Bomb
Squadron (Heavy), they left on August
13, having commenced operations on
June 3.

Their place was taken by a new RAF
RCM squadron, No 223, which reformed
here on August 23 and equipped with
Liberator B VIs. The immediate task for
those and 214 Squadron's Fortress IIs and
IIIs was to seek for evidence that V2s were
being radio-controlled, which operations
under Spitfire cover were flown in daylight. To the end of the war both squadrons flew RCM operations, 223 Squadron
receiving some Fortress IIIs in April 1945
before disbanding here on July 29 1945.
At that time 214 Squadron moved to the
Middle East, and the run-down of Oulton
began. It passed to Maintenance Command on October 3 1945 to become 119
Sub-Storage Site to 274 MU Swannington. Mosquitoes were stored here then,
until 274 MU disbanded in November
1947.

Rackheath, Norfolk
TG285145. E of Norwich

Rackheath came into use at the end of

1943. In February-March 1944 the 467th Bomb Group arrived with B-24s and first operated, against Bourges airfield, on April 10 1944.

Subsequently the targets for B-24s included the docks at Kiel, chemical factory at Bonn, textile works at Stuttgart, aircraft factory at Brunswick, steel works at Osnabruck and power station at Hamm. Intruders attacked the airfield on the late evening of April 22 1944 as the B-24s circled prior to landing back from Hamm. Two Liberators were shot down and the airfield was strafed.

On D-Day the 467th attacked shore installations and bridges near Cherbourg and on July 25, after some interdiction sorties, attacked troops and supply centres at Montreuil during the St Lô break out. The Group supplied fuel to mechanised forces in France during September, operated during the airborne invasion of Holland and during the Ardennes offensive. After supporting the Rhine crossing it concentrated on communications targets. Its 212th and final mission came on April 25 1945. The bombing accuracy of the 467th was reckoned to be the best in the 8th AF.

The control tower remains, but the airfield site is now occupied by light industry.

Rattlesden, Suffolk

TL965555. Make for Felsham, airfield to SE. Remnants of runways reached along narrow roads

For nearly a year the 447th Bomb Group had been heavily engaged in action from Rattlesden, where the control tower and a hangar still mark the airfield's site, standing amid agricultural land. Action was fierce. On November 2 1944 came a display of heroism and selfless devotion of one man for another. Among those flying that day was 2nd Lieutenant Robert E. Femoyer, a B-17 Navigator. Flak was hurled against his aircraft and Femoyer was seriously wounded by shrapnel. He stayed at his station refusing sedation. For two hours he continued to navigate the bomber home. His devotion cost him his life. He died soon after being lifted from the battered bomber.

Rattlesden was allotted to the USAAF on October 1 1942 and two months later the first Americans moved in, ground echelons of two squadrons to follow. They were flying some of the first B-26 Marauders to operate from Britain, from Rougham where the Group, the 322nd,

became consolidated in April 1943.

At the end of November 1943 the 447th Bomb Group ('K in a square') arrived from the USA and, using B-17Gs, went into action against V-1 sites on December 24 1943. Thereafter it was in the thick of battle and on April 19 1944 was despatched to Berlin. Station keeping by the 3rd Air Division was bad. Straggling, as ever, brought a heavy pasting from enemy fighters, the 447th losing 11 of its aircraft, the heaviest loss ever sustained in one raid — and at a time when the 8th AF bombing offensive was at a peak. The Group sustained further heavy losses on May 12 when penetrating to distant Leipzig.

Between December 1943 and May 1944 the Group was primarily engaged preparing for the invasion by attacking submarine pens, naval units, German industrial targets, ports and V-1 sites, as well as airfields and marshalling yards. June 1944 found it in direct support to the Normandy invasion, then the break-out at St Lô. It assisted in the liberation of Brest in September 1944 and made supply drops to the French Resistance. It gave general support to the Dutch landings before, in October, resuming its part in the strategic air offensive, concentrating on oil targets until December 1944 when it took its part in the Ardennes battle by bombing marshalling yards, rail bridges and communications centres in the battle zone. Then the Group resumed operations against oil, transport and communications targets to the close of hostilities. The 447th left Rattlesden in August 1945. The station was

The 'Milk Wagon', 43-37756, a B-17G of the 447th Bomb Group at Rattlesden. Some 70 'milk bottles' denoting sorties can be seen on the nose.

returned to the RAF in October 1945 and
the land finally relinquished in the mid-
1960s.

Raydon, Essex

*TM061391. Roydon-Hintlesham road
crosses part of site, E of village*

It was to Raydon, built by the US Army,
that some of the original P-51s came for
the USAAF in Europe. They arrived at
the end of 1943 and entered the hands of
the 357th Fighter Group, second to have
them. Compared with the Thunderbolt
the Mustang presented an image of speed
and nimbleness, and brought back to East
Anglia the sound of the Spitfire IX, a note
like a heavy version of the Allison which
powered the Mustang 1s which the RAF
used. The 8th AF was eager to obtain
P-51s and the 357th was transferred at the
end of January 1944 to Leiston, which
brought the 358th Fighter Group in its
place flying P-47s. Thus, the scene now
was of these heavily built and bulky
machines.

The 358th was already operational
when it moved to Raydon and, in the
hands of the 9th AF, it carried out some
bomber escorts for B-26s based in Essex.
It had long been decided that the fighters
of the 9th would be based in the south of
England prior to the invasion. For the
358th a move to High Halden came early
in April 1944.

The vacuum this left was quickly filled
by the arrival of the 353rd Fighter
Group's P-47s which came to Raydon
from Metfield in mid-April 1944. This
unit had already achieved notoriety, for
much of the pioneering of low-level strafing and bombing methods in support of
the 8th AF bomber operations had been
worked out by the 353rd. Its fighter-
bomber activities reached fever pitch
when the Group moved to Raydon. It gave
close support for the immediate period of
the invasion, and was particularly busy
during the September airborne landings in
Holland for which it was awarded a Distinguished Unit Citation for persistent
attacks, particularly on ground defences
during the days of re-supply between September 18 and 23. To the end of the war
the 353rd rendered very valuable support
to the bombers high above, having converted to P-51s in October 1944. Keeping
enemy fighters engaged when on the
ground was a very useful tactic which
prevented refuelling, and ensured the
enemy had a rough time throughout any
operation.

*Thunderbolt 'Arkansas Traveler' on dis-
persal at Raydon in June 1944 (USAF).*

The 652nd Weather Squadron was here
between October and December 1945
before Raydon was taken over by the
RAF at the end of that year and vacated
in the summer of 1958. There are two T2
hangars to be seen, one a Home Office
store, the other in private hands.

Ridgewell, Essex

*TM740415. 2 miles S of Stoke-by-Clare,
SE of Ashen*

Newly formed 90 Squadron left Bottes-
ford for Ridgewell on December 29 1942,
the recently built satellite for Stradishall
then coming off Care & Maintenance. As
it touched down the first Stirling bounced
and careered into a ditch. Luckily the
crew was safe, but the remainder of the
squadron returned to its old home. It was
an inauspicious opening for the three-
runway station.

The squadron arrived next day and flew
its first sorties, minelaying, on Janury 8
1943. The Stirlings were then slotted into
3 Group's offensive which, at the time,
was directed mainly at French west coast
ports, although on February 4 they raided
Turin and on March 1/2 1943 made their
first raid on Berlin.

On February 1943 the first major
operation had come and the pulse of
Ridgewell quickened as bomb trolleys
trundled around the perimeter track,
loaded with GP, HE and lots of SBCs full
of incendiaries. Seven Stirlings were despatched to Hamburg.

March 5/6 1943 really witnessed the
start of the 1943 bombing offensive in
strength when Essen was the target and
90 Squadron despatched seven aircraft.
From then onwards it attacked a variety
of Main Force targets with mining operations interspersed. Already the Stirling's
low operational ceiling was bringing fearsome experiences for the crews. Courageous, indeed, was Sergeant William

Davine during a raid on Duisburg. He was terribly wounded during the bomber's first run up, but continued to give instructions for a second run and the crew nursed him and the battered bomber home. The same night Pilot Officer Gordon William Young's machine was attacked four times by fighters but he managed to get home, whilst Pilot Officer F. Shippard's Stirling was attacked by a fighter 15 miles off the enemy coast. He brought BF473 home by holding the control column between his knees to prevent the aircraft climbing.

At the end of May 1943 90 Squadron moved to West Wickham and the 4th Bomb Wing Substitution Unit, USAAF, moved in as the station was put under Care & Maintenance.

B-17Fs of the 381st Bomb Group arrived in June 1943. Their first operation took place against Antwerp on June 23, the first of 296 raids mounted from Ridgewell. Without doubt the most memorable was that against Schweinfurt on August 17 1943 when the 381st lost 11 aircraft, the highest loss by any Group on that raid.

Twice the 381st was awarded a Distinguished Unit Citation, the first time after it fought its way to Bremen against flak and fighters on October 8 1943, the second for its part in the 1st Air Division operations on January 11 1944. The target list was long — Le Mans, Munster, Offenburg, Kiel, St Nazaire, Kassel, Leipzig and the nitrate plant at Heoya in Norway. Like other Groups, the 381st supported the build up to D-Day and aided US troops across Europe. Its final raid was made on April 25 1945, the late war operations being mainly against transport targets.

On July 15 1945 Ridgewell was transferred to the RAF for Maintenance Command. No 94 MU was here from September 10 1946 to March 31 1957. A visit to the site shows that runways have been torn up, but that two hangars remain in good condition on an expanse of farmland. The Ashen-Yeldham road built on the line of the perimeter track crosses the west part of the old airfield giving a good general view. Near Ashen there is still a dispersal area where it is easy to imagine a B-17 resting.

Rivenhall, Essex

TM820210. N of village

Rivenhall opened late in 1943 under control of the US 9th AF. The 363rd Fighter Group, which arrived in January 1944,

A B-17G settles on the runway at Ridgewell (USAF).

A view across the same area in 1978. The hangar remains.

received P-51s here, commencing operations on February 23 1944. It performed bomber escorts then gradually switched to a fighter-bomber ground-attack role, including dive-bombing in its repertoire. The Group moved to Staplehurst in April 1944.

In its place came the 397th Bomb Group which arrived mid-April for its part in the pre-invasion softening up. It operated on D-Day, attacking strongpoints and landing areas. It supported ground forces, attacked POL targets and defended areas. To impede enemy retreat it had a particular task in reducing bridges across the Loire, and of the 86 missions the Mustangs flew from Rivenhall, 32 were against bridges.

The Group advanced to Hurn on August 5 1944. On October 1 38 Group, RAF, took over the station and early in October Nos 295 and 570 Stirling IV transport squadrons arrived, after licking their Arnhem sores. Their task was to work up for the Rhine crossing, the squadrons participating in many large-scale exercises whilst continuing drops to the Resistance forces in Europe. Some 60 Horsas were towed out of Rivenhall for the Rhine crossing. In May 1945 the squadrons helped to carry the occupation force into Norway. Martinets of 1677 Target Towing Flight were also here from October 10 to December 28 1944.

The Stirling squadrons stayed until January 1946 when they disbanded, parts of 295 Squadron leaving the station at the end of December 1945. Rivenhall then became a camp for displaced persons. In 1956 Marconi took over part of the site. Two hangars and some buildings are still here, and the main runway is virtually intact.

Rougham (Bury St Edmunds), Suffolk

TM880645. E of Bury St Edmunds on A45

'There are Marauders at Rougham'. The news spread fast, but they weren't there long and must have fled when they heard me coming! All there was to be closely seen was an equally rare creature, an A-20C which had not once been an RAF machine. Its tail poked across the barbed wire on the perimeter of the Ipswich road by a large tree which still remains. Already the B-17s of the 94th Bomb Group had arrived. For the specialist an interesting feature of them was that some carried the 'DF' coding, more at home on the B-17s at Bassingbourn. It seems these were 'foggy codes' designed to fox the enemy. Apparently this was a little used ruse. The base was generally known as Rougham, but was later re-designated Bury St Edmunds. There is now a rose garden in the Abbey grounds by which to remember the Americans.

Rougham opened in August 1942 and in December the 322 Bomb Group moved in. It took many months for the Group to be established and not until March 1943 did its Marauders arrive, two squadrons of the Group being sited at Rattlesden.

The B-26 was a heavy aeroplane whose high wing loading meant long take-off runs, and even a span extension did not remove inherent problems. Added to this, the engines were temperamental. And, amazingly, the Americans decided to use B-26s in a low-level role. Royal Air Force observers were incredulous, for their handling of the aircraft suggested that, like the Mitchell, it was only suitable for medium level saturation bombing. It would need strong fighter escort too. A chance to use the Marauder was brushed aside by the RAF's 2 Group, which suggested the Boston was a much better aeroplane. British advice went unheeded.

As a result East Anglians were treated to some spectacular low flying by seemingly quite fast and quite large aeroplanes. Well do I remember a Sunday afternoon in April 1943 when three B-26s raced so low over Wilbraham Fen that one could read the fin serials with ease — and they had to be low for that to happen.

By early May the 450th and 452nd Squadrons were ready for battle — or so they thought. chosen for attack was a power station near Ijmuiden, a fringe target in a heavily defended zone. On May 14 the Marauder crews set off. Low they raced across the North Sea to avoid radar detection. Enemy reception was intense, and although they did their best their aim was bad and all 12 aircraft sustained flak damage.

Command structure was displeased with this poor result and ordered the 322nd to strike again, at once, at the same target. On May 17 the Marauders took off again, with a second target at Haarlem for

Rougham's Fortresses airborne during a training flight on September 6 1943 (USAF).

half the force. Some 1½ hours later a B-26 circled Rougham and landed. It had aborted and in so doing might have alerted the enemy. It later transpired that the B-26s had made landfall at the wrong point, crossing a most heavily defended area, and before long found themselves over Amsterdam and its strong defences. Little wonder that these and enemy fighters brought down the entire force.

One can but imagine the feelings of other crews at Rougham. But the outcome was as the RAF had expected, the Marauder was not for low-level attack. It is likely that the crews were insufficiently trained and unaware of what was required in this type of operation. An error in navigation was nearly always fatal, as the RAF found. The B-26s were moved into Essex in June 1943 and replaced by B-17s of the 94th Bomb Group ('A in a square').

Immediately upon arrival from Earls Colne the 94th commenced operations, flying 324 in all from Rougham and being twice awarded a Distinguished Unit Citation, the first for its part in the Regensburg shuttle raid on August 17 1943. The second was awarded for the action on January 11 1944. Winter weather was reducing the number of high-level raids, but when a spell of fine weather seemed likely a maximum effort was ordered against aircraft factories in the Brunswick area. Optimism was exceeded by reality and, as the bombers approached their targets, the weather conditions declined. The 94th pressed on. Enemy reaction was savage as a result of which seven Rougham B-17s were lost in action.

One of the 47th Bomb Wing B-45s at Sculthorpe.

The B-45s of the 47th were replaced by B-66s and the 19th Strategic Reconnaissance Squadron re-equipped with RB-66s.

The 94th ranged widely in its attacks, raiding the ball bearing works at Eberhausen, oil installations at Merseburg, shipyards at Kiel, etc, as well as bombing tactical targets and V-weapon sites.

Unlike most USAAF Groups, the 94th did not immediately return to America. Instead, it carried out a widespread leaflet-dropping campaign, mainly to assist displaced persons. It was mid-December before the 94th left for the USA. Rougham returned to the RAF on December 20 1945 and passed to Bomber Command on September 11 1946. It was abandoned in 1948.

The main entrance to the one-time base now leads to Rougham Industrial Estate. The Nissen Hut which served as the guard room is still there and a blister hangar — which never housed aircraft — stands alongside. The control tower is in private hands, and both 'T' hangars remain.

Rowley Mile, Suffolk
See Newmarket Heath

Sculthorpe, Norfolk
TF860315. 5 miles W of Fakenham, at junction of A148/B1454

'This is the base the enemy most fears,' said the tall American. He could well have been right. As far as one could see, along the disused runway sat, wingtip to wingtip, a line of North American B-45 jet bombers. Beyond, guarded by fearsome looking warriors armed to the teeth, was the nuclear stores area. This was Sculthorpe in the winter of the Cold War, when the base swarmed with all that America has meant in the last few decades.

Sculthorpe, built in 1942, became an RAF station in January 1943. Its first occupants were Horsa gliders there for storage, but in May 1943 the station ceased to be a satellite of West Raynham when, with Group Captain P.C. Pickard as Station Commander, 342 Free French Squadron moved in flying a collection of Boston IIIs and a few Douglas Havocs for training. July witnessed their departure.

Dynamic Sir Basil Embry came to 2 Group in mid-1943. His experience of the Mosquito as a night fighter had convinced him of its superlative qualities. It was he who argued the fighter-bomber case and did much to promote its development. He wanted 2 Group to rid itself of cumbersome bombers and operate only Mosquitoes, and in this he largely succeeded.

On July 20/21 1943 464 and 487 Squadrons left Methwold and moved rapidly to Sculthorpe where they were soon training with Mosquito FB VIs, essential, argued Embry, for invasion support, and especially at night. Once Operation *Starkey* was over 21 Squadron joined the others resident at Sculthorpe.

By October the three Mosquito VI squadrons were ready for action, flying into battle in spectacular style, in Mosquito style. They flew to Exeter and from there by carefully selected routes, deep into France to attack power stations. With them, of course, flew Sir Basil. It was unusual for a Group Commander to fly on operations, but then none surely could class Sir Basil Embry as anything other than highly individualistic. He had with him David Atcherley, one of the great Atcherley twins — what a combination with which to inspire anyone else!

The Mosquitoes of Sculthorpe were grouped as 140 Airfield which would operate as one unit, and which was planned to transport itself rapidly to any other station. Soon they were busy attacking targets in France. Then came discovery of just how advanced the building of flying-bomb sites had become. In December Sculthorpe's Mosquitoes began attacking them. Then the weather turned sour, and in any case that long haul to France was hardly acceptable. Therefore, on December 31 1943, the three squadrons set off for Le Ploy site. They were moving to Hunsdon — and bombing a target en route.

It was now that Sculthorpe, amply supplied with three runways, passed to 100 Group. On January 17 1944 No 214 Squadron began to arrive from Downham Market, having relinquished Stirlings and receiving some B-17s transferred from the US 8th AAF. Two days later a radio counter-measures detachment of the 8th Air Force arrived, under Colonel G.A. Scott, equipped with B-17Fs. All of these aircraft carried jamming and radio devices for the radio counter-measures role. Not until April 20/21 1944 did 214 Squadron venture into action, during raids on two French marshalling yards. All the operations in the role were on a small scale and barely underway when the jammer squadrons packed and left for Oulton in May 1944. Sculthorpe closed, to be converted for use by ultra-heavy bombers.

The station re-opened in December 1948 under Group Captain Parker and wa held on Care & Maintenance. Its long runways were ideal for American B-29s and in February 1949 the 92nd Bomb Group arrived, prior to operating over Korea. The B-29 Groups of Strategic Air Command rotated to British bases for Temporary Duty (TDY), usually staying for about three months. Often only one squadron was sited on one base.

To Sculthorpe on August 22 1949 came the first B-50As to be stationed in Britain, belonging to the 63rd Squadron of the 43rd Bomb Group. Among them was 46-010, 'Lucky Lady II', the first aircraft to make a non-stop flight around the globe, with the aid of probe and drogue in-flight refuelling. Thus the B-50s had with them KB-29M tankers. Among those who visited the Group was Her Majesty Queen Mary.

A succession of SAC Bomb Groups had stays at the base, among them the 2nd, 22nd, 97th and the 301st, the 97th being the first to operate B-50Ds from Sculthorpe. In January 1951 the USAF took over the base, which left only four RAF officers on the station. Great interest was always occasioned by brief visits of eight-engined RB-36s and B-36s to the base. Strategic Air Command used Sculthorpe for less time than it used most East Anglian bases, for on May 31 1952 Sculthorpe accepted permanent residents in the form of B-45 Tornado jet bombers of the 84th and 85th Squadrons, 47th Bomb Group (later Bomb Wing). A third squadron formed here in March 1954, the 86th. RB-45Cs of the 19th Tactical Reconnaissance Squadron (Night Photo Jet) arrived in mid-May 1954, staying until August 1959 when they left for Alconbury. There the 86th Squadron was detached between September 1955 and August 1959. The 8554th Tow Target Flight arrived in June 1954 flying TB-26B Invader target tugs and L-5 Sentinels. Additionally the base was home for the 49th Air Division which flew C-119 Packets, C-47 Dakotas, L-20s and T-33s, and which controlled the American tactical force in Britain. For some time the entire 47th Bomb Group/Wing was based at Sculthorpe, nominally flying 75 B-45s, a mighty force for a foe to reckon with.

The Americans publicly displayed their strength at Sculthorpe on May 29 1954. Few attended — people did not visit air displays much before the 1960s; but those who attended went so far as to sit on the runway during the flying display, surely a unique event!

It was in January 1958 that RB-66s began to replace the RB-45Cs in the 19th

Squadron, then the 47th received B-66s. KB-29P tankers had arrived in January 1956, greatly extending the range of the forces here, and were replaced in January 1957 by KB-50Ds. KB-50J jet-assisted tankers came in April 1958, the last seven leaving for America on March 22 1964.

Use was made of the ranges off Stiffkey in the 1950s. For this purpose radio-controlled drones were brought to Britain and manned by some personnel from Sculthorpe.

On June 22 1962 the 47th Bomb Wing was de-activated, and Sculthorpe's offensive posture ended. The American flag still flies at Sculthorpe which is a Standby Base. In recent years Super Mystères and F-100s of the French Air Force have been stored here, funded from the Mutual Defence Aid Pact.

Seething, Norfolk

TG320995. Off A 146, SW of Loddon

Seething is one of the few airfields built during the war expressly for the Americans which is still active. Usually, during the summer, the airfield holds a flying display, but the field is now but a former shadow of itself. The Americans arrived at the end of 1943, the 448th Bomb Group bringing its Liberators in December 1943 and remaining here until July 1945, during which period 262 operations were flown, the first on December 22 1943.

Targets ranged widely including the synthetic oil plant at Politz, aircraft engine factory at Rostick, marshalling yards at Cologne, the I.G. Farben works at Ludwigshaven, U-Boat building facilities at Kiel, a ball bearing plant at Berlin, the aircraft factory at Gotha, airfield at Hanau and the V-1 factory at Fallersleben.

Like other 2nd Air Division Groups the 448th took an active part in the run-up to D-Day and operated in support of the invasion. In September 1944 it supplied American forces at Nijmegen, an activity repeated at Wesel during the Rhine crossing. Thereafter it operated against communication targets, making its last raid on April 25 1945 when the target was marshalling yards at Salzburg.

Shepherd's Grove, Suffolk

TM990730. On the A143 NE of Ixworth

Flight Lieutenant D.R. Campbell was on finals here, landing back from a bombing raid on Rees. Suddenly an enemy aircraft opened fire on his Stirling, setting it ablaze. Campbell landed the burning

An F-84F Thunderstreak of the 81st Fighter Bomber Wing's 78th Squadron at Shepherd's Grove.

transport of 196 Squadron, and all except the rear gunner escaped the inferno.

During and after the war Shepherd's Grove was much a Stirling base. The station took its name from a small wood nearby. Although built for USAAF use in 1943, the station opened under 3 Group, RAF, on April 3 1944 as a satellite of Stradishall. Between April and October 1944 it was the Stirlings of 1657 Conversion Unit which were based here.

When Stradishall again became operational at the end of 1944, Shepherd's Grove was transferred to 38 Group and had its own SHQ. Nos 196 and 299 Stirling IV transport squadrons moved in late in January 1945, continuing their SOE supply drop sorties and took part in the Rhine crossing airborne operation when both squadrons towed gliders out of Shepherd's Grove. No 1677 Target Towing Flight's Martinets were here from January 28 to April 18 1945.

After the war the two Stirling squadrons flew mail and stores overseas, 196 Squadron using a number of Stirling Vs between January and March 1946, at which time the squadrons were withdrawn. The station was taken over by 60 Group in May 1946.

Shepherd's Grove now became a satellite of Watton, the Radio Warfare Establishment there positioning some of its Ansons and Lancasters at Shepherd's Grove. The station fell from use in February 1950 and was put on Care & Maintenance.

In 1951 it returned to active life and was loaned to the USAF. The station hit the headlines when, on August 27 1951, No 116 Squadron of the 81st Fighter-Interceptor Wing brought along their F-86A Sabres, the first to be based in Britain, and soon joined by those of the 92nd Squadron. These were the first

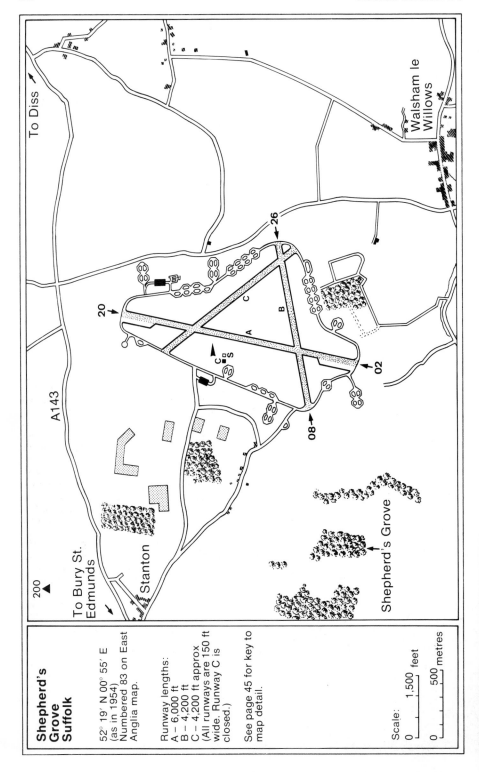

Shepherd's Grove Suffolk

52° 19′ N 00° 55′ E
(as in 1954)
Numbered 83 on East
Anglia map.

Runway lengths:
A – 6,000 ft
B – 4,200 ft
C – 4,200 ft approx
(All runways are 150 ft
wide. Runway C is
closed.)

See page 45 for key to
map detail.

Scale:

0 _____ 1,500 feet

0 _____ 500 metres

To Diss

Walsham le Willows

200

A143

To Bury St. Edmunds

Stanton

Shepherd's Grove

26

20

02

08

C

B

A

C
S

foreign aircraft assigned to the air defence of Britain.

In November 1952 the 116th Squadron was re-designated 78th Fighter Squadron. It became the 78th Fighter-Bomber Squadron on April 1 1954 and began receiving F-84F Thunderstreaks later that year. The 78th moved to Woodbridge in December 1958.

Almost at once building of a Thor complex took place and a Flight of 82 Squadron arrived in 1959 to operate them until July 1963. After their removal the site was returned to civilian use.

Shipdham, Norfolk

TM985075. Off A1075, SE of Shipdham village

There was nothing fundamentally wrong with the B-24 Liberator, but when it was committed to action in Europe in the autumn of 1942 it was simply not ready for the intended high-level day bombing role. In one respect it was vastly superior to the B-17, and that was in terms of combat radius. This, though, was not a feature in much demand in north-west Europe, at least as far as the US bomber offensive went in 1942-1943.

Although the snags were small and irritating, and the armament none too good, they amounted to quite a lot which made early B-24 operations trying, to say the least. It fell to the 44th Bomb Group at Shipdham to iron out the problems of making the good design a really potent weapon in Europe. Thus Shipdham, the first American heavy bomber base in Norfolk, became the ancestral home of the 8th AF Liberators.

By mid-summer 1942, three-runway Shipdham was all but ready to receive the Americans who brought in their 319th Bomb Group (Medium) during September. This unit, like others, came to pre-

An aerial view of Shipdham taken in 1978.

pare for its part in the north-west African Operation *Torch*, and moved out in October to Horsham St Faith, its place being taken almost immediately by advance elements of the 44th. This Group's initial equipment was the B-24D, and it was the second Group to bring them to Britain.

Eager, perhaps impatient, to operate, the unit went into action against Cap de la Hague at the tip of the Cherbourg peninsula on November 7 1942, but the operation was plagued with problems. When the 93rd BG went overseas the 44th found itself alone to work out the B-24, and losses became heavy on these early raids. As the British had found, it was never easy to operate more than one type of bomber on a daylight operation, for differences in speed, cruise altitude and fields of fire usually differed radically, as between the B-17 and the B-24. It was found best to operate the 44th's B-24s behind the B-17s, which meant that the defenders were well tuned for action by the time Shipdham's Liberators went into action. They did so against Germany for the first time on January 27 1943.

These early raids demanded much courage, so much so that the 44th was awarded a Distinguished Unit Citation for its operation on May 14. The Liberators, carrying incendiary loads, flew behind the B-17s to attack Kiel and as they ran in had none of the massed firepower of the foreging B-17 Groups. Worse still their formation had to open up when under attack, but still the crews fought on to bomb Kiel.

Like the 389th, at Hethel the 44th was taken off operations in June 1943 and low-level training followed, giving welcome relief from difficult operations. On June 28 the 44th left Shipdham for Libya where ten operations were flown, including its first raid on Rome on July 19, attacks during the Sicilian campaign and then the Ploesti raid. On that occasion Colonel Leon Johnson was awarded the Medal of Honour for courageously leading the B-24s despite their being pestered by flak and fighters, and the raid also won the Group its second Distinguished Unit Citation. Austria and Italy were attacked during the period overseas.

Barely was the Group back at Shipdham than, in mid-September 1943, it went overseas again, this time to Tunis for more raids in the Mediterranean Theatre.

Once back at Shipdham it settled down to a bombing campaign which did not end until April 24 1945. As with other B-24 Groups the 44th operated widely and distantly; bombed, dropped supplies, supported the Normandy invasion and the airborne attack on Holland. In mid-June 1945 came the time to bid farewell to Shipdham and leave the base to run down.

After a long period of inactivity the airfield re-opened to flying in June 1970, two of the runways having been refurbished. Arrow Air Services use it for taxi and charter work. On the south side hangars remain, also a wrecked control tower on private property. Nearby is a site used by contractors. The best view is probably the distant one from the Dereham road with a runway visible in good state. One can so easily imagine a B-24 coming in on low approach.

Snailwell, Cambridgeshire

TL650665. Off A142, to right just N of Newmarket

Drive along the Newmarket bypass towards Bury and the odds are that you will pass directly over the site of Snailwell airfield without realising it. If you look ahead at the right moment you will see the one remaining blister hangar, and the long line of trees from the main entrance which stood at the impressive gateway to the left of the Norwich road, seen just after leaving Newmarket. Gone the tower into which a Typhoon rammed itself while taking off on March 22 1943 when armed with two 500 lb bombs. It is not the Typhoons, though, which live clearly in the local memory; it is the Lysanders, Tomahawks and especially Mustangs, for this was a busy Army Co-operation Command station.

Snailwell opened in March 1941. On April 1 Lysanders of 268 Squadron arrived from Westley, for that airfield could not be enlarged to take the Tomahawk with which 268 Squadron soon began to equip. Snailwell was laid down as a second satellite for Duxford, planned to open about May 1 1941. It slipped into Army Co-operation hands before becoming a permanent airfield for fighter aircraft. Three months after 268 Squadron arrived a Station HQ was established here and, although attached to Duxford, the station now functioned in its own right.

Throughout 1941 Snailwell echoed to the unmistakable tinny note of the Lysander as countless army exercises were worked out with the many troops in the area. Not until 1942 did 268 see any action, and then only by way of detachment to Ibsley in Hampshire whence the

Tomahawks flew Channel patrols with the Spitfires of 501 Squadron.

Snailwell lay in countryside as picturesque as its name, the road alongside offering a view of the field, but all aircraft were dispersed by or among the eastern trees.

From March 1942 Snailwell's residents took on a more imposing appearance as the heavy Typhoons of 56 Squadron moved in from Duxford. Within days the beautiful lines of the Mustang 1 had joined 268 Squadron which, on June 29 1942, took its new toys into action when two aircraft flew the first of a very large number of *Lagoons* — searches for enemy shipping between Texel and the Hague — which tasks were carried out from Snailwell at dawn most days and often repeated later during daylight hours.

The Typhoons had not long been here when they started to practice low-level *Rhubarb* operations under Squadron Leader 'Cocky' Dundas, and from May 29 Flights were detached to Manston and West Hampnett in a brief attempt to use the Typhoons against low-flying fighter-bombers.

On June 1 1942 56 Squadron flew to join its comrades at Duxford where the Typhoon Wing, led by Wing Commander Gillam and Group Captain John Grandy, took off on the first Typhoon Wing sweep, from Mardyck to Boulogne, after which '56' landed back at Snailwell. Similar operations followed then, early on August 19, the Duxford Wing — including 56 Squadron — flew to West Malling, spending the day there and making sorties to the Dieppe area during the landings. It was upon this day that the Typhoon was first pitted against the FW 190, which pilots found they could not out-manoeuvre, but could outpace. On August 24 56 Squadron moved to Matlaske.

Army Co-operation Command still held sway at Snailwell, for a new squadron, No 168, was formed from No 268 on June 15 1942. It flew Tomahawks using Snailwell and Bottisham. It had a Battle and a Master II for dual training at Snailwell.

In March 1942 Whirlwinds of 137 Squadron had been briefly based here for ground attack training, and they came again in August 1942 to practice with Bostons of 107 Squadron which would land to allow the crews to exchange tactical ideas. It was whilst 137 Squadron was here that, in early September, the Squadron's Commanding Officer first tried out the Whirlwind as a fighter-bomber before his squadron moved to Manston on September 12 for a fighter-bomber role.

A brief stay by Blenheims of 614 Squadron was followed by Americans flying P-39 Airacobras. Their 347th Squadron was based here whilst its companions used Duxford, which was too full to accommodate the entire Group. They left for King's Cliffe on December 8 and two days later the second Typhoon squadron to use Snailwell arrived from Duxford. This was No 181 which, two days later, received its first 'Bomphoons' and became the earliest such Typhoon fighter-bomber squadron. 'A' Flight moved to Ludham for operations in February.

This was a busy period for, as well as *Lagoons*, 268 Squadron had, on January 11 1943, given close support when Mitchells went into action for the first time. Some FW 190s had engaged them and 268 Squadron shot down its first enemy aircraft for the loss of one pilot. On February 12 seven pilots of '268' flew to Amersfoort in Holland, there to attack the SS barracks before shooting down a Do 217 landing at Soesterburg. The Typhoons moved out to Gravesend on March 24, their place quickly being taken by Mustangs of 170 Squadron, the ground crews for which arrived in Horsa gliders. Not long after a Glider MU was established at Snailwell, but no gliders were ever held here, the unit looking after those on bomber stations.

Early in May 1943 309 (Polish) Squadron also brought in Mustang 1s and between June 28 and October 1943 flew *Lagoons*. On October 4 they flew an eight-aircraft *Distil* operation off Denmark, trying to shoot down minesweeping Ju 52s.

Operating alongside 309 was 613 Squadron whose Mustangs began *Lagoons* in mid-July. They operated

Snailwell was long the haunt of RAF Mustangs like the example seen here belonging to 268 Squadron.

almost daily until October 8 1943, their role being threefold: reconnaissance for enemy ships, some PR and a few ASR Walrus escorts, all undertaken under 12 Group, which took control of the station when Army Co-operation Command disbanded at the end of May 1943. No 613 Squadron left in mid-November when 309 Squadron resumed *Lagoons* which continued until January 1944.

Close association with Duxford and AFDU had brought No 1426 Enemy Aircraft Flight here with its assortment of German aircraft in July 1943, and the famous He 111, AW177, was operating from here when it crashed on the runway at Polebrook on November 10 1943. That autumn also saw detachments of 116 and 288 Squadrons using the station for radar calibration and AA support duties.

February 8 1944 brought an abrupt change. No 309 Squadron had flown its last *Lagoon* on this day and the squadron began to equip with Hurricane II/IVs, worked up and moved north on April 3. As a pointer to the future 417 Repair & Salvage Unit formed here on January 1 1944, leaving for Lasham and an important role in the invasion on March 1.

Snailwell now assumed far less importance. No 527 Squadron flying six Blenheim IVs, eight Hurricanes and four DH Hornet Moths arrived from Castle Camps on February 28 1944 and stayed until late April flying calibration sorties. Then the station was relieved of aircraft.

On May 7 the 41st Base Complement Squadron, USAAF, moved in, the 33rd and 41st MR Squadrons arriving soon after, and having a few A-20Gs here in summer. The Americans stayed until autumn, the RAF having closed its SHQ on July 15.

Snailwell's final fling came in 1945 when some Master IIs arrived for the training of pilots for the post-war Belgian Air Force, Snailwell and Bottisham housing personnel of the Belgian Air Force Training Squadron. They left in early 1946 and the station became surplus to needs.

Snailwell is worth a visit for anyone with a sense of nostalgia. The airfield is now given over entirely to agriculture, but the village is as delightful as any and has a trout farm and a beautiful brook by which to pause on any tour of East Anglian airfields. The views of the distant chalk uplands on a fine day are among the best in the region. If you listen carefully you might even hear the ghost of a Lysander!

Snetterton Heath, Norfolk

TM005895. On A11(T), 7 miles SW Attleborough

As the cars race around the circuit on a fine summer's day it is worth remembering the Snetterton of the war years, for the 96th Bomb Group based here had the highest loss rate of any unit in the 8th AF. From Snetterton B-17s made some shuttle raids on Germany which meant flying on to Russia or the Mediterranean, and

Snetterton Heath photographed from a 58 Squadron Canberra on March 29 1965 (DoE).

making another attack when flying home. The 96th undertook some operations which involved crossing the Alps and landing at Italian bases from where they made raids on Roumania which involved tremendously long and exhausting flights. Plenty of Snetterton remains — the perimeter tracks have formed the basis of the race circuit, and there are 'T' hangars.

This base was built between autumn 1942 and mid-1943, yet opened in January 1943 although it was not yet ready to receive the intended Group. Instead, the 386th Bomb Group trained to fly B-26s and moved in early in July 1943, staying only a week before moving to Boxted. Meanwhile the 96th had assembled at Great Saling and was moved north to Snetterton in mid-June 1943.

It commenced operations on May 14 1943, attacking strategic targets in Germany, Poland and Czechoslovakia. For its part in the Regensburg raid of August 17 1943 the Group received a Distinguished Unit Citation. It received its second such award when leading the 45th Combat Wing on April 19 1944 when it penetrated deep and through dense cloud and AA fire to reach Poland.

The list of the 96th's targets is as wide as any, and includes airfields at Augsburg where the Messerschmitt factory was sited; Bordeaux, lair of the anti-shipping raiders; marshalling yards at Kiel, Hamm, Brunswick and Gdynia; aircraft factories at Chemnitz, Hanover and Diosgyor; oil refineries at Merseburg and Brux; chemical works at Wiesbaden, Neukirchen and the great I.G. Farben complex at Leverkusen. The Group supported the Normandy landings and the St Lô break-out, dropped supplies to the Maquis in France and in 1945 carried out some attacks upon communications targets behind the front.

Once the war was ended the 96th flew food to the Dutch and in a transport role moved personnel to Morocco, France, Germany and Ireland. They stayed in Britain longer than most and did not leave until December 1945.

The airfield was then put under Care & Maintenance under the control of 262 MU for which hangars on the north side of the main road were available. For a long time Snetterton was maintained in excellent condition, becoming one of the tidiest wartime airfields then in East Anglia. The RAF left in the late 1940s and the site was privately bought in 1952. Quidenham Church nearby has a memorial to the 96th Bomb Group.

Somersham, Cambridgeshire

TL350770. S of village

Few East Anglian airfields cloaked themselves in such anonymity as Somersham. A visit to the site during the war showed that it contained little, although in 1941 it served as a Q-site for Wyton. The local population was largely ignorant of what was going on, and usually any action came at night. Occasionally by day a Lysander or Hudson would land and to the skilled eye the secret would have been out. Somersham was the airfield where the special duties squadrons practised pick-up operations conducted in France and Belgium. Little wonder they used the airfield rarely, and at night. Its use apparently spanned the years 1942-1944, but its history has yet to come fully to light. It probably does not have much history.

Stansted, Essex

TL535230. SE of Stansted Mountfichet, E of M11

Third London Airport? Whether the inhabitants around like it or not, that is what Stansted is. If air travel expands much the site could become far busier. It is a waste that the 10,000-foot runway should be used mainly for training purposes.

As long ago as July 4 1942 the 817th US Engineering Air Battalion arrived to build the 1,919-acre airfield, which opened in July 1943, after more engineers had arrived, as an Air Depot for US forces in Britain. By October 1943 an airfield existed with the customary three runways, a main NE/SW 6,000 × 150-foot runway and two subsidiaries, both 2,000 × 150 feet, running roughly NW/SW and N/S. To Stansted came many a Marauder to be prepared for combat in the ETO, at the site on the south side. But it was the arrival of the 344th Bomb Group with B-26s which really brought the station to life.

The Group commenced operations on March 6 1944, flying daylight raids on France, Belgium and Holland and concentrating its attacks on bridges in May 1944. For its July operations it was awarded a Distinguished Unit Citation.

The Group moved to France in late September 1944, leaving the 30th Air Depot Group in residence. After the war the airfield was used as an American transit centre. On August 12 1945 the Americans moved out and the RAF took over, siting 263 MU here. Some German POWs were held here pending repatriation.

On December 14 1946 the airfield opened for civilian use and was base for that brave enterprise London Aero Motor Services (LAMS), which bought six surplus Halifax VIIIs from the RAF to conduct a charter cargo service, particularly for perishables. Halifaxes were costly to operate, cargo capacity was limited and LAMS fell by the wayside. In the summer of 1947 Kearsley Airways began charter flights with three Dakotas and a Proctor. During the following October 263 MU moved to Hitcham, Suffolk, keeping Stansted as its satellite.

In December 1948 the Minister of Civil Aviation considered the use of Stansted as 1) the principal charter airfield in the London area, 2) a base for charter aircraft and 3) main diversion airfield for the London area. During April 1949 the airfield was passed from the Air Ministry to the Ministry of Civil Aviation.

Meanwhile the USAF was interested in operating jet aircraft from Stansted and approached the Secretary of State with plans for its improvement, including a 10,000 × 200-foot runway with an LCN of 100, and 11 hard standings for large aircraft.

Stansted from the air in 1977.

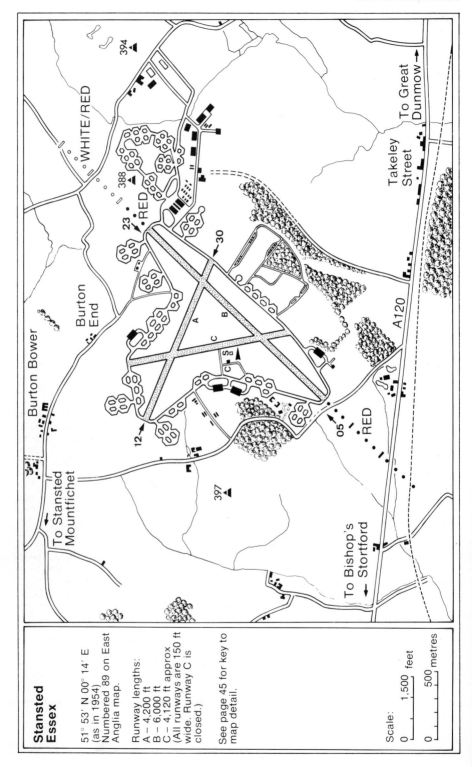

Stansted
Essex

51° 53′ N 00° 14′ E
(as in 1954)
Numbered 89 on East
Anglia map.

Runway lengths:
A – 4,200 ft
B – 6,000 ft
C – 4,120 ft approx
(All runways are 150 ft
wide. Runway C is
closed.)

See page 45 for key to
map detail.

Scale:

0   1,500   feet

0   500 metres

A general view across Stansted showing the wartime T2 hangar still in place.

Agreement was reached and the 803rd US Engineering Aviation Battalion commenced construction work in February 1954, the work continuing until December 8 1956. During runway improvement a new parallel taxiway served as a runway and over 66,000 passengers staged through, mainly troops being transported in Yorks. There were 10,731 aircraft movements. In 1956 44,734 passengers used the airfield and there were 15,026 aircraft movements.

April 1957 saw the final withdrawal of the US engineers. More discussions took place and in mid-1958 the USAF informed the British that they had decided only to make use of the airfield in the event of war. The Air Ministry decided in November that it no longer needed the aerodrome.

Stansted then came into use for the refurbishing by Airwork of F-86 Sabres discarded by the RAF and being passed to other NATO air forces. A large number of ex-RAF Prentices was brought here awaiting destruction or civilian buyers. With them rested some of the last Avro Tudor airliners. Charter flights by Skyways, among others, continued.

The Ministry of Aviation Fire Service Training School moved in from Pengham Moors, Cardiff, in November 1960, setting itself up in the south-eastern corner, the wartime US church then becoming the main lecture room. Unusual aircraft for fire practice were by no means a new feature for it was from Stansted that

the Handley-Page 88, test-bed for the Victor bomber, had made its first and its final flight before crashing on August 26 1951.

In August 1961 Aviation Traders transferred its Carvair production line from Southend, the first example flying from Stansted in the summer of 1962.

Trooping flights were continued in 1961, 1962 and 1963 and were by then being augmented by charter flights between the UK and America and Canada by KLM, CPA and Capitol Airlines which used Boeing 707s and DC-8s. Passengers totalled 105,157 in 1963-1964 with 27,139 movements. Since 1960 training of pilots by BEA, BOAC and foreign airlines steadily increased to exceed all other movements. Some decline came in 1964 when BEA training was transferred to Malta and the BEA Trident training base transferred to Shannon. In 1964 British United Airways lost its trooping contract and at the end of that year such flights ended here. But flying was still considerable for in 1964-1965 there were 36,378 movements.

Government White Papers in 1961 and 1964 recommended Stansted become one of Britain's four major airports, but a public enquiry showed intense local opposition and expansion was abandoned in favour of the suggested Maplin complex. This was abandoned in 1974 and the Government is now considering alternatives.

Stansted has the capacity to handle

about one million passengers a year and has one of the longest runways in the country. In 1976/77 300,000 passengers passed through Stansted and the new M11 motorway to London seems likely to bring more use of the airport.

Since 1949 Stansted has been the home of the civil aviation radar and radio facilities unit, under varying names, and this still operates from here. Its aircraft and a wide assortment of large passenger aircraft and cargo carrying CL-44s can now be seen at Stansted.

Steeple Morden, Cambridgeshire

TL302420. 2 miles N of A505, between Litlington and Steeple Morden village

Those living locally had it all worked out. This new aerodrome being produced from fields to the east of their village was a very secret place. Since no hangars were visible they were obviously underground — and no amount of arguing would, for a long time, convince them that satellite airfields in 1940-1941 did not have hangars anyway, nor even watch offices.

When, by September 1940, Wellington 1s, 1as and 1cs of 11 Operational Training Unit based at nearby Bassingbourn began flying from their satellite, one had only to take off for its home station to convince everyone that it had gone to earth. An aura of secrecy somehow was induced to make Steeple Morden something special.

In the main it was used for circuit flying, leaving the main cross-country and bombing exercises to be flown from the parent station. Then, to add to the tales, the Germans came — unconventionally.

It was a partly cloudy night, one upon which disorientation would be easily possible. Intruder activity was well underway in the area, and many of the main Blitz operations took the Luftwaffe over the region during their transit flights. On the night of February 15/16 1941 the main target was Birmingham. Among the participants was a Junkers Ju 88A-5 of III/KG 1, V4+GS, Werk Nr 6214. Quite a new machine it was too, built by Junkers Flugzeugbau MW AG of Dessau and partly by the Heinkel works at Oranienburg. The Luftwaffe had accepted it on November 11 1940.

Evidently the crew had become completely lost and believed they were over France. They were not, they were over Cambridgeshire when, in bright moonlight, they switched on their landing light. Challenged by a Blenheim crew they fired

their signal cartridges and proceeded to land cross-wind over Steeple Morden's goose neck flare path. As soon as they touched down the aircraft's starboard undercarriage leg collapsed and the propeller, wing tip and engine cowling were damaged as the machine slewed across the grass. An Armadillo raced to the machine, black and with dark green spinners, and the crew of four were soon in custody suitably dazed by their experience. Unfortunately the Ju 88 was too badly damaged to be of much use, but the Radio Department at Farnborough investigated its equipment. Parts were used to maintain Ju 88s flown in Britain, including at Duxford. Another tale added piquancy to this mysterious airfield.

Meanwhile 11 OTU flew on, and in 1942 supplied some of the force for the '1,000 bomber' raids. When 11 OTU left Bassingbourn in September 1942 Steeple Morden fell quiet until October 26 when the 3rd US Photo Group came under Colonel Elliott Roosevelt. Runways were laid and hangars added. Then, between January 13 and May 4 1943, Blenheim 1s of 17 OTU used the station. and were afterwards stored here.

In July 1943 the Americans arrived in the form of the 355th Fighter Group flying P-47s, and commenced operations in September 1943, making a sweep over Belgium on the 14th. Thereafter the Group soon switched to bomber escorts and by April 1944 was flying P-51B Mustangs, later switching to P-51Ds and P-51Ks.

Its travels took the Group far — to distant Berlin, for instance, and to Karlsruhe, Gelsenkirchen and Minden. But it was not merely as an escort formation that it excelled, for the 355th was credited with the highest score of enemy aircraft destroyed on the ground by any Group. The unit armed its aircraft with bombs and attacked airfields, locomotives, vehicles, radio stations and bridges.

On D-Day it gave fighter cover to the Allies and later supported the St Lô break-out. Interdiction and escort duties were continued to the end of the war, the Group leaving for Germany and participation in the occupation force. As well as over 300 aircraft claimed in combat, the Group also laid claim to over 500 destroyed on the ground.

During its stay at Steeple Morden the 355th had some odd companions. The 17 OTU Blenheims may well have been the last Mk 1s to have seen much active service. The Americans, ever ready to accept a good thing, had a Mosquito T III here and for target towing a B-26 of ancient vintage. After the war the 4th Fighter Group spent some four months at the airfield.

There is very little left of the station now, but you can lean over a wooden gate which now bars the route which many a P-47 and P-51 took as it crossed the road to dispersal on the north side. Steeple Morden closed on September 1 1946 and was sold for agricultural use in the early 1960s.

Stradishall, Suffolk

TL720515. By A143, 7 miles NE Haverhill

'Gentlemen, we are at war. Your target for this first attack is — Berlin'. Pause, for gasps of astonishment. 'I need hardly add that this is going to be a difficult operation.' Luckily in September 1938 it never came to that, although incredibly Berlin *was* the target chosen for Stradishall's Heyfords, and had the Munich crisis turned to war ... but the result is too awful to contemplate. Fortunately, Heyfords had left Stradishall before war came.

For over 30 years, and with barely a break, Stradishall was an active station. It opened on February 3 1938 under Group Captain J.H. Herring, DSO, MC. No 9 Squadron with Heyford IIIs and 148 Squadron with Wellesleys moved in on March 10. The latter re-equipped with Heyford IIIs and Ansons in November 1938, policy changing to operating Wellesleys in the Middle East only. Late in 1938 runway building commenced. No 9 Squadron re-equipped with Wellington

The Ju 88 after its landing at Steeple Morden (IWM).

1s in February 1939 and 148 Squadron the following month. On July 15 1939 9 Squadron moved out and was replaced on August 15 by 75 Squadron's Wellingtons and Ansons. These and 148 Squadron moved to Harwell on September 9 1939 and the station was put on to Care & Maintenance until the end of October 1939 when an abrupt, though brief, change of role took place.

When Stradishall re-opened it did so to accommodate two new squadrons, No 254 formed on October 30 and 236 formed the following day. Both received Blenheim 1F fighters, 254 moving to Sutton Bridge on December 9 1939 and 236 to Martlesham Heath the next day.

The station reverted to being a bomber base with the arrival of Wellington 1as of 214 Squadron on February 8 1940. This, the Federated Malay States squadron, came to be very much Stradishall's own wartime unit and stayed until October 1 1942. It was an active squadron, taking part in many operations from Stradishall, where No 148 Squadron reformed on April 30 1940, only to leave on May 23. No 150 Squadron with a few Battles recuperated here between June 6 and July 1940 after its mauling in France. No 215 Squadron had a brief stay in January 1941.

Like other 3 Group stations, Stradishall had its share of intruders, the worst incident coming early in 1941 when bombs badly damaged a hangar. As the Ju 88 careered across the field an object fluttered down. It turned out to be the German crew's target map. On February 20 two bombs fell on the main runway. This was at a time when Wellingtons were being flown to the Middle East by 3 Group Training Flight, sometimes known as the Reserve Squadron. That duty continued until the end of April 1941 when the Flight moved to Newmarket whose longer run was more suitable for the overloaded bombers.

In 1941 No 1419 Flight moved to Newmarket. It became No 138 (Special Duties) Squadron on August 25 1941, equipped with Whitley Vs and a few Lysanders. In November the unit moved to Stradishall and was based here for 90 days under Wing Commander Farley. Whilst here it flew 50 sorties, to France, Poland, Holland, Norway and Czechoslovakia. In March 1942 the squadron moved to Tempsford.

No 214 Squadron converted to Stirlings in April 1942, and these were used until the squadron moved from Stradishall. On

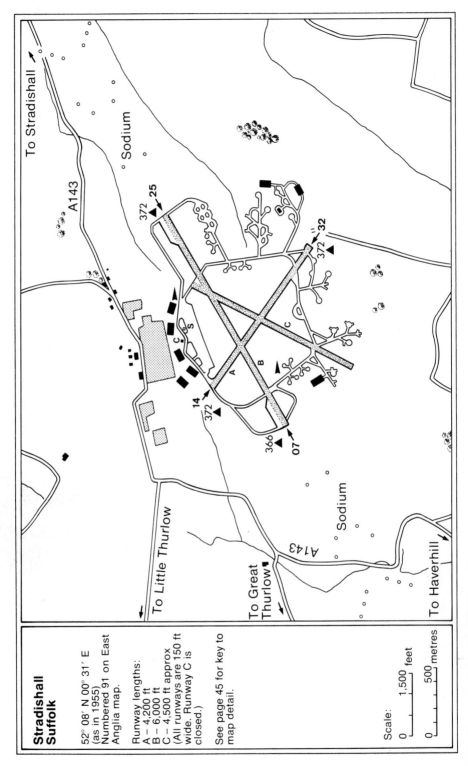

Stradishall
Suffolk

52° 08′ N 00° 31′ E
(as in 1955)
Numbered 91 on East
Anglia map.

Runway lengths:
A – 4,200 ft
B – 6,000 ft
C – 4,500 ft approx
(All runways are 150 ft
wide. Runway C is
closed.)

See page 45 for key to
map detail.

Scale:

0   1,500   feet

0   500   metres

April 6 1942 No 109 Squadron's HQ and 'C' Flight arrived, later joined by the remainder of the squadron. They flew Wellingtons and, from Stradishall, apart from radio reconnaissance duties, carried out the first trials with *Window*. The squadron broke up on July 4, 'B' Flight leaving for Gransden to become 1474 Flight. Headquarters and the Wireless Development Flight stayed at Stradishall and 109 Squadron was re-organised on a two-Flight basis with a mixture of Wellington VIs, 1cs and IVs. Apparently only two of the rare Mk VI high-altitude Wellingtons were ever here and it is said that some operations were flown by one of them over Germany. On July 24 an extra Flight equipped with six Mosquito IVs was formed, the squadron moving to Wyton on August 6 1942 after the Wellington VIs had left Stradishall.

Nudged out of Bourn by XV Squadron's arrival, No 101 Squadron, flying Wellington IIIs, was at Stradishall from August 13, leaving for 1 Group on September 30. Chedburgh had opened as a second satellite on September 7.

On October 1 1942 No 1657 Conversion Unit formed with 16 Stirling 1s and a few Oxfords, and stayed until December 15 1944. During that period the Oxfords of 1521 BAT Flight were here, until March 15, and Stradishall became the main station of 32 Base in May 1943, controlling Ridgewell and Chedburgh.

The station became operational again when, on December 17 1944, No 186 Squadron arrived from Tuddenham, flying Lancaster IIs in 3 Group and operating to the end of the war. This squadron disbanded on July 17 1945.

Stradishall left 3 Group and passed to 47 Group Transport Command. During August 1945 Nos 51 and 158 Squadrons arrived flying Stirling CVs. No 158 Squadron disbanded on January 1 1946, but 51 Squadron continued flying Stirlings until March 1946 when it was equipped with Yorks, later moving to Waterbeach in August.

Stradishall reverted to 3 Group on September 19 1946 and 35 Squadron flying Lancaster B1 (FEs) arrived from Graveley. No 115 Squadron, similarly equipped, joined them in September and two other squadrons — Nos 149 and 207 — in November 1946. Lancasters remained until February 1949, then Stradishall was put on to Care & Maintenance on February 18.

It re-opened on July 6 1949 and, on September 1, No 203 Advanced Flying

Above: *By one of Stradishall's hangars stands a Heyford of 9 Squadron (Bruce Robertson).* Below: *A Wellington 1c of 214 Squadron being towed into a Stradishall hangar in 1941 (IWM).*

After the war Stradishall became a fighter station. Meteor 8s are seen here, nearest 'K' WF740 then 'G' WK893, both of 245 Squadron (L. Tavender).

School arrived to train fighter pilots using mainly Meteor 4s and 7s and an assortment of Spitfires — Mks 14, 16 and 18 — into the early 1950s. Vampire 5s were used until 1951, Harvards for slightly longer.

No 203 AFS was re-designated 226 Operational Conversion Unit but the mixture of aircraft was unchanged, although Meteor PR9s replaced the Spitfires in mid-1951. Tempest 5s and Beaufighter TT10s were briefly used for target towing, but it was the Martinet which bore the brunt of the task, outliving these types and not being withdrawn until early 1954, by which time Mosquito TT35s had taken over the role. In mid-1952 the Meteor 8 became standard equipment, along with the Meteor 7. A few Oxfords were used between 1949 and 1955, Vampire T11s from 1953 to 1955. Add to these a Balliol, Tiger Moths and Mosquito T3s and it can be seen what a wide assortment of aircraft were used by 226 OCU before it closed on June 1 1955.

Stradishall had passed from 81 Group to 11 then 12 Groups and in March 1955 again became an operational station, with the formation on March 31 1955 of 125 Squadron, initially flying Meteor NF11s and re-equipping with Venom NF3s in January 1956 before disbanding on May 10 1957. Between June 9 and July 18 253 Squadron worked up with Venom NF2s before moving to Waterbeach. No 89 Squadron reformed here on December 15 and also flew Venom nightfighters. Another night fighter squadron, No 152, was here with Meteor NF 12/14s in the second half of 1956 and was at Stradishall again in 1957-1958, arriving with 263 Squadron on August 18 1957 and leaving with them on July 8 1958.

The longest-staying resident at this time was 89 Squadron which, in October 1957, converted to an assortment of Javelin 2s and 6s. No 85 Squadron, similarly equipped, was based here from November 30 1958 until September 7 1959.

By then Stradishall had become mainly a Hunter station, for No 1 Squadron with Hunter 6s arrived on July 2 1958 and 54 Squadron on August 1 1958. Whilst here they converted to Hunter 9s, 1 Squadron leaving for Waterbeach on November 7 1961 and 54 Squadron on November 21. The station had been under 12 Group since the autumn of 1959.

In 1960 Stradishall briefly housed 208 Squadron from April 1 to May 30 flying Hunter 9s, 111 Squadron from July 15 to September 13 and 43 Squadron from September 23 to October 13, all Hunter-armed.

The final stage in its history came on December 1 1961 when Stradishall was transferred to Training Command and 1 Air Navigation School arrived with Varsities, Meteor 14s and 7s. The jets were used until the start of 1966, but late in 1965 the first Dominie T1s arrived to replace them. Dominies and Varsities remained in use until August 27 1970 when 1 ANS moved to Finningley.

Visit the station now and one is confronted by a high wire fence surrounding the buildings, for Stradishall became Highpoint Prison in July 1977. Before that it was used as a transit camp for Ugandan Asians.

Sudbury (Acton), Suffolk

TL895435. NE of town on B1115, W of Great Waldingfield. Lay-by-cum-gateway on the roadside offers good view

The visitor to Sudbury town may notice a memorial to the USAAF on the town hall. Parts of the airfield remain and it is in agricultural use. From March 1944 to August 1945 the airfield was home for the 486th Bomb Group.

That Group had a chequered career. It arrived flying B-24s although assigned to the 3rd Air Division, a B-17 organisation. There were insufficient B-17s to equip the 8th Air Force so Sudbury and Lavenham Wings temporarily used B-24 Liberators. The two Groups were placed in the 92nd Combat Wing, operating together to ease the tactical problems which always arose when mixed aircraft type formations operated.

On May 7 1944 the 486th went into action against rail targets at Liège, and it was later employed in pre-invasion operations. It supported the D-Day landings and backed up the American advance across Europe. In July the Group began to receive B-17s introduced to operations in August 1944, the first raid being against Berlin on August 6. Thereafter the Group's operations from Sudbury were mainly strategic, targets ranging widely to include marshalling yards at Stuttgart, Mainz and Cologne, airfields at Kassel and Munster, the docks at Kiel and Bremen, oil refineries at Merseburg and Hamburg and numerous factories.

Sudbury was short-lived as an active airfield, and after the Americans moved out in August 1945 it quietened down. Ashdown Rawlinson Ltd have an agricultural contractor's business there utilising a 'T' hangar. The perimeter track runs near the B1115 and another hangar remains among some huts on the eastern side.

Swanton Morley, Norfolk

TG010185. NW of village

Tactical support for the invasion of Europe by day was assured. What was needed was equivalent effective operations against the Wehrmacht by night. In March 1944 Mitchells of 98 Squadron arrived at Swanton Morley to work out tactics for such night attacks, first tried over a road through the Stanford Battle Area on March 29/30. A day later all the great names in 2 Group gathered at nearby Bylaugh Hall to discuss the result of the trial. It was resolved that attacks would be made either against large targets lit by flares or by single Mosquitoes strafing roads, each crew being allocated a precise area to patrol and attacking every sign of enemy movement. On April 25/26 a large-scale exercise based upon Swanton Morley took place, and the plan was laid. Once the invasion had begun these trials evolved into operations, and until the end of the war the night interdictor work of Mosquitoes played a vital role in the reduction of the Wehrmacht.

Building the airfield at Swanton Morley commenced in early 1939 and, since only one large 'K' hangar was to be placed here, the station was constructed fairly quickly, opening in September 1940. At the end of October 105 Squadron arrived flying Blenheim IVs and took a very active part in the 2 Group day and night bombing campaign, switching to anti-shipping duties in 1941. For three weeks in May 1941 the Blenheims were away at Lossiemouth and between July and October they were in Malta. No 152 Squadron had Spitfires here between August and December 1941.

The main event of that year, however, came on November 15 when Geoffrey de Havilland Jr brought to the station the first Mosquito bomber to enter RAF service. It provided everyone with a shattering aerobatic performance which amazed crews accustomed to the poor old Blenheim. The Mosquito, though, was to be a rare commodity for months, and only a handful were with 195 Squadron when it moved to Horsham St Faith on December 9 1941.

Immediately 226 Squadron moved in during December, just as it was going through the process of converting to Boston IIIs. The unit was quickly thrown into action during the 'Channel Dash' before it was ready for operations. It was on March 8 1942 that the planned introduction came when 88 and 226 Squadrons flew to Thorney Island for a low-level attack on the Matford Works at Poissy near Paris. They set out from Thorney Island and the six Bostons successfully bombed the factory. Wing Commander Butler leading 226 either flew too low or was caught by the blast of exploding bombs, for his Boston soon crashed. Then followed *Circus* operations and in

August 226 Squadron flew from Thruxton to lay smoke to screen the Dieppe landings.

Shortly before, an even more portentous event had taken place. The 15th Bomb Squadron (Light) had arrived at Swanton Morley and by the end of June 1942 seemed ready to fly some of 226's Bostons on operations. On the afternoon of June 29 four Americans climbed into a Boston at Swanton Morley to become the first of their nation to carry out a bombing attack in Europe. July 4 was chosen as the day when 12 Bostons, nine crewed by Americans with each Flight being led by experienced RAF personnel, set off to make low-level attacks on Dutch airfields. They took a pasting from enemy gunners in this highly eventful operation. Nevertheless the Americans were now on the scene and from then onwards their power would only increase.

Circus operations continued from Swanton Morley until poor weather set in late in the year. Then practices for the Eindhoven raid occupied the Boston crews. Twelve Bostons of 226 Squadron participated and one was lost. Withdrawal of the Boston IIIs reduced operational capability until the Mk IIIA became available. Then *Circus* and *Ramrod* operations were resumed and continued throughout the year, until February 14 1944 when the squadron moved to Hartford Bridge. Its equipment had changed in mid-1943 when Mitchell IIs arrived to allow more Bostons to be used elsewhere. With the Mitchells 226 Squadron had flown many *Ramrods* in daylight against Continental targets including V-sites.

Other units had shared Swanton Morley with their main occupants. No 1515 Blind Approach Training Flight formed here on September 20 1941, equipped with eight Oxfords, and remained here until May 1942. No 1508 BAT Flight arrived on August 29 1943 and apart from a short spell away was at Swanton Morley until June 1944. On September 4 1943 305 Squadron arrived to work up on Mitchells leaving the station on November 13 to receive Mosquitoes.

In December 1943 1482 B&G Flight of 2 Group arrived form Great Massingham flying Mitchells, Venturas and Martinets. On April 1 1944 this unit disbanded here to become the nucleus of 2 Group Support Unit whose task was to hold trained aircrew who could quickly replace any lost during the invasion action. No 2 GSU flew a variety of aircraft types including

Above: *Swannington from the air in 1978.*
Below: *Stop butts remain in good condition at Swannington.*

A general view across the airfield site in 1978.

Mosquito IIIs and Hurricanes for fighter attack training, and in September 1944 held six Ansons of 2 Group Communication Flight. The unit moved to Fersfield in mid-December 1944.

Earlier months of that year had seen plenty of activity at Swanton Morley. In March-April No 98 Mitchell squadron and three others with Mosquitoes — 464, 487 and 613 — were here for night interdictor training. Typhoons of 3 Squadron had been here between November 1943 and February 1944.

When 2 Group moved out in December 1944 the station was passed to 100 Group which based the Bomber Support Development Unit here until it disbanded after the war. It flew mainly Mosquitoes. The

100 Group Mosquito Servicing squadron was here in early 1945. The airfield's proximity to 100 Group HQ at Bylaugh meant that their Communications Flight was here, just as the 2 Group Communications Flight had been.

In March 1949 No 4 School of Signalling arrived for training purposes, flying Anson 1s (later T22s) and Proctor 4s. In 1951 the unit was redesignated 4 Radio School and continued flying Anson 22s. Prentices replaced the Proctors. The School continued to function here until December 1957 when it moved to Hullavington.

Swanton Morley remains a grass field, ideal for ATC gliding purposes. The return of Wattisham to operational status brought the Central Servicing Establishment here, and servicing schedules for all types of aircraft and their sophisticated equipment are now worked out. Being one of the last pre-war airfields to be laid down, it is a mixture of the elegance of the expansion period and the hurried compromise demanded by the war.

Swannington, Norfolk

TG141205. 1 mile N of Swannington, by the Brandiston Road which encircles the site

Just how great a threat to Allied victory flying-bombs were is not generally realised. By day anti-aircraft gunners and fighter pilots located them, even if they could not destroy them. At night their exhaust glare was easily visible, but their high speed and low altitude made them difficult targets. Mosquito XIXs with narrow band centimetric radar could catch them, but were a precious commodity in June 1944. So great was the V-1 threat that Flights of the only two Mosquito XIX squadrons in 100 Group, at Swannington, went to West Malling almost at the beginning of the flying-bomb campaign and within days of having started bomber support operations.

Flying-bombs were released in salvoes, which could come at any time, night or day, and this meant having costly standing patrols. Even then, destroying the V-1s was difficult. During July and August 1944 85 Squadron managed to shoot down 30, while 157 claimed 40.

Construction of Swannington began on November 3 1942 and the station opened on April 1 1944 in 100 Group. Both 85 and 157 Squadrons arrived at the station in early May 1944 and the airfield came to life. Each unit had an enviable record during night fighting. No 85 had been led by Wing Commander John Cunningham and 157 Squadron was the first to be issued with Mosquito fighters. The first to be equipped with AI MkX radar, the two squadrons commenced night operations on June 5/6, the night of the Normandy invasion. No 85 Squadron operated over the beach-head area and No 157 flew patrols over Dutch airfields. Flight Lieutenant J.G. Benson of 157 Squadron was, on June 12/13, the first to claim a kill, a Ju 188 at Compiègne. No 85's first success came on June 14/15, a Ju 88 shot down at Florennes.

The two squadrons returned to Swannington in August 1944 and already had engaged some He 111s carrying V-1s. Bomber support duties were resumed from Swannington in September 1944. Thereafter both units supported many Bomber Command night operations, 85 Squadron ultimately being credited with 43 kills and 157 with 28. Mosquito XIXs were used almost to the end of the war, by which time Mk XXXs with engines rated for higher altitudes were available. They flew their last operational sorties on May 2/3 1945, giving high-level support during a raid on Kiel.

On June 27 1945 85 Squadron moved to Castle Camps. No 157 Squadron disbanded at Swannington on August 16 and the station closed in 100 Group on September 30 1945. No 274 MU formed October 1 1945 to store Mosquitoes with sunstations at North Creake and Oulton. The airfield closed to flying on June 30 1947, the MU disbanded in November, and the site was sold on February 22 1957.

Swannington is now given over to agri-culture, a narrow road encircling the site. The control tower is still to be seen to the west of an industrial area on the north side. Large container vehicles use the narrow winding roads, so take care if you visit the airfield. The best view is across fields from the north from where the tower may be seen and some huts. On the west side the road crosses runway remnants and part of the perimeter track. This road also passes close to the stop butts which are in remarkably good condition.

Teversham, Cambridgeshire
See Cambridge

Thorpe Abbotts, Suffolk
TM185890. Turn off A143 at Thorpe Abbotts; by-road encircles airfield and joins perimeter track.

This is a place of sorrow, indeed, because the 100th Bomb Group based here endured extremely heavy losses, set against which were three special awards for courageous action.

The Americans moved in to open the station, satellite to Horham and with the usual two T2 hangars, in April 1943. The 100th Bomb Group arrived in June from Podington where it had been held briefly until it was able to assemble and until Thorpe Abbotts was ready. The first operation was flown on June 25 1943, the first major mission coming on August 17 when the target was Regensburg after which 'the Bloody Hundreth' flew on to North Africa during the first shuttle bombing raid.

Winter surrounds a B-17G of the 100th Bomb Group at Thorpe Abbotts (USAF).

Between June 1943 and June 1944 the Group (identified by a 'D' in a square) took part in many raids on strategic targets, operating from Thorpe Abbotts. These reached a climax in March 1944, for on the 4th, 6th and 8th the 100th fought their way to Berlin, receiving a second Distinguished Unit Citation.

Support to the invasion and St Lô break-out followed and in the summer of 1944 oil targets in particular felt the weight of their bombs. Then the unit helped pave the way for the capture of Brest. Between October and December 1944 it hammered transport and ground defences during the assault on the Siegfried Line. Meanwhile the Group had been active in dropping supplies to the French Resistance, being awarded the Croix de Guerre with Palms for this duty performed between June and December 1944.

During its 306 missions the 100th suffered heavy losses and its last raid came on April 20 1945. The Group was one of the last to leave Britain for it did not vacate Thorpe Abbotts until December 1945, although the RAF had moved in during June 1945. The site closed in April 1956, the control tower, runways and perimeter tracks still being visible.

Nearby is the site of Pulham St Mary airship station, but the famous airship hangar has long since been dismantled. The site was used as an ammunition depot during the war, No 53 MU forming here on August 12 1940. The Officer's Mess and some sheds still stand. No 53 MU disbanded on February 1 1958 and the airfield was sold on August 1 1962.

Covered by hundreds of signatures, the war-weary B-17 'Squawkin Hawk 1' is seen shortly before returning to the USA (USAF). Above right: Summer 1978 saw work in progress to remove the main runway from Thorpe Abbotts.

Tibenham, Norfolk

TM145885. Off A140 N of Diss; turn off left on B1134 and turn right for airfield

For 17 months Tibenham housed B-24s of the 445th Bomb Group which arrived here in November 1943 and returned to the USA in May-June 1945, having flown 282 operations. The Group's first mission, the first from Tibenham, was a raid on Kiel on December 13 1943, after which it bombed such varied targets as the synthetic oil depot at Lutzkendorf, a chemical factory at Ludwigshaven, the famed marshalling yards at Hamm, an airfield at Munich, underground oil stores at Ehmen and an ammunition centre at Duneburg. For the Group's part in the attack on the Gotha aircraft factory on February 24 1944 it received a Distinguished Unit Citation.

The unit took part in the pre-invasion attacks on France and operated in support of the US Army on D-Day and at St Lô and during the Ardennes offensive. Tibenham's Liberators were particularly active on March 24 1945 when they dropped food, medical supplies and ammunition to airborne forces at Wesel. In the afternoon of the same day they operated again, bombing the landing ground at Stormede. Leaflets were dropped on France in the summer of 1944 and they ferried fuel to the American forces. For their drops of supplies to the French Resistance between December 1943 and February 1945 they were awarded the Croix de Guerre. Their final operation took place on April 25 1945.

Tibenham's Group had one unwanted distinction: it had the highest casualty figures for any one operation in the 8th Air Force, when in September 1944 they lost a staggering 30 aircraft.

The RAF retrieved the station in July 1945 and, although the main runway was lengthened in 1955, the airfield closed in March 1959. Runways and the perimeter track remain intact and the Norfolk Gliding Club has used the station since 1960.

Tuddenham, Suffolk

TL760715. Turn off A11 at Barton Mills; airfield SE of village

This station opened in October 1943 in 3 Group. No 90 Squadron flying Stirling IIIs arrived in mid-October, commencing mining operations on October 17. The unit also flew SOE sorties from Tuddenham. Stirling IIIs were replaced by Lancaster IIIs in May 1944, their first operation coming against Dreux on June 10. Until the end of the war 90 Squadron operated from here, by night and day, against a variety of strategic and some tactical battle targets. It took part in the June raid on Villers Bocage and helped the break-out from Caen. In September it was involved in the destruction of Le Havre and participated in the attack on West Kapelle in October. Thus, for the last year of the war, Tuddenham was a very busy Lancaster base.

'C' Flight of 90 Squadron was hived off to form the nucleus of 186 Squadron on October 5 1944, this new unit moving to Stradishall in December 1944. In March 1945 138 Squadron, which was no longer required as a special duties squadron at Tempsford, was re-organised as a bomber squadron and moved to Tuddenham for Lancaster operations.

After the war both squadrons remained in Bomber Command and re-equipped with Lancaster B1 (FE)s so that they could be available for overseas service. They were joined by two others similarly equipped in April 1946, Nos 149 and 207. In strength each was only a half squadron so that Tuddenham held on average 24 Lancasters. The bomber squadrons vacated Tuddenham in November 1946 when post-war re-arrangement on permanent stations was available. Tuddenham then closed to flying and was held for possible future use.

The airfield passed to the USAF on December 12 1954 as a sub-station of Pickenham. In July 1959 107 Squadron in 3 Group reformed from 'C' Flight of 77 Squadron and received three Thor missiles. This unit disbanded in July 1963 and the site was disposed of.

Upwood, Cambridgeshire

TL270845. Off B1096, 2 miles SW Ramsey

Upwood opened in January 1937 and its four 'C' Type hangars still stand out clear on the fringe of the Fens. To Wyton went the RAF's first Blenheims and to Upwood the first Fairey Battles. Underpowered, poorly armed, yet twice as fast as the Hawker Hind it replaced, the Battle began to reach 63 Squadron at Upwood in May 1937, the unit having arrived on March 3 with Hinds and Audaxes. No 52 Squadron, which brought Hinds to Upwood a few days before 63 Squadron, arrived rearmed with Battles at the end of 1937.

The Battle's range was too short to enable it to attack Germany from Britain, and poor manoeuvrability and insufficient armament rendered it useless for ground-attack purposes. Only by raiding Germany from advanced bases in France could Battles be of any use. They stood by during the Munich crisis as a mobile squadron for advanced deployment, but on the outbreak of war both 52 and 63 Squadrons switched to a training role in 6 Group and moved out of Upwood.

They were replaced there by Blenheim Is of 35 and 90 Squadrons, providing operational training for 2 Group. In April 1940 these were amalgamated, becoming 17 OTU which shared Blenheim bomber training for home and overseas squadrons with 13 OTU at Bicester. Daily, the sky around Upwood seemed full of Blenheim Is and IVs, on circuits or training sorties to the bombing ranges off Holbeach. Many who were later to achieve fame in 2 Group passed through Upwood, and sadly a large number would fly only a few sorties before being posted missing. Bostons were tried briefly in 1941. It was at Upwood that the 'Woods brothers'

A B-24 lead-ship of the 445th Bomb Group at Tibenham (USAF).

Lancasters of 90 Squadron were based at Tuddenham at the end of the war.

In the mid-1950s squadrons of Canberras were based at Upwood.

developed Synthetic Night Flying using a Battle. For this, the pilot was masked and could only pick out the take-off lane by sodium flares placed along its sides. A Blenheim, Oxford and Anson were also involved in the trials, all types used by 17 OTU here.

At the end of April 1943 17 OTU left Upwood, to re-equip with Wellingtons. Runway building had then commenced. Halifaxes and Lancasters of the PFF NTU used the station from mid-June 1943, but spent more time at Warboys because of the runway building. The station fully re-opened to them on November 1 1943.

In February 1944 No 139 Squadron brought in its Canadian-built Mosquito XXs from Wyton for night operations under 8 Group. Part of their fleet was fitted with H2S and 139 Squadron led many night operations marking for other Mosquito bomber squadrons when they operated beyond the range of *Oboe*. The PFF NTU finally left for Warboys in March 1944 and was replaced by Lancas-

ters of 156 Squadron based at Upwood until June 1945 and much engaged in the bomber offensive, principally as a marker squadron in the pathfinder force.

No 105 Squadron arrived in June 1945, making the station all-Mosquito equipped, although a few Lincolns were here in the autumn for trials. No 105 Squadron disbanded on February 1 1946 and 139 Squadron moved to join 109 Squadron at Hemswell to become the post-war marker force for Bomber Command. In February 1946 Liberators of 53 Squadron arrived and stayed until July.

Like so many stations Upwood needed a thorough clean-up after the war and when this had been achieved 7 Squadron arrived on July 30 1946 when Mepal closed. Its Lancaster BI (FE) aircraft were joined by others of 148 and 214 Squadrons in November.

During 1949 the three squadrons re-equipped with Lincoln IIs and flew a number of overseas detachments, taking part in the policing operations in Malaya and Aden where bombs were dropped in anger.

No 214 Squadron disbanded on December 30 1954, No 148 on July 1 1955 and No 7 on January 1 1956, as each unit prepared itself for participation in the V-Force.

The Lincolns were then replaced by Canberra 2s, forming the Upwood Wing established by first posting in 18 Squadron in May 1955, 61 Squadron in June 1955, 50 Squadron in January 1956 and

Shortly after introduction to service a Battle stands by one of Upwood's hangars (MoD).

35 Squadron in June 1956. In the autumn of 1956 Upwood's Canberras took part in the Suez campaign.

When the build-up of the V-Force permitted it the Canberra force began to be reduced. No 40 Squadron which had arrived in October 1956 amalgamated with 50 Squadron two months later. No 18 Squadron disbanded on February 1 1957 and No 61 on March 31 1958. Strength was somewhat restored when 21 Squadron flew in from Waddington in October 1958, but disbanded on January 15 1959. Flying virtually ended at Upwood when 35 Squadron disbanded on September 11 1961. As a reminder of that squadron's long association with Upwood a Canberra now stands at the entrance to the station bearing 35's markings.

Upwood then settled down to being a station for RAF clerical and accounts training, and remains an active RAF base although flying has ceased.

Warboys, Cambridgeshire

TL290795. 7 miles NE Huntingdon, off A141; airfield by road to W of village

Such was the intensity of Blenheim training by 17 OTU Upwood in 1941 that a satellite field at Warboys had to come rapidly into use. However, nearby Wyton, operational from the start of the war, had just as great a need and so in September 1941 Warboys became its second satellite. For a few weeks Stirlings of XV Squadron flew from Wyton as well as Alconbury, and while runways were being laid at the latter.

A new squadron, No 156, formed under Wyton's control at Alconbury in February 1942 and on August 5 1942 began to move to Warboys to make way for the Americans at Alconbury. From Warboys they mounted their first operation, against Osnabruck, on August 9. Then they became part of 3 Group's Pathfinder Force still using Wellington IIIs. Their first operation under the new system came on August 18 with Flensburg as target. Moments after take-off a flare ignited in Flight Sergeant Case's Wellington and the flares were then jettisoned five miles from the airfield. A more successful flare dropping raid was that against Frankfurt on August 24, but two Wellingtons were lost and Captain J.M. Hodgson's aircraft was badly damaged by flak which stripped off a lot of its fabric. The first raid on Italy — Genoa — came on November 7 and more Italian sorties

followed in December.

On the last day of the year three Lancaster 1s arrived for squadron conversion. The final Wellington raid from Warboys was mounted on January 23 1943 against Lorient which was again the target when Lancasters came into use on January 26. Thereafter they flew as part of the Pathfinder Force from Warboys making their first Berlin raid on March 1 and taking part in the highly successful Essen sortie on March 5. Warboys had been raised to full station status on January 1 1943, and in March that year 1507 BAT Flight began to use the airfield. No 156 Squadron operated from here until March 1944 when they moved to Upwood.

In June 1943 the Pathfinder Navigational Training Unit reached Upwood and some of its Halifax IIs and Lancasters were based at Warboys. When 156 Squadron vacated that station the PFF NTU moved completely to Warboys, on March 5 1944, continuing to use Lancasters and some Mosquitoes.

Two days later a formation of six Mosquito bombers came to Warboys signalling the arrival of 1655 Mosquito Conversion Unit. This was the organisation responsible for conversion of crews to Mosquitoes of Bomber Command, and it also used some Oxford trainers for bombing practice and navigational training. By the close of 1944 they were flying Mosquito IVs and Canadian-built XXs, and training crews to use *Oboe* and H2S. No 1655 MCU disbanded at the end of December 1944, to reform as 16 OTU. This left behind the H2S and *Oboe* training commitments which were passed to the PFF NTU, then flying some of the Mosquitoes of 1655 MCU. That duty continued until the war ended.

An aerial view of Warboys taken by 543 Squadron on June 5 1967 (DoE).

No 571 Mosquito Squadron arrived at Warboys from Oakington on July 24, forced out of its base by the arrival of Transport Command. They disbanded here on September 28 1945, most of the crews being posted to 98 Squadron in Germany.

Warboys closed as an airfield in January 1946. It was resurrected in 1959 to become a base for Thors in a complex set in the middle of the old airfield.

Greenwoods Transport Ltd now hold the site both of the Thors and the remaining Type T2 hangar, and have hired out this and other sheds to various concerns whilst having a transport depot in the one-time Thor complex. The airfield is now cultivated, but the watch office remains in quite fair condition. Part of one runway may be seen at the north end of the field and sections of the perimeter track. There are also a number of huts to be seen. The best preserved item, though, is the old D/F radio station still complete with radio masts and in civilian hands.

Waterbeach, Cambridgeshire

TL495665. 6 miles NE Cambridge on A10.

'You should see for yourself. There's a huge oblong patch of water miles wide stretching to the Wash. I wouldn't have thought it possible. Come and have a look.' I climbed into the station's Anson and off we set. Once aloft the sight was incredible, as if the sea really reached Waterbeach shore. A few islands protruded, Witchford being safe on the Isle of Ely. Beyond, it was exactly as he had described. There was this huge extent of water leading to the sea. 'Look at that, it's about to go,' cried the skipper. We circled and a farm house collapsed into a swirling mass of water.

Those days have probably gone, for after the 1947 floods a huge drainage ditch encircles the Fens. You cross it when travelling to Lakenheath from Newmarket and you can see it when taking off from Marham.

Waterbeach is of the Fens. They are inseparable. It stands close to the site of Denny Abbey, and when the land was requisitioned in 1939 there was much opposition, for fine agricultural land was being taken. Drainage was surprisingly good because a base layer of sand and gravel lay close to the surface.

By mid-1940 hangar building was much under way and to prevent the Germans from landing Ju 52s the aerodrome

Below: *The control tower still stands at Warboys.* Above: *Near to Warboys a wartime D/F station remains in good condition.*

surface was festooned with poles and trip wires. Late 1940 they were removed, then the Germans arrived but not, of course, in Ju 52s. They first paid a call on December 30 1940, and on February 3 1941 the crew of a Dornier 17Z neatly placed a stick of nine bombs along the face of the western hangar and damaged the watch office and runway. Intruder activity, though, was less here than at other stations.

Waterbeach opened on January 11 1941, at the time when a concrete track was being laid into dispersals cut into an orchard to the south of the flying field. Personnel accommodation, to prewar standards, was good and the runways almost complete when on the afternoon of March 19 1941 Wellington Ics of 99 Squadron flew in and dispersed around the perimeter track. There was plenty of mud to contend with when it rained, for grass had yet to take hold on the airfield. But the problem on March 1941 when 99 Squadron took off for Cologne was dust. So much was thrown up that only six crews could get away and Newmarket was again briefly used before operations were resumed on March 30, against Brest. On April 9 the first Berlin raid from Waterbeach was mounted. The squadron stood by to attack the *Bismarck* on May 25 and next day searched for the *Hipper*. Six

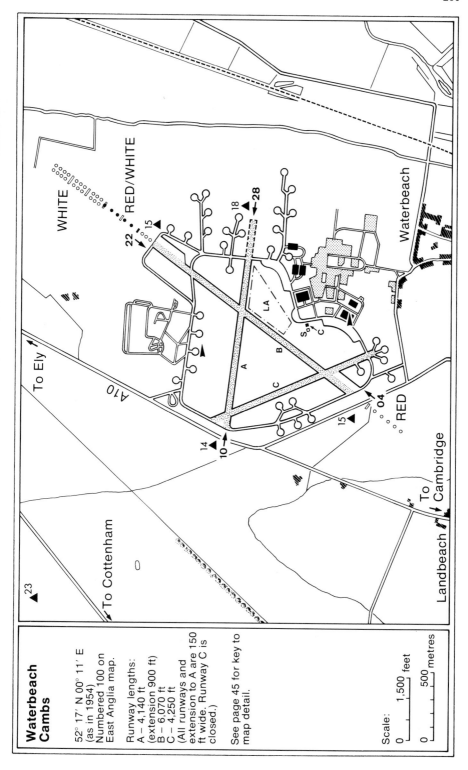

Waterbeach
Cambs

52° 17' N 00° 11' E
(as in 1954)
Numbered 100 on
East Anglia map.

Runway lengths:
A – 4,140 ft
(extension 900 ft)
B – 6,070 ft
C – 4,250 ft
(All runways and
extension to A are 150
ft wide. Runway C is
closed.)

See page 45 for key to
map detail.

Scale:

0 _____ 1,500 feet

0 _____ 500 metres

Above: *The aircraft most associated with Waterbeach, the Short Stirling. W7459 is seen here.* Below: *After the Stirlings came the Lancasters. Mk II JJ-O:LL734 of 514 Squadron is seen here returning from a daylight raid on France in July 1944 (IWM).*

crews took part in the July day raid on Brest, a target they were to attack frequently, and the dusk procession west over Cambridgeshire was something one almost came to expect each day.

In March 1941 the squadron had received the first of a handful of Wellington IIs from which 4,000 lb 'Cookies' were dropped. The IIs were unpopular, for engine overheating was encountered and crews considered them a risky invention until they proved later to be superior to the Mk Ics.

There were a number of bad accidents in 1941. On May 5 'J Johnny' took off and crashed north-west of the airfield. A bright glare lit the sky for miles around, but the bomb load did not explode. On December 7 'Q Queenie' set off for Aachen. Engine trouble arose over the sea and the crew turned back. On final approach the other engine cut and the aircraft crashed. All personnel on the station were ordered into the air-raid shelters. Five of the crew raced from the burning aircraft, then the 4,000 lb bomb exploded.

On a grey November day in 1941 a Stirling circled the station. Its landing heralded the arrival of a type always to be associated with Waterbeach. Conversion training for Stirling crews soon began and 1651 Conversion Unit formed in January 1942, 99 Squadron leaving for overseas in March 1942. For almost two years the Stirlings droned round the circuit, for landing and taking-off in the large bomber needed skill and a lot of training. The accident rate due to swing on take-off and landing was high, but once airborne safely the Stirling was a delight to fly, as manoeuvrable as a fighter.

An overshoot to the west meant an almost certain outcome: the aircraft would trip as it crossed the drainage ditch along the Ely road. Many times in 1942-1943 one would see a Stirling literally ditched and looking very sorry for itself.

Stirlings stayed, rapidly increasing in number and diversity of appearance until November 1943 when Waterbeach again became an operational station, head of 33 Base from September. On November 23 1943 the Main Party of 514 Squadron arrived, also 1678 Conversion Flight, both with Lancaster IIs.

It was at Waterbeach that the Supermarine Swift entered service and troublesome it was.

These aircraft had the built-in ability to carry a 8,000 lb bomb, but usually delivered lighter loads of mixed 4,000 lb bombs and incendiaries. At the time of their arrival they were much involved with the Battle of Berlin, but were soon attacking targets widely in Germany and France. They took part in the invasion support operations aiding the break out from Caen, following on with raids on V-1 targets and oil depots. The Mk IIs were gradually phased out, flying their last sorties on September 23 1944. This meant that 1678 Conversion Flight was no longer needed and it disbanded after DS654 landed early on June 12 1944. No 514 Squadron fought a tough war to the bitter end, taking part in the Dresden and Chemnitz raids of 1945. Come VE-Day and they were dropping food to the Dutch, then repatriating POWs. They disbanded on August 27 1945.

Suddenly the station took on a new look. No 47 Group Transport Command took over on September 12 1945. Almost immediately Liberators of 59 and 220 Squadrons moved in. Some wore Coastal Command colours, others were in Far East bomber trim, and there were Mks 3, 6, and 8. Almost at once they began trooping flights to India and the Middle East, a duty which petered out in the New Year.

In August 1946 Avro Yorks of 51 Squadron arrived, able to carry mixed loads — 'passenger-cum-freight' — on trunk routes mainly to India. An abrupt change took place in November-December 1947 when Dakotas of Nos 18, 53, 62 and 77 Squadrons moved in and 46

The interior of a Waterbeach hangar. The Javelin 9 is XH768 of 25 Squadron (Wilf Manderfield).

Group took command. They were soon barely in evidence at Waterbeach, being detached to Germany in the summer of 1948 for their part in the Berlin Airlift, following flying on routes to the Middle East. No 18 Squadron returned in October 1949, disbanding on February 20 1950. It was this same month which saw the demise of 53 and 62 Squadrons. No 77 had disbanded in December 1949, and their place was partly taken by that exclusive club, No 24 (Commonwealth) Squadron which arrived on June 8 1949.

The importance of Transport Command diminished by 1950. No 24 Squadron left in March 1950 and in April Fighter Command took control of Waterbeach bringing 63 Squadron in on the 13th of the month and 56 Squadron the following month, both flying Meteor 4s, which were exchanged for Mk 8s in late 1951. In July 1950 the Meteors were involved in the RAF display at Farnborough and the distinguished 56 Squadron was one of the first to appear with post-war squadron colours. At the same time the Korean War broke out which induced the Americans to place an F-84 Thunderjet Group in Britain to provide escort for their bombers. Some F-84s used Waterbeach for training during August 1950, the only time when the Americans used the station.

On a dreary day in February 1954 the station received its first Supermarine Swift, and 56 Squadron tried to make a success of this aeroplane which gave much trouble. There were some bad accidents and in March 1955 the Swifts were withdrawn and 56 Squadron re-equipped, disappointingly, with Meteor 8s. These they flew until May 1955 when Hunter 5s began to arrive. No 63 Squadron were more fortunate since they re-equipped with Hunter 6s in November 1956.

A new squadron, No 253, formed at Waterbeach in April 1955, equipped with Venom night fighters, the three squadrons comprising a day and night fighter Wing intact until 253 Squadron disbanded in August 1957. It was replaced in September by 153 Squadron which in June 1958 was re-numbered 25 Squadron and continued to fly Meteor night fighters. No 63 Squadron disbanded on October 24 1958.

No 56 Squadron moved out in July 1959 during which month No 46 Squadron brought in their Javelin 2s, remaining here until May 1961. No 25 Squadron gave up their Meteors and successively flew Javelin 7s and 9s, staying until November 1961. Crews for No 60 Javelin

Within protecting revetments stands another Javelin 9 of 64 Squadron.

Hunters of 1 Squadron lined up at Waterbeach and photographed moments before operational flying ceased at the station.

Squadron trained at Waterbeach in early 1961, leaving on June 25 for the Far East. No 64 Squadron's Javelin 9s were based here from July 27 1961 until July 13 1962.

A further change came in January 1962 when 38 Group took over Waterbeach, and in January 1962 Hunter FGA 9s of Nos 1 and 54 Squadrons arrived for ground-attack and transport escort duties.

On the afternoon of August 8 1963 a Pakistani pilot in Hunter XG264 of 54 Squadron landed at Waterbeach. To him had fallen the distinction of being last man home. He halted in front of my camera, stood up and as best he could saluted. That salute could well have been a tribute to all who had courageously flown from the station. The Hunters left in the next few days for West Raynham.

Flying here had not quite finished for, with the runway in good state, Varsities from 5 FTS Oakington flew circuits here until they were withdrawn, and a few similar flights were made by Oakington's Jetstreams.

The airfield building element of the Army's Royal Engineers are currently based at Waterbeach, and in recent years the Burma Star Day has brought aeroplanes back to the runway.

At the north end drivers of heavy goods vehicles attend the testing station. Gone are the concrete revetments once sheltering fighters, together with some of the bomber dispersals. Who, though, accurately can predict what the future holds?

Waterbeach from the air on March 25 1947 (DoE).

Wattisham, Suffolk

TM025510. Off B1078, six miles SW Needham Market

Moments before midnight on September 3 1939 the order was given to Wattisham — stand by for operations. Shortly before 1500 hours on September 4 ten Blenheims — five each of Nos 107 and 110 Squadrons — set off to attack German warships off Wilhelmshaven. The weather was very bad, the attack ineffectual, and it cost five Blenheim crews, four from 107 Squadron. From the attack would be remembered the name of Kenneth Doran, DFC who led the raid. Tragic, indeed, that he should lose his life many years later in the Turkish Airways DC-10 crash in France.

Wattisham, a refined pre-war station with four C-type hangars, opened in March 1939. The arrival of Blenheims of 107 Squadron in April 1939 and 110 Squadron in May brought associations with its most famous residents. It was not long before the dynamic qualities of Basil Embry were electrifying the station. Courage, such as he always displayed, was needed when the Blenheim squadrons were hurled into action in May 1940 incurring heavy losses. Then the big blow struck — Embry was missing. How he spent his lonely hours escaping cannot be better told than in his biography *Mission*

Completed (Methuen).

The two squadrons endured the whole operations pattern of 2 Group with detachments to Lossiemouth, Manston and Malta, all connected with anti-shipping operations as hazardous and horrific as any during the war. No 107 Squadron moved to Great Massingham on May 11 1941 and 110 left for the Far East on March 17 the following year.

Association with 2 Group was far from ended. No 226 Squadron had arrived flying Blenheims in May 1941 and stayed, except for detachments, until December 9 1941 when it left for Swanton Morley. It was at once replaced by a depleted 18 Squadron, part of which was still in Malta. 18 Squadron remained at Wattisham until August 1942 by which time it was flying Blenheim VDs. It then went to the Middle East. At the end of May 1942 and in June, 13 Squadron was briefly here taking part in the '1,000-bomber' raids in an intruder role.

An unusual occurrence was the arrival at Wattisham of 236 Squadron on February 9 1942, with Beaufighter Ics under 16 Group control. They flew anti-shipping patrols and the highlight of their stay came in May. It was known that the Germans always mounted a noon parade along the Champs Elysées in Paris. What better than to delight the inhabitants of that sad, beautiful city by tickling up the parade? Flight Lieutenant A.K. Gatwood and Sergeant G. Fern volunteered without knowing what they were letting themselves in for. They were to shoot up the parade and throw out a tricolour — when cloud suitably covered their sortie.

They tried on May 13 but cloud ran out. Only on their fifth attempt, on June 12, was the attack possible. They landed on Thorney Island to refuel. Cloud broke over the French coast but they flew on low. At 1202 hours they were over the Champs Elysées, but no troops were to be seen. Had the Germans discovered the plan? They hurled out their tricolour over the Arc de Triomphe and sprayed the Gestapo headquarters in the Ministry of Marine building. They were not intercepted except by a crow which crashed into their starboard engine. They landed safely at Northolt after a sortie in the best traditions of Wattisham. On July 7 1942 No 236 Squadron moved to Oulton.

The RAF vacated the station in September 1942, and the Americans moved in and runways were laid. Instead of a planned bomber base the Americans used Wattisham as a depot for fighter aircraft, and an additional technical site was established in the southern corner of the airfield. The 68th Observation Group, flying P-39Ds, were at Wattisham between October and December 1942.

In May 1944 the 479th Fighter Group arrived, the last Fighter Group to join the US 8th Air Force, their P-38Js beginning operations on May 26 1944 for bomber escort and ground support duties. During the Normandy invasion they flew patrols over the armies and made fighter sweeps, strafing targets of opportunity. For their attacks on French airfields between August 18 and September 5 1944 they received a Distinguished Unit Citation and a second one after combats during a Munster raid on September 26. Bomber escort and ground-attack continued to the end of the war and on April 24 1945 the Group were credited with the last enemy aircraft shown down by the 8th Air Force during the war. Since September 1944 they had been flying P-51s. After the USAAF left the RAF once again took over the station.

During October 1946 No 245 Squadron flying Meteor IIIs arrived from Bentwaters, followed next month by Nos 56 and 266 Squadrons which stayed until April 16 1947. Runway work then took place while the station served as a centre

for the establishment of servicing schedules. On October 27 1950 No 257 Squadron arrived, followed on November 22 by 263 Squadron. They flew Meteor 4s and equipped with Meteor 8s the following year. No 152 Squadron reformed here on June 30 1954 with Meteor NF12s and 14s and moved to Stradishall on August 28 1957. No 257 Squadron hit the headlines in November 1954 when they became the first squadron to receive Hunter 2s, No 263 being issued with them in March the following year. In August 1956 263 Squadron equipped with Hunter 6s and a year later on August 29 moved to Stradishall, 257 having disbanded on March 31 1957. Previously the Hunters had been away at Wymeswold whilst the runway was strengthened, 263 Squadron moving to make way for Lightnings.

Before they arrived 111 Squadron, 'The Black Arrows', moved into Wattisham in June 1958 and flew many displays from the station. No 41 Squadron arrived with Javelins in June 1958 and in 1960 were the first squadron to receive Javelin 8s. They disbanded in December 1963.

In April 1961 Lightning 1as replaced 111 Squadron's Hunters heralding a long association between Wattisham and the Lightning. With them were Lightnings of 56 Squadron which had arrived here in

'Two-six; heave!' Ground crews lift the tail of a 110 Squadron Blenheim at Wattisham in 1940 (IWM).

Briefly the Lightnings of 56 Squadron formed a display team, the 'Firebirds', seen here on the ASP at Wattisham (Peter Corbell).

July 1959 and later fielded a team, 'The Firebirds', although this aircraft was rather unsuitable for display flying.

No 56 Squadron was here until January 1971 when they moved to Cyprus. No 29 Squadron took up residence on May 10 1967 and received Lightings and the two squadrons, 111 and 29, saw out the main Lightning era until 56 Squadron returned to replace 111 in 1975. A highlight of the Lightning days was undoubtedly the annual contribution to the Queen's Birthday fly-past when a host of these hefty, impressive machines would be lined-up for the fly-past over London.

Nos 29 and 111 Squadrons were removed after elements of the squadrons re-equipped with Phantoms at Coningsby. Wattisham is now the home for the Phantoms of 23 and 56 Squadrons.

Control towers at many airfields were modified in the 1950s, including that at Wattisham (MoD, via Bruce Robertson).

Watton, Norfolk

TL945000. E of Watton town on B1108

On days when clouds hung low in 1941 East Anglian airfields were subject to sudden enemy attack by raiders dipping out of the overcast often undetected by radar. One such day was February 18, when an He 111 operating over Norfolk attacked Watton. Response was fast, and the weapons which engaged the bomber were of the Parachute and Cable variety (PAC). Fired, in effect, was a miniature aerial minefield, and the Heinkel flew straight into it. The bomber came down near Ovington in Norfolk, one of the few to be credited to PAC and probably the only one to fall to the weapon in East Anglia.

The Heinkel, of 4/KG 53, the Condor Legion, A1 + CM, its markings blotted out with lamp black, had been badly mauled. One cable had penetrated the port wing leading edge and cut through to the main spar severing the port aileron control rod. Another sliced into the port wing nearer the tip and a third hit had penetrated the starboard wing. Evidently this Heinkel He 111H-3 Wk Nr 3349 had been sent on an armed reconnaissance to the Humber region, and was shot down about 0755 hours. The crew of five was taken prisoner.

Watton's claim to fame, though, rests in the years when it was a station for 2 Group Blenheims. So much courage of an outstanding order was shown by so many crews that it would be invidious to single out any one.

Twice the station encountered crippling losses, the first when 82 Squadron attacked enemy formations near Gembloux in May 1940 and were all but wiped out. The second came in August 1940 when again the squadron was ambushed, on a high level raid on Aalborg in Denmark, only one of 12 Blenheims returning. Through these bad days of 1940 Watton sustained an appalling casualty rate, and fought on through the dark winter nights before switching to the anti-shipping raids of 1941. In the summer it was busy mounting *Circus* operations and took part in the August low-level raid on Cologne's power stations. The airfield's career at this time was inseparably bound up with that of Bodney.

Watton opened at the start of 1939, first residents being the Blenheims of 34 Squadron which arrived in late February. A few days later 21 Squadron moved in,

the two squadrons working up until August 1939 when 34 Squadron moved to the Far East. Their place was taken in late August by 82 Squadron, both units now flying Blenheim IVs whose first operations, photographing enemy airfields, came on September 27.

In March 1940 the satellite at Bodney came into use for both squadrons. Although operations were usually from the parent station, Bodney was used more than most, both squadrons alternating their stays at the two aerodromes.

No 21 Squadron moved to Lossiemouth to watch for enemy shipping off the Scottish coast, returning to Watton in late October. Whilst it was away 105 Squadron took its place, reforming after its mauling in France as a Blenheim squadron, and operating by day against Continental targets. No 18 Squadron were also briefly here.

Cloud-cover day raids, night Main Force attacks and fighter-escorted day raids occupied the squadrons in 1941, but the anti-shipping campaign was their prime employment.

In May 1941 21 Squadron was detached to operate from Malta against shipping. In July it used Manston as a base for *Channel Stop* and in September made a few raids on Norwegian coastal shipping, again from Lossiemouth. In December it went to Malta again and then to North Africa for the desert war.

Meanwhile 82 Squadron had been hurled against shipping too and, apart from a spell in Malta in May-June 1941, used Watton as their base for daylight operations throughout 1941. No 82 was one of the squadrons sent to reinforce the RAF in the Far East, leaving Watton in March 1942. Throughout 1941 Blenheims left Britain for overseas after preparation at Watton.

One other aspect of the station's 1941 career deserves mention, for it was here that 90 Squadron reformed on May 7 to operate Fortress 1s, although these early B-17s flew from Bodney and not the parent station. Three Blind Approach Training Flights operated under 2 Group and one of these, No 1508 flying Blenheim 1s was briefly Watton-based, from December 20 1941 to January 19 1942.

No 2 Group relinquished Watton in January 1942. Their place was taken by Master IIs of 17 (P) AFU formed on January 29, the only mid-Anglia training unit. No 17 (P) AFU trained pilots after their elementary course and in some cases after flying training overseas so they

Above: *From Watton Blenheims were very active in the early years of the war. One of 21 Squadron's aircraft is seen here.* Below: *In the latter part of the war American Mosquitoes operated from Watton (M. Havelaar).*

could acclimatise to the European environment. This unit left Watton and Bodney in May 1943 for Calveley.

In mid-1943 the Americans took over the station and built a runway. Its first tenants were the 3rd Strategic Air Depot who established a base known as Neaton and situated on the south side of the airfield at a new complex. Its task was the maintenance of B-24s for the 2nd Air Division.

On April 22 1944 the 803rd Reconnaissance Group moved in to use B-17s, B-24s and mainly Mosquito PR XVIs for weather reporting and reconnaissance, becoming the 25th Bomb Group (R) on August 9 1944. They played an important part in the 8th Air Force campaign flying ahead of the bombers to report on weather conditions and wind speeds for bombing, two squadrons using Mosquitoes.

The Americans left in the summer of 1945 and the RAF took control of Watton on September 27. Watton became the home of the Radio Warfare Establishment which evolved into the Central Signals Establishment. This organisation was responsible for the development of radio and radar warfare for the RAF and generally looked after the introduction of ECM apparatus and navigational aids, etc. For this purpose it was later organised into three squadrons. No 192 flying Canberras, Washingtons and Comets after using Lincolns and Mosquitoes in 1953-1955; No 527 a calibration unit flying Canberras; and No 116 equipped with Varsities which checked on navigational aids having earlier used Ansons and Mosquitoes. Additionally, Development Squadron flew Varsities in 'A' Flight and some of the last RAF Lincolns in 'B'

Flight.

August 21 1958 saw dramatic alterations to squadron numbering when 192 Squadron became 51, 527 changed to 245 and 116 altered to 115, the latter two squadrons moving to Tangmere in September 1958. The Development Squadron became No 151 and in November 1958 90 Group which had administered the station became Signals Command.

A further change came in September 1963 when 245 and 115 Squadrons returned, 245 becoming 98 Squadron. No 51 Squadron had left in March 1963 and transferred to Bomber Command.

In the 1950s the Royal Navy also had a squadron here for radio and radar work, flying Gannets and Venoms.

Flying has ceased at Watton now, although a major control and air traffic organisation is based there.

Wendling, Norfolk

TF925150. 2 miles N of A47(T) at Wendling

Built in 1942, and with the customary two T2 hangars, Wendling was the home of the 392nd Bomb Group, fourth Liberator Group to join the 8th Air Force and the first to be fully equipped with nose turreted B-24Hs. These began to arrive in

Britain, albeit in small numbers, in August 1943 as the 392nd moved into Wendling. Commencing operations on September 6 1943, they flew 285 missions from this station.

Targets were the same as for other 2nd Division Groups, although the 392nd did not take part in any Middle East ventures. For its participation in the attack on an aircraft factory at Gotha on February 24 1944 it received a Distinguished Unit Citation. The unit attacked municipal targets in Berlin, a tank factory at Kassel, oil refinery at Gelsenkirchen, steel plant at Brunswick, marshalling yards at Osnabruck and later the railway viaduct at Bielefeld which was eventually brought down by 22,000 lb bombs dropped by Lancasters of 617 Squadron.

Coastal defences and choke points were bombed on D-Day and the Group assisted at St Lô and in the Ardennes battle. It also took part in the airborne support operations at Nijmegen and the Rhine crossing. After its last bombing raid on April 24 1945 the unit dropped food to the Dutch. The Group left Wendling in June 1945, and the station was returned to the RAF on June 25, eventually closing in November 1961. A turkey farm now sprawls across the site, but a memorial to the 392nd can be found on the Beeston road.

Westley, Suffolk

TM825645. W of Bury St Edmunds on A45, immediately W of old army camp. Now a housing estate

Visit the site of this small airfield immediately west of Bury and you will find a large housing estate covering most of where it used to be. Small and insignificant, it might well have been an 'action station' had the invasion of Britain come about.

In 1938 this airfield was built with two small hangars. It was the home for the West Suffolk Aero Club, which acquired two Taylorcraft Plus C monoplanes. The unit was not big enough to be incorporated into the Civil Air Guard Scheme, and the field too small for RAFVR use. Thus, private flying continued until the war came, when the airfield closed.

Proximity to the then thriving Bury Barracks certainly influenced its future, for between April and July 1941 241 Squadron was here flying Lysanders. Their immediate task was to co-operate with the Army in the vicinity and watch East Coast Areas for any invading forces.

At the end of 1940 Army Co-operation Command pressed for faster and less vulnerable aircraft, the failure of the American Curtiss Tomahawk as a front-line fighter resulting in their being transferred to Army Co-operation Command. This brought about another problem. In order to take off, the fighter needed a longer runway than that available at Westley and so, as soon as Snailwell was ready, the Lysanders moved out of Westley. This left the station vacant although communications aircraft used it.

On August 21 1942 652 (AOP) Squadron arrived flying Tiger Moths and equipped with Auster 1s in late 1942. The small field was ideal for Austers and during 1943 other squadrons trained here. Austers, for all their ruggedness, were very light aeroplanes. Too light, for on one

A formation of Liberators of the 392nd Bomb Group setting out from Wendling on November 24 1944 (USAF).

occasion a Stirling pilot from Ridgewell made a very low run over Westley. The slipstream was such that it managed to overturn one of the Austers!

Auster squadrons continued to use Westley for training until the summer of 1944 when it became devoid of aircraft.

West Raynham, Norfolk

TF850245. 2 miles from village, off A1065

Passing West Raynham when on the Swaffham-Fakenham road one sees Bloodhound missiles of 85 Squadron on the skyline. Although Raynham is no longer a fighter station is retains an important role in the defence of the United Kingdom. Action radius of the Bloodhounds enables them to produce a defensive screen over East Anglia.

West Raynham, a typical expansion period airfield, opened in 1939. The first occupants were Blenheims of 101 Squadron which arrived in May 1939. West Raynham was deprived of an active operational career when it became the main training station for 2 Group at the start of the war, few operations being flown until 101 Squadron began operational flying in July 1940. No 76 Squadron based here as a training unit with Ansons and Hampdens in April-May 1940 disbanded on May 20.

By then a wide assortment of aircraft were on the station. No 2 Group Target Towing Flight formed on February 22 1940, absorbing some aircraft of 101 Squadron including a Battle target-tower, Blenheim Is and IVs, and an Avro Tutor. No 139 Squadron came to re-establish

itself on May 30 1940 and left for Horsham St Faith on June 10. Two days later 18 Squadron reformed with Blenheim IVs. They stayed until September 9 1940 when they left for the satellite at Great Massingham. During the autumn and winter of 1940 No 101 Squadron flew actively in 2 Group's campaign and, after a detachment for anti-shipping operations from Manston in April-May 1941, the squadron re-armed with Wellington Ics, flying a few sorties in 2 Group before moving to Oakington on July 6 1941.

In May-June 1941 West Raynham had been used as the headquarters for the RAF Fortress I Squadron, No 90, although the aircraft were based at Massingham. No 1420 Flight arrived on July 20 1941 and disbanded here in November. No 101 Squadron was replaced on July 6 1941 by another Blenheim squadron, No 114, which operated from West Raynham until August 1942. They then re-equipped with Blenheim VDs (commonly called Bisleys) before moving to North Africa on November 13 1942. In August 1942 No 18 Squadron returned from Massingham and, similarly equipped, left for North Africa in October 1942. One of their pilots was the celebrated Wing Commander H.G. Malcolm, VC. In May 1942 614 Squadron's Blenheims had operated from West Raynham on the '1,000-bomber' raids.

During 1941 Lysander target towers had replaced the Battles in 2 TT Flight which, on January 1 1941, became 1482 Bombing & Gunnery Flight and subsequently flew Blenheim IVs, Boston IIIs and Defiant target tugs from West Raynham. In November 1942 four Martinets

Wendling from the air in 1978.

replaced the Defiants; a Blenheim V flight was formed; and the first Ventura joined the unit.

No 180 Squadron formed at West Raynham on September 13 1942, their Mitchells being stationed at Massingham. No 1482 Flight moved to Great Massingham on May 19 1943, soon after 342 (Free French) Boston Squadron had arrived on April 7 1943. This unit moved to Sculthorpe on May 5 1943. No 1482 Flight was back at Raynham between September 17 and December 1943 when their Hurricanes and Mitchells left for Swanton Morley.

On December 1 1943 West Raynham was transferred from 2 Group to 100 Bomber Support Group which brought in 141 Squadron on December 4 and 239 Squadron on December 10 1943, both units taking a very active part in bomber support operations with Mosquitoes to the end of the war. No 141 Squadron left for Little Snoring on July 3 1945 and 239 was disbanded seven days later on July 10.

After the war the Central Fighter Establishment (CFE) moved in from Tangmere. This became a very large organisation responsible for carrying out tactical and operational trials of all new fighter aircraft types and training leaders for fighter squadrons. The Air Fighting Development Squadron watched over the tactical development of the Meteor, Vampire, Venom, Swift, Hunter and finally the Lightning, although AFDS flew the latter at Coltishall. The Day Fighter Leader School used Meteor 4s then 8s and evolved into the Day Fighter Combat School and later Fighter Leader School. The

Night Fighter Leader School initially flew Mosquito 36s and later Meteor 11s and 14s, and became the All Weather Wing of CFE in 1951. These changes of names really meant little, but at least reflected tactical alterations from night fighting to all-weather operations.

The Fighter Command Instrument Training Squadron moved to West Raynham in February 1950 successively flying Oxfords, Mosquito 3s and Mk 7s before becoming part of CFE in December 1952. Working alongside CFE was the Naval Air Fighting Development Unit which conducted trials with a Wyvern, Attackers and later Sea Venoms from West Raynham.

Gradually the Central Fighter Establishment reduced its size. In 1959 AFDS and AWDS moved to Coltishall leaving the brightly spined Hunters of DFCS, and AWFCS, at Raynham. These closed during 1962 leaving the two elements at Coltishall to proceed to Binbrook in October 1962.

West Raynham became an operational station again in August 1960 with the arrival of Javelin 8s of 85 Squadron based here until May 1963 when the Target Facilities Squadron now flying Canberra T11s from the airfield was renumbered 85 Squadron before moving out to Binbrook.

The station then passed to 38 Group and when Waterbeach closed to flying in August 1963 its two Hunter squadrons, Nos 1 and 54 flying FGA 9s, arrived. It was from West Raynham that a pilot of No 1 Squadron was flying in April 1968 when he mounted his own 50th anniversary tribute to the Royal Air Force by

An assortment of aircraft in use for tactical trials at CFE West Raynham (MoD).

flying between the spans of Tower Bridge. Feelings at the time were right behind him, although his manoeuvre was hazardous, for the government had indeed directed a calculated insult to the Royal Air Force. In 1967 the Hunter squadrons made news when they tried to sink the wrecked tanker *Torrey Canyon*

The Hunters left in July 1969. During part of their stay, between October 1964 and November 1965, they had as companions the Kestrel Evaluation Squadron which tested the revolutionary concept of the Harrier.

Two Canberra target facility squadrons arrived, Nos 85 and 100, the latter reforming in February 1972. No 85 Squadron disbanded in December 1975 and 100 Squadron moved to Marham. West Raynham then closed to flying.

Wethersfield, Essex

TL720335. On B1053 SE of Finchingfield

'We've had the OK from HQ USAFE,' said the Base Commander. 'The Captain here will be flying you.'

We made the journey to the helicopter in the inevitable giant limousine, although the Piasecki was only a stone's throw away. Kitted out we wandered over to the strange, banana-shaped object. 'I think I should tell you that we've never flown one of these before in such a strong wind,' said the pilot. 'There is quite a chance that when we start a gust could bring the main rotor on to the cabin roof. It could be sticky.' Then he added, 'If we have an engine failure — and there have been some — then the helicopter will drop tail first, and you will hear the rotor blades break up on impact. Best sit up front for the whole journey. You're still keen to come aren't you?'

I readily admitted I was, a flight in an H-21 would not be life's most common experience. In the event all went well and we did some fire fighting training before returning at almost no forward speed in a gale.

Then there was that memorable day when the Americans introduced the F-100 Super Sabres to us. Films, chit-chat about the noise, a banquet and then one of life's most embarrassing incidents. Resting in the Mess I joined a very smart gentleman in civilian dress with whom I sat talking. I asked if he was local. No, he was not. I wondered if he was a newsman, but he looked far too impressive. At last he admitted that he was the current Chief of the Air Staff... not one of life's best

moments!

And surely, no recollections of Wethersfield could be complete without remembering the day when the Americans introduced the Starfighter, which they called 'The Missile with a Man in it'. It was not the aeroplane that was so impressive, it was the man. There he stood, by his mount, wearing stetson and spurs, an incredible sight.

No doubt others will have more action-packed memories of Wethersfield which was established in December 1941 as a satellite for Ridgewell although little used. It opened as an RAF station under Bomber Command in January 1944, and the USAAF arrived in February in the form of the 416th Bomb Group, flying A-20Gs and Hs. The clear-nosed machines were used as leadships when the Group began operations against tactical targets and V-weapon sites in France. Support to the invasion and interdictor operations by day followed, but like other 9th Air Force units the 416th was soon beyond effective operational range and in September moved to Melun Villaroche, south of Paris.

The transfer took place during the run-up to the Arnhem venture. The plan was that after this operation RAF airborne squadrons would move into stations vacated by the 9th Air Force, but this could not take place until the Stirling squadrons had recovered from their terrible mauling over Arnhem.

It was November when the Stirling IVs arrived in the hands of 196 and 299 Squadrons. Supply dropping operations were resumed and glider training was just underway when bad drainage problems were encountered and the squadrons had to move out to Shepherd's Grove in two stages.

For Operation *Varsity*, the Rhine Crossing, 9th Air Force C-47s assembled here, 81 lifting paratroops of the 6th Airborne Division into battle.

On October 19 1945, 1677 Target-Towing Flight arrived, staying until it was disbanded on January 25 1946. In mid-October 1945 the Operational & Refresher Training Unit equipped with Halifaxes and a Flight of Stirlings had arrived and became No 1385 Heavy Transport Support Conversion Unit on April 1 1946 when they gave up using Stirlings. The Unit remained until July 1946 when the station closed and was placed on Care & Maintenance.

Thereafter Wethersfield lay dormant. Its position had one attraction in the post-

Above: *The 20th Fighter Bomber Wing was long associated with Wethersfield. An F-84F of the 55th Squadron is seen here.* Below: *For long the incumbents of Wethersfield were F-100 Super Sabres of the 20th Fighter Bomber Wing.*

war world; it was sited well away from heavily populated areas. Positioning of airfields did not usually bother the local populace much during the war because nobody was then concerned with the noise. They were, instead, interested in the trade airfields generated.

In the early 1950s the main runway was lengthened and the airfield generally improved. With the Cold War intensifying the Americans returned in April 1952. On June 1 1952 the 20th Fighter Group arrived bringing Republic F-84G Thunderjets via Labrador and Iceland. This tactical element was closely tied to the 49th Air Division which also controlled Sculthorpe, and the activities of the two bases were related. The in-flight tankers

for the 20th became based at Sculthorpe. One of the three squadrons of the 20th, the 79th, was positioned at Woodbridge, for purposes of dispersal and to allow easier training, as the nominal strength of the Group was 75 F-84s.

On February 8 1955 the 20th Fighter-Bomber Group became the 20th Fighter-Bomber Wing but little else changed until the autumn when F-84F Thunderstreaks began to replace the ageing Thunderjets. The most obvious feature of the new-comers was the multiplicity of stores they could carry, and one never ceased to be amazed how happily the F-84s seemed to fly with highly asymmetric loads.

Then came the F-100s. Invitations to see them flooded the area, for the local population had awoken to jet noise, and worse was at hand. The Americans were going to base the first so-called 'Century Fighters', the F-100Ds, here. In a huge publicity exercise they brought a few F-100s for everyone to have a good look at and flew a few brave souls in these supersonic machines. They explained how the run-up pens would be placed behind a shield of trees as far as possible from nearby Finchingfield. Yes, the harmless re-heats would roar and they were sorry that their flight plan was the best they could achieve. I noticed that the climb out would be over my home... I told them that at least *I* did not mind. I imagine I was in the great majority of one. To round off the day the F-100Cs of the Sky-blazers gave as shattering a display as Wethersfield would ever witness, and it was very noisy.

F-100D and 100F Super Sabres began to equip the 20th in June 1957 and a year later the unit was renamed the 20th Tactical Fighter Wing. Thereafter the USAF's Armed Forces Days began to appeal to huge crowds and some splendid shows were devised. The 23rd Squadron (Detachment) Helicopter had its Piasecki H-21Bs here in 1956-58 and later a few HH-43Bs were on hand for rescue and fire fighting.

By the summer of 1970 the F-100s were quite outdated and the 20th began to re-arm with F-111s, not here but at Upper Heyford. On April 1 1970 the 66th Combat Support Group took over Wethersfield and on July 1 1970 RAF Wethersfield assumed the role of a Dual Operating Base and prepared to host dual-based

CONUS units. The base mission was changed in September 1970 to that of a Standby Deployment Base and then the Support Group became the 66th Combat Support Squadron.

On June 1 1976 the 66th was redesignated Operation Location A (OLA), 10th Tactical Reconnaissance Wing, RAF Wethersfield and on August 1 1976 became Detachment 1 (Det 1), 10th TRW, RAF Wethersfield. During 1977 assigned military strength fell from 138 men to nine. In 1977 RAF Phantoms from Wattisham were detached here whilst their runway was being attended to, and it seems likely that if UK expansion of the USAF ever takes place Wethersfield will have a part to play.

Weybourne, Norfolk

TG120435. Off A149, 3 miles W of Sheringham

What constitutes an airfield? The answer must simply be that an airfield is a place where aeroplanes persistently land and take off. What, then, does one say about Weybourne?

In summer 1936 anti-aircraft gunners began to use new ranges on the north Norfolk coast firing upon targets towed by Wallace biplanes from Bircham Newton. Such gunnery practice continued, from Stiffkey Marshes, into the 1950s.

Weybourne, though, was special for here was built a catapult launch from which radio-controlled Queen Bee targets could be sent out to sea. After the gunners had tried to shoot them down or disable them, the aircraft could either be brought

Radio-controlled Queen Bee N1846 sits on Weybourne's catapult awaiting launching out to sea (Bruce Robertson).

down in the sea — or upon the sea if they were of the floatplane variety — or landed in a field close by for further use.

Such activities began at Weybourne after 'X' Flight of No 1 Anti-Aircraft Co-operation Unit arrived on May 16 1939. On June 6 1939 the first Queen Bee launch took place for gunners. Subsequently a number of such exercises were carried out, not without moments of concern. N1846 was launched on June 29 and, damaged by gunfire, landed on the sea and was repaired, only to be hit by 3.7 inch anti-aircraft fire on August 2 and sunk. The Flight left Weybourne just after the war started. Then more conventional firing took place from the AA camp against towed targets.

In January 1941 'T' Flight, 1 AACU, formed here receiving a salvage boat and a seaplane tender in February. The first catapult launch was made on April 8 1941, the Queen Bee flying out to sea and not being heard of again. The exercises on April 22 were more successful, resulting in a Queen Bee landing on the beach after being hit. Thereafter a steady flow of targets and shoots took place.

Excitement came on June 6 1941 when the Prime Minister and a large distinguished company arrived to watch a demonstration of 'Z' battery firing. The Queen Bee V4797 approached and ran into a salvo of 160 UP rockets, then landed, unscathed on the sea to be retrieved by the salvage boat SS *Rad-*

The anti-aircraft camp site at Weybourne photographed in 1978 when being dismantled.

stock. There was not time for a repeat performance.

Subsequent training using UP weapons was more successful, but more often than not an aerial was shot away and control of the target lost. On June 18 1941 another demonstration of rocket power was held for the Prime Minister. After no less than 45 minutes of firing a near burst put a Queen Bee out of control and it spun into the sea. A second attempt to demonstrate the weapons resulted in no hits and the Queen Bee was finished off by Bofors fire.

Landing the Queen Bees on a site close to the RA camp was far from easy as so often they had sustained some damage. On August 23 after 91 rounds of fire damaged a Queen Bee it was brought on to the air strip only to pass through a hedge and into an adjacent meadow. 'T' Flight was disbanded on April 29 1942 and the aircraft side of activity ceased at Weybourne, although gunners continued to use the range firing against towed targets.

Witchford, Cambridgeshire

TL520780. 2 miles S of Ely on A10, also visible from A142

For hundreds of years the isles of the Fens have provided sanctuary and succour. At Ely, close by Witchford, the legendary Hereward the Wake made his stand against the Normans. In the past, when floods came, local people fled to protecting high ground, the Isle of Ely, upon which Witchford stands. Help to the needy was what Witchford's fliers would remember too.

In the late autumn of 1944 the Dutch, seeing the Allies advancing, decided to give them special support. Dutch railway workers in the north of Holland went on strike. By way of retaliation the enemy flooded large areas effectively cutting off the region of Holland which had virtually revolted. Food supplies soon ran low, and the Germans thought they could starve the Dutch into submission. Starve them they did, to the extent that the Dutch scoured their precious fields for bulbs and were forced to eat their pets to remain alive.

The Allies had their hands full with offensive action, but by February 1945 felt bound to do something about aiding the Dutch. What could be done? The solution lay with delivery of food to keep the population alive. How could it be achieved? It had to be by day which was

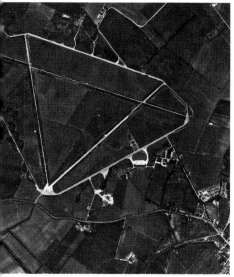

An aerial view of Witchford taken by 58 Squadron on March 29 1965 (DoE).

clearly hazardous. Thus, a Lancaster and crew of 115 Squadron, Witchford, were detached to Netheravon, there to conduct trials whereby food would be packed in bags in Small Bomb Containers and dropped from low level. This might seem easy, but the food sacks repeatedly burst on impact until the delivery aircraft flew low enough to drop their loads effectively.

On April 6 1945 practice drops of food supplies were demonstrated to VIPs at Witchford from varying types of Lancasters, for some at the station had special bomb doors to allow carriage of 12,000 lb bombs. Next day Major R.P. Martin demonstrated the art to Bomber Command officers at Lacey Green, by delivering six SBCs with 1,245 lb of food, one fifth the possible load.

No 115 Squadron flew their final wartime bombing raid against Bad Oldesloe on April 24 1945. Next day came the first food drop by Lancasters. Each carried five packs of provisions, weight in all 59,551 lb. Weather was clear, apart from April showers, and when the Lancasters arrived over the Hague at very low level they saw crowds everywhere. Here was salvation for many, and it seemed the entire city was on holiday. But for all concerned there were moments of bitter disappointment as many sacks burst open upon hitting the ground, dispersing the precious flour. So desperate were some of the Dutchmen that they seized handfuls of

the manna to eat immediately.

The following day the Lancasters went again, this time to Rotterdam, and some supplies fell in drainage ditches. As the sacks fell they did so among the people and some were hit whilst others waited in carts and lorries to carry away all they could. One of the saddest moments came when a target indicator from the PFF hit a house, which was soon a mass of flames.

On six more days 115 Squadron participated in the drops, including sweets for children, and tobacco for which appeals had been seen in huge white letters on roof tops. Then, like so many other squadrons of Bomber Command, 115's Lancasters joined in Operation *Exodus*, the return of POWs from French airfields.

Those supply drops, though, must be something countless East Anglians remember. My recollection of hundreds of Lancasters truly at roof top height remains vivid, for it was the only time when one saw the might of Bomber Command low in daylight. It was as if the whole of Bomber Command was making a fly-past in jubilation that the slaughter was over.

Witchford, as muddy as any airfield could ever be, was just a collection of two 'T' Hangars, three runways and some concrete or metal huts. Placed on the side of the Isle of Ely its surface sloped considerably, which led to drainage problems.

It opened in June 1943 under 3 Group. No 196 Squadron arrived with their Wellington Xs on July 19 and almost at once re-equipped with Stirling IIIs which began Main Force operations in August. Witchford became part of 33 Base under Waterbeach in September 1943. No 513 Squadron formed here with Stirling IIIs but disbanded before operating. In November 1943 196 Squadron switched to 38 Group and Leicester East, their place being taken in late November by the Lancaster IIs of 115 Squadron. They had been the first to equip with radial-engined Lacaster IIs which they operated intensively until April 1944 when Lancaster Is and IIIs were received. Witchford's Lancasters took part in the general run of 3 Group's campaign — Berling, the Ruhr, softening-up for the Normandy invasion. One memorable night was April 18 1944 when, as the bombers were returning from Rouen, an Me 410 joined the circuit and shot down two Lancaster IIs as they were circling to land. Such events were rare at this time.

From Witchford the Lancasters operated — sometimes as many as 30 at a time — to the end of hostilities, through daylight phases in close army support, against V-weapons and oil targets. The squadron left Witchford in August 1945.

The station wound down to Care & Maintenance and closed in March 1946. Despite its poor state a hangar was used as a storage depot by the Americans between 1950 and 1952, but most of the airfield is now farmland with few traces of its former use. One of the wartime hangars may be seen on the west side of the field, also an entrance on the Cambridge road. Opposite on the A10(T) is a golf course, but during the war it was the site of a camp for Italian POWs, who had a good view of Witchford's active days.

Woodbridge, Suffolk

TM330487. S of B1084, S of Bentwaters

Flying Officer R.F. Limbert and crew were among 29 who, flying Lancasters of 514 Squadron from Waterbeach, set off at midday on November 15 1944 to bomb the Hoesch Benzin works at Dortmund. Aboard LM288 was a 4,000 lb 'Cookie', fifteen 500 pounders and flares. Flak on the run in to Dortmund was quite heavy, but it was not this that soon brought alarm.

Above them were other Lancasters and, at the moment of bomb release, 'C Charlie' was directly below one of these other aircraft. A falling 500-pounder smashed into their port outer engine and another rammed against the port inner badly

A photograph of Lancaster LQ-K: ME315 of 405 Squadron, Gransden Lodge, after forced landing at Woodbridge.

damaging it. One more penetrated the fuselage beside the main spar and yet another hit the starboard outer engine. Their own bombs released they made for home, miraculously scraping in at Woodbridge.

On November 27 1944 Flight Lieutenant R.A. Pilcher of 514 Squadron was running up on Cologne in mid-afternoon when his Lancaster was hit by flak. After bombing came the problem of return. Their mid-upper gunner had been wounded, and by a combined effort of the remainder of the crew who tied a rope on to the control column they managed to hold the aircraft on course and force-landed at Woodbridge.

Lancasters of 514 Squadron were despatched on August 11 1944 for an afternoon raid on the marshalling yards at Lens. Their bomb aimer in LL697 had given the 'steady' when a bomb from an aircraft above crashed into the nose of the Lancaster. Warrant Officer Brickwood held the aircraft on course, but the nose of the Lancaster had been sliced off and the bomb aimer had fallen with it. All the instruments on the pilot's panel apart from the altimeter were out of action. Seeing their plight Warrant Officer D. Beaton escorted LL697 back to a forced landing at Woodbridge. These episodes were typical of many in which Woodbridge became involved.

In the early years of the war bringing damaged or lost aircraft back to a safe haven had been a great problem particularly at night, and especially if the weather turned bad. The number of bombers which crashed in East Anglia simply because their crews became lost, or because aircraft were short of fuel and often damaged, was considerable. Usually, they were ordered to land at any aerodrome which could receive them, but not all airfields could accept them at night, and some runways were too short or not strong enough.

In 1942 the bomber offensive was assuming massive proportions, and it was decided to build three airfields specifically to accommodate aircraft which were damaged, short of fuel or suffering from undercarriage or brake trouble. A crash landing on an airfield to which others were returning could be fatal. So could a return if fog descended on the operating stations. All these factors led to the construction of three specialised airfields, at Carnaby, Manston and Woodbridge, of which the latter proved to be the busiest by day and night.

Woodbridge is now the home of the USAF's rescue Hercules and 'Jolly Green Giant' helicopters.

These three airfields were sited along the East Coast so that crippled bombers could land immediately after crossing the coast. Each had a runway 3,000 yards long and 250 yards wide with an undershoot and overshoot at each end of 500 yards. The runway at each was laterally divided into three lanes. The south lane lined with green lights at night, white by day, was the emergency lane into which any aircraft could land without first contacting flying control. The centre lane was lined by white lights at night, the northern by yellow. By day the lines of lights clearly defined the three sections of the runway.

Coupled with this was the use of FIDO at the three bases. Investigation into fog dispersal by petrol burning from a long line of jets by the runway edge had commenced in November 1942. It was found that, after entering the fog zone and descending to 100 feet, touchdown then became virtually visual. The main burner lines for the runway lighting began 250 yards from the touchdown end of the runway which was sealed from fog intrusion by a cross line of burners. FIDO was installed at 15 airfields, Woodbridge, Gravely and Foulsham among them. It had become operational in November 1943. Woodbridge opened on November 15. Its usefulness was at once apparent for 36 aircraft landed there in November 1943, one needing 3,000 yards of runway

plus 200 yards of overshoot.

The site chosen was almost ideal as it was nearly fog free and had no obstructions for miles. But it was in the middle of a forest owned by the Forestry Commission and before construction could commence more than a million small trees had to be cleared, which much displeased the local population. Actual construction began in July 1942 and when completed the runway was 1,000 longer than normal runways and five times wider. It covered 159 acres.

Woodbridge received its first emergency landing on July 18 1943, long before it opened — a B-17 short of fuel. This was the first of 4,120 emergency landings made to the end of June 1945.

The airfield lighting system consisted of contact and Drem lights on the runway, while funnel and approach lights were used for the perimeter. A fateful incident on December 17 1943 led to the realisation that this was inadequate. Five Halifaxes were diverted here and haze was at 300 feet so that the pilots could not see any lights. None of the aircraft had beam approach equipment and the direction finder could not home them in. One crew landed, but the others crashed in the vicinity with the cost of 13 lives. Therefore by the end of April 1944 sodium and incandescent lights had been installed on the south side of the runway to within a mile of the coast at Orford.

Over 60 aircraft were handled in January 1944, 72 the next month, 48 being USAAF aircraft. Fog Investigation and Dispersal Operation equipment began to be installed in February 1944. In March 130 landings were made, followed by 159 in April. These totals seemed to increase steadily and June 1944 was a busy month when, for the first time, the station came under enemy attack. Several bombs fell close on June 28, the nearest being only 300 yards from the FIDO fuel store tanks containing over a million gallons of petrol. Flying-bombs also penetrated the area and a sharp eyed controller thinking one to be an aircraft tried homing it with his Aldis Lamp. Luckily he was unsuccessful.

Incidents came fast at Woodbridge. In the early hours of June 22 a Lancaster damaged by fighters and with 11,000 lb of bombs aboard touched down in the green lane. On landing it swerved and came to rest on the south side of the amber lane. Personnel were warned away because a B-17 was landing on the green lane. This swerved and cut the Lancaster in half. Since the green lane was free another Lancaster was allowed to land, and in doing so its undercarriage collapsed and the bomber slid to a halt blocking the lane. The controller was about to close the runway until wreckage could be cleared when yet another Lancaster requested an emergency landing. The pilot had so little fuel that he landed over the wreckage, illuminated by searchlights, touching down beyond the debris. This all took place within 13 minutes.

The early hours of July 13 1944 were memorable. An aircraft landed and when ground crew arrived they found it was German. The occupants on realising their error were trying to destroy the aircraft when an NCO wrenched open a door beneath the aircraft and the pilot fell out. There was a struggle and then the other two occupants surrendered. Interrogation revealed they had been on a flight from Holland to Berlin and, with little fuel left, landed unaware of their position.

The machine itself was a fairly new Ju 88G night fighter, a considerable prize because it carried the latest German radar, Lichtenstein SN-2 which had proved so effective against RAF bombers. The Ju 88 was flown to Farnborough and the radar tested. As a result Bomber Command used a revised system against SN-2 during a raid on Kiel on July 23 1944.

The 1,000th emergency landing at Woodbridge came in August. One of the most spectacular arrivals then was a B-17 with a 16-foot hole in the belly under the spar and another 6 × 8-foot hole in the fuselage side. More than 50 per cent of the starboard mainplane was missing, all due to heavy calibre flak. It was a write-off, but many of the arrivals were repaired and flown out.

October 1944 found the station a quagmire due to the heavy rain. Masses of water rested on the runway which the drainage system could barely cope with. Many of the 306 landings were aided by FIDO. The first fatal accident occurred during November when a Lancaster crashed into the runway. By the end of 1944 2,719 aircraft had made use of Woodbridge, and 570 aircrew had been treated at the sick quarters.

Records were broken monthly. In 2½ hours on a January day 950 diverted aircrew arrived, but the activity lessened when better weather came.

The station was closed on March 19 1945 for five days when two Halifax squadrons towed in 68 Hamilcar and Horsa gliders. Sixty combinations then took part in the Rhine crossing assault, Operation Varsity. For various reasons only 38 Hamilcars and 11 Horsas landed correctly.

As an extensively damaged Halifax approached on April 9 1945, one of the crew was seen to be dangling beneath. The mid-upper gunner had in fact fallen through the floor but his parachute harness was caught in the rear of the shattered bomb bay. Apart from 3½ hours suffering exposure he was uninjured, although his oxygen mask and goggles scraped the runway surface as the bomber landed.

By the end of June 1945 4,120 landings had been made, an outstanding contribution to the war effort. Post-war the station remained in use, with only 244 landings in one year. The station was also used for experimental work which included the dropping of 'Tallboy' and 'Grand Slam' bombs at Orfordness by Lancasters operating from Woodbridge. The Blind Landing Experimental Unit also worked from here as well as Martlesham.

On May 15 1946 the maiden flight of the DH 108 tailless jet took place here, but by then Woodbridge was a shadow of its former self although experimental work at Martlesham was transferred there. It was finally abandoned by the RAF on March 15 1948.

The USAF gained administrative control of Woodbridge on June 5 1952 and it became the home of the 79th Fighter-Bomber Squadron of the 20th Fighter-Bomber Wing, first with F-84Gs and in 1957 F-100s. A new squadron operations block had been constructed in 1953 and a new fire station in 1956, base housing being brought fully into use in April 1957. These dwellings were built by the British Government in a deal by which tobacco was accepted in payment, so that the scheme quickly became known as 'Tobacco Housing'.

Operational control of Woodbridge was taken over by the 81st TFW on July 8 1958, and then the station prepared to receive another squadron, although facilities were none too adequate. Runway repairs came in December, and the ends were resurfaced and turn-offs placed at the 3,000- and 6,000-foot intervals. In December 1958-January 1959 the 78th Tactical Fighter Squadron moved in. At the time it was converting from F-84Fs to F-101s, and it arrived from Shepherd's Grove. Phantoms of the 81st TFW first touched down at Woodbridge on March 2 1966, the 78th TFS receiving its first F-4D on April 23 1969.

In mid-September 1969 it was announced that the 79th TFS would move to Upper Heyford and that the 67th Aerospace Rescue & Recovery Squadron would come from Moron AFB in Spain. They arrived in December flying HC-130 Hercules and HH-3E 'Jolly Green Giant' helicopters and remain there today. Woodbridge seems likely to stay a USAF base in the foreseeable future.

Wormingford, Essex

TL920308. 1 mile SE of village

The first sight of a P-38 Lightning was a memorable experience; it was such a strange-looking machine. An aura of interest in the P-38 was aroused long before any reached Britain. Their coming was preceded by exaggerated stories of speed and capability. Among the last to serve the 8th Air Force were those of the 55th Fighter Group at Wormingford.

The station was prepared during 1943 for the US 9th Air Force whose 362nd Fighter Group arrived in November 1943 equipped with P-47Ds. They first operated on February 8 1944 escorting B-24s bombing a V-1 site in the Pas de Calais. The 362nd concentrated on bomber escorts before moving to Headcorn in mid-April 1944.

Their place was taken by P-38J Lightnings of the 55th Fighter Group which had led a prominent life when at Nuthampstead from where they had moved making way for B-17s of the 398th Bomb Group. Although P-38s were operational in 1942 the 55th were the first to take them into combat. They moved to Wormingford when their use as fighter-bombers was under review. Lightnings could not readily engage in low-level strafing; instead they operated along the lines of the A-20s with a 'drop snoot' leadship, and made shallow dive attacks on tactical targets interspersed with escort missions. Among their final operations were patrols over shipping in the Channel,

P-51 Mustangs of the 55th Fighter Group at Wormingford (USAF).

their ample duration making them ideal. By mid-1944 the P-38 was dated. During June the 55th began to re-equip with P-51Ds which type had lately entered service. Low-level operations continued, the Group giving general support to the St Lô breakthrough and busily attacking gun emplacements. Throughout that summer similar operations and bomber escorts were flown. The 55th was awarded a Distinguished Unit Citation for its bomber escort duties and strafing of airfields during the period. September saw the lead-in to the airborne landings in Holland.

The 55th was active during the winter Ardennes offensive and received a second Distinguished Unit Citation for extensive low-level attacks on communications in February 1945 immediately prior to Operation *Clarion*. Whilst the Allies crossed the Rhine Wormingford's P-51s strafed locomotives, trucks, and oil targets near Wesel, and their final operation was flown on April 21 1945.

On July 22 1945 they left Wormingford for Kaufbueren. After the war the station was used by RAF Training and Technical Training Commands until January 1947. Some civil flying followed and then the site was sold off for agricultural use in the early 1960s.

Wratting Common, Cambridge-shire

TL645510. By B1052, 2½ miles NE of Balsham, Cambridgeshire

To the local people it was West Wickham aerodrome when it opened in May 1943. Astride the East Anglian heights it was a typical bomber airfield, three of whose hangars can still be seen. Now the remnants of the station, never a very flourishing one, ring to the sound of farm implements on land owned by Lord Vestey, or to the hustle and bustle of a commercial vehicle haulage business. Essential tasks were performed here, but with rather less glamour than at other airfields in the area.

In the general re-organisation of Stirling squadrons in 32 Base run by Stradishall, 90 Squadron moved from Ridgewell to the airfield, then known as West Wickham, on May 31 1943. The unit arrived at the height of the Stirling bomber's career, resuming action with a mining operation on June 3/4. The Battle of the Ruhr was being fiercely waged and during June No 90 Squadron's targets included Krefeld, Mulheim and Wuppertal. It took part in

the destruction of Hamburg in July and 15 crews set off from West Wickham for the famous Peenemünde raid. Twice they attacked Turin in August and then West Wickham underwent a sudden transformation. The station's name had brought confusion with another similarly named airfield, and on August 21 it became known as Wratting Common which really lies just to the north.

Stirling operations continued with less frequency until mid-October when 90 Squadron moved to Tuddenham. The Ladder Plan whereby 3 Group squadrons would equip with Lancaster Is and IIIs became effective in November. To make room for 514 Squadron at Waterbeach No 1651 Conversion Unit moved into Wratting and 90 Squadron had to make way for them. No 1651 CU arrived on November 20 becoming part of 32 Base.

Stirling training was a costly business, and a very large number of accidents occurred at Wratting, mainly due to incorrect handling on take-off and landing. Basic operational training was conducted as crews converted from twins at OTUs to four-engined aircraft. Most then proceeded to 3 LFS at Feltwell and, when there were sufficient Lancasters in the Group, the Stirling Conversion Unit wound down, moving out on November 10 1944 to Woolfox Lodge.

In their place in late October 1944 had come 195 Squadron, an offshoot of 115 Squadron, Witchford, which commenced operations on November 2 1944 with a day raid on Homberg. Operations followed 3 Group's normal pattern with a concentrated effort against oil targets. Thus Nordstern, Castrup Rauxel, and Wanne Eickel figured prominently in battle orders, along with many other well-known German target areas such as Munich, Duisburg, Dortmund and Kiel. The Lancasters took part in the famous Dresden raid but their most eventful operation took place on December 12

Nissen huts and a Type T2 hangar at Wratting Common

Wratting Common photographed from 10,000 feet by a Canberra of 58 Squadron on March 27 1956 (DoE).

1944. Witten was the target for 18 crews and enemy fighters penetrated to 195's leading formation which was broken up, a rare event on day raids at this time. Three Lancasters were shot down and another badly damaged put down in Belgium. To add confusion fog came down at Wratting and 11 crews had to be diverted.

The final operation was against Bad Oldesloe on April 24, a railway installation. Then the Lancasters flew eight supply drops to the Dutch before bringing home released POWs to Tangmere and Westcott. No 195 Squadron disbanded on

August 14 1945 and flying ceased at Wratting Common. For a while the station housed some of the personnel needed for transport operations from Stradishall. A period of Care & Maintenance was followed by closure in April 1946. The camp then held displaced persons.

A total of 1,367 sorties were flown from here during the course of 79 operations, and a tonnage of 6,144.6 was delivered. Now, a long line of conifers stretches across the old airfield where three hangars and a few huts may be seen.

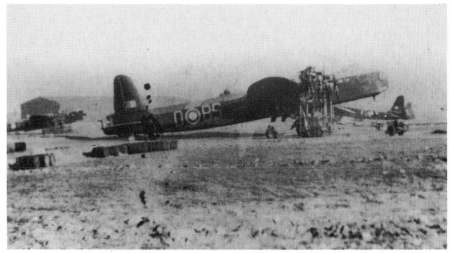

Very rare picture showing Stirlings of 1651 Conversion Unit on dispersal at Wratting Common (Richard Gunton).

Wyton, Cambridgeshire

TL285741. NE of Huntingdon, at junction of A141/B1090

Few aeroplanes arrive amid the sort of euphoria which courted the Bristol Blenheim, supposedly able to outpace existing fighters. Sadly the latter were only of the biplane variety. To Wyton came the initial Blenheims for the RAF, the first example inauspiciously completing its arrival on March 19 1937 with a ground loop. Nevertheless, the Blenheim and Wyton have become inseparably linked in history. It was Blenheim N6125 which, a few moments after war was declared, made the first Bomber Command sortie, to seek out and photograph the German fleet in the Schillig Roads preparatory to bombing attack. Unlucky it was for 139 Squadron that when they participated in that raid the following day the weather and an element of bad map reading defeated their part in the operation.

Wyton became linked with the Mosquito in 1942. From this station in December No 109 Squadron's Mosquitoes first operated *Oboe*, the blind bombing device which in 1943 brought hitherto unknown accuracy to the bomber offensive. From Wyton six Mosquitoes of 109 Squadron set out on March 5 and successfully marked the Krupp works for a devastating attack.

Wyton was the station from where the first Master Bomber operated, Wing Commander J.H. Searby, whose task it was to control the attack on the V-weapons research establishment at Peenemünde. Thus, Wyton's place in RAF history is assured, and it is good that it remains an active station.

It is an airfield with a very long history, for the present massive aerodrome has swallowed the small field where in World War 1 a procession of RFC men learnt to fly a wide variety of aircraft types from a site that opened in 1916. Reserve and training squadrons passed through, the aerodrome buildings being on the west side where a few modern buildings now stand. Testimony of the workmanship of those days could be seen after the last war, for those wooden buildings still remained. Sadly they have gone now, but the site is still in use. Between the wars, incidentally, Alan Cobham's circus made use of the field.

When building of the new aerodrome started at the end of 1935 the hangars were sited on the south side. RAF expansion, though, brought the first personnel and aircraft to Wyton, which opened in July 1936, before the hangars were ready. When No 139 Squadron reformed on September 3 1936 an attempt was soon made to house their Hinds in one of the old wooden sheds. The roof sagged so much when the doors were opened that they could not be closed again. Hinds had to be picketed out until No 1 Hangar opened in November. Then they moved in among the decorators and the smell of paint.

Next month on December 1 114 Squadron reformed as winter rain was reducing the airfield to mud. Not, however, reducing the area of the old airfield and from there flying was still possible. Old airfields, it seems, were very carefully sited.

On March 1 1937 Wyton passed to 2 Group and Blenheims began to arrive, but 114 Squadron having prematurely given up Hinds took on charge some Audaxes when the Blenheim conversion programme slipped. Long-nosed Blenheims replaced the Mk Is in 1939 and with these the two squadrons went to war. They flew few sorties before late November 1939 when they moved to France, their place being taken by Battles of XV and 40 Squadrons which had returned to convert to Blenheims.

An expected move to France did not come about and both squadrons were at Wyton when the western storm broke in May 1940. The harshness of battle was at once evident when on May 19 40 Squadron was committed to action against Dutch targets. Appalling casualty lists were opened. May 12 hammered the Blenheim's limitations home when half the force of XV Squadron failed to return. This put XV Squadron out of the fight for a few days, but soon Wyton's squadrons were to be seen daily, in vics of three, usually 12 to a formation, heading for terrifying action. The carnage during this period was simply horrific, and all to no avail.

Once France fell both squadrons, using Alconbury for dispersal, settled down to a regular day bomber and reconnaissance role using cloud cover, sometimes flying solo, occasionally in formation. They had

been joined in late May 1940 by the tattered remnants of 57 Squadron which had virtually been wiped out in France and which, after reforming, had been detached to Lossiemouth on June 24 as an anti-invasion measure and for possible operations over Scandinavia. This squadron returned to Wyton on October 29 1940, when the station's Blenheim days were nearly over.

On November 1 1940 Wyton and its three squadrons were switched to 3 Group. All re-equipped with Wellington Ics. No 57 Squadron moved to Feltwell, but the other two stayed on although 40 Squadron moved completely to Alconbury on February 2 1941. Both squadrons flew night raids. From early 1941 No 4 Blind Approach Training Flight which became 1504 BAT Flight was at Wyton, moving to Graveley on August 5 1942.

In January 1941 Wyton had begun to take on greater importance, for Short Brothers established a working party there to support the entry of the Stirling into 3 Group. During March 1941 XV Squadron began to equip with the new four-engined bomber. The change brought big problems for this was an exacting aeroplane. Nevertheless, XV Squadron were not to be trifled with, and when they took the new type into action they did it in style — against Berlin.

The number of Stirlings ready for action was, for many months, small. In the summer XV Squadron tried to sink the *Scharnhorst* at La Pallice and at the end of the year raided Brest in daylight.

Blenheims of 40 Squadron warm-up at Wyton in 1940 (IWM).

These sorties were afforded much publicity at the time, but had little effect on the warships. In an attempt to hit them XV Squadron carried out some radio-controlled night raids, but effective equipment was a year away.

The Stirlings operated into 1942, usually from Wyton whilst training was undertaken at Alconbury, a trail of crashes being none too good for morale. Yet it would be very wrong to think of the Stirling as unpopular; indeed, many who flew in this sturdy, manoeuvrable bomber thought highly of it and when they later encountered the Lancaster rated that a frail, tinny contraption!

The next major change for Wyton came in August 1942 with the establishment of the pathfinder force within 3 Group. The Stirlings moved to Bourn and in their place on August 15 came Lancasters of 83 Squadron on loan from 5 Group. Their task was to provide part of the flare force for marking, and during ensuing months they improved their accuracy and speed handsomely, developing tactics which culminated in the use of target indicators in place of flare bundles. No 83 Squadron continued to operate from Wyton until April 1944 and moved to Coningsby on April 20. By then Wyton housed Mosquitoes.

The first Mosquito came from Stradishall in early September 1942 in the hands of 109 Squadron which arrived on August 7 headed by Squadron Leader H.E. Bufton. Under the watchful eye of Air Commodore Don Bennett they worked up their technique and made their first raid against Lutterade power station, a calibration operation to test the effectiveness of *Oboe*. Thereafter until July 1943 109 Squadron performed, and during the Battle of the Ruhr both 109 and 83 Squadrons, leaders and backers-up, played a great part in the bombing accuracy. In June 1943, when 2 Group was shoved into Fighter Command much against its wishes 139 Squadron at Marham was switched to night nuisance raids and 105 became the second *Oboe* squadron. Then 139 Squadron was changed with 109 to keep the *Oboe* markers together at Marham. No 139 Squadron operated by night on a small but accurate scale into 1944, leaving Wyton in February 1944.

In January 1944 No 1409 Meteorological Reconnaissance Flight arrived with Mosquitoes from Oakington. Their role was as vital as any Wyton unit, for each day they gathered weather forecast material to permit planning of the night's raids over the Continent, often penetrating very deeply into Germany and in daylight, and feeding data to both Bomber Command and the 8th Air Force. This they did from Wyton until the end of the war, and flew the vital weather reconnaissance flights prior to the launching of the D-Day landings.

On September 15 1944 No 128 Squadron reformed at Wyton and, equipped with Mosquito XVIs, became part of the Light Night Striking Force until the end of hostilities. Expanding the station's capability, 163 Squadron also reformed here with Mosquitoes on January 25 1945, disbanding at Wyton on August 19 that year.

The peacetime phase for Wyton began when 156 Squadron brought in their Lancasters. The squadron disbanded on September 25 1945 but their Lancasters remained at dispersals long after the owners had gone. No 1688 BDT Flight arrived on March 19 1946, disbanding at Wyton in November.

In August 1946 XV Squadron returned with Lancasters and 44 Squadron also arrived. They were joined by 138 and 90 Squadrons in November and soon after the four squadrons re-equipped with Lincoln IIs which were based here for the next 3½ years, often being away on *Sunrays* to give them mobility practice overseas. Nos 90 and 138 Squadrons disbanded on September 1 1950. XV Squadron left in November 1950 and during January 1951 44 Squadron moved to Marham.

The station which, since the end of the war, had housed Technical Training Command Communications Flight (and which now flies as 26 Squadron using Devons and Jet Provosts), underwent great change in the 1950s. The main runway was lengthened and the St Ives-Ramsey road was closed to permit this, ready for much heavier aircraft.

In 1952 Wyton became the home of the strategic reconnaissance force. At that time this meant Lancasters of 82 Squadron, Mosquitoes of 58, 540 and 541 Squadrons which had some Meteor PR 10s on strength. Their Mosquito PR 34s were replaced by Canberra PR 3s, first used by 540 Squadron, and later PR 7s. No 58 Squadron was the first to equip with Canberra PR 9s. In 1958 No 237 OCU was based at Wyton. Meteor 7s were available for training, and 100 Squadron had a detachment of Canberras here for special duties.

Certainly the biggest change came with the arrival of Valiant B(PR) 1s of 543

Squadron in November 1955 which greatly enhanced the strategic reconnaissance ability of the station.

The part played in the post-war world by the RAF's reconnaissance squadrons is little known, but much of it has been for civilian and often humanitarian purposes. In 1961, for instance, the Wyton Valiants photographed British Honduras to assess the damage by the hurricane there, carried out a photo survey of Agadir following the earthquake, and kept a photographic eye on the volcanic eruption on Tristan da Cunha. The following year they photographed the Solomon Islands for mapping purposes and in 1964 three Valiants produced photographs so that more accurate maps could be drawn up of Rhodesia and Bechuanaland.

Victor B(SR) 2s replaced the Valiants at the end of 1964 and 543 Squadron's operational effectiveness was greatly increased. In 1965 they photographed Saddleworth Moor in the hunt for the Moors Murderers. In 1967 they produced a complete photo coverage of Denmark for mapping purposes, and kept a watch over the oil pollution from the *Torrey Canyon*. Of course, the Victors had a strategic role too, four being able to obtain full coverage of the North Atlantic in six hours, or one being able to cover an area the size of the UK in two hours employing radar photography in cloudy conditions. The Victors have long since

gone, a similar task now being performed by Vulcans based at Scampton.

When Watton closed 51 Squadron moved to Wyton bringing their specialised aircraft and skills, Comet 2s later being replaced by special Nimrods.

Wyton has become the home for Canberra PR 9s of 39 Squadron and, with the closure of Cottesmore, 360 Squadron flying Canberra T 17s. Wyton is thus the last fully operational Canberra station in the RAF.

It is apt that this survey of East Anglian airfields should end with an active RAF station, for East Anglia has been so much the home of the Royal Air Force. To the uninitiated the Service exists only as an instrument of war. The part played by the Royal Air Force for humanitarian reasons is so often overlooked. At Wyton the Service fulfils peacetime and wartime needs whether it is keeping an eye on a potential foe or the North Sea oil rigs — or aiding us all by just photographing the new roads which are rapidly being built in East Anglia for the benefit of the area. It is sad that so many of these have been built on the foundations of the runways which once criss-crossed so much of East Anglia. It is, though, perhaps satisfying that when one switches on the lights the electricity from a nuclear power station may have its basic foundation in the runways of Bradwell Bay!

Present occupants of Wyton are Canberras. One of 39 Squadron's aircraft is seen here (MoD).

Index of units referred to in the text

Luftwaffe

JG 26 - 82
KG 1 - 188
KG 2 - 88, 102
KG 27 - 86
KG 53 - 82, 208
NJG 2 - 55
NJG 4 - 159
4/121 - 167
3/122 - 146

Royal Air Force

FLIGHTS
5 ASR - 87, 155
403 - 66
1359 - 56
1401 - 66, 98
1402 - 141
1403 - 66, 162
1409 - 66, 168, 255
1418 - 120, 150
1420 - 211
1426 - 105, 183
1428 - 172
1429 - 107
1444 - 172
1473 - 113, 115
1474 - 120, 191
1482 - 125, 193, 211, 212
1483 - 150, 164, 165
1489 - 156
1499 - 135
1503 - 162
1504 - 121, 131, 225
1505 - 131
1507 - 199
1508 - 193, 208
1515 - 193
1517 - 120, 135
1521 - 191
1525 - 98

1611 - 66
1612 - 66
1616 - 135
1627 - 135
1677 - 119, 175, 179, 213
1678 - 108, 115, 142, 202, 203
1686 - 73
1688 - 114, 165, 225
1692 - 125, 143
1693 - 68
1694 - 125
1696 - 135
1699 - 172
Battle of Britain Memorial - 92, 154
Meteorological - 162
Wireless Investigation - 120

MISCELLANEOUS UNITS
1 AACU - 64, 66, 139, 216
7 AACU - 135
A & AEE - 151, 152
2 AATF - 135
3 AATF - 135
15 ACHU - 59
18 ACHU - 68
5 AEF - 82
AFDU - 104, 183
AFDS - 91, 212
203 AFS - 191
206 AFS - 170
15 Air Beam Training Flight - 68
1 ANS - 192
2 APC - 66, 99
2 APS - 77
ASRTU - 99
AWW/CFE - 212
BAFTS - 183
BBU - 154
BDU - 113, 120, 165
BLEU - 154

BSDU - 115, 194
2 CAACU - 134, 141, 144
CBE - 150
CCEBTS - 68
CCPP - 67
CFE - 91, 125, 212
Conversion Units
1385 - 213
1651 - 202, 222
1653 - 85
1655 - 199
1657 - 179, 191
1665 - 123, 158
CSE - 160, 194, 209
CUAS - 81, 102
DFCS - 212
DFLS - 212
22 EFTS - 69, 78, 84, 146
45 ERFTS - 134
ERS - 96
FCITS - 212
4 FIS - 80
3 Fighter School - 61
1 FTS - 170
2 FTS - 100
3 FTS - 114
5 FTS - 121, 170, 204
2 GDC - 144
2 Group CF - 194
3 GFAF - 150
2 GRU - 65
2 GSU - 114, 193
2 GTF - 114, 211
3 LFS - 113, 115, 165
MAEE - 109
Maintenance Units
12 - 114
25 - 132
53 - 196
54 - 165
94 - 131, 175
258 - 166
262 - 132, 184
263 - 185

274 - 144, 166, 172, 195
NAFDU - 212
NFLS - 212
NTU - 198, 199
OATS - 68
Operational Conversion Units
226 - 60, 91, 191
231 - 58
237 - 58, 131, 226
ORTU - 155, 213

Operational Training Units
10 - 60
11 - 54, 188
16 - 199
17 - 188, 197, 198
20 - 137
23 - 168
52 - 95
17 (P) AFU - 68, 69, 208
3 PRU - 167, 168
22 RFS - 81
RNATTS - 141
1 RNZAF Unit - 112, 148
4 RS/SS - 194
417 RSU - 183
7 RTC - 109
18 RTC - 142
RWE - 179, 209
SDRDU - 115
1 TAMU - 131
TCCF - 226
TICU - 68
WDF - 191
Warwick Training Unit - 66, 98
Washington Conversion Unit - 191
74 Wing - 105
157 Wing - 67

SQUADRONS
Royal Air Force
1 - 192, 204, 212
2 - 80, 117
3 - 76, 152, 156, 194
6 - 92
7 - 61, 78, 131, 158, 164, 167, 168, 198
9 - 129, 130, 131, 158, 164, 167, 168, 198
10 - 55, 131, 170
11 - 61
12 - 131
XV - 46, 72, 131, 150, 151, 163, 168, 224, 226

16 - 80
17 - 82, 83, 92, 94, 152
18 - 124, 132, 170, 172, 198, 199, 203, 204, 205, 208, 211
19 - 52, 77, 78, 94, 100, 101, 102, 104, 116, 135, 146, 156
21 - 64, 68, 114, 132, 160, 171, 172, 178, 199, 208
22 - 87, 111, 151, 154
23 - 75, 83, 91, 134, 143, 144, 207
24 - 56, 170, 204
25 - 74, 77, 84, 90, 91, 94, 152, 204
26 - 80, 91, 226
27 - 170
29 - 75, 92, 94, 101, 152, 207
30 - 170
33 - 64
34 - 64, 134, 208
35 - 64, 100, 121, 150, 151, 163, 191, 197, 199
37 - 112, 160
38 - 148, 149, 161
39 - 61, 227
40 - 46, 56, 199, 224, 225
41 - 91, 92, 206
42 - 64, 87
43 - 134, 192
44 - 131, 150, 158, 225, 226
46 - 170, 204
49 - 64, 158
50 - 198
51 - 56, 191, 203, 209, 227
52 - 197
53 - 98, 120, 198, 203, 204
54 - 92, 192, 204, 212
55 - 131, 151
56 - 60, 61, 75, 76, 104, 105, 152, 156, 182, 204, 206, 207
57 - 113, 131, 151, 224, 225
58 - 226
59 - 56, 148, 203
60 - 204
61 - 68, 198, 199
62 - 203, 204
63 - 46, 197, 204
64 - 59, 60, 61, 76, 86, 90, 105, 114, 133, 151, 204
65 - 52, 60, 95, 105, 126, 129, 133, 135, 156
66 - 85, 86, 100, 102
68 - 76, 84, 88, 90
71 - 95, 126, 154

72 - 86
73 - 82, 83, 92, 160
74 - 86, 91, 133, 134
75 - 111, 112, 113, 130, 158, 162, 189
76 - 75, 211
77 - 114, 203, 204
78 - 55
80 - 92
82 - 68, 181, 208, 226
83 - 225
85 - 75, 82, 84, 92, 94, 95, 152, 192, 194, 211, 212, 213
86 - 87, 170
87 - 92
88 - 53, 172, 193
89 - 192
90 - 68, 125, 131, 150, 157, 174, 197, 208, 211, 222, 225
91 - 83, 105, 147
92 - 105
97 - 72, 100, 120, 121
98 - 114, 115, 192, 194, 200, 209
99 - 61, 161, 162, 164, 200
100 - 151, 213
101 - 61, 72, 84, 168, 191, 211
102 - 56, 130
103 - 130
104 - 55
105 - 53, 68, 70, 130, 132, 148, 150, 193, 198
106 - 74
107 - 124, 125, 135, 197, 205
108 - 55
109 - 120, 150, 191, 224, 225
110 - 135, 207
111 - 82, 94, 101, 116, 152, 192, 206, 207
113 - 158
114 - 132, 171, 224
115 - 107, 121, 130, 143, 148, 149, 150, 151, 162, 163, 191, 209, 217, 222
116 - 183, 209
118 - 59, 88, 89, 135, 147
119 - 59, 67, 68, 134
122 - 52, 156
124 - 60, 76
125 - 192
126 - 52, 59, 60, 76, 114, 129
128 - 225

129 - 53, 59, 60
133 - 87, 126
137 - 88, 155, 156, 182
138 - 164, 189, 197, 225
139 - 132, 133, 148, 150,
   172, 198, 211, 224, 225
140 - 114
141 - 75, 89, 91, 144, 212
142 - 120
148 - 151, 189, 198
149 - 137, 138, 149, 150,
   160, 161, 162, 163, 191,
   197
150 - 189
151 - 77, 83, 84, 86, 87, 88,
   90, 152
152 - 87, 146, 192, 193, 206
153 - 204
154 - 88, 116
156 - 46, 47, 198, 199, 225
157 - 75, 83, 95, 194
158 - 191
161 - 121, 165
162 - 73
163 - 225
165 - 59, 60, 75, 105
166 - 61
167 - 146, 147
168 - 70
169 - 125, 144
170 - 183
171 - 165, 166
174 - 116
180 - 114, 125, 212
181 - 105, 183
182 - 76, 154
186 - 191, 197
190 - 124
192 - 113, 115, 120, 209
195 - 132, 147, 156, 222, 223
196 - 179, 213, 217
198 - 75
199 - 131, 138, 165, 166
202 - 91
204 - 131
206 - 64, 65, 98
207 - 64, 150, 151, 163, 191,
   197
208 - 131, 192
209 - 109
211 - 161
214 - 85, 100, 112, 131, 151,
   159, 172, 178, 189, 198
215 - 55, 130, 189
217 - 87
218 - 85, 99, 100, 149, 150,

160, 167
219 - 76
220 - 64, 167, 203
221 - 65, 98
222 - 74, 86, 87, 102, 155
223 - 172
226 - 135, 193, 205
227 - 121
228 - 134
229 - 65, 91, 147, 156
233 - 64
234 - 59, 60, 74
235 - 65, 98
236 - 172, 189, 205
238 - 170
239 - 80, 212
241 - 69, 70, 210
242 - 86, 104, 152, 170
245 - 60, 133, 134, 156, 206,
   209
247 - 54, 75
248 - 59, 65
253 - 146, 192, 204
254 - 59, 64, 65, 141, 189
255 - 87
257 - 83, 86, 87, 134, 152,
   206
263 - 74, 134, 192, 207
264 - 75, 91, 94, 102, 116,
   132, 152
266 - 105, 134, 135, 156, 206
268 - 80, 88, 182, 183
269 - 64
271 - 119
274 - 61
275 - 134
277 - 152
278 - 59, 77, 78, 87, 88, 89,
   90, 147, 155, 156
279 - 59, 60, 66, 67
280 - 59, 66, 139, 140
288 - 59, 99, 183
295 - 175, 176
296 - 106
297 - 106
299 - 179, 213
301 - 85
303 - 52, 91, 129
304 - 85, 98
305 - 193
307 - 84, 91, 133
309 - 52, 183
310 - 77, 102, 104, 157
311 - 107, 130
312 - 77, 102, 157
313 - 77, 157

315 - 52
316 - 52, 90, 91, 129
320 - 53, 66, 90, 113
340 - 135
341 - 75
342 - 125, 177
360 - 227
402 - 75, 89
405 - 120
407 - 66, 140
410 - 83
411 - 88, 117, 146, 156
415 - 66, 98
416 - 75, 89, 90
418 - 74, 75, 90, 95
419 - 84, 162
422 - 56
423 - 56
453 - 156
455 - 138, 140
456 - 77, 83
461 - 60
462 - 115
464 - 113, 114, 160, 178, 194
466 - 56
485 - 88, 146, 156
486 - 75, 83, 156
487 - 113, 114, 147, 159,
   160, 178, 194
488 - 75, 76
489 - 138, 140
500 - 56
501 - 76, 182
504 - 89, 92, 152
512 - 119
513 - 217
514 - 115, 202, 203, 218, 222
515 - 47, 89, 143, 144
519 - 98, 140
521 - 66, 98, 140, 168
524 - 99, 140
527 - 83, 183, 209
529 - 135
540 - 226
541 - 226
543 - 226
570 - 175
571 - 100, 170, 200
575 - 119
598 - 67
601 - 94, 104, 155
602 - 147, 156
603 - 147
604 - 87
605 - 75, 76, 83, 84, 114,
   144

608 - 66, 100
609 - 74, 105
610 - 88, 146, 147
611 - 76, 89, 90, 102, 147,
   156
613 - 90, 114, 183, 194
614 - 183
616 - 52, 86, 95, 126
617 - 58
618 - 58
620 - 85, 124
622 - 163
623 - 100
627 - 120, 170
635 - 100
652 - 70, 135, 210
655 - 117
657 - 170
658 - 135
679 - 135
692 - 120, 121
695 - 66, 68, 133, 134, 135
Fleet Air Arm
762 - 127, 128
798 - 127, 128
809 - 131
810 - 59
814 - 59
819 - 59, 67, 139
827 - 59, 140
841 - 89
855 - 67

**United States Army Air
Force/USAF**

GROUPS
2 - 138, 178
3 - 188
4 - 75, 95, 126, 133
20 - 214, 221
22 - 178
25 - 209
34 - 157
43 - 138, 178, 181
44 - 77
47 - 132, 178, 179
55 - 56, 222
68 - 206
78 - 105
81 - 60, 221
91 - 55
92 - 47, 178
93 - 47, 77, 128, 129, 163,
   181

94 - 106, 136, 176, 177
95 - 47, 51, 59, 117, 118,
   132
96 - 59, 136, 184
97 - 56, 150, 178
100 - 136, 195
301 - 47, 56, 178
306 - 47, 163
310 - 128
319 - 53, 133, 181
320 - 129
322 - 51, 173, 176
323 - 106, 132
339 - 117
344 - 185
352 - 69
353 - 159, 174
354 - 73
355 - 188
356 - 154
357 - 142, 174
358 - 142, 174
359 - 59, 108
361 - 70, 145
362 - 221
363 - 175
364 - 131
365 - 119
381 - 175
385 - 123
386 - 73, 123
387 - 85
388 - 136
389 - 129, 181
390 - 117, 136
391 - 154
392 - 209, 210
394 - 69
397 - 175
398 - 221
409 - 145
410 - 119
416 - 213
435 - 163
445 - 196
446 - 77, 78
447 - 173
448 - 179
452 - 96
453 - 171
457 - 118
458 - 133
466 - 54
467 - 173
479 - 206
482 - 47

486 - 192
487 - 141
489 - 127
490 - 108
491 - 166
492 - 92, 159, 166
493 - 145
496 - 127

SQUADRONS
1 - 51
5 - 127
15 - 192
19 - 179
23 - 215
30 - 51
33 - 183
36 - 172
38 - 56
41 - 183
53 - 51
63 - 178
65 - 138
67 - 221
78 - 181, 221
79 - 214, 221
84 - 178
85 - 51, 178
86 - 179
91 - 60
92 - 60, 179
116 - 179, 181
329 - 77, 163
334 - 95
335 - 95, 126
336 - 95
346 - 88
347 - 183
353 - 56
374 - 145
375 - 145
376 - 145
450 - 176
452 - 176
527 - 51
554 - 178
652 - 174
784 - 54
803 - 209
7523 - 51

*MISCELLANEOUS
UNITS*
7560 Air Base Group - 51
1 ADSU - 118
49 Air Division - 178, 214

322 Air Division - 163
11th CCRG - 47
513 TAW - 163

WINGS
10 - 51
48 - 138
55 - 56
81 - 60, 179
406 - 60